The Enjoyment of Music

ALSO BY JOSEPH MACHLIS

The Enjoyment of Music

An Introduction to Perceptive Listening

Sixth Edition Shorter

JOSEPH MACHLIS

Professor of Music Emeritus,
Queens College of the City University of New York

WITH

KRISTINE FORNEY

Professor of Music, California State University, Long Beach

W. W. NORTON & COMPANY
New York • London

Acknowledgments

PHOTOGRAPHS:

Paul Klee. *Heroic Strokes of the Bow.* 1938. Colored paste on newspaper on dyed cotton fabric, 28¾ × 10⅞″. Collection, The Museum of Modern Art, New York. Nelson A. Rockefeller Bequest. (p. 85)

Clavichord by Christian Kintzing. Courtesy of The Metropolitan Museum of Art, Purchase, Gift of George Bashlow, Helen C. Lanier, Mr. and Mrs. Jason Berger in honor of Angna Enters, Mrs. Harold Krechmer, Miss Erika D. White, Burt N. Pederson, Risa and David Bernstein, Miss Alice Getty, John Solum, Carroll C. Beverly, and Garry S. Bratman, and The Crosby Brown Collection of Musical Instruments, by exchange, and The Barrington Foundation Inc. Gift, and Rogers Fund, 1986. (1986.239) Photograph by Sheldan Collins. (p. 129)

Henri Matisse. *The Cowboy,* plate 14 from *Jazz.* Paris, Tériad, 1947. Pochoir, printed in color, sheet, 16⅝ × 25⅝″. Collection, The Museum of Modern Art, New York. Gift of the artist. (p. 138)

Vasily Kandinsky. *Painting Number 199.* 1914. Oil on canvas, 64⅛ × 48⅜″. Collection, The Museum of Modern Art, New York. Nelson A. Rockefeller Fund (by exchange). (p. 274)

Robert Motherwell. *Elegy to the Spanish Republic, 108.* (1965–67). Oil on canvas, 6′10″ × 11′6¼″. Collection, The Museum of Modern Art, New York. Charles Mergentime Fund. (p. 311)

Robert Rauschenberg. *First Landing Jump.* 1961. "Combine painting": cloth, metal, leather, etc.; overall, including automobile tire and wooden plank on floor, 7′5⅛″ × 6′ × 8⅞″. Collection, The Museum of Modern Art, New York. Gift of Philip Johnson. (p. 313)

TRANSLATIONS:

Excerpt from *Le Nozze di Figaro* by W. A. Mozart, translation of the libretto © 1968 by Lionel Salter. Reprinted by kind permission of Deutsche Grammophon GmbH, Hamburg. (pp. 184–90)

Translations of *Erlkönig* by Franz Schubert and *Ich grolle nicht* by Robert Schumann are from *The Ring of Words* by Philip L. Miller. Reprinted by permission of Doubleday & Company, Inc., and Philip L. Miller. (pp. 207–08)

Excerpt from *Die Walküre* by Richard Wagner, translation of the libretto © 1967 by William Mann. Reprinted by kind permission of Deutsche Grammophon GmbH, Hamburg. (pp. 254–55)

Poetry (*Ancient Voices of Children* by George Crumb) from Federico García Lorca, *Selected Poems.* Copyright 1955 by New Directions Publishing Corporation. Reprinted by permission of New Directions Publishing Corporation. Translation by W. S. Merwin. (p. 325)

Library of Congress Cataloging-in-Publication Data

Machlis, Joseph, 1906–
    The enjoyment of music/Joseph Machlis with Kristine Forney.—6th ed., shorter
      p. cm.
    Includes index.
    ISBN 0–393–96070–6
    1 Music appreciation. I. Forney, Kristine. II. Title.
    MT6.M134E5   1991
    780—dc20   90–25297
                        CIP
                        MN

Cover illustration by Nenad Jakesevic and Sonja Lamut
Cover design by Mike MacIver

ISBN 0–393–96070–6

W. W. Norton & Company, Inc., 500 Fifth Avenue, New York, N.Y. 10110
W. W. Norton & Company, Ltd., 10 Coptic Street, London WC1A 1PU

3 4 5 6 7 8 9 0

For Earle Fenton Palmer

Contents

PART FIVE
MORE MATERIALS OF FORM   137

PART SIX
EIGHTEENTH-CENTURY CLASSICISM   147

PART EIGHT
THE TWENTIETH CENTURY 259

Preface

The new, shorter version of *The Enjoyment of Music,* Sixth Edition, follows the chronological format recently introduced. This version is intended for those who find that the Sixth Edition contains more material than they have time for. The Shorter maintains the overall structure of the Sixth Edition, having the same Parts and Units, but cuts its general length by more than a third. This is achieved through abridging biographical and historical details and through a careful selection of repertory representative of major styles and composers.

This edition represents a major reorganization of material. In the first five editions, the chapters were organized according to individual composers. The chapter on Beethoven, for example, presented various aspects of his creativity—a symphony, a concerto, a piano sonata, a string quartet. In the sixth edition, all these types are represented, but in divisions organized according to genres. The Classical era is therefore subdivided into units entitled The Symphony, Chamber Music, The Concerto, and the like, each discussing works of Haydn, Mozart, and Beethoven. This new organizaion thus constitutes a subtle shift of emphasis from the personalities of composers to their works, a shift very much in line with present-day trends in education.

One of the most notable changes in this revision is the addition of Listening Guides that supplement the prose descriptions of the chosen musical repertory. These outline the works in question, presenting their themes and details of their structure, usually with timings to assist students in following specific musical events. It is not necessarily suggested that all pieces be studied in such detail, but the Listening Guides can be effective teaching tools to facilitate our students' comprehension of what they hear.

The section on the elements of music has been slightly reorganized so that most of the basic concepts and building blocks of music are presented in the beginning of the book, while more advanced concepts needed for particular style periods—such as formal structures for the Classical era—have been placed in later chapters. The opening chapters also include new material on musical ensembles—choral groups, orchestra, and band. The section on notation that was formerly a part of the elements of music now appears in the Appendix, so that it may be introduced when needed or simply used for reference.

Other unique features of this edition include two new chapters in the twentieth-century music section: one on the American popular scene, including discussion of ragtime, jazz, blues, and musical theater; and one on non-Western music and its influence on the contemporary scene. This revision has also focused attention on social history and the role of the musician in society. This socio-historical emphasis includes consideration of the role of women in the musical world as performers, composers, teachers, and patrons; a work of the nineteenth-century composer Clara Schumann is included in the basic repertory.

The book has been completely redesigned so as to take full advantage of the newest technological developments in book production, including the use of a second color for highlighting. Some information has been presented in tabular form for ease in reviewing. This includes, in addition to the Listening Guides, a listing of the principal works of each composer with dates and original titles, that can serve as reference and summary. Brief transitional passages that link eras present comparative tables of style traits for consecutive eras, such as Renaissance-Baroque, Baroque-Classic, and Classic-Romantic.

Whenever possible, operatic scenes studied in class have been made available on videocassettes, which should enliven and enrich the teaching of opera. Among the operas included are three favorites: Mozart's *The Marriage of Figaro,* Verdi's *La traviata,* and Wagner's *Die Walküre.* Several other standard works have made their way into this edition: Palestrina's *Pope Marcellus Mass,* Bach's Prelude and Fugue in C minor from Volume I of the *Well-Tempered Clavier*, and Schoenberg's *Pierrot lunaire.* The section on contemporary music has, of course, been updated to include more recent composers such as John Adams.

A new sound package has been created with the student in mind. Three 90-minute cassettes accompany the book, and include the thirty-five selections for which there are Listening Guides in the book. At the top of each Listening Guide you will find a pictograph indicating exactly where the particular piece is located in the new cassette package. Careful attention has been given to the choice of recordings, preference going to those that reflect contemporary concepts of performance practice. As a result, the recordings of Medieval and Renaissance music feature historical instruments and choirs of the correct size, while performances of Baroque works accord with present-day scholarship in regard to tempo, dynamics, ensemble size, and other aspects of interpretation.

I am heavily indebted to David Hamilton and Claire Brook for their devoted reading of the manuscript, and to Kristine Forney for her imaginative assistance in revising the text. I hope that the changes introduced in the sixth edition will make this a better book, one that truly enhances our students' enjoyment of music.

Joseph Machlis

Prelude:
Listening to Music Today

We are currently experiencing the most radical technological revolution the world has yet known. This age of supertechnology in which we live has touched every aspect of our everyday lives, including when and how we hear music. From the moment we are awakened by our clock radios, our daily activities unfold against a musical background. We listen to music while on the move—on our car stereos, on planes, or with our walkman or diskman while running or biking, and at home for relaxation. We can hardly

Avery Fisher Hall, Lincoln Center, New York, as seen by members of the New York Philharmonic from the stage. (Photo by Norman McGrath)

Bruce Springsteen in concert at the Spectrum, a sports stadium in Philadelphia.
(J. Jay/Star File)

avoid it in grocery and department stores, in restaurants, in elevators, in offices—everywhere, music is much in evidence. We can experience music in live concerts—at outdoor festivals, the symphony, the opera, or ballet—or we can hear it at the movies or on television. The advent of MTV (Music Television Video) has revolutionized the way we listen to popular music; now it is a visual experience as well as an aural one. This increased dependency on our eyes—one of our more highly developed senses—makes our ears work less hard, a factor we shall attempt to counteract in this book.

Music media too are rapidly changing. The LP record will be largely unknown to the next generation of music listeners. Cassettes, a relatively recent development, are already being replaced by compact disks, and video disk players will soon be a part of our home stereo systems.

We have learned to accept new sounds in our music experiences, many produced by synthesizers rather than traditional instruments. Much of the music we hear on television, at the movies, and in pop groups is synthetic. These electronic musical instruments can very accurately reproduce the familiar sounds of violins or trumpets, and they can produce totally new timbres and noises for special effects. Composers too have succumbed to the technological revolution—the tools of music composition, formerly a pen, music paper, and perhaps a piano, now more likely include a synthesizer, computer, and laser printer. In short, modern technology has placed at our disposal a wider diversity of music—from every period in history and from every corner of the globe—than has ever before been available.

Given this diversity, we must choose a path of study. In this book, we will focus on the classics of Western art music. Our purpose is to expand the listener's experience through a heightened appreciation of the musical heritage of Europe and its offshoots in America. But no music exists in a vacuum. In discussing the traditions of Western art music, we will touch briefly on popular music, especially blues and jazz, and on the musics of other cultures. The varied musics of Africa and Asia, the worlds of European and American folk music, the remarkable flowering of American jazz in the twentieth century, the vibrant history of popular and theatrical music—each of these is in itself a subject worthy of serious study.

The language of music cannot be translated into the language of words. You cannot deduce the actual sound of a piece from anything written about it; the ultimate meaning lies in the sounds themselves. Unlike popular music, which is intended to be immediately accessible and to speak to its audience without explanation, the world of art music brings us into contact with sounds and concepts that are not always so quickly grasped. What, you might wonder, can be said to prepare the nonmusician to understand and appreciate these sounds? A great deal. We can discuss the social and historical context in which a work was born. We can learn about the characteristic features of the various style periods throughout the history of music, so that we can relate a particular piece or style to parallel developments in literature and the fine arts. We can read about the lives and thoughts of the composers who left us so rich a heritage, and take note about what they said about their art. We can acquaint ourselves with the elements out of which music is made, and discover the plan made by a composer for combining these

Listening to a favorite tape on his Walkman helps this biker pass the time. (Photo courtesy of Sony Corporation of America)

in any one work. All this knowledge—social, historical, and biographical, technical, and analytical—can be interrelated. What will emerge is a total picture of the work, one that will clarify, in far greater degree than you may have thought possible, the form and meaning of a piece.

There are people who claim they prefer not to know anything about the music they hear, that to intellectualize the listening experience destroys their enjoyment of music. Yet they would never suggest that the best way to enjoy a football game is to know nothing about the rules of the game. A heightened awareness of musical processes and styles brings the listener closer to the sounds, and allows them to hear and comprehend more.

In the course of our discussion we will be building a vocabulary of musical terms that help us understand what the composer tried to communicate. Some of these terms will be familiar to you in another context from which they were borrowed in order to take on a different—perhaps more specific— meaning. Others come from a foreign language, such as the directions for musical expression, tempo, and dynamics which are traditionally given in Italian. We will begin building this vocabulary in the next chapters by breaking music into its constituents, its building blocks—the elements or materials of music. We will then analyze how a composer proceeds to shape a melody, how that melody is fitted with accompanying harmony, how music is organized in time, and how it is structured so as to assume logical, recognizable forms. In doing so we will become cognizant of the basic principles that apply to all styles of music, classical and popular alike, to music from all eras, and beyond that, to other arts as well.

"To understand," said the painter Raphael, "is to equal." When we come to understand a great musical work we grasp the "moment of truth" that gave it birth. For a short time we become, if not the equal of the master who created it, at least worthy to keep the same company. We receive the message of the music, we fathom the intention of the composer. In effect, we listen perceptively—and that is the one sure road to the enjoyment of music.

PART ONE

The Materials of Music

"There are only twelve tones. You must treat them carefully."—PAUL HINDEMITH

Henri Matisse (*1869–1954*) Tristesse du roi, *1952*. (Musée National d'Art Moderne, Paris. Scala/Art Resource)

UNIT I

■

The Elements of Music

1

Melody: Musical Line

"It is the melody which is the charm of music, and it is that which is most difficult to produce. The invention of a fine melody is a work of genius."—JOSEPH HAYDN

Melody is that element of music which makes the widest and most direct appeal. It is generally what we remember and whistle and hum. The melody is the musical line—or curve if you prefer—that guides our ear through a composition. The melody is the plot, the theme of a musical work, the thread upon which hangs the tale.

The Nature of Melody

A *melody* is a succession of single tones or pitches perceived by the mind as a unity. Just as we hear the words of a sentence not singly but in relation to the thought as a whole, so too do we perceive the tones of a melody in relation to one another. We derive from them the impression of a beginning, a middle, and an end.

We can describe three characteristics of any melody: its range, its shape, and the way it moves. A melody goes up and down, its individual tones being higher or lower than one another. By *range* we mean the distance between its lowest and highest tones. A melody may have a narrow, medium, or wide range. *Shape* is determined by the direction a melody takes as it turns upward or downward. This movement can be charted on a kind of line graph that may take the form of an ascending or descending line, an arch, or a wave, to list a few possibilities. *Type of movement* depends upon

Characteristics of melody

7

whether a melody moves stepwise or leaps to a tone several degrees away or farther. Melodies that move principally in stepwise motion are called *conjunct* (joined or connected), while a melody that moves with many leaps is described as *disjunct* (disjointed or disconnected).

These characteristics are illustrated by the examples below.

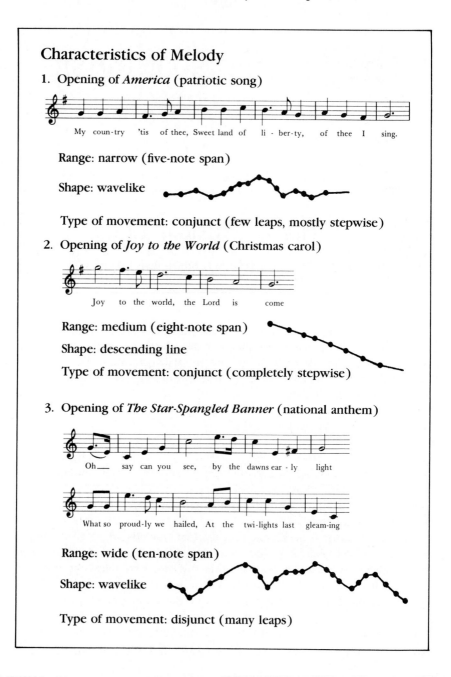

Characteristics of Melody

1. Opening of *America* (patriotic song)

    My coun-try 'tis of thee, Sweet land of li - ber-ty, of thee I sing.

    Range: narrow (five-note span)

    Shape: wavelike

    Type of movement: conjunct (few leaps, mostly stepwise)

2. Opening of *Joy to the World* (Christmas carol)

    Joy to the world, the Lord is come

    Range: medium (eight-note span)

    Shape: descending line

    Type of movement: conjunct (completely stepwise)

3. Opening of *The Star-Spangled Banner* (national anthem)

    Oh__ say can you see, by the dawns ear - ly light

    What so proud-ly we hailed, At the twi-lights last gleam-ing

    Range: wide (ten-note span)

    Shape: wavelike

    Type of movement: disjunct (many leaps)

The Structure of Melody

We can examine the structure of a melody in much the same way that we analyze the form of a sentence. A sentence can be divided into its component units or phrases; the same is true for a melody. A *phrase* in music, therefore, denotes a unit of meaning within a larger structure. The phrase ends in a resting place or *cadence*, which punctuates the music in the same way that a comma or period punctuates a sentence. The cadence may be either inconclusive, leaving the listener with the impression that more is to come, or it may sound final, giving the listener the sense that the melody has reached the end. If the melody is set to words, the text phrase and the musical phrase will coincide. Many folk and popular tunes consist of four phrases set to a four-line poem. An example is the well-known American tune, *Amazing Grace*. Its four phrases are of equal length. Notice that the first and third lines of the stanza rhyme, as do the second and fourth. The first three cadences are inconclusive (incomplete), with an upward inflection like a question at the end of the second phrase. The fourth phrase, with its downward inflection, provides the answer: that is, it gives the listener a sense of finality. One tone serves as home base, around which the melody revolves and to which it ultimately returns.

A melody has to be carefully shaped in order to maintain the listener's interest. What makes a striking effect is the climax, the high point in a melodic

Phrase

Cadence

The Structure of Melody: Phrasing

Amazing Grace (early American melody)

Four text phrases = four musical phrases

A - ma - zing grace how sweet the sound

That saved a wretch like me!

I once was lost, but now am found

Was blind, but now I see.

line that usually represents the peak of intensity. The climax gives purpose and direction to the melodic line. It creates the impression of crisis met and overcome. The American national anthem, for example, contains a splendid climax in the last phrase on the words "O'er the land of the free." There can be no doubt in anybody's mind that this song is about freedom.

2

Rhythm: Musical Time

"In the beginning was rhythm."—HANS VON BÜLOW

Rhythm—the Greek word for "flow"—is the term we use to refer to the controlled movement of music in time. Since music is an art that exists solely in time, rhythm shapes all the relationships within a composition, down to the minutest detail.

The Nature of Rhythm

It is rhythm that causes people to fall in step when the band plays, to nod or tap with the beat. Upon the tick-tock of the clock or any series of noises we hear, we automatically impose a pattern. We hear the sounds as a regular pulsation of strong and weak beats. In other words, we organize our perception of time by means of rhythm. The ancients believed that, in its most general sense, rhythm was the controlling principle of the universe. Certainly, it can be perceived in all the arts. The symmetrical proportions of architecture, the balanced grouping of painting and sculpture, the repeated movements of the dance, the regular meters of poetry— each in its own sphere represents our deep-seated need for rhythmical arrangement. But it is in music, the art of ideal movement, that rhythm finds its richest expression.

Meter

If we are to grasp the flow of music through time, time must be organized. Musical time is usually organized in terms of a basic unit of length, known

Beat
as a *beat*—the regular pulsation to which we may tap our feet. Some beats are stronger than others—these are known as *accented* or *strong* beats. In much of the music we hear, these strong beats occur at regular intervals— every other beat, every third beat, every fourth, and so on—and thus we perceive the beats in groups of two, three, four, or more. These groups are

In architecture, symmetry and repetition of elements are expressions of rhythm. The Sydney Opera House, Bennelong Point, Sydney Harbor, 1972. (Photo courtesy Australian Tourist Commission)

known as *measures* each containing a fixed number of beats. The first beat of the measure generally receives the strongest accent.

Meter, therefore, denotes the fixed time patterns within which musical events take place. Although meter is one of the elements of rhythm, it is possible to draw a subtle distinction between them: rhythm refers to the overall movement of music in time and the control of that movement while meter involves the actual measurement of time.

Metrical Patterns

Most meters are organized into simple patterns of two, three, or four beats grouped together in a measure. These meters depend on the regular recurrence of accent. Simplest of all is a succession of beats in which a strong beat alternates with a weak one: ONE-two, ONE-two, or, in marching, LEFT-right, LEFT-right. This pattern of two beats to a measure is known as *duple meter* and occurs in many nursery rhymes and marching songs.

Triple meter is another basic pattern consisting of three beats to a measure—one strong beat and two weak—and is traditionally associated with such dances as the waltz and the minuet.

Quadruple meter also known as *common time*, contains four beats to the measure, with a primary accent on the first beat and a secondary accent on the third. Although it is sometimes not easy to tell duple and quadruple meter apart, quadruple meter usually has a broader feeling.

Meters in which each beat is divided into three (rather than two) are known as *compound meters*. Most frequent among them is *sextuple meter*:

Measure

Simple meters

Compound meters

six beats to the measure with a primary accent on the first beat and a secondary accent on the fourth. Marked by a gently flowing effect, this pattern is often found in lullabies and boat songs. The following examples illustrate the four basic patterns.

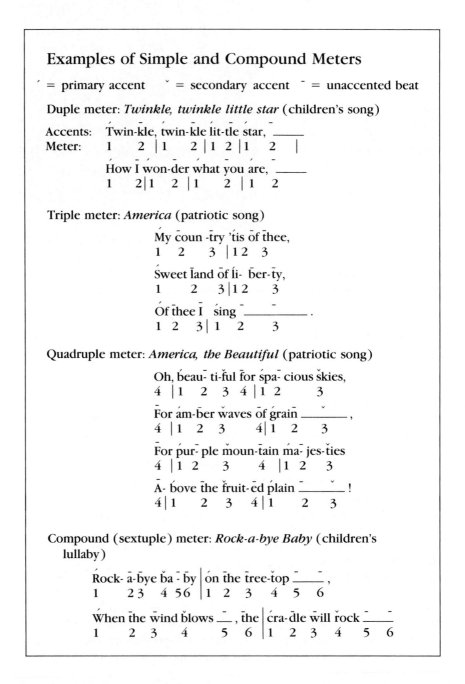

Examples of Simple and Compound Meters

´ = primary accent   ˘ = secondary accent   ‾ = unaccented beat

Duple meter: *Twinkle, twinkle little star* (children's song)

Accents: Twin-kle, twin-kle lit-tle star, ‾‾‾‾‾
Meter: 1   2 | 1   2 | 1 2 | 1   2 |

          How I won-der what you are, ‾‾‾‾‾
          1   2 | 1   2 | 1   2 | 1   2

Triple meter: *America* (patriotic song)

          My coun-try 'tis of thee,
          1   2   3 | 1 2 3

          Sweet land of li- ber-ty,
          1   2   3 | 1 2   3

          Of thee I sing ‾‾‾‾‾‾‾‾‾ .
          1 2   3 | 1   2   3

Quadruple meter: *America, the Beautiful* (patriotic song)

          Oh, beau- ti-ful for spa- cious skies,
          4 | 1   2   3 4 | 1 2   3

          For am-ber waves of grain ‾‾‾‾‾‾ ,
          4 | 1   2   3   4 | 1 2   3

          For pur- ple moun-tain ma- jes-ties
          4 | 1 2   3   4 | 1 2   3

          A- bove the fruit-ed plain ‾‾‾‾‾ !
          4 | 1   2   3 4 | 1   2   3

Compound (sextuple) meter: *Rock-a-bye Baby* (children's lullaby)

          Rock- a-bye ba - by | on the tree-top ‾‾‾‾ ,
          1   2 3   4 5 6 | 1 2   3   4   5   6

          When the wind blows ‾ , the | cra-dle will rock ‾‾‾
          1   2   3   4   5 6 | 1   2   3   4   5   6

Several additional characteristics of meter should be explained. In some cases, a piece will not begin with an accented beat. For example, *America, the Beautiful* (see page 12) begins with an *upbeat*, or on the last beat of the measure—in this case on beat 4. Composers devised a number of ways to keep the recurrent accent from becoming monotonous. They used ever more complex rhythmic patterns within the measure, and learned how to vary the underlying beat in different ways. The most common of these procedures is *syncopation*, a term used to describe a deliberate upsetting of the rhythm through a temporary shifting of the accent to a weak beat or to an *offbeat* (in between the beats). This technique is characteristic of the Afro-American dance rhythms out of which jazz developed. The examples that follow illustrate the technique.

Syncopation

Syncopation

1. Slightly syncopated tune: *Good Night, Ladies*

> Good night, la-dies, _____ good night, la-dies _____
> 1   2 |1   2 |1   2 |1   2

2. Highly syncopated tune: *I Got Rhythm*

> I got rhy- thm, I got mu- sic
> 1 2   3   4 |1 2   3   4 |

> I got my girl, who could ask for a-ny-thing more _____
> 1 2   3   4 |1   2   3   4

To sum up: music is an art of movement in time. Rhythm, the artistic organization of musical movement, permeates every aspect of the musical process. It binds together the parts within the whole: the notes within the measure, the measures within the phrase.

3

Harmony: Musical Space

"Music, to create harmony, must investigate discord."—PLUTARCH

We are accustomed to hearing melodies against a background of harmony. To the movement of the melody, harmony adds another dimension—depth. Think of harmony as occurring on a vertical plane: it describes the simultaneous happenings in music. Harmony is to music what perspective is to

Harmony lends a sense of depth to music, as perspective does to painting.
Meindert Hobbema (*1638–1709*) The Avenue, Middelharnis. (Courtesy of the
Trustees, The National Gallery, London)

painting. The supporting role of harmony is apparent when a singer is accompanied by a guitar or piano. The singer presents the melody while the instrument provides the harmonic background.

Interval

Scale

Octave

Chord

Harmony pertains to the movement and relationship of intervals and chords. An *interval* may be defined as the distance—and relationship—between two tones. A series of tones arranged in consecutive order, ascending or descending, is called a *scale.* These tones are identified either by syllables—*do-re-mi-fa-sol-la-ti-do*—or by numbers—1–2–3–4–5–6–7–8 (1). Thus, the interval *do-re* (1–2) is a second, *do-mi* (1–3) is a third, *do-fa* (1–4) a fourth, *do-sol* (1–5) a fifth, *do-la* (1–6) a sixth, *do-ti* (1–7) a seventh, and from one *do* to the next is an *octave.*

A *chord* may be defined as a combination of two or more tones that constitutes a single block of harmony. As you see from the example below, melody constitutes the horizontal aspect of music, while harmony, consisting of blocks of tones (the chords), constitutes the vertical.

The Function of Harmony

Chords have meaning only in relation to other chords: that is, only as each chord leads into the next. Harmony therefore implies movement and progression.

Triad

The most common chord in our music is a certain combination of three tones known as a *triad.* Such a chord may be built, for example, by combining the first, third, and fifth degrees of the scale: *do-mi-sol.* The triad is a basic formation in our music. In the next example, the melody of *Old MacDonald* is harmonized by triads.

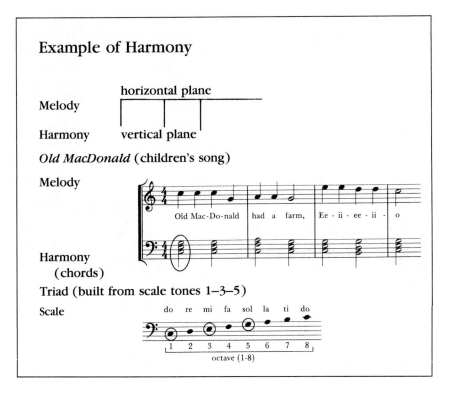

It is apparent that melody and harmony do not function independently of one another. On the contrary, the melody implies the harmony that goes with it, and each constantly influences the other.

Tonality

A system of music must have set procedures for organizing tones into intelligible relationships. One of the first steps in this direction is to select certain tones and arrange them in a family or group. In such a group, one tone assumes greater importance than the rest. This is the first tone of the scale, *do*, also called the *tonic* or keynote, which serves as a home base *Tonic* around which the others revolve and to which they ultimately gravitate. We observed this principle at work earlier with the tune *Amazing Grace* (Chapter 1, page 9). It is this sense of a home base that helps us recognize when a piece of music ends.

The principle of organization around a central tone, the tonic, is called *tonality*. The particular scale chosen as the basis of a piece determines the identity of the tonic and the tonality. Two different types of scale are commonly found in Western music written between about 1650 and 1900: *major* and *minor*. What characterizes these two types are the intervals upon which they are built. More about the formulation of scales later (see Chapter 14, pages 89–90). For the moment, it is sufficient to offer the following observation concerning the differences usually attributed to major and minor scales: music in major may be thought of as bright while minor sounds more subdued. Indeed, in the nineteenth century, the minor was regarded as more somber than the major. For this reason, a composer would hardly choose a minor tonality for a triumphal march or grand finale of a piece. For now, we shall regard major and minor as scale types and tonalities, each with its own unique quality of sound.

Diatonic vs. chromatic

We will observe later that we make a distinction between notes that belong to a particular scale and tonality and those that do not. The term *diatonic* describes melodies or harmonies that are built from the tones of a major or minor scale; *chromatic* (from the Greek word *chroma* meaning color) describes the full gamut of notes available in the octave.

Consonance and Dissonance

Harmonic movement, as we shall see, is generated by motion toward a goal or resolution. This striving for resolution is the dynamic force in our music. It shapes the forward movement, imparting focus and direction. Movement in music receives its maximum impetus from *dissonance*, a combination of tones that sounds discordant, unstable, in need of resolution.

Dissonance introduces the necessary tension into music. Without it, a work would be intolerably dull and insipid. What suspense and conflict are to the drama, dissonance is to music. The resolution of dissonance results in *consonance*, a concordant or agreeable combination of tones that provides a sense of relaxation and fulfillment in music. At their extremes, dissonance can be harsh sounding while consonance is more pleasing to the ear. Each complements the other; both are a necessary part of the artistic whole.

Harmony is a much more sophisticated phenomenon than melody. Historically, it appeared much later, about a thousand years ago, and its real development took place only in the West. Indeed, we may consider the great achievement of Western music to be harmony (hearing in depth), even as in painting it is perspective (seeing in depth). Our harmonic system has advanced steadily over the past ten centuries. Today it is adjusting to new needs. These constitute the latest chapter in man's age-old attempt to impose order upon the raw material of sound—to organize tones in such a way that they will manifest a unifying idea, a selective imagination, a reasoning will.

4

Musical Texture

"Ours is an age of texture."—GEORGE DYSON

In writings on music we encounter frequent references to its fabric or *texture*. Such comparisons between music and cloth are not as unreasonable as may at first appear, since the melodic lines may be thought of as so many threads that make up the musical fabric.

Types of Texture

The simplest texture is *monophonic* or single-voice texture. ("Voice" refers to an individual part or line, even when we speak of instrumental music.) Here the melody is heard without either a harmonic accompaniment or other vocal lines. Attention is focused on the single line. All music up to about a thousand years ago of which we have any knowledge was monophonic.

To this day the music of the Oriental world—of China, Japan, India, Java, Bali, and the Arab nations, for example—is largely monophonic. The melody may be accompanied by a variety of rhythm and percussion instruments that embellish it, but there is no third dimension of depth or perspective that harmony alone confers upon a melody.

When two or more melodic lines are combined, we have a *polyphonic* or many-voiced texture. Here the music derives its expressive power and its interest from the interplay of several lines. Polyphonic texture is based on counterpoint. This term comes from the Latin *punctus contra punctus*, "point against point" or "note against note"—that is to say, one musical line against the other. *Counterpoint* is the art of combining in a single texture two or more simultaneous melodic lines, each with a rhythmic life of its own.

It was a little over a thousand years ago that European musicians hit upon the device of combining two or more lines simultaneously. At this point Western art music parted company from that of the monophonic Orient. There ensued a magnificent flowering of polyphonic art that came to its high point in the fifteenth and sixteenth centuries. This development of counterpoint took place at a time when composers were mainly preoccupied with sacred choral music, which, for the most part, is many-voiced.

In the third type of texture a single voice takes over the melodic interest while the accompanying voices surrender their individuality and become blocks of harmony, the chords that support, color, and enhance the principal part. Here we have a single-melody-with-chords or *homophonic* texture. Again the listener's interest is directed to a single line, but this line, unlike

Monophonic

Polyphonic

Counterpoint

Homophonic

17

the melody of Oriental music, is conceived in relation to a harmonic background. Homophonic texture is heard when a pianist plays a melody in the right hand while the left sounds the chords, or when the singer or violinist carries the tune against a harmonic accompaniment on the piano. Homophonic texture, then, is based on harmony, just as polyphonic texture is based on counterpoint.

We have said that melody is the horizontal aspect of music while harmony is the vertical. The comparison with the warp and woof of a fabric consequently has real validity. The horizontal threads, the melodies, are held together by the vertical threads, the harmonies. Out of their interaction comes a weave that may be light or heavy, coarse or fine. A composition need not use one texture or another exclusively. It may be principally homophonic with polyphonic texture interspersed on occasion, or the reverse.

Contrapuntal Devices

Imitation

When several independent lines are combined, composers try to give unity and shape to the texture. A basic procedure for achieving this end is *imitation*, in which a theme or motive is presented in one voice and then restated in another. While the imitating voice restates the theme, the first voice continues with counterpoint. Thus a polyphonic texture is achieved. We have spoken of the vertical and horizontal threads in musical texture. To these, imitation adds a third, the diagonal (see the example below).

Canon and round

The length of the imitation may be brief or may last the entire work. In the latter case, we have a strict type of composition known as a *canon*. (The name comes from the Greek word for "law" or "order.") The simplest and most popular form of canon is a *round*, in which each voice enters in succession with the same melody. A round is a perpetual canon for singing voices; commonly known examples include the childrens' songs *Row, Row, Row Your Boat* and *Frère Jacques* (Brother John).

Inversion

Retrograde

Retrograde inversion
Augmentation

Diminution

Contrapuntal writing is marked by a number of devices that have flourished for centuries. *Inversion* is a technique that turns the melody upside down; that is, it follows the same intervals but in the opposite direction. Where the melody originally moved up by a third, the inverted version moves down by a third. *Retrograde* refers to a statement of the melody backwards, beginning with its last note and proceeding to its first. These two techniques can be combined in the *retrograde inversion* of a melody: upside down and backwards. *Augmentation* calls for the melody to be presented in longer time values, often twice as slow as the original. Think of it as augmenting or increasing the time it takes to play the melody. The opposite technique is called *diminution* in which the melody is presented in short time values, thus diminishing the time it takes to be played. These devices are illustrated on page 19 using a theme from the Sonata for Violin and Piano by César Franck.

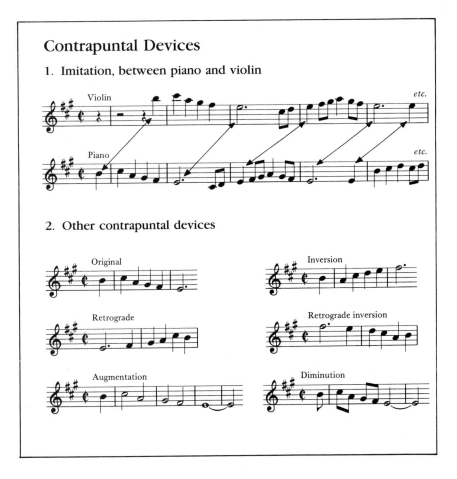

Contrapuntal Devices

1. Imitation, between piano and violin

2. Other contrapuntal devices

Musical Texture and the Listener

Different types of texture require different types of listening. Monophonic music—the simplest type, since it has only a single melodic line—hardly figures in the music of the West at present. Homophonic music poses no special problems to music lovers of today. They are able to differentiate between the principal melody and its attendant harmonies, and to follow the interrelation of the two. They are helped in this by the fact that most of the music they have heard since their childhood consists of melody and chords.

The case is different with polyphonic music, which is not apt to appeal to those who listen with half an ear. Here we must be aware of the independent lines as they flow alongside one another, each in its own rhythm. This requires much greater concentration on our part. Only by dint of repeated hearings do we learn to follow the individual voices and to separate each within the contrapuntal web.

Examples of Musical Texture

Monophonic—one melodic line, no accompaniment

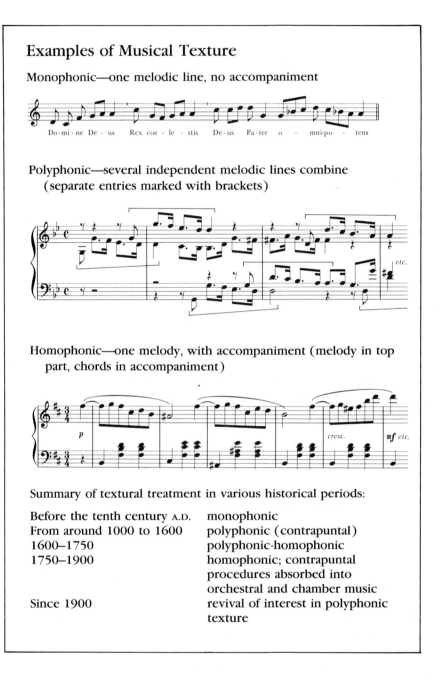

Polyphonic—several independent melodic lines combine
  (separate entries marked with brackets)

Homophonic—one melody, with accompaniment (melody in top
  part, chords in accompaniment)

Summary of textural treatment in various historical periods:

Before the tenth century A.D.	monophonic
From around 1000 to 1600	polyphonic (contrapuntal)
1600–1750	polyphonic-homophonic
1750–1900	homophonic; contrapuntal procedures absorbed into orchestral and chamber music
Since 1900	revival of interest in polyphonic texture

5

Musical Form

"The principal function of form is to advance our understanding. It is the organization of a piece which helps the listener to keep the idea in mind, to follow its development, its growth, its elaboration, its fate."
—ARNOLD SCHOENBERG

Form is that quality in a work of art which presents to the mind of the beholder an impression of conscious choice and judicious arrangement. Form represents clarity and order in art. It shows itself in the selection of certain details and rejection of others. Form is manifest too in the relationship of the parts to the whole. It helps us to grasp the work of art as a unity.

Structure and Design in Music

Our lives are composed of sameness and differentness: certain details are repeated again and again, others are new. Music mirrors this dualism. Its basic law of structure is *repetition and contrast*—unity and variety. Repetition fixes the material in our minds and ministers to our need for the familiar. Contrast sustains our interest and feeds our love of change. From the interaction of the familiar and the new, the repeated elements and the contrasting ones, result the lineaments of musical form. These are to be found in every type of musical organism, from the nursery rhyme to the symphony.

Repetition and contrast

One further principle of form that falls between repetition and contrast is *variation*, where some aspects of the music are altered but recognizable. We hear this formal technique when we listen to a new arrangement of a well-known popular song. The tune is recognizable, but many features of the known version may be changed.

Variation

The principle of form is embodied in a variety of musical structures. These utilize procedures worked out by generations of composers. No matter how diverse, they are based in one way or another on repetition and contrast. The forms, however, are not fixed molds into which composers pour their material. What gives a piece of music its aliveness is the fact that it adapts a general plan to its own requirements. All faces have two eyes, a nose, and a mouth. In each face, though, these features are found in a wholly individual combination. The forms that students in composition follow are ready-made formulas set up for their guidance. The forms of the masters are living organisms in which external organization is delicately adjusted to inner content. No two symphonies of Haydn or Mozart, no two sonatas of Beethoven are exactly alike. Each is a fresh and unique solution to the problem of fashioning musical material into a logical and coherent form.

Two-Part and Three-Part Form

Binary form

Ternary form

The principles of form may be illustrated through two of the most basic and common patterns in music. Two-part or *binary form* is based on a statement and a departure, without a return to the opening section. Three-part or *ternary form*, on the other hand, extends the idea of statement and departure by bringing back the first section. Formal patterns can be simply outlined: binary form as **A-B** and ternary form as **A-B-A**, as illustrated in the following chart.

The Building Blocks of Form

Theme

When a melodic idea is used as a building block in the construction of a musical work, it is known as a *theme*. The theme is the first in a series of musical situations, all of which must grow out of the basic idea as naturally as does the plant from the seed. The process of spinning out a theme, of weaving and reweaving threads of which it is composed, is the essence of musical thinking: every measure in a musical work takes up where the one before left off and brings us inexorably to the next.

The most tightly knit kind of expansion in Western music is known as *thematic development*. To develop a theme means to unfold its latent energies, to search out its capacities for growth and bring them to fruition. Thematic development is one of the most important techniques in musical composition, demanding of the composer imagination, master craftsmanship, and intellectual power.

Thematic development

In the process of development, certain procedures have proved to be particularly effective. The simplest is repetition, which may be either exact or varied; or the idea may be restated at another pitch. Such a restatement at a higher or lower pitch level is known as a *sequence*. The original idea may also be varied in regard to melody, harmony, rhythm, or other elements that we have not yet discussed, such as loudness or softness, tempo, or particular instrumental sound. It may be attended by expansion or contraction of the note lengths as well as by bold and frequent changes of tonality.

Sequence

A basic technique in thematic development is the breaking up of the theme into its constituent motives. A *motive* is the smallest fragment of a theme that forms a melodic-rhythmic unit. Motives are the cells of musical growth. Through fragmentation of themes, through repeating and varying motives and combining them in ever fresh patterns, the composer imparts to the musical organism the quality of dynamic evolution and growth.

Motive

These musical building blocks can be seen in action even in simple songs, such as the popular national tune *America*. In this piece, the opening three-note motive ("My country") is repeated in sequence almost immediately at a different pitch level on the words "Sweet land of." A fine example of a sequence occurs later in the piece: the musical motive set to the words "Land where our fathers died" is repeated beginning on a slightly lower note for the words "Land of the pilgrim's pride."

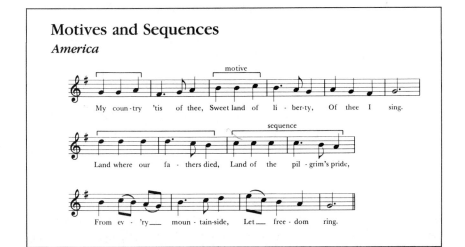

Motives and Sequences
America

In subsequent chapters we shall examine the great forms of Western music. No matter how imposing their dimensions, they all show the principle of repetition and contrast, of unity and variety, that we have traced here. In all its manifestations our music displays the striving for organic form that binds together the individual tones within a phrase, the phrases within a *Movement* section, the sections within a *movement* (a complete, comparatively independent division of a large-scale work), and the movements within a work as a whole; even as, in a novel, the individual words are bound together in phrases, sentences, paragraphs, sections, chapters, and parts.

An essential principle in music, form distributes the areas of activity and repose, tension and relaxation, light and shade, and integrates the multitudinous details, large and small, into the spacious structures that are the glory of Western music.

6

Tempo and Dynamics

"The whole duty of a conductor is comprised in his ability to indicate the right tempo."—RICHARD WAGNER

The Pace of Music

Meter tells us how many beats there are in the measure, but it does not tell *Tempo* us whether these beats occur slowly or rapidly. The *tempo*, by which we mean the rate of speed, the pace of the music, provides the answer to this vital question. Consequently, the flow of music in time involves both meter and tempo.

Tempo carries emotional implications. We hurry our speech in moments of agitation. Our bodies press forward in eagerness, hold back in lassitude. Vigor and gaiety are associated with a brisk gait as surely as despair demands a slow one. In an art of movement such as music, the rate of movement is of prime importance. We respond to musical tempo physically and psychologically. Our pulse, our breathing, our entire being adjusts to the rate of movement and to the feeling engendered thereby on the conscious and subconscious levels.

Because of the close connection between tempo and mood, tempo markings indicate the character of the music as well as the pace. The tempo terms are generally given in Italian, as in the following list:

solemn (very, very slow)	*grave*
broad (very slow)	*largo*
quite slow	*adagio*

a walking pace	*andante*
moderate	*moderato*
fast (cheerful)	*allegro*
lively	*vivace*
very fast	*presto*

Frequently encountered too are modifying adverbs such as *molto* (very), *meno* (less), *poco* (a little), and *non troppo* (not too much).

Of great importance are the terms indicating a change of tempo. The principal ones are *accelerando* (getting faster) and *ritardando* (holding back, getting slower); *a tempo* (in time) indicates a return to the original pace.

Loudness and Softness

Dynamics denote the degree of loudness or softness at which the music is played. In this area, as in that of tempo, certain responses seem to be rooted in the nature of our emotions. Mystery and fear call for a whisper, even as jubilation and vigorous activity go with full resonance.

Dynamics

The principal dynamic indications are:

very soft	*pianissimo* (*pp*)
soft	*piano* (*p*)
moderately soft	*mezzo piano* (*mp*)
moderately loud	*mezzo forte* (*mf*)
loud	*forte* (*f*)
very loud	*fortissimo* (*ff*)

Dynamic contrasts in music are analagous to light and shade in painting. **Rembrandt van Rijn** (*1606–69*) Les disciples d'Emmaus. (*Musée Jacquemart-André, Paris*)

Of special importance are the directions to change the dynamics. Such changes are indicated by words or signs. Among the commonest are:

growing louder   *crescendo* (————————)
growing softer   *decrescendo or diminuendo* (————————)
sudden stress   *sforzando* (*sf*), "forcing"—accent on a single note or chord

Tempo and Dynamics as Elements of Musical Expression

The markings for tempo and dynamics contribute to the expressive content of a piece of music. These so-called expression marks steadily increased in number during the late eighteenth and nineteenth centuries, as composers tried to indicate their intentions ever more precisely. In this regard it is instructive to compare a page of a Handel score (early eighteenth century) with one of Mahler (late nineteenth century; see facing page).

A page from the score of The Royal Fireworks Music *by* **George Frideric Handel.** (Note the absence of expression marks.)

Crescendo and diminuendo are among the important expressive effects available to the composer. Through the gradual swelling and diminishing of the tone volume, the illusion of distance enters music. As orchestral style developed, composers quickly learned to take advantage of this effect.

A page from the score of **Gustav Mahler's** *Symphony No. 2.* (Observe the profusion of expression marks.)

UNIT II

■

Musical Instruments
and Ensembles

7

Musical Instruments I

"With these artificial voices we sing in a manner such as our natural voices would never permit."—JOHN REDFIELD

Properties of Musical Sound

Pitch

Any musical sound can be described in terms of four qualities or properties: pitch, duration, volume, and timbre. By *pitch* we mean the location of a tone in the musical scale in relation to high or low. The pitch is determined by the rate of vibration, which to a large extent depends on the length of the vibrating body. Other conditions being equal, the shorter a string or column of air, the more rapidly it vibrates and the higher the pitch. The longer a string or column of air, the fewer the vibrations per second and the lower the pitch. *Duration* depends on the length of time over which the vibration is maintained. We hear tones as being not only high or low but also short or long. *Volume* (dynamics) depends on the degree of force of the vibrations as a result of which the tone strikes us as being loud or soft.

Duration

Volume

The fourth property of sound is tone color or *timbre*. (The word retains its French pronunciation, *tám'br.*) This is what makes a note on the trumpet sound altogether different from the same note played on a violin or a flute. Timbre is influenced by a number of factors, such as the size, shape, and proportions of the instrument, the material of which it is made, and the manner in which vibration is set up.

Timbre

The composer has available two basic mediums—human voices and musical instruments. When writing for a group of instruments, the composer will try to make each instrument do the things for which it is best suited, taking into account its capacities and limitations. There are, to begin with, the limits of each instrument's range—the distance from its lowest to its highest tone, beyond which it cannot go. There are also the limits of dynamics—the degree of softness or loudness beyond which it cannot be played. There are technical peculiarities native to its low, middle, and high registers, as a result of which a certain combination of notes may be executed more easily on one instrument than on another. (By *register*, we mean a specific area in the range of an instrument or voice, such as low, middle, or high.) These and a host of similar considerations determine the composer's choices.

Register

The Voice as a Model for Instrumental Sound

The human voice is perhaps the most natural of all musical instruments. Each person's voice has a particular quality or character and range. The standard designations for vocal ranges, from highest to lowest, are *soprano, mezzo-soprano*, and *alto* (short for *contralto*) for female voices, *tenor, baritone,* and *bass* for male voices.

Vocal ranges

Throughout the ages, the human voice has served as a model for instrument builders and players, who have sought to transfer its lyric beauty and expressiveness to their instruments. Critics today still praise a violinist or a cellist for having a "singing tone" and Chopin taught his piano pupils that "everything must be made to sing."

String Instruments

The string family includes two types of instruments: those that are bowed and those that are plucked. The bowed string family has four members: violin, viola, violoncello, and double bass, each with four strings that are set vibrating by drawing a bow across them. The bow is held in the right hand while the left hand is used to *stop* the string by pressing a finger down at a particular point, thereby leaving a certain portion of the string free to vibrate. By stopping the string at another point, the violinist changes the length of the vibrating portion, and with it the rate of vibration and the pitch.

The *violin* was brought to its present form by the brilliant instrument makers who flourished in Italy from around 1600 to 1750. Most famous among them were the Amati and Guarneri families—in these dynasties the secrets of the craft were transmitted from father to son—and the master builder of them all, Antonio Stradivari (c. 1645–1737). Pre-eminent in lyric melody, the violin is also capable of brilliance and dramatic effect, of subtle nuances from soft to loud, of the utmost rhythmic precision and great agility in rapid passages. It has an extremely wide range.

Violin

Violinist Itzhak Perlman (Photo Julian Kreeger)

Yo-Yo-Ma, cellist. (Photo © Martha Swope)

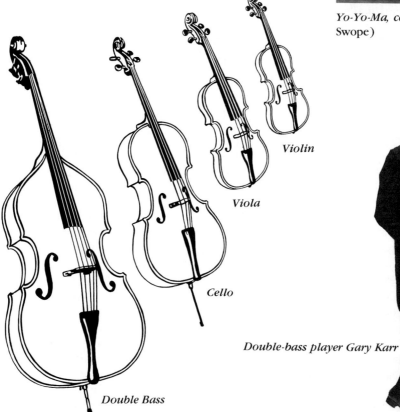

Violin

Viola

Cello

Double Bass

Double-bass player Gary Karr

The *viola* is somewhat larger than the violin, and is lower in range. Its strings are longer, thicker, heavier. The tone is husky in the low register, somber and penetrating in the high. The viola is an effective melody instrument, and often serves as a foil for the more brilliant violin by playing a secondary melody. It usually fills in the harmony, or may *double* another part, that is, reinforce it by playing the same notes an octave higher or lower. *Viola*

The *violoncello*, popularly known as *cello*, is lower in range than the viola and is notable for its lyric quality, which takes on a dark resonance in the low register. Cellos enrich the sonority with their full-throated songfulness, they accentuate the rhythm, and together with the basses, they supply the foundation for the harmony of the string choir. *Violoncello*

The *double bass*, known also as *contrabass* or *bass viol*, is the lowest in range of the string section. Accordingly, it plays the bass part—that is, the foundation of the harmony. *Double bass*

These four string instruments constitute the string section of the orchestra, which has come to be known as "the heart of the orchestra." This term indicates the versatility and importance of this section.

The string instruments are pre-eminent in playing *legato* (smooth and connected), though they are capable too of the opposite quality of tone, *staccato* (short and detached). A special effect, *pizzicato* (plucked), is executed by the performer's plucking the string with a finger instead of using the bow. *Vibrato* denotes a throbbing effect achieved by a rapid wrist-and-finger movement on the string that slightly alters the pitch. In *glissando* a finger of the left hand slides along the string while the right hand draws the bow, thereby sounding all the pitches of the scale. *Tremolo*, the rapid repetition of a tone through a quick up-and-down movement of the bow, is associated with suspense and excitement. No less important is the *trill*, a rapid alternation between a tone and the one above it. *Double-stopping* involves playing two strings simultaneously. Thereby the members of the violin family, essentially melodic instruments, became capable of harmony. The *mute* is a small attachment that fits over the bridge, muffling (and changing) the sound. *Harmonics* are crystalline tones in the very high register. They are produced by lightly touching the sring at certain points while the bow is drawn across the string. *Special effects*

Two plucked string instruments, the harp and the guitar, are in common use. The *harp* is one of the oldest of musical instruments. Its plucked strings produce an ethereal tone that sounds lovely, both alone and in combination with other instruments. Pedals are used to tighten the strings, hence to raise the pitch. Chords on the harp are frequently played in broken form—that is, the tones are sounded one after another instead of simultaneously. From this technique comes the term *arpeggio* which means a broken chord (*arpa* is the Italian for harp). *Harp*

The *guitar*, too, is an old instrument, dating back at least to the Middle Ages. It has always been widely used as a solo instrument, and is associated today with folk and popular music as well as classical styles. The standard acoustical (as opposed to electric) guitar is made of wood, has a fretted fingerboard and six nylon strings, which are plucked with the fingers of the right hand or with a pick. *Guitar*

Woodwind Instruments

In woodwind instruments, the tone is produced by a column of air vibrating within a pipe that has little holes along its length. When one or another of these holes is opened or closed, the length of the vibrating air column within the pipe is changed. The woodwind instruments are capable of remarkable agility by means of an intricate mechanism of keys arranged to suit the natural position of the fingers.

The woodwinds are a less homogeneous group than the strings. Nowadays they are not necessarily made of wood, and they represent several methods of setting up vibration: by blowing across a mouth hole (flute family); by blowing into a mouthpiece that has a single reed (clarinet and saxophone families); or by blowing into a mouthpiece fitted with a double reed (oboe and bassoon families). They do, however, have one important feature in common: the holes in their pipes.

Flute

The *flute* is the soprano voice of the woodwind choir. Its timbre ranges from the poetic to the brilliant. Its tone is cool and velvety in the expressive low register, and smooth in the middle. In the upper part of the range the timbre is bright, birdlike, and stands out against the orchestral mass. The present-day flute, made of a silver alloy rather than wood, is a cylindrical tube that is held horizontally. It is closed at one end. The player's lips are used to blow across a mouth hole cut in the side of the pipe at the other end. The flute is much prized as a melody instrument and offers the performer complete freedom in playing rapid repeated notes, scales, and trills.

Piccolo

The *piccolo* (from the Italian *flauto piccolo*, "little flute") has a piercing tone that produces the highest notes in the orchestra. In its upper register it takes on a shrillness that is easily heard even when the orchestra is playing fortissimo.

Oboe

The *oboe* is made of wood. Its mouthpiece is a double reed consisting of two slips of cane bound together so as to leave between them an extremely small passage for air. Oboe timbre is generally described as plaintive, nasal, reedy. The instrument is associated with pastoral effects and with nostalgic moods. The pitch of the oboe is not readily subject to change, for which reason it is chosen to sound the tuning note for the other instruments of the orchestra.

English horn

The *English horn* is an alto oboe. Its wooden tube is wider and longer than that of the oboe and ends in a pear-shaped opening called a *bell*, which largely accounts for its soft, somewhat mournful timbre. The instrument is not well named, for it is neither English nor a horn.

Clarinet

The *clarinet* has a single reed, a small flexible piece of cane fastened against its chisel-shaped mouthpiece. The instrument possesses a beautiful liquid tone, as well as a remarkably wide range from low to high and from soft to loud. Almost as agile as the flute, it has an easy command of rapid scales, trills, and repeated notes.

Bass clarinet

The *bass clarinet* is one octave lower in range than the clarinet. Its rich singing tone, flexibility, and wide dynamic range make it an invaluable member of the orchestral community.

James Galway, flute virtuoso. (Photo by Brian Davis)

Heinz Holliger playing the oboe.

Richard Stoltzman playing the clarinet in Carnegie Hall.

Bernard Garfield, principal bassoonist of The Philadelphia Orchestra.

Bassoon

The *bassoon* is a double-reed instrument. Its tone is weighty and thick in the low register, dry and sonorous in the middle, reedy and intense in the upper. Capable of a hollow-sounding staccato and wide leaps that create a humorous effect, it is at the same time a highly expressive instrument.

Contrabassoon

The *contrabassoon*, known also as *double bassoon*, produces the lowest tone in the orchestra. Its function in the woodwind section may be compared to that of the double bass among the strings, in that it supplies a foundation for the harmony.

Saxophone

The *saxophone* is of more recent origin, having been invented by the Belgian Adolphe Sax in 1840. It was created by combining the features of several other instruments—the single reed of the clarinet, the conical tube of the oboe, and the metal body of the brass instruments. The saxophone blends well with either woodwinds or brass. In the 1920s it became the characteristic instrument of the jazz band.

8

Musical Instruments II

"Lucidity is the first purpose of color in music."—ARNOLD SCHOENBERG

Brass Instruments

The principal instruments of the brass family are the trumpet, French horn, trombone, and tuba. These instruments have cup-shaped mouthpieces (except for the horn, whose mouthpiece is shaped like a funnel). The tube flares at the end into a bell. The column of air within the tube is set vibrating by the tightly stretched lips of the player, which act as a kind of double reed. To go from one pitch to another involves not only mechanical means, such as a slide or valves, but also variation in the pressure of the lips and breath. This demands great muscular control. Wind instrument players often speak about their *embouchure* referring to the entire oral mechanism of lips, lower facial muscles, and jaws.

Trumpet

The *trumpet*, highest in pitch of the brass choir, possesses a firm, brilliant timbre that lends radiance to the orchestral mass. It is associated with martial pomp and vigor. Played softly, the instrument commands a lovely round tone. The muted trumpet is much used; the mute, a pear-shaped device of metal or cardboard, is inserted in the bell, achieving a bright, buzzy sound. Jazz trumpet players have experimented with various kinds of mutes to produce different timbres, and these are gradually finding their way into the symphony orchestra.

French horn

The *French horn*—generally referred to simply as *horn*—is descended from the ancient hunting horn. Its golden resonance lends itself to a variety

Trumpeter Wynton Marsalis.
(Photo by Marcus Devoe)

Steven Johns playing the tuba. (Photo by
Jane Hamborsky)

*Barry Tuckwell plays the French
horn.* (Photo by Richard Holt/
EMI, Ltd.)

Christian Lindberg, trombonist

of uses: it can be mysteriously remote in soft passages, and nobly sonorous in loud. The timbre of the horn blends equally well with woodwinds, brass, and strings, for which reason it serves as the connecting link among them. Although capable of considerable agility, the horn is at its best in sustained utterance; for sheer majesty, nothing rivals the sound of several horns intoning a broadly flowing theme in unison. The muted horn has a poetic faraway sound. Horn players often "stop" their instrument by plugging the bell with their hand; the result has an ominous rasping quality.

Trombone

The *trombone*—the Italian word means "large trumpet"—has a grand sonorousness that combines the brilliance of the trumpet with the majesty of the horn, but in the tenor range. In place of valves it has a movable U-shaped slide that alters the length of the vibrating air column in the tube. Composers use the trombone to achieve effects of nobility and grandeur.

Tuba and sousaphone

The *tuba* is the bass instrument of the brass choir. Like the string bass and contrabassoon, it furnishes the foundation for the harmonic fabric. The tuba adds body to the orchestral tone, and a dark resonance ranging from velvety softness to a rumbling growl. The *sousaphone* is an adaptation of the tuba designed by the American bandmaster John Philip Sousa, for use in marching bands.

Percussion Instruments

The percussion family comprises a variety of instruments that are made to sound by striking or shaking. Some are made of metal or wood. In others, such as the drums, vibration is set up by striking a stretched skin.

Pitched percussion instruments

The percussion instruments fall into two categories: those capable of being tuned to definite pitches, and those that produce a single sound in the borderland between music and noise (instruments of indefinite pitch). In the former class are the *kettledrums*, or *timpani*, which are generally used in sets of two or three. The kettledrum is a hemispheric copper shell across which is stretched a "head" of plastic or calfskin held in place by a metal ring. A pedal mechanism enables the player to change the tension of the head, and with it the pitch. The instrument is played with two padded sticks, which may be either soft or hard. Its dynamic range extends from a mysterious rumble to a thunderous roll. The *glockenspiel* (German for "set of bells") consists of a series of horizontal tuned steel bars of various sizes. The player strikes these with mallets, producing a bright metallic sound. The *celesta* which in appearance resembles a miniature upright piano, is a kind of glockenspiel that is operated by a keyboard: the steel plates are struck by small hammers and produce a sound like a music box. The *xylophone* consists of tuned blocks of wood laid out in the shape of a keyboard. Struck with mallets with hard heads, the instrument produces a dry, crisp timbre. The *marimba* is a more mellow xylophone of African and Latin-American origin. The *vibraphone* combines the principle of the glockenspiel with resonators, each containing revolving disks operated by electric motors. This instrument is featured in jazz combinations, and has been used by a

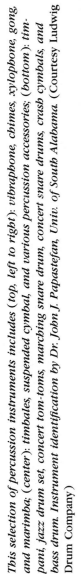

This selection of percussion instruments includes (top, left to right): vibraphone, chimes, xylophone, gong, and marimba; (center): timbales, suspended cymbal, and various percussion accessories; (bottom): timpani, jazz drum set, concert tom-toms, marching snare drum, concert snare drum, crash cymbals, and bass drum. Instrument identification by Dr. John J. Papastefan, Univ. of South Alabama. (Courtesy Ludwig Drum Company)

number of contemporary composers. *Chimes* or *tubular bells* consist of a set of tuned metal tubes of various lengths suspended from a frame and struck with a hammer.

Unpitched percussion instruments

In the other group are the percussion instruments that do not produce a definite pitch. The *side drum* or *snare drum* is a small cylindrical drum with two heads stretched over a shell of metal. It is played with two drumsticks and owes its brilliant tone to the vibrations of the lower head against taut snares (strings). The *tenor drum* is larger in size, with a wooden shell, and has no snares. The *bass drum*, played with a large soft-headed stick, produces a low heavy sound. The *tom-tom* is a name given to American Indian or Oriental drums of indefinite pitch. The *tambourine* is a small round drum with "jingles"—little metal plates—inserted in its rim. It is played by striking the drum with the fingers or elbow, by shaking, or by passing the hand over the jingles. *Castanets* are widely used in Spain. They consist of little wooden clappers moved by the player's thumb and forefinger. The *triangle* is a slender rod of steel bent in the shape of a triangle. It is open at the upper end and, when struck with a steel beater, gives off a bright tinkling sound. *Cymbals* are two large circular brass plates of equal size. When struck sidewise against each other, they produce a shattering sound. The *gong*, or *tam-tam*, is abroad circular disk of metal, suspended in a frame so as to hang freely. When struck with a drumstick, it produces a deep roar.

Other Instruments

Besides the instruments just discussed, several others, especially those of the keyboard family, are frequently heard in solo and ensemble performances.

Piano

The *piano* was originally known as the *pianoforte*, Italian for "soft-loud," which indicates its wide dynamic range and its capacity for nuance. Its strings are struck with hammers controlled by a keyboard mechanism. The piano cannot sustain tone as well as the string and wind instruments, but in the hands of a fine performer it is capable of producing a singing melody. Each string (except in the highest register) is covered by a damper that stops the sound when the finger releases the key. There are three pedals. If the one on the right is pressed down, all the dampers are raised, so that the strings continue to vibrate, producing that luminous haze of sound which the great piano composers used to such advantage. The pedal on the left shifts the hammers to reduce the area of impact on the strings, thereby inhibiting the volume of sound; hence it is known as the "soft pedal." The middle pedal (missing on upright pianos) is the sustaining pedal, which sustains only the tones held down at the moment the pedal is depressed. The piano is pre-eminent for brilliant scales, arpeggios, and trills, rapid passages, and octaves. It has a wide range from lowest to highest pitch, spanning eighty-eight keys or semitones.

Organ

The *organ*, once regarded as "the king of instruments," is a wind instrument; air is fed to its pipes by mechanical means. The pipes are controlled by two or more keyboards and a set of pedals. Gradations in the volume of tone are made possible on the modern organ by means of swell boxes. The organ possesses a multicolored sonority that is capable of filling a huge space. Electrically amplified keyboards, capable of imitating pipe organs and other timbres, are commonplace today. A number of sound production methods have been explored, including vibrating metal reeds, oscillators, and, most recently, digital waveform synthesis.

The instruments described in this chapter and in the previous one form a vivid and diversified group. To the composer, performers, and listener alike, they offer an endless variety of colors and shades of expression.

Misha Dichter at the piano. (Photo by J. Henry Fair)

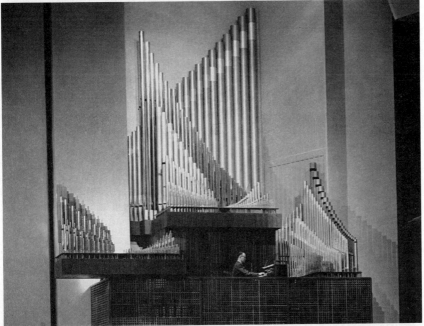

Performing on the modern Holtkamp Organ at Furman University, Greenville, South Carolina. (Photo courtesy H. Neil Gillespie)

9

Musical Ensembles

Choral Groups

Chorus

By choral music, we mean music performed by many voices in a chorus or choir. A *chorus* is a fairly large body of singers who perform together; their music is usually sung in several parts. A chorus most often consists of both men and women, but the term can also refer to a men's chorus or a women's chorus. A *choir* is traditionally a smaller group, often connected with a

Choir

church. The standard voice parts in both chorus and choir correspond to the voice ranges explained earlier: sopranos, altos, tenors, and basses.

In early times, choral music was often performed without accompaniment.

A cappella

This singing style is known as *a cappella* (meaning "in the church style"). The organ eventually became coupled with the choir in church music, and by the eighteenth century, the orchestra had established itself as a partner of the chorus.

There are many smaller, specialized vocal ensembles as well, such as a madrigal choir, chamber chorus, or glee club. These groups might perform a cappella secular works, popular music, or college songs.

Chamber Ensembles

Chamber music is ensemble music for up to about ten players, with one player to a part, as distinct from orchestral music, in which a single instrumental part is performed by anywhere from two to eighteen players. The essential trait of chamber music is its intimacy; its natural setting is the home.

Many of the standard chamber music ensembles depend on string players. Most common is the string quartet, consisting of two violins, viola, and cello.

The Tokyo String Quartet (Peter Oundjian, Kikuei Ikeda, violins; Sadao Harada, viola; and Kazuhide Isomura, cello) enjoys an international reputation. (Photograph by Christian Steiner)

Other popular combinations are the duo sonata, the piano trio and quartet, the string quintet, as well as larger groups—sextet, septet, and octet. Winds too have standard chamber combinations, especially woodwind and brass quintets. These ensembles are outlined below.

Standard Chamber Ensembles

DUO SONATA	Solo instrument and piano		
TRIO			
String trio	Violin 1	or	Violin
	Violin 2		Viola
	Cello		Cello
Piano trio	Piano		
	Violin		
	Cello		
QUARTETS			
String quartet	Violin 1		
	Violin 2		
	Viola		
	Cello		
Piano quartet	Piano		
	Violin		
	Viola		
	Cello		
QUINTETS			
String quintet	Violin 1	or	Violin 1
	Violin 2	(more rarely)	Violin 2
	Viola 1		Viola
	Viola 2		Cello 1
	Cello		Cello 2
Piano quintet	Violin 1 ⎱		
	Violin 2 ⎰		
	Viola ⎱ string quartet		
	Cello ⎰		
	Piano		
Woodwind quintet	Flute		
	Oboe		
	Clarinet		
	French horn (not a woodwind instrument)		
	Bassoon		
Brass quintet	Trumpet 1		
	Trumpet 2		
	French horn		
	Trombone		
	Tuba		

(Above) The Boston Symphony Orchestra with its conductor Seiji Ozawa. (Photograph by Christian Steiner) *(Below) The seating plan of the orchestra.*

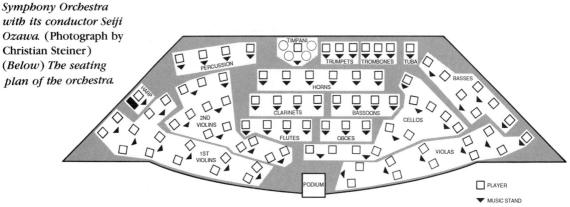

The Orchestra

Instruments have traditionally been grouped into several large standard ensembles. Most popular among these are the orchestra, which has varied in size and makeup throughout its history but features strings as its core. From the twenty-piece group of the Baroque era and the forty-odd instruments of the Classical orchestra, the modern orchestra has grown into an ensemble of more than a hundred players. The performers are divided into the four instrumental families we have studied, and approximately two-thirds of the orchestra consists of string players. In large cities, orchestral musicians give full time to rehearsal and performance.

The instruments of the orchestra are arranged so as to secure the best balance of tone. Most of the strings are near the front, as are the gentle woodwinds. Brass and percussion are at the back. The seating plan for the Boston Symphony Orchestra is shown on the facing page; this arrangement varies from one orchestra to another.

The Band

The band is a much-loved American tradition, be it a concert, marching, military, jazz or rock ensemble. The earliest wind and percussion groups were used for military purposes. Musicians accompanied soldiers to war, playing their brass and percussion instruments from horseback to spur the troops on to victory, and their fifes and drums from among the ranks of the foot soldiers. Concert wind groups originated in the Middle Ages. In northern Europe, a wind band of three to five musicians played each evening, often from the high tower of a local church or city hall. From these traditions grew the military bands of the French Revolution and American Civil War. One American bandmaster, John Philip Sousa (1854–1932), achieved world fame with his brass band and the repertory of marches that he wrote for it.

Today the *concert band*, an ensemble ranging anywhere from forty to eighty members or more, is an established institution in most secondary schools, colleges, and universities and in many communities as well. Modern composers like to write for this ensemble since it traditionally plays new compositions. The *marching band*, best known in the United States, is a popular group for entertainment at sports events and parades. Besides its core of winds and percussion, this group often includes a spectacular display of drum majors/majorettes, flag twirlers, and the like. The precise instrumentation of *jazz bands* depends on the particular music being played, but generally includes a reed section made up of clarinets and saxophones of various sizes, a brass section of trumpets and trombones, and a rhythm section of percussion, piano, and strings, especially double bass and electric guitar.

Concert band

Marching band

Jazz band

A performance by the Wind Symphony of California State University, Long Beach, Larry Curtis conducting. (Photo courtesy CSULB Photographic Services)

Britten's Young Person's Guide to the Orchestra

A helpful introduction to the orchestra is Benjamin Britten's *Young Person's Guide to the Orchestra*, which was written expressly for the purpose of illustrating the timbre of each orchestral instrument. The work, composed in 1946, is subtitled *Variations and Fugue on a Theme by Purcell* and is based on a dance tune by Henry Purcell, the great seventeenth-century English composer.

Britten's plan was to introduce the sound of the entire orchestra playing together, then the sonorities of each instrumental family as a family—woodwinds, brass, strings, percussion—and then to repeat the statement by the full orchestra. Once the listener has the theme well in mind, the composer features each instrument in the order of highest to lowest in range within each family. In this section, we encounter variations of the theme, each presented by a new instrument and with differing accompanying instruments. (See Listening Guide 1 for the order of instruments.) Finally, the work closes with a grand *fugue*, a polyphonic form popular in the Baroque era (1600–1750), which is also based on Purcell's theme. Just as in the variations, the fugue presents its subject, or theme, in rapid order in each instrument.

Listening Guide 1

BRITTEN: *Young Person's Guide to the Orchestra*
(*Variations and Fugue on a Theme by Purcell*)

Date: 1946

Theme: Based on a dance from Henry Purcell's incidental music to the play *Abdelzar* (*The Moor's Revenge*)

Form: Theme and variations, followed by a fugue

I. THEME: 8 measures in D minor, stated six times to illustrate the instrumental families of the orchestra:

1. entire orchestra
2. woodwinds
3. brass
4. strings
5. percussion
6. entire orchestra

II. VARIATIONS: 13 short variations, each illustrating a different instrument or family of instruments:

	Variations	Solo Instrument	Accompanying Instruments
Woodwinds	1	flutes, piccolo	violins, harp, triangle
	2	oboes	strings and timpani
	3	clarinets	strings and tuba
	4	bassoons	strings and snare drum
Strings	5	violins	brass and bass drum
	6	violas	woodwinds and brass
	7	cellos	clarinets, violas, harp
	8	double basses	woodwinds and tambourine
	9	harp	strings, gong, and cymbal
Brass	10	French horns	strings, harp, and timpani
	11	trumpets	strings and snare drum
	12	trombones, tuba	woodwinds and high brass
Percussion	13	percussion	strings

(Order of introduction: timpani, bass drum and cymbals, timpani, tambourine and triangle, timpani, snare drum and wood block, timpani, castanets and gong, timpani, whip, whole percussion section)

III. FUGUE: subject based on a fragment of the Purcell theme, played in imitation by each instrument of the orchestra in same order as in variations:

Woodwinds:	piccolo
	flutes
	oboes
	clarinets
	bassoons
Strings:	first violins
	second violins
	violas
	cellos
	double basses
	harp
Brass:	French horns
	trumpets
	trombones, tuba
Percussion:	percussion

Full orchestra at end

TRANSITION I

■

Hearing Musical Styles

The Concept of Style

"A good style should show no sign of effort. What is written should seem a happy accident."—SOMERSET MAUGHAM

Style may be defined as the characteristic manner of presentation in any art. The word may refer to the element of flexibility that shapes each type of art work to its function. We distinguish between the style of a novel and that of an essay, between the style of a cathedral and that of a palace. The word may also indicate the creator's personal manner of expression—the distinctive flavor that sets one artist apart from all others. Thus we speak of the style of Dickens or Thackeray, of Raphael or Michelangelo, of Wagner or Brahms. In a larger sense we often identify style with national culture, as when we speak of French, Italian, or German style; or with an entire civilization, as when we contrast the musical style of the West with that of the Orient.

It is the difference in the treatment of the elements of music that makes one musical work sound very different from another, the music of another culture widely divergent from ours. We have seen that a violin and a piano have individual qualities of sound and unique capabilities, and that one melody, with its characteristic ups and downs, does not sound just like another. But it is differing concepts of how to combine the elements of music that produces varying musical styles.

Musical Styles in History

Since all the arts change from one age to the next, one very important use of the word "style" is in connection with the various historical periods. Here the concept of style enables us to draw the proper connection between the artists and their time, so that the art work is placed in its socio-historical frame. No matter how greatly the artists of a particular era may vary in personality and outlook, when seen in the perspective of time they turn out to have certain qualities in common. The age has put its stamp upon all. Because of this we can tell at once that a work of art—whether music, poetry, painting, or architecture—dates from the Middle Ages or the Renaissance, from the eighteenth century or the nineteenth. The style of a period, then, is the total art language of all its artists as they react to the artistic, political, economic, religious, and philosophical forces that shape their environment.

Scholars will always disagree as to precisely when one style period ends and the next begins. Each period leads by imperceptible degrees into the following one, dates and labels being merely convenient signposts. The following outline shows the main style periods in the history of Western music. Each represents a conception of form and technique, an ideal of beauty, a manner of expression and performance attuned to the cultural climate of the period—in a word, a style! (The dates, naturally, are approximate.)

350–600 A.D.	Period of the Church Fathers
600–850	Early Middle Ages—Gregorian Chant
850–1150	Romanesque period—Development of the staff in musical notation, about 1000
1150–1450	Gothic period
1450–1600	Renaissance period
1600–1750	Baroque period
1725–1775	Rococo period
1750–1825	Classical period
1820–1900	Romantic period
1890–1915	Post-Romantic period—including Impressionism
1900–	Twentieth century

PART TWO

Medieval and Renaissance Music

"Music was originally discreet, seemly, simple, masculine, and of good morals. Have not the moderns rendered it lascivious beyond measure?"—JACOB OF LIÈGE

Sandro Botticelli (*1445–1510*) Adoration of the Magi (National Gallery of Art, Washington. Andrew W. Mellon Collection.)

UNIT III

■

The Middle Ages

10

The Culture of the Middle Ages

"Nothing is more characteristic of human nature than to be soothed by sweet modes and stirred up by their opposites. Infants, youths, and old people as well are so naturally attuned to musical modes by a kind of spontaneous feeling that no age is without delight in sweet song."—BOETHIUS (c. 480–524)

The relics of the ancient civilizations—Sumer, Babylonia, Egypt—bear witness to a flourishing musical art; however, only a few fragments have descended to us of the music of antiquity. The centuries have forever silenced the sounds that echoed through the Athenian amphitheater and the Roman circus. Those sounds and the attitudes they reflected, in Greece and throughout the Mediterranean world, formed the subsoil out of which flowered the music of later ages. They became part of the heritage of the West.

The Middle Ages extended over the thousand-year period between the fall of Rome, commonly set at A.D. 476, and the flowering of the culture of the modern world. The first half of this millennium, from around 500 to 1000 and often referred to as the Dark Ages, should not be viewed as a period of decline, but rather of ascent, during which Christianity triumphed over paganism throughout Europe. In this society all power flowed from the king, with the benign approval of the Church and its bishops. The two centers of power, Church and state, were bound to clash, and the struggle between them shaped the next chapter of European history. The concept of a strong, centralized government as the ultimate dispenser of law and order found its embodiment in Charlemagne (742–814), the legendary em-

Feudalism

51

peror of the Franks in whose domains Roman, Frankish, and Teutonic elements intermingled. This progressive monarch, who regretted until his dying day that he did not know how to write, encouraged education and left behind him an ideal of social justice that illumined the "darkness" of the early Medieval world.

The monastic influence

The culture of this period was largely shaped by the rise of monasteries. It was the monks who preserved the learning of the ancient world and transmitted it, through their manuscripts, to European scholars. In their desire to enhance the church service, they extensively cultivated music. Because of their efforts, the art music of the Middle Ages was largely religious. Women too played a role in the preservation of knowledge and in music for the church, for nuns had an important societal role in this era. One woman stands out in particular, Hildegard of Bingen, abbess of an abbey in a small town in West Germany. She is remembered today for her writings on natural history, medicine, and for her poetry and music for special services of the church.

The High Middle Ages, from around 1000 to 1400, witnessed the building of the great cathedrals and the founding of universities throughout Europe. Cities emerged as centers of art and culture, and with them came the townsman, the bourgeois, who was destined to play an ever expanding role in civic life. Developing national literatures played their part in shaping the languages of Europe: the *Chanson de Roland* in France, Dante's *Divine Comedy* (1307) in Italy, Chaucer's *Canterbury Tales* (1386) in England. These literary landmarks have their counterparts in painting with Giotto's frescoes for the Arena chapel in Padua (1306; see page 57) and Orcagna's *Last Judgment* for Florence (c. 1355).

The Virgin, seen as the sweetly-loving Mother of God, in this detail of a statue from the Ile-de-France, c. 1200, by an unknown artist. (Museum of Fine Arts, Boston. William Francis Warden Fund)

Although feudal society was male-dominated, idealizing as it did the figure of the fearless warrior, women's status was raised by the universal cult of Mary, the mother of Christ, and was further enhanced by the concepts of chivalry that emerged from the age of knighthood. In the songs of the court minstrels, the woman was adored with a fervor that laid the foundation for our concept of romantic love. This poetic attitude found its perfect symbol in the image of the faithful knight who worshiped his lady from afar and was inspired by her to deeds of daring and self-sacrifice.

The age of knighthood

The Middle Ages, in brief, encompassed a period of enormous ferment and change. Out of its stirrings emerged the profile of what we today know as Western civilization.

11

Music of the Medieval World

"When God saw that many men were lazy, and gave themselves only with difficulty to spiritual reading, He wished to make it easy for them, and added the melody to the Prophet's words, that all being rejoiced by the charm of the music, should sing hymns to Him with gladness."—ST. JOHN CHRYSOSTOM (345–407)

Sacred Music

The early music of the Christian Church was shaped by Greek, Hebrew, and Syrian influences. It became necessary in time to assemble the ever growing body of music into an organized liturgy. The task extended over several generations but is traditionally associated with the name of Pope Gregory the Great, who reigned from 590 to 604.

Like the music of the Greeks and Hebrews from which it descended, *Gregorian chant* (also known as *plainchant* or *plainsong*) consists of a single-line melody. In other words, it is monophonic in texture and lacks the dimension of harmony and counterpoint. Its freely flowing vocal line is subtly attuned to the inflections of the Latin text. Gregorian melody is generally free from regular accent.

Gregorian chant

The Gregorian melodies, numbering more than three thousand, formed an anonymous body of music whose roots reached deep into the spiritual life of the people. In melodic style, Gregorian chant avoids wide leaps and dynamic contrasts. Its gentle rise and fall constitute a kind of disembodied musical speech, "a prayer on pitch."

At first the Gregorian chants were handed down orally from one generation to the next. As the number of chants increased, however, singers needed

Neumes

to be reminded of the general outlines of the different melodies. Thus came into being *neumes*, little ascending and descending signs that were first written above the words to suggest the contour of the melody, and which developed into a musical notation with square notes on a four-line staff (see facing page).

Text settings

As far as the setting of text is concerned, the melodies fall into three main classes: *syllabic*, that is, one note to each syllable of text; *neumatic*, generally with groups of two to four notes to a syllable; and *melismatic*, with a single text syllable extending over longer groups of notes. The melismatic style, descended from the rhapsodic improvisations of the Orient, became a prominent feature of Gregorian chant and exerted a strong influence on subsequent Western music.

Modes

From Gregorian chant to the Baroque era, Western music made use of a variety of scale patterns or *modes*. In addition to major and minor modes, there were others that lacked a strong sense of gravitation to the tonic note. The modes served as the basis for European art music for a thousand years. With the development of polyphony, or many-voiced music, a harmonic system evolved, based on modes. The adjective *modal* consequently refers to the type of melody and harmony that prevailed in the early and later Middle Ages. It is frequently used in opposition to *tonal*, which refers to the harmony based on the major-minor tonality that came later.

The Mass

The Mass is the most solemn ritual of the Roman Catholic Church. It constitutes a re-enactment of the sacrifice of Christ. The name is derived from the Latin *missa*, "dismissal" (of the congregation at the end of the service). The aggregation of prayers that make up the Mass fall into two categories: those that vary from day to day throughout the church year

Proper and Ordinary

dependent upon the particular feast celebrated, the *Proper*; and those that remain the same in every Mass, the *Ordinary*. (A chart of the organization of the Mass with the individual movements of the Proper and Ordinary appears in Chapter 13, page 72.) The liturgy, which reached its present form about nine hundred years ago, is supported by Gregorian melodies for each item of the ceremony. In this way, Gregorian chant was central to the celebration of the Mass, which was and remains today the most important service in the Catholic Church.

A *Gregorian Melody:* Haec dies

A fine example of Gregorian chant is *Haec dies*, the Gradual from the

Gradual

solemn Mass for Easter Day. *Gradual* is the name of the fourth item of the Proper or variable part of the Mass. Derived from the Latin word for steps (because the melody may have been sung from the steps of the altar), the term was applied to the singing of portions of a Psalm in a musically elaborate,

Responsorial

melismatic style. The Gradual is performed in a *responsorial* manner, that is, as a series of interchanges between soloist and chorus in which one answers the other. The solo passage is known as a *verse*, the choral answer

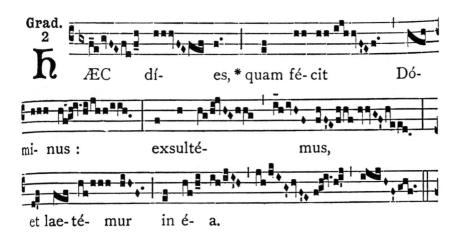

Grad. 2

ℏ ÆC dí- es, * quam fé- cit Dó-

mi- nus : exsulté- mus,

et lae- té- mur in é- a.

The opening of the chant, Haec dies, *in Gregorian notation.*

is the *respond.* The Gradual therefore involves the contrast between two dissimilar bodies of sound, and is monophonic in texture.

Haec dies opens with a brief introductory passage for a soloist. The choral response occupies the first half of the melody. The second half is given over to the verse of the soloist, which is followed by a brief choral conclusion. (See Listening Guide 2 for the text, which is drawn from two Psalms.) The melody moves by step or small leap within a narrow range and consists of a series of tiny motives that grow like cells and expand in a natural process of variation. Striking is the way in which certain key words are extended over a series of notes. This melismatic treatment brings into prominence such important words as *Dominus* (Lord) or *exsultemus* (we will rejoice), setting them apart from the others.

Melismatic setting

Listening Guide 2

🖭 1A/1

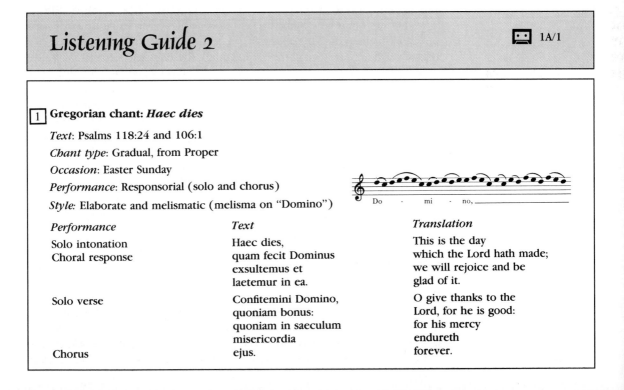

1 **Gregorian chant: *Haec dies***

Text: Psalms 118:24 and 106:1

Chant type: Gradual, from Proper

Occasion: Easter Sunday

Performance: Responsorial (solo and chorus)

Style: Elaborate and melismatic (melisma on "Domino")

Do - mi - no, _____

Performance	Text	Translation
Solo intonation	Haec dies,	This is the day
Choral response	quam fecit Dominus exsultemus et laetemur in ea.	which the Lord hath made; we will rejoice and be glad of it.
Solo verse	Confitemini Domino, quoniam bonus: quoniam in saeculum misericordia	O give thanks to the Lord, for he is good: for his mercy endureth
Chorus	ejus.	forever.

The Rise of Polyphony: The Notre Dame School

Toward the end of the Romanesque period (c. 850–1150) began the single most important development in the history of Western music: the emergence of polyphony. (You will remember that *polyphony* combines two or more simultaneous melodic lines.) This occurred at about the same time that European painting began developing the science of perspective. Thus hearing and seeing in depth came into European culture together.

Once several melodic lines proceeded simultaneously, the flexible prose rhythms of single-line music disappeared. Polyphony contributed to the increased use of regular meters that enabled the different voices to keep together. This music had to be written down in a way that would indicate precisely the rhythm and the pitch, which necessitated a more exact notational system not unlike the one in use today. (For an explanation of our modern notational system, see Appendix I, Musical Notation).

Organum   The earliest kind of polyphonic music was called *organum*, which developed when the custom arose of adding to the Gregorian melody a second voice that paralleled the plainchant at the interval of a fifth or fourth above or below. In the forefront of this development were the composers whose center was the Cathedral of Notre Dame in Paris during the twelfth and

Léonin   thirteenth centuries. Their leader, Léonin, is the first composer of polyphonic music whose name is known to us. He lived in the latter part of the twelfth century and appears to have won considerable fame.

It was self-evident to the Medieval mind that the new must be founded on the old. Therefore composers of organum based their pieces on preexisting Gregorian chant, such as the *Haec dies* melody. While the tenor sang the melody in enormously long notes, the upper voice moved freely and rapidly above it. This is known as *organal style*. In such a setting, the chant was no longer recognizable as a melody. Its presence was symbolic, anchoring the new in the old, inspiring and guiding the added voice.

Pérotin   While Léonin limited himself to polyphony in two parts, his successor Pérotin extended the technique by writing for three and four voices. Toward the end of Pérotin's life, clerics began composing new texts for the previously textless upper voices of organum. The addition of these texts resulted in

Motet   the *motet*, the most important form of early polyphonic music. The term "motet" derives from the French word *mot*, referring to the words that were added to the vocal lines. These might present two different Latin texts at the same time; or one might have Latin words while another French. The motet is, then, a vocal composition, either sacred or secular, which may or may not have had instrumental accompaniment.

The early motet illustrates how Medieval composers based their own works on what had been handed down from the past. They selected a fragment of Gregorian chant, such as the *Haec dies* we have just studied, and, keeping the notes intact, gave them precise rhythmic values, usually of very long notes that contrasted with the more active movement of the other parts. This served as the structural skeleton of the piece, to which the composer added one, two, or three freely-composed countermelodies. (A

Polyphony emerged as a stylistic factor of prime importance in Western music at about the same time that European painting began to reflect the science of perspective. **Giotto** (*c. 1267–1337*) Lamentation. (Arena Chapel, Padua. Scala/Art Resource)

countermelody is a melody heard against another.) In the motet, a sacred text might be combined with a quite secular—even racy—one. The basic Gregorian theme, hidden among the voices, fused these disparate elements into a unity—if not in the listener's ear, at least in the composer's mind.

Countermelody

Secular Music of the Jongleurs, Troubadours, and Trouvères

Alongside the learned or art music of the cathedrals and choir schools there sprang up a popular literature of songs and dances that reflected every aspect of Medieval life. The earliest secular songs that have been preserved were set to Latin texts, which suggests their origin in university towns rather than in the villages. Typical are the student or Goliard songs of the period. In these works, both poetry and music celebrate the joys of the bottle, the impermanence of love, the beauty of springtime, and the cruelty of fate.

The *jongleurs* emerged as a class of musicians who wandered among the courts and towns. These were versatile entertainers who played instruments, sang and danced, juggled and showed tricks along with animal acts, and performed plays. In an age that had no newspapers, they regaled their audience with gossip and news. These actor-singers were viewed as little better than vagabonds and thus lived on the fringe of society.

On an altogether different social level were the poet-musicians who flourished at the various courts of Europe. The *troubadours* were Medieval poet-musicians who lived in Provence, the region roughly equivalent to southern France, while the *trouvères* were active in the provinces to the north. Both terms mean the same thing—finders or inventors— implying that these musicians performed original material, as distinguished from the Church

Heinrich von Meissen, called "Frauenlob" or champion of ladies, is exalted by musicians playing drum, flute, shawm, fiddles, psaltery, and bagpipe. Frauenlob was a minnesinger (singer of courtly love), the German counterpart of the troubadour. (Heidelberg University Library)

musicians who based their art on melodies that had been handed down from the past.

Roles of secular music

Secular music became an integral part of Medieval court life, supplying the necessary accompaniment for dancing, dinner, and after-dinner entertainment. It was indispensable in ceremonies for visiting dignitaries, at tournaments and civic processions; military music supported campaigns, strengthened the spirit of warriors departing on the Crusades, and greeted them upon their return.

Courtly poetry

The poems of the troubadour and trouvère repertory ranged from simple ballads to love songs, political and moral ditties, war songs, laments, and dance songs. They exalted the virtues prized by the age of chivalry—valor, honor, nobility of character, devotion to an ideal, and the quest for perfect love. Like so many of our popular songs today, many of them dealt with the subject of unrequited passion. The object of the poet's desire was generally unattainable, either because of her exalted rank or because she was already wed to another. This poetry, in short, dealt with love in its most idealized form. Significantly, the songs in praise of the Virgin Mary were cast in the same style and language, sometimes even to the same melodies, as served to express love of a more worldly kind.

Moniot d'Arras

One of the last trouvères was Moniot d'Arras, a monk in the abbey of St. Vaast. Characteristic is his folklike love song *Ce fut en mai* (It happened in May), a monophonic tune probably sung against an improvised instrumental accompaniment which tells of an unhappy lover who finds solace in religious feeling.

Guillaume de Machaut and the French Ars Nova Motet

The breakup of the feudal social structure brought with it new concepts of life, art, and beauty. This ferment was reflected in the musical style that made its appearance at the beginning of the fourteenth century in France and somewhat later in Italy, known as *Ars Nova* (new art). The music of the French Ars Nova shows greater refinement than the *Ars Antiqua* (old art), which it displaced. Writers such as Petrarch, Boccaccio, and Chaucer were turning from the divine comedy to the human; painters would soon begin to discover the beauties of nature and the attractiveness of the human form. So, too, composers turned increasingly from religious to secular themes. The Ars Nova encompassed developments in rhythm, meter, harmony, and counterpoint that transformed the art.

Its outstanding figure was the French composer-poet Guillaume de Machaut (c. 1300–77). He took holy orders at an early age, became secretary to John of Luxembourg, King of Bohemia, and was active at the court of Charles, Duke of Normandy, who subsequently became King of France. He spent his old age as a canon of Rheims, admired as the greatest musician of the time.

Machaut's double career as cleric and courtier impelled him to both religious and secular music. His poetry reveals him as a proponent of the ideals of Medieval chivalry—a romantic who exalted the moral and social code of an age that was already finished.

Machaut: Hareu! hareu! le feu—Helas!—Obediens

The secular motet came to full flower in the art of Machaut. He expanded the form of the preceding century to incorporate the new developments made possible by the Ars Nova, especially the greater variety and flexibility of rhythm. Characteristic is the motet *Hareu! hareu! le feu/Helas! ou sera pris confors/Obediens usque ad mortem.* Since the three simultaneous parts have different texts, the listener is obviously expected to follow the general idea rather than the individual words. The top voice, the *triplum*, sings a poem on a favorite theme of fourteenth-century verse—the suffering of the lover who is consumed by his desire. At the same time, the middle voice, the *duplum*, sings a fifteen-line poem in a similar vein. (See Listening Guide 3 for the texts.)

The bottom voice is the structural one, called the *tenor*, from the Latin *tenere* (to hold), so called because it "held" the long notes. The tenor is taken from a plainsong Gradual that refers to Christ, but Machaut chooses only the section that goes with the words *obediens usque ad mortem* (obedient even unto death), a sentiment appropriate to the chivalric love described in the other poems. The notes of the tenor are arranged in a rhythmic pattern that is repeated again and again.

This procedure identifies *Hareu! hareu! le feu* as an *isorhythmic motet* (*iso* means "the same"), based on a repeating rhythm or an *ostinato*. The

Isorhythmic motet
Ostinato

slow-moving tenor was probably played on an instrument, such as the slide trumpet (an early type of trumpet, with a single slide rather than a double, like today's trombone). The upper two voices move at a much faster rate, in a compound meter we could call 6/8 time. Though they occupy the same range, the triplum generally stays at the top of that range, the duplum near the bottom. This highly stylized art, which delights in structural sophistication, tells us something of the society for which it was created.

Listening Guide 3   📼 1A/2

MACHAUT: *Hareu! hareu! le feu—Helas!— Obediens*

Date: mid–14th-century

Genre: Isorhythmic motet, 3-voiced

Text: 3 different texts (2 French, 1 Latin)

Form: Based on rhythmic ostinato pattern: short-long-long-long-short. Repetitions of ostinato: 6 in very long notes, 6 in diminution (half as long)

TRIPLUM VOICE

Form	Text	Rhyme Scheme	Translation
Long note ostinato			
1	Hareu! hareu! le feu, le feu, le feu	a	Help! Help! Fire! Fire! Fire!
	D'ardant desir, qu'einc si ardant ne fu,	a	My heart is on fire with burning desire
	Qu'en mon cuer a espris et sousteneu	a	Such as was never seen before.
2	Amours, et s'a la joie retenu	a	Love, having started it, fans the flames,
	D'espoir qui doit attemprer telle ardure.	b	Withholding all hope of joy which might put out such a blaze.
	Las! se le feu qui ensement l'art dure,	b	Alas, if this fire keeps on burning,
3	Mes cuers sera tous bruis et esteins,	c	My heart, already blackened and shrivelled.

	Qui de ce feu est ja nercis et teins,	c	Will be burnt to ashes.
	Pour ce qu'il est fins, loyaus et certeins;	c	For it is true, loyal, and sincere.
4	Si que j'espoir que deviez yert, eins	c	I expect I shall be mad with grief
	Que bonne Amour de merci l'asseure	b	Before gentle Love consoles it
	Par la vertu d'esperance seure.	b	With sound hope.
5	Car pour li seul, qui endure mal meint;	d	It alone, suffering much Hardship,
	Pitié deffaut, ou toute biauté meint;	d	Is devoid of Pity, abode of all beauty.
	Durtés y regne et Dangiers y remeint,	d	Instead, Harshness rules over it and Haughtiness flourishes.
6	Desdeins y vit et Loyautez s'i feint	d	Disdain dwells there, while Loyalty is a rare visitor
	Et Amours n'a de li ne de moy cure.	b	And Love pays no heed to it or to me.
	Joie le het, ma dame li est dure,	b	Joy hates it, and my lady is cruel to it.

Diminution of ostinato

1	Et, pour croistre mes dolereus meschiés,	e	To complete my sad misfortune,
2	Met dedens moy Amours, qui est mes chiés,	e	Love, my sovereign lord,
3	Un desespoir qui si mal entechiés	e	Fills me with such bitter despair
4	Est quietous biens a de moy esrachiés,	e	That I am left penniless,
5	Et en tous cas mon corps si desnature	b	And so wasted in body
6	Qu'il me convient morir malgré Nature.	b	That I shall surely die before my time.

DUPLUM VOICE

Long note ostinato

1	Helas! ou sera pris confors	a	Alas, where can I find consolation
	Pour moy qui ne vail nés que mors?	a	Who am as good as dead?
2	Quant riens garentir ne me puet	b	When my one salvation
3	Fors ma dame chiere qui wet	b	Is my dear lady,
	Qu'en desespoir muire, sans plus,	c	Who gladly lets me die in despair,
4	Pour ce que je l'aim plus que nulz,	c	Simply because I love her as no other could.
5	Et Souvenir pour enasprir	d	And Memory, in order to keep
	L'ardour de mon triste desir	d	My unhappy desire alive,
6	Me moustre adés sa grant bonté	e	Reminds me all the while of her great goodness.

Diminution of ostinato

1	Et sa fine vraie biauté	e	And her delicate beauty,
2	Qui doublement me fait ardoir.	f	Thereby making me want her all the more.
3	Einssi sans cuer et sans espoir.	f	Deprived thus of heart and hope
4	Ne puis pas vivre longuement,	g	I cannot live for long.
5	N'en feu cuers humeins nullement	g	No man's heart can long survive
6	Ne puet longue duree avoir.	h	When once aflame.

Early Instruments and Instrumental Music

The fourteenth century witnessed a steady growth in the scope and importance of instrumental music. Though the central role in art music was still reserved for vocal works, instruments gradually found more and more uses. As we have seen, they could play a supporting role in vocal music, doubling or accompanying the singers. Instrumental arrangements of vocal works grew increasingly popular. In dance music, where rhythm was the prime consideration, instruments found early and abiding employment.

Unlike the "learned" vocal music of church and court, instrumental music was rarely written down; rather, it was improvised, much like jazz. We can therefore only speculate about the extent and variety of instrumental repertory during the Middle Ages. But our speculation can be guided by an ever growing body of knowledge acquired from graphic representations, historical documents, and surviving instruments.

These old instruments were more limited in range and volume than their modern counterparts; yet today we have abandoned the notion that they were nothing more than primitive versions of their descendants. It has become increasingly clear that instruments were perfectly suited to the purposes of the societies that devised them. Thus, while early instruments fall into the same general families as modern ones—that is, strings, woodwinds, brass, percussion, and keyboard—they are also divided into "soft" or "indoor" and "loud" or "outdoor" categories according to their use.

Among the most commonly used soft instruments were the *recorder*, an endblown flute with a breathy tone; the *lute*, a plucked string instrument of Middle Eastern origin with a more rounded back than a guitar; and the *rebec* and *vielle*, the two principal bowed string instruments of the Middle Ages. The loud category of instruments, used principally for outdoor occasions, includes the *shawm*, an ancestor of the oboe with a loud, nasal tone, and the *slide trumpet*, which developed into the early trombone known as the *sackbut*. Percussion instruments of the time include small drums known as *nakers*, usually played in pairs, and a larger, cylindrical drum called the *tabor*.

Several types and sizes of organ were already in use in the Middle Ages. There were large ones, requiring a team of men to pump their giant bellows and often several more to manipulate the cumbersome slider mechanisms that opened and closed the pipes. At the other end of the scale were *portative* and *positive* organs, miniatures with keyboards and a few ranks of pipes. One type of small organ, the *regal,* took its name from one of the reedy stops of the larger organs.

Of the purely instrumental pieces left to us from the Middle Ages, most are simple monophonic dance melodies. One common type was the *saltarello*, a lively Italian "jumping" dance. These melodies reflect, however, only the skeletal framework from which Medieval musicians performed, adding *embellishments* or melodic decorations to the written music over an improvised percussion accompaniment and possibly a *drone*, a sustained single note commonly used in folk music around the world.

Embellishments
Drone

The Virgin surrounded by angel musicians performing the motet Ave Regina caelorum *by* Walter Frye, the English composer. Accompanying instruments include (counterclockwise from top left): shawm, harp, portative organ, lute, vielle, recorders, and hammer dulcimer. Mary, Queen of Heaven, *by the* **Master of the St. Lucy Legend,** *c. 1485.* (National Gallery of Art, Washington. Samuel H. Kress Collection)

The revival of early music has burgeoned in recent decades, as scholars and performers have endeavored to reconstruct the appropriate performing conditions. A growing number of ensembles specialize in this repertory, and their members have mastered the playing techniques of old instruments. Their concerts and recordings have made the public aware of the sound of old instruments to a degree that was undreamed of fifty years ago. What was once considered esoteric or "scholarly" has now become the regular fare of many music lovers.

UNIT IV

The Renaissance

12

The Renaissance Spirit

". . . we here in the West have in the last two hundred years recovered the excellence of good letters and brought back the study of the disciples after they had long remained as if extinguished. The sustained industry of many learned men has led to such success that today this our age can be compared to the most learned times that ever were."—LOYS LE ROY (1575)

The Renaissance (c. 1450–1600) is one of the most beautiful if misleading names in the history of culture: beautiful because it implies an awakening of intellectual awareness, misleading because it suggests a sudden rebirth of learning and art after the presumed stagnation of the Middle Ages. History moves continuously rather than by leaps and bounds. The Renaissance was the next phase of a cultural process that, under the leadership of the Church, the universities, and princely courts, had begun long before.

The Arts in the Renaissance

Philosophical developments

What the Renaissance does mark is the passing of European society from an exclusively religious orientation to a more secular one; from an age of unquestioning faith and mysticism to one of belief in reason and scientific inquiry. The focus of human destiny was seen to be life on earth rather than in the hereafter. There was a new reliance on the evidence of the senses rather than on tradition and authority. Implied was a new confidence in people's ability to solve their problems and rationally order their world. This awakening found its symbol in the culture of Greek and Roman antiquity. Renaissance society discovered the summit of human wisdom not only in the Church fathers and saints, as their ancestors had done, but also in Homer and Virgil and the ancient philosophers.

The Renaissance painter preferred realism to allegory and psychological characterizations to stylized stereotypes. These characteristics are exemplified in Madonna and St. Anne *by* **Leonardo da Vinci** (*1452–1519*) (© Photo P.M.N., The Louvre, Paris)

Historical developments

Historians used to date the Renaissance from the fall of Constantinople to the Turks in 1453 and the emigration of Greek scholars to the West. Today, we recognize that there are no such clear demarcations in history. But a series of momentous circumstances around this time help to set off the new era from the old. The development of the compass made possible the voyages of discovery that opened up a new world and demolished old superstitions. The revival of ancient letters was associated with the humanists, and was spurred by the introduction of printing. This revival had its counterpart in architecture, painting, and sculpture. If the Romanesque found its grand architectural form in the monastery and the Gothic in the cathedral, the Renaissance lavished its constructive energy upon palace and château. The gloomy fortified castles of the Medieval barons gave way to spacious edifices that displayed the harmonious proportions of the classical style. (The term *classical* in this context refers to the culture of the Ancient Greeks and Romans, whose art embodied the ideals of order, stability, and balanced proportions.) In effect, Renaissance architecture embodied the striving for a gracious and reasoned existence that was the great gesture of the age.

Artistic developments

So, too, the elongated saints and martyrs of Medieval painting and sculpture were replaced by the David of Donatello and the gentle Madonnas of Leonardo. Even where artists retained a religious atmosphere, the Mother of Sorrows and the symbols of grief gave way to smiling madonnas—often posed for by very secular ladies—and dimpled cherubs. The human form, denied for centuries, was revealed as a thing of beauty; also as an object of anatomical study. Nature entered painting along with the nude, and with it an intense preoccupation with the laws of perspective and composition.

The human form, denied for centuries, was revealed in the Renaissance as a thing of beauty. David *by* **Donatello** (*c. 1386–1466*). (Alinari/Art Resources)

Medieval painting had presented life as an allegory; the Renaissance preferred realism. The Medieval painters posed their figures frontally, impersonally; the Renaissance developed psychological characterization and the art of portraiture. Medieval painting dealt in types; the Renaissance concerned itself with individuals. Space in Medieval painting was organized in a succession of planes over which the eye traveled as over a series of episodes. The Renaissance created unified space and the simultaneous seeing of the whole. It discovered the landscape, created the illusion of distance, and opened up endless vistas upon the physical loveliness of the world.

The Renaissance came to flower in the nation that stood closest to the classical Roman culture. Understandably the great names we associate with its painting and sculpture are predominantly Italian: Donatello (c. 1386–1466), Botticelli (c. 1445–1510), Leonardo da Vinci (1452–1519), Michelangelo (1475–1564), Raphael (1483–1520), and Titian (1488–1576). With masters who lived in the second half of the century, such as Tintoretto (1518–94) and Veronese (1528–88), we approach the world of the early Baroque. From the multicolored tapestry of Renaissance life emerge figures that have captured the imagination of the world: Lorenzo de' Medici and Ludovico Sforza, Lucrezia Borgia and Isabella d'Este. Few centuries can match the sixteenth for its galaxy of great names. The list includes Erasmus (1466–1536) and Martin Luther (1483–1546), Machiavelli (1469–1527) and Galileo (1564–1642), Rabelais (1494?–1553) and Cervantes (1547–1616), Marlowe (1564–93) and Shakespeare (1564–1616). *Intellectual developments*

The Renaissance marks the birth of modern European temper and of Western society as we have come to know it. In that turbulent time was shaped the moral and cultural climate we still inhabit.

The Musician in Renaissance Society

The painting and poetry of the Renaissance abound in references to music. Nothing more clearly attests to the vast importance of the arts in the cultural life of the time. The pageantry of the Renaissance unfolded to a momentous musical accompaniment. Throwing off its Medieval mysticism, music moved toward clarity, simplicity, and a frankly sensuous appeal.

Musicians of the sixteenth century were supported by the chief institutions of their society—the Church, city, and state; royal and aristocratic courts. As the influence of the art spread, professional possibilities widened. Musicians could find employment as choirmasters, singers, organists, instrumentalists, copyists, composers, teachers, instrument builders, music printers, and publishers. There was a corresponding growth in the basic musical institutions: church choirs and schools, publishing houses, civic wind bands. So too were there increased opportunities for apprentices to study with master singers, players, and instrument builders. *Musicians as professionals*

The rise of the merchant class brought with it a new group of patrons of music. This development was paralleled by the emergence, among the cultivated middle and upper classes, of the amateur musician. When, in the early sixteenth century, the system for printing type was made available to music, printed music books became available—and affordable. This in turn made possible the rise of the great publishing houses. As a result, there was a dramatic upsurge of musical literacy.

13

Renaissance Music

"He who does honor and reverence to music is commonly a man of worth, sound of soul, by nature loving things lofty." —PIERRE DE RONSARD to FRANCIS II (1560)

Renaissance Musical Style

A cappella music

The vocal forms of the sixteenth century were marked by smoothly gliding melodies conceived entirely in relation to the voice. The Renaissance achieved an exquisite appreciation of *a cappella* music. (You will recall that this term refers to a vocal work without instrumental accompaniment.) Its polyphony was based on a principle called *continuous imitation*. The motives wandered from vocal line to vocal line within the texture, the voices imitating one another so that the same theme or motive was heard now in the soprano or alto, now in the tenor or bass.

Most church music was written in a cappella style. Secular music, on the other hand, was divided between purely vocal works and those in which the singers were supported by instruments. The period also saw the growth of solo instrumental music, especially for lute and the keyboard instruments. In the matter of harmony, the Renaissance leaned toward fuller chords. There was a turning away from the parallel fifths and octaves favored by Medieval composers to the more euphonious thirds and sixths; also a greater use of dissonance was linked with the text, although in sacred music this

Word painting

tendency was carefully controlled. The expressive device of *word painting*, or musically pictorializing words from the text, was much favored: an unexpected, harsh dissonance might coincide with the word "death" or an ascending line might lead up to the word "heavens" or "stars."

Cantus firmus

Polyphonic writing offered the composer many possibilities, such as the use of a *cantus firmus* (fixed melody) as a basis for elaborate ornamentation in the other voices. Triple meter had been especially attractive to the Medieval mind because it symbolized the perfection of the Trinity. The new era, much less preoccupied with religious symbolism, showed a greater interest in duple meter.

The composers of the Flemish school were pre-eminent in European music from around 1450 to the end of the sixteenth century. They came from the southern Lowlands, which is now Belgium, and from the adjoining provinces of northern France and Burgundy. In their number were several who wrote their names large in the history of music.

Music played a prominent part in the ritual of the Church. There were several types of music for church services in addition to the monophonic Gregorian chant, such as polyphonic settings of the Mass, motets, and hymns. These were normally based on counterpoint and, especially in the early sixteenth century, on pre-existent music. Such works were sung by professional singers, usually churchmen, trained from childhood in the choir schools.

Sacred Music: The Motet

The Renaissance motet now became a sacred form with a single Latin text, for use in the Mass and other religious services. Motets in praise of the Virgin Mary were extremely popular, because of the many brotherhoods of laymen all over Europe devoted to Marian worship. These works were in three or four voices, sometimes based on a chant or other cantus firmus. Until this point the voices had been equal in importance. Now the interest shifted to the top voice or melody, with the lower parts serving as a background and sometimes played on instruments.

Dufay: Alma redemptoris mater

Guillaume Dufay (1397?–1474) was one of the earliest composers of the Burgundian School to make his career in Italy, where he spent his formative years. He was also active at the court of Philip the Good, Duke of Burgundy (1419–67), which for several decades rivaled that of the kings of France in the brilliance of its art. He spent his last years in his native Cambrai in northern France, where he continued to compose up to his death.

In the music of Dufay and his Burgundian colleagues, the rhythmic complexities of fourteenth-century music were abandoned in favor of an uncomplicated, more accessible style. The meandering vocal lines of the past were replaced by well-defined melodies and clear-cut rhythms, with something of the charm of folksong. Harmony grew simpler and more consonant, foreshadowing a language based on triads and sense of key. Eventually, Dufay expanded the standard musical texture from three voices to four.

Dufay's style is well exemplified in his Latin motet *Alma redemptoris mater* for three voices on a text praising the Virgin Mary. (In such works, some or all of the voices may be played on instruments as well). Several important characteristics distinguish his music from that of earlier times. To begin with, the cantus firmus, drawn from a Gregorian chant, has been elevated to the highest part, where the listener can easily hear it. Instead of being a mystical symbol, it is now a graceful melody that delights the ear. As a result, this voice dominates the others. Also, instead of following the sacred chant slavishly, Dufay adapts it both rhythmically and melodically to his own expressive purpose. Equally significant, Dufay has replaced the open fifths and octaves that impart so stark a color to Medieval music with the gentler thirds and sixths. As a result, he seems to have moved a considerable distance away from Machaut's archaic sound.

Dufay's motet opens with an extended melisma on the first vowel of *Alma*. (See Listening Guide 4.) Dufay's prime concern is the flow of the melodic lines. The motet is in triple meter and in several sections. It opens in three-part harmony, but toward the end the sopranos divide to make four voice parts. In effect, harmony is moving toward the four-part structure that will become the standard, in which each of the four voices—soprano, alto, tenor, bass—occupies its respective register instead of crowding the others in the same range. This means, too, that the separate voices can take on greater independence, with an attendant broadening of the musical space.

Listening Guide 4   1A/3

DUFAY: *Alma redemptoris mater*

Date: mid-15th century

Genre: Latin motet

Subject: Honors the Virgin Mary

Setting: 3 voices and/or instruments

Basis: Gregorian chant *Alma redemptoris mater* paraphrased in top voice

Text	Translation	Setting
Alma redemptoris mater,	Gracious mother of the Redeemer,	Solo, then homophonic in 3 voices, oriented to top voice
quae pervia caeli porta manes,	Abiding at the doors of Heaven,	
et stella maris, succurre cadenti,	Star of the sea, aid the falling.	
surgere qui curat populo.	Rescue the people who struggle.	
Tu quae genuisti, natura mirante,	Thou who, astonishing nature,	More polyphonic, movement in all voices
tuum sanctum genitorum:	Hast borne thy holy Creator:	
Virgo prius ac posterius,	Virgin before and after,	Homophonic texture returns in long, sustained chords in all voices until the end
Gabrielis ab ore sumens illud Ave,	Who heard the Ave from the mouth of Gabriel,	
peccatorum miserere.	Be merciful to sinners.	Sopranos divide to make 4 voice parts
	Trans. by DR. YVETTE LOURIA	

Opening of Gregorian chant *Alma redemptoris mater* with melisma on "Alma"

Opening top line (notes of chant marked), with melisma on "Alma"

An engraving from the late sixteenth century of singers and instrumentalists performing the Mass. A Religious Service by **Collaert** *after* **Stradanus.** (The Metropolitan Museum of Art, Whittelsey Fund)

The Renaissance Mass

With the rise of polyphony, composers concentrated their musical settings on the invariable portion of the Mass that was sung daily, known as the Ordinary. Thus came into prominence the five sections known as the musical setting of the Mass: Kyrie, Gloria, Credo, Sanctus, and Agnus Dei. (Today these sections of the Mass are recited or sung in the language of the country—the *vernacular*.) The opening section, the Kyrie—a prayer for mercy—dates from the early centuries of Christianity, as its original Greek text attests. It is an **A-B-A** form that consists of nine invocations: three of "Kyrie eleison" (Lord, have mercy), three of "Christe eleison" (Christ, have mercy), and again three of "Kyrie eleison." There follows the Gloria (Glory to God in the highest). This is a joyful hymn of praise which is omitted in the penitential seasons, Advent and Lent. The third movement is the confession of faith, Credo (I believe in one God, the Father Almighty). It includes also the *Et incarnatus est* (And He became flesh), the *Crucifixus* (He was crucified), and the *Et resurrexit* (And He rose again). Fourth is the Sanctus (Holy, Holy, Holy), which concludes with the *Hosanna* (Hosanna in the highest) and the *Benedictus* (Blessed is He who comes in the name of the Lord), after which the *Hosanna* is repeated as a kind of refrain. The fifth and last part, the Agnus Dei (Lamb of God, who takes away the sins of the world), is sung three times. Twice it concludes with "Miserere nobis" (Have mercy on us), and the third time with the prayer "Dona nobis pacem" (Grant us peace). A summary of the order of the Mass, with its Proper and Ordinary movements, follows. (Remember that we studied an example of a Gradual for Easter Sunday, *Haec dies.*)

Sections of the mass

Movements and Order of the Mass

Proper	*Ordinary*
Introit	
	Kyrie
	Gloria
Collect	
Epistle	
Gradual	
Alleluia (or Tract)	
Evangelium	
	Credo
Offertory	
Secret	
Preface	
	Sanctus
Canon	
	Agnus Dei
Communion	
Post-Communion	
Ite missa est	

Like the motet, the polyphonic setting of the Mass was usually based on a fragment of Gregorian chant. This became the cantus firmus that served as the foundation of the work, supporting the florid patterns that the other voices wove around it. When used in all the movements of a Mass, the Gregorian cantus firmus helped to weld the work into a unity. It provided composers with a fixed element that they could embellish with all the resources of their artistry.

Josquin Desprez   Perhaps the greatest master of the Renaissance mass was the Franco-Flemish composer Josquin Desprez (c. 1440–1521). The older generation of musicians had been preoccupied with solving the technical problems of counterpoint—problems that fit the intellectual climate of the waning Middle Ages. Josquin appeared at a time when the humanizing influences of the Renaissance were wafting through Europe. The contrapuntal ingenuity that he inherited from the Flemish composer Johannes Ockeghem he was able to harness to a higher end—the expression of emotion. His music is rich in feeling, in serenely beautiful melody and expressive harmony. Its clarity of structure and humanism bespeak the spirit of the Renaissance.

Josquin composed at least seventeen complete settings of the Mass. He used a variety of techniques, basing much of the music on pre-existent models, both monophonic and polyphonic, secular and sacred. His *La sol fa re mi* Mass, written while he was in Italy, is based on the five-note figure in the title (A G F D E), which serves as an ostinato that pervades the work.

At the time of Josquin's death, major religious reforms were sweeping across northern Europe. After the revolt of Martin Luther (1483–1546) the desire for a return to true Christian piety brought about a reform movement in the Catholic Church. This movement became part of the Counter Reformation whereby the Church strove to recapture the minds of its people. Among its manifestations were the activities of Franciscans and Dominicans among the poor; the founding of the Society of Jesus (Jesuits) by St. Ignatius Loyola (1491–1556); and the deliberations of the Council of Trent, which extended—with some interruptions—from 1545 to 1563.

Counter Reformation

In its desire to regulate every aspect of religious discipline, the Council took up the matter of church music. The cardinals were much concerned over the corruption of the traditional chant by the singers, who added all manner of embellishments to the Gregorian melodies. They objected to the use of instruments other than the organ in religious services, to the practice of incorporating popular songs in Masses, to the secular spirit that was invading sacred music, and to the generally irreverent attitude of church musicians. They pointed out that in polyphonic settings of the Mass the sacred text was made unintelligible by the overelaborate contrapuntal texture. The committee assigned to deal with the problem contented itself with issuing general recommendations for a more dignified service. The authorities favored a pure vocal style that would respect the integrity of the sacred texts, that would avoid virtuosity and encourage piety.

Palestrina: Gloria *from* Pope Marcellus Mass

"I have held nothing more desirable than that what is sung throughout the year, according to the season, should be more agreeable to the ear by virtue of its vocal beauty."

Giovanni Pierluigi, called da Palestrina after his birthplace (c.1525–94), met the need for a reformed church music in so exemplary a fashion that for posterity he has remained *the* Catholic composer. He served as organist and choirmaster at various churches including that of St. Peter's in Rome. Palestrina's music gives voice to the religiosity of the Counter-Reformation, its transports and its visions. A true Italian, he was surpassingly sensitive to the needs of the human voice. It was from this vantage point that he viewed his function as a church composer.

Palestrina wrote over a hundred Masses, of which the most famous is his mass for Pope Marcellus, one of his patrons. It is popularly believed that this Mass was written to satisfy the new strict demands placed on polyphonic church music by the Council of Trent. Since the pontifical choir sang without instrumental accompaniment at this time, the *Pope Marcellus Mass* was probably performed a cappella. It was written for six voice parts—soprano, alto, two tenors, and two basses, a typical setting for the all-male church choirs of the time. The highest voice was sung by boy sopranos or male falsettists, the alto part by male altos or countertenors (tenors with very

Council of Trent

high voices), and the lower parts were distributed among the normal ranges of the male voice.

The Gloria from the *Pope Marcellus Mass* exhibits the salient characteristics of Palestrina's conservative style. As was typical, the work begins with a monophonic intonation of the opening line "Gloria in excelsis Deo" (Glory be to God in the highest), followed by a carefully constructed polyphonic setting of the remaining text. Notable is the way Palestrina balances the harmonic and polyphonic elements of his art so that the words of the sacred text are clear and audible, an effect desired by the Council of Trent. (See Listening Guide 5 for the text and anaylsis.)

Palestrina's style incarnates the pure a cappella ideal of vocal polyphony, in which the individual voice fulfills its destiny through submergence in the group. His music remains an apt symbol of the greatness art can aspire to when it subserves a profound moral conviction.

Listening Guide 5   📟 1A/4

PALESTRINA: Gloria, from *Pope Marcellus Mass*

Date: published 1567

Genre: Mass, setting of Ordinary

Voices: 6 (SATTBB); Frequent textural changes, reduction of voices

Opening of "Gloria," showing 4 voice parts (of six), in clear word declamation

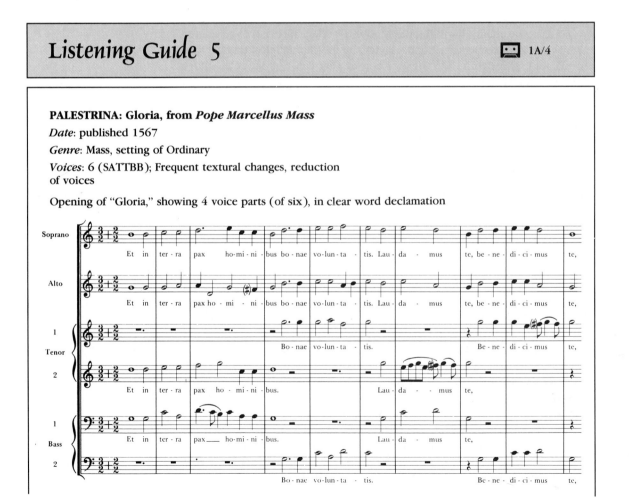

Text	Translation	Voices
18 Gloria in excelsis Deo	Glory be to God on high,	1
et in terra pax hominibus	And on earth peace to men	4
bonae voluntatis.	of goodwill.	4
Laudamus te,	We praise Thee,	4
Benedicimus te.	We bless Thee.	4
Adoramus te.	We adore Thee.	3
Glorificamus te.	We glorify Thee.	4
Gratias agimus tibi propter	We give Thee thanks for	5
magnam gloriam tuam.	Thy great glory.	3
Domine Deus, Rex caelestis,	Lord God, heavenly King,	4
Deus Pater omnipotens.	God the Father Almighty.	3
Domini Fili	O Lord, the only-begotten Son,	4
unigenite, Jesus Christe.	Jesus Christ.	6/5
Domine Deus, Agnus Dei,	Lord God, Lamb of God,	3
Filius Patris.	Son of the Father.	6
Qui tollis	Thou that takest	4
peccata mundi,	away the sins of the world	4
miserere nobis.	have mercy on us,	4
	have mercy on us,	5
19 Qui tollis peccata mundi,	Thou that takest away the sins	5/4
suscipe deprecationem nostrum.	of the world, receive our prayer.	
Qui sedes ad dexteram Patris,	Thou that sittest at the right hand,	3
miserere nobis.	of the Father, have mercy on us.	3
Quoniam tu solus sanctus.	For thou alone art holy.	4
Tu solus Dominus.	Thou only art the Lord.	4
Tu solus Altissimus.	Thou alone art most high.	4
Jesu Christe, cum Sancto Spiritu	Jesus Christ, along with the Holy Ghost	6/3/4
in gloria Dei Patris.	in the glory of God the Father	5
Amen.	Amen.	6

Secular Music in Court and City Life

"I am not pleased with the Courtier if he be not also a musician, and besides his understanding and cunning (in singing) upon the book, have skill in like manner on sundry instruments."—BALDASSARE CASTIGLIONE (1528)

The secular music of the Renaissance was intended for both the professional and the amateur. Court festivities included music performed by professionals for the entertainment of noble guests and dignitaries. With the rise of the middle class, music making in the home became increasingly popular. Most middle- and upper-class homes had a lute (a plucked-string instrument with a rounded body) or a keyboard instrument, and the study of music was considered part of the proper upbringing for a young lady or—in lesser degree—gentleman. Women began to play a prominent part in the performance of music both in the home and at court. During the later sixteenth century in Italy, a number of professional women singers achieved great fame. In addition, dances provided a popular outlet for music at all levels of society.

Amateur music making

Music played an increasingly important role in the celebrations of sixteenth-century nobility. The Wedding at Cana *by* **Paolo Veronese** (*1528–88*). (The Louvre, Paris)

From the union of poetry and music came two important secular forms: the chanson and the madrigal. In both of these, music was used to enhance the poetry of such major literary figures as Petrarch and Pierre de Ronsard. In this domain the intricate verse forms of French and Italian poetry helped to shape the ensuing musical forms.

The chanson

The fifteenth-century *chanson* was the characteristic genre at the court of the dukes of Burgundy and the kings of France, who were great patrons of the arts. It was usually for three voices, with one or both lower voices played by instruments. Chansons were set to the courtly love poetry of the French Renaissance, the poems being in the form of a *rondeau*, a *ballade*, or a *virelai*. These fixed forms established the character of the setting and the repetition of sections. If there was a recurrent refrain of one or two lines, this naturally was reflected in the music. Some chansons were in a more popular style, with simpler, more direct expressions of love. One such example is the rondeau *L'autre d'antan* (The Other Year) by the Flemish master, Johannes Ockeghen (c. 1410–97).

Roland de Lassus

The Renaissance chanson culminates in the towering figure of Roland de Lassus (c. 1532–94). This northern master wrote about a hundred and fifty chansons, most of them on the verses of such famous French poets as Pierre de Ronsard and Clément Marot. The texts cover a wide range of emotions from amorous to bawdy to religious. The sixteenth-century chanson is most often set for four voices, generally in a chordal or homophonic style. Typical of this genre is *Bon jour mon coeur* by Lassus, set with many musical subtleties to a poem by Ronsard.

Monteverdi and the Italian Madrigal

In the madrigal the Renaissance found one of its chief forms of secular music. The sixteenth-century *madrigal* was an aristocratic form of poetry-and-music that came to flower at the small Italian courts, where it was a favorite diversion of cultivated amateurs. The text was a short poem of lyric or reflective character, rarely longer than twelve lines, marked by elegance of diction and refinement of sentiment. Conspicuous in it were the affecting words for weeping, sighing, trembling, dying that the Italian madrigalists learned to set with such a wealth of expression. Love and unsatisfied desire were by no means the only topics of the madrigal. Included, too, were humor and satire, political themes, scenes and incidents of city and country life, with the result that the Italian madrigal literature of the sixteenth century presents a vivid panorama of Renaissance thought and feeling.

In this highly stylized, sixteenth-century painting, four aristocratic singers perform from part books in an imaginary landscape. The couple in back are beating time, as was customary. Concert in the Open Air. *Anonymous* (Italian School). (Bourges, Musée de Berry)

Instruments participated, duplicating or even substituting for the voices. Sometimes only the top part was sung while the other lines were played on instruments. During the first period of the Renaissance madrigal—the second quarter of the sixteenth century—the composer's chief concern was to give pleasure to the performers, often amateurs, without much thought to virtuosic display. In the middle phase (c. 1550–80), the Renaissance madrigal became a conscious art form directed toward the listener.

The final phase of the Italian madrigal (1580–1620) extended beyond the late Renaissance into the world of the Baroque. The form became the direct expression of the composer's personality and feelings. Certain traits were carried to the point of mannerism: rich chromatic harmony, dramatic declamation, vocal virtuosity, and vivid depiction in music of emotional words. It was in the art of Claudio Monteverdi (1567–1643) that the late Renaissance madrigal came to full flower.

Monteverdi spent twelve fruitful years at the court of the Duke of Mantua. In 1613 he was appointed choirmaster of St. Mark's in Venice, and retained that post until his death thirty years later. Into his operas and ballets, madrigals and religious works he injected an emotional intensity that was new to music. The new-born lyric drama of the Florentines he welded into a coherent musical form and tightened their shapeless recitative into an expressive line imbued with drama. He originated what he called the *stile concitato* (agitated style), introducing such novel sound-effects as the string tremolo and pizzicato as symbols of passion. Monteverdi aspired above all to make his music express the emotional content of poetry. "The text," he declared, "should be the master of the music, not the servant."

Monteverdi: Ohimè! se tanto amate

Monteverdi's madrigal books, published between 1587 and 1634, span the transition from Renaissance to Baroque style. *Ohimè! se tanto amate*, from his *Fourth Book of Madrigals* (1603), a superb example of his style, is a setting for five voices of a poem by Guarini. The words are in the courtly manner of much madrigal poetry, both tongue-in-cheek and exaggeratedly romantic in their subtle suggestions of sexual desire. Notable is the way

Claudio Monteverdi

Principal Works

Operas, including *Orfeo* (1607), *Arianna* (1608, music lost), *Il ritorno d'Ulisse* (The Return of Ulysses, 1640), *L'incoronazione di Poppea* (The Coronation of Poppea, 1642); other dramatic music includes ballets and *Il Combattimento di Tancredi e Clorinda* (The Combat of Tancredi and Clorinda, 1624)

Secular vocal music, including 9 books of madrigals, 2 books of *Scherzi musicali,* canzonettas

Sacred vocal music, including Vespers (1610), Masses, Magnificats, spiritual madrigals, motets, and psalms

Monteverdi uses the conventional "sigh" motive based on the descending interval of a third, and plays on it with the key word "Ohimè!"—the unhappy lover's "Alas!"—against a harmonic background now consonant, now dissonant. This motive becomes the unifying element of the piece. (See Listening Guide 6 for the text.)

Other basic words in the text are set in an equally telling manner. The phrase "S'io moro" (If I die) is set for three voices instead of five to suggest the ebbing strength of the dying lover, but upon its return is carried by all five voices. "Languido e doloroso" (languid and sad) calls forth an ascending chromatic scale with a harsh dissonance to bring out the sadness in "doloroso." And in the witty wordplay of the final line Monteverdi makes the lover sigh "a thousand times." This vivid depiction of the text through music, known as word painting, was a hallmark of the Italian madrigal. This is music of amorous dalliance, as elegant as the courtly lifestyle out of which it sprang.

Listening Guide 6   🔲 1A/5

Monteverdi: *Ohimè! se tanto amate*

Date: published 1603, *Fourth Book of Madrigals*

Genre: Italian madrigal, 5 voices (SSATB)

Poem: 8-line madrigal (aabcbcdd) by Battista Guarini

Text

Ohimè! se tanto amate
di sentir dir *ohimè,* deh, perché fate
chi dice *ohimè* morire?
S'io moro, un sol potrete
languido e doloroso *ohimè* sentire;
Ma se, cor mio, volete
che vita abbia' da voi, e voi da me,
avrete mille e mille dolci *ohimè.*

Translation

Alas, if you so love
to hear me say alas, then why do you slay
the one who says it?
If I die, you will hear only
a single, languid, sorrowful alas;
but if, my love, you wish
to let me live and wish to live for me,
you will have a thousand times a sweet alas.

Opening of madrigal, showing "sighs" of falling thirds on "ohimè" (alas)

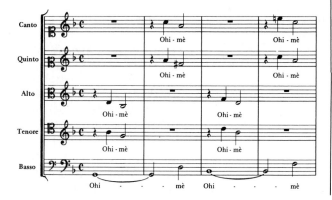

Harsh dissonances, set to "e doloroso"
(and sorrowful)

Repetitions of "mill'e mille dolc'ohimè"
(sweet alas thousands and thousands of
times)

The English Madrigal

Just as English poets took over the Italian sonnet, so the composers of England
adopted the Italian madrigal and developed it into a native art form. All the
brilliance of the Elizabethan age is reflected in the school of madrigalists
who flourished in the late sixteenth century during the reign of Elizabeth
I (1558–1603) and on into the reign of the Stuart dynasty. Among the most
important figures were Thomas Morley (1557–1603), John Wilbye (1574–
1638), Thomas Weelkes (c. 1575–1623), and Orlando Gibbons (1583–
1625).

The first collection of Italian madrigals published in England appeared in 1588 and was called *Musica transalpina*—Music from beyond the Alps. The madrigals were "Englished"—that is, the texts were translated. In their own madrigals the English composers preferred simpler texts. New, humorous madrigal types were cultivated, some with refrains of nonsense syllables such as *fa la la*. Typical of the lighter vein of the English madrigal is John Farmer's popular *Fair Phyllis*, set to a pastoral text in a gay mood.

The Renaissance madrigal impelled composers to develop new techniques of combining music and poetry. In doing so it prepared the way for one of the most influential forms of Western music—the opera.

Instrumental Dance Music

The sixteenth century witnessed a remarkable flowering of instrumental dance music. With the advent of music publishing, printed dance music became readily available for solo instruments as well as small ensembles. Venice, Paris, and Antwerp took the lead as centers of the new publishing industry. The dances were often fashioned from vocal works such as madrigals and chansons, and were published in simplified four-part versions that were played instead of sung.

A number of dance types became popular during the sixteenth century, several of which survived into the Baroque era. The stately court dance known as the *pavane* often served as the first number of a set and was followed by one or more quicker dances, especially the Italian *saltarello* (hopping dance) and the French *galliard* (a more vigorous version of the saltarello). Less courtly was the *ronde* or round dance, a lively romp associated with the outdoors in which the participants formed a circle.

Dance types

It was through dance pieces such as these that Renaissance composers explored the possibilities of purely instrumental forms. From these humble beginnings sprang the imposing structures of Western instrumental music.

TRANSITION II

■

From Renaissance to Baroque

"The (Venetian) church of St. Mark was . . . so full of people that one could not move a step . . . a new platform was built for the singers, adjoining . . . there was a portable organ, in addition to the two famous organs of the church, and the other instruments made the most excellent music, in which the best singers and players that can be found in this region took part."—F. SANSOVINO (1604)

The stylistic changes that mark the shift from the Renaissance to the Baroque are dramatic; indeed, the new era that dawned at the onset of the seventeenth century can be viewed as a revolution in music. We have already suggested that the madrigal, as the favorite musical form of the late Renaissance, gave

Venetian painters captured the splendid pageantry of their city in their canvases. Singers and instrumentalists took part in this religious ceremony. **Gentile Bellini** (*c. 1429–1507*), Procession in Piazza San Marco (Accademia, Venice)

This drawing by **Giovanni Antonio Canal** (*1697–1768*), *called "Canaletto," shows singers crammed into a pulpit at St. Mark's, reading from a large choirbook.* (Hamburg, Kunsthalle)

rise to a new style, one that focused more and more on the emotional content of the text.

The highly polyphonic style of the late Renaissance did not die away suddenly in favor of the more intimate solo song of the Baroque. In Venice, famous throughout Europe for its magnificent Basilica of St. Mark's and the impressive line of choirmasters and organists who worked there, a new, grandiose style had evolved. The chief characteristic of the Venetian school was *polychoral* singing, involving the use of two or three choirs that either answered each other antiphonally, making possible all kinds of echo effects, or sang together. (*Antiphonal* performance suggests groups singing in alternation, and then together.) This Venetian tradition reached its high point in the works of Giovanni Gabrieli (c. 1557–1612), who fully exploited the possibilities of multiple choirs. The use of such large forces drew him away from the subtle complexities of the old contrapuntal tradition to a broad homophonic style.

Antiphonal style

This music, belonging as it does to the final decades of the sixteenth century, leaves the world of the Renaissance behind. The splendor of its sound brings us into the next great style period—the Baroque.

A Comparison of Renaissance and Baroque Styles

Renaissance (1450-1600)	*Baroque (1600-1750)*
Dufay, Josquin, Palestrina, Monteverdi (early works)	Monteverdi (late works), Purcell, Vivaldi, Handel, Bach
Modal harmony	Major and minor tonality
Imitative polyphony, multi-voiced	New monodic or solo style; one voice and accompaniment
A cappella vocal music	Concerted music (voices and instruments)
Religious vocal forms dominant: mass and motet	New religious vocal forms: oratorio, Lutheran cantata
Secular vocal forms: chanson, madrigal	Secular vocal forms: opera, cantata, masque
Instrumental forms beginning, derived from vocal forms: dance music	Instrumental forms developing: sonata, concerto grosso, sinfonia, suite
Instruments unspecified	Specified instruments
Works built on pre-existant melody (cantus firmus)	Freely-composed works
Performances at church and court	Rise of public theaters

PART THREE

More Materials of Music

"In any narrative—epic, dramatic, or musical—every word or tone should be like a soldier marching towards the one, common, final goal: conquest of the material. The way the artist makes every phrase of his story such a soldier, serving to unfold it, to support its structure and development, to build plot and counterplot, to distribute light and shade, to point incessantly and lead up gradually to the climax—in short, the way every fragment is impregnated with its mission towards the whole, makes up this delicate and so essential objective which we call FORM."—ERNST TOCH

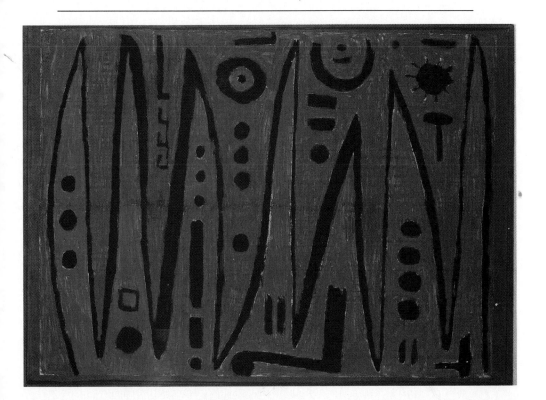

Paul Klee (*1879–1940*) Heroic Strokes of the Bow. 1938. (Collection, The Museum of Modern Art, New York. Nelson A. Rockefeller Bequest)

UNIT V

◼

The Organization of Musical Sounds

14

Tonality, Key, and Scale

"All music is nothing more than a succession of impulses that converge towards a definite point of repose."—IGOR STRAVINSKY

At the beginning of this book we discussed various elements of music. Now that we have had occasion to hear how these are combined in a number of works, we are ready to consider the materials of music on a more advanced level.

In Chapter 3 we described our perceptions of harmony in terms of *tonality*, a principle of organization whereby we hear a piece of music in relation to a central tone, the tonic, and according to a *scale* or group of notes that is either major or minor. When we listen to a composition in the key of C major we hear a piece built around the central tone C, the major scale on C, and the harmonies formed from that scale.

By a *key*, then, we mean a group of related tones with a common center *Key* or tonic. These tones revolve around the central tone, the tonic or keynote, to which they ultimately gravitate. This "loyalty to the tonic" is fostered in us by much of the music we hear.

Tonality, needless to say, resides in our minds rather than in the tones themselves. It underlies the whole system of relationships among tones as embodied in keys, scales, and the harmonies based on them. Specifically, tonality refers to those relationships as they were manifest in Western music from around 1600 to 1900.

The Miracle of the Octave

A string of a certain length, when set in motion, vibrates at a certain rate per second and produces a certain pitch. Given the same conditions, a string half as long will vibrate twice as fast and sound an octave higher. A string twice as long will vibrate half as fast and sound an octave lower. When we sound two tones other than the octave together, such as C–D or C–F, the ear hears two distinctly different tones. But when we strike an octave such as C–C or D–D, the ear recognizes a very strong similarity between the two tones. Indeed, if one were not listening carefully one would almost believe that a single tone was being sounded. This "miracle of the octave" was observed at an early stage in all musical cultures, with the result that the octave became the basic interval in music. (An interval, we saw, is the distance and relationship between two tones.)

The method of dividing the octave determines the scales and the characters of a musical system. It is precisely in this particular that one system differs from another. In Western music the octave is divided into twelve equal intervals. The fact is apparent from the look of the piano keyboard, where counting from any tone to its octave we find twelve keys—seven white and five black. These twelve tones are a half tone (*semitone*) apart.

Half steps and whole steps

That is, from C to C sharp is a half step, as is from C sharp to D. The *half step* is the smallest unit of distance in our musical system. From C to D is a distance of two half steps, or a *whole step*.

Chromatic scale

The twelve semitones into which Western music divides the octave constitute what is known as the *chromatic scale*. No matter how vast and intricate a musical work, it is made up of the twelve basic tones and their higher and lower duplications. Hence the statement of the composer Paul Hindemith

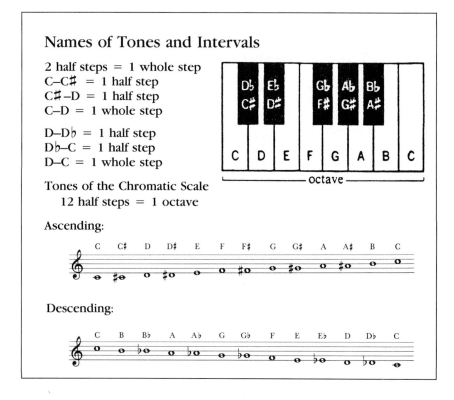

Names of Tones and Intervals

2 half steps = 1 whole step
C–C♯ = 1 half step
C♯–D = 1 half step
C–D = 1 whole step

D–D♭ = 1 half step
D♭–C = 1 half step
D–C = 1 whole step

Tones of the Chromatic Scale
    12 half steps = 1 octave

Ascending:

Descending:

quoted at the beginning of this book: "There are only twelve tones. You must treat them carefully."

On the keyboard above, you will note that the black keys are named in relation to their white-key neighbors. When the black key between C and D is thought of as a semitone higher than C, it is known as C sharp (♯). When the same key is thought of as a semitone lower than D, it is called D flat (♭). Thus D sharp is the same tone as E flat, F sharp is the same tone as G flat, and G sharp is the same tone as A flat. Which of these names is used depends upon the scale and key in which a particular sharp or flat appears.

The Major Scale

We have noted that a *scale* (from the Italian *scala*, "ladder") is a series of tones arranged in consecutive order, ascending or descending. Specifically, a scale presents the tones of a key.

Much of Western art music is based on two contrasting scales, the *major* and the *minor*. These consist of seven different tones, with the octave *do* added at the end of the series. The major scale has the familiar *do-re-mi-fa-sol-la-ti-do* pattern already mentioned. If you play the white keys on the piano from C to C you will hear this series. Let us examine it a little more closely.

We notice that there is no black key on the piano between E–F (*mi-fa*) and B–C (*ti-do*). These tones, therefore, are a half step apart, while the others are a whole step apart. Consequently, when we sing the *do-re-mi-fa-sol-la-ti-do* sequence we are measuring off a pattern of eight tones that are each a whole step apart except tones 3–4 (*mi-fa*) and 7–8 (*ti-do*). This scale implies certain relationships based upon tension and resolution. We have already indicated one of the most important of these—the thrust of the seventh tone to the eighth (*ti* seeking to be resolved to *do*). There are others: if we sing *do-re* we are left with a sense of incompleteness that is resolved when *re* moves back to *do*; *fa* gravitates to *mi*; *la* descends to *sol*.

Most important of all, the major scale defines the two poles of traditional harmony: the *do* or tonic, the point of ultimate rest; and the *sol* or dominant, representative of the active harmony. Tonic going to dominant and returning to tonic becomes a basic progression of harmony. It will also serve, we shall find, as a basic principle of form.

The Minor Scale

Whether the major scale begins on C, D, E, or any other tone, it follows the same pattern in the arrangement of the whole and half steps. Such a pattern is known as a *mode*. The *minor mode* complements and serves as a foil to the major. It differs from the major primarily in that its third degree is lowered a half step; that is, the scale of C minor has an E flat instead of E natural. The minor is pronouncedly different from the major in mood and coloring. *Minor*, the Latin word for "smaller," refers to the fact that the distinguishing interval C–E flat is smaller than the corresponding interval C–E natural in the major ("larger") scale.

Mode

Like the major, the pattern of the minor scale, given in the table below, may begin on any of the twelve tones of the octave. In each case, there will be a different group of seven tones out of twelve; that is, each scale will include a different number of sharps or flats. This gives us twelve keys according to the major mode and twelve keys according to the minor mode.

Chromaticism

When seven tones out of twelve are selected to form a major or minor key, the other five become extraneous in relation to that key and its tonic note. They enter the composition only occasionally, mainly to embellish the melody or harmony. In order for a piece to sound firmly rooted in a key, the seven notes of the key should prevail. If the five foreign tones become too prominent in the melody and harmony, the relationship to the key center is weakened and the key feeling becomes ambiguous. The distinction between the tones that do not belong within the key area and those that do *Chromatic* is expressed in the contrasting terms "chromatic" and "diatonic." ***Chromatic***

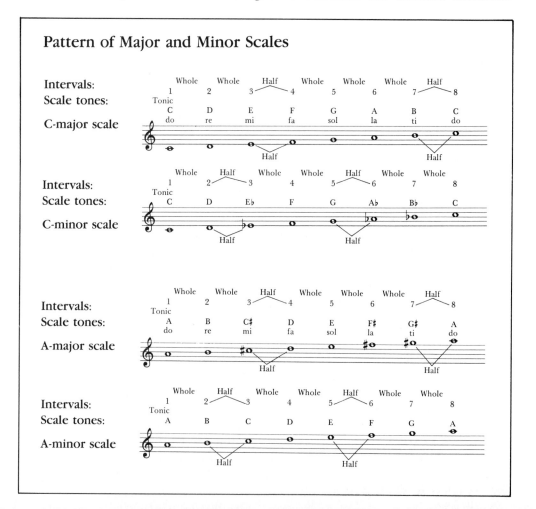

Pattern of Major and Minor Scales

refers to the twelve-tone scale, including all the semitones of the octave, whereas *diatonic* refers to music based on the seven tones of a major or minor scale, and to harmonies that are firmly rooted in the key. We can best associate chromatic music with the Romantic era. In contrast, music of the Classical era tends to be diatonic, centering around a keynote and its closely related harmonies.

Diatonic

15

The Major-Minor System

"Form follows function."—LOUIS SULLIVAN

Transposition

Suppose a certain melody begins on G. If you felt that the song lay a little too high for your voice, you might begin on F instead of G and shift all the tones of the melody one step lower. Someone else might find that the song was too low. That person could begin on A and sing each tone of the melody one step higher than it was written. That act of shifting all the tones of a musical composition a uniform distance to a different level of pitch is called *transposition*.

When we transpose a piece we shift it to another key. We change the level of pitch, the keynote, and the number of sharps or flats. But the melody line remains the same because the pattern of its whole and half steps has been retained in the new key.

Why does a composer choose one key rather than another? In former times external factors strongly influenced this choice. Up to around the year 1815, for example, the brass instruments were not able to change keys as readily as they are now. In writing for string instruments composers considered the fact that certain effects, such as playing on the open strings, could be achieved in one key but not in another. Several nineteenth-century composers seemed to associate a certain emotional atmosphere or color with various keys.

Choice of key

Modulation

If a piece of music can be played in one key as in another, why not put all music in the key of C and be done with it? Because the contrast between keys and the movement from one key to another is an essential element of musical structure. We have seen that the tones of the key form a group of "seven out of twelve," which imparts coherence and focus to the music. But this closed group may be opened up, in which case we are shifted— either gently or abruptly—to another area centering on another keynote. Such a change gives us a heightened sense of activity. It is an expressive gesture of prime importance.

The process of passing from one key to another is known as *modulation*. The twelve major and twelve minor keys may be compared to so many rooms in a house, with the modulations equivalent to corridors leading from one to the other. We shall see that modulation was a common practice of the Baroque and was refined as a formal procedure in the Classical era. In the Romantic era modulations were more frequent and abrupt. There came into being a hyperemotional music that wandered restlessly from key to key in accord with the need for excitement of the mid- and late-Romantic era.

Active and Rest Chords

Just as melodies have inherent active and rest poles, so do the harmonies built around these tones. The three-note chord or *triad*, built on the first scale tone, is known as the I chord or the *tonic* and serves as a point of rest. But rest only has meaning in relation to activity. The chord of rest is counterposed to other chords, which are active. The active chords seek to be completed, or *resolved* in the rest chord. This striving for resolution is the dynamic force in our music. It shapes the forward movement, imparting to it direction and goal.

Dominant

The fifth scale step, the *dominant*, is the chief representative of the active principle. We therefore obtain two focal points: the active triad, the V chord, which seeks to be resolved to the restful tonic chord. The triad built on the

Subdominant

fourth scale step (*fa*) is known as the *subdominant* (meaning below the dominant). The movement from the subdominant to the tonic (IV to I) is familiar from the chords traditionally associated with the "Amen" sung at the close of many hymns.

The Key as a Form-Building Element

By marking off an area in musical space with a fixed center, the key provides the framework within which musical growth and development take place. The three main harmonies of the key—tonic (I), dominant (V), and sub-dominant (IV)—become the focal points over which melodies and chord progressions unfold. In brief, the key is the neighborhood inhabited by a tune and its harmonies.

At the same time the contrast between keys may further the cause of variety. Composers pitted one key against another, thereby achieving a dra-matic opposition between them. They began by establishing the home key. Presently they modulated to a related key, generally that of the dominant (for example, from C major to G major, or from G major to D major). In so doing they created a tension, since the dominant key was unstable com-pared to the tonic. This tension required resolution, which was provided by the return to the home key.

The progression or movement from home key to contrasting key and back outlined the basic musical pattern of statement-departure-return. The home key was the symbol of unity; the foreign key ensured variety and contrast.

PART FOUR

The Baroque Era

"Provided only that we abstain from receiving anything as true which is not so, there can be nothing so remote that we cannot reach it, nor so obscure that we cannot discover it."—RENÉ DESCARTES

Peter Paul Rubens (*1577–1640*). The Garden of Love. (Museo del Prado, Madrid)

UNIT VI

■

The Baroque and the Arts

16

The Baroque Spirit

"I do not know what I may appear to the world; but to myself I seem to have been only like a boy playing on the seashore, and diverting myself in now and then finding a smoother pebble or a prettier shell than ordinary, whilst the great ocean of truth lay all undiscovered before me."—SIR ISAAC NEWTON (1642–1727)

The Baroque era stretched across a turbulent century and a half of European history. It opened shortly before the year 1600, a convenient signpost that need not be taken too literally, and may be regarded as having come to a close with the death of Bach in 1750.

The term "baroque" was probably derived from the Portuguese *barroco*, a pearl of irregular shape much used in the jewelry of the time. The period from 1600 to 1750 was a time of change and adventure. The conquest of the New World stirred the imagination and filled the coffers of the Old. The middle classes gathered wealth and power in their struggle against the aristocracy. Empires clashed for mastery of the world. Appalling poverty and wasteful luxury, magnificent idealism and savage oppression—against contradictions such as these unfolded the pomp and splendor of Baroque art: an art bold of gesture and conception—vigorous, decorative, monumental.

The transition from the classically minded Renaissance to the Baroque was foreshadowed in the art of Michelangelo (1475–1564). His turbulent figures, their torsos twisted in struggle, reflect the Baroque love of the dramatic. In like fashion the Venetian school of painters—Titian, Tintoretto, Veronese—captured the dynamic spirit of the new age. Their crowded canvases are ablaze with color and movement.

Baroque art

The bold and vigorous Baroque style was foreshadowed in this dramatic drawing by **Michelangelo** *(1474–1564),* Studies for the Libyan Sibyl. *(The Metropolitan Museum of Art, Purchase, 1924, John Pulitzer Bequest)*

Politics

The Baroque was the era of absolute monarchy. Rulers throughout Europe took as their model the splendor of the French court at Versailles. Louis XIV's famous "I am the State" summed up a way of life in which all art and culture served the cult of the ruler. Courts large and small maintained elaborate musical establishments including opera troupes, chapel choirs, and orchestras. Baroque opera, the favorite diversion of the aristocracy, aimed at a lofty pathos that left no room for the frailties of ordinary people. It centered on the gods and heroes of antiquity, in whom the occupants of the royal box and their courtiers found a flattering likeness of themselves.

Scientific frontiers

The Baroque was also an age of reason. The findings of Kepler, Galileo, and Copernicus in physics and astronomy, of Descartes in mathematics and Spinoza in philosophy were so many milestones in the intellectual history of Europe. Harvey explained the circulation of the blood. Newton's theory of gravitation revealed a universe based upon law and order. The philosopher Locke expressed the confidence of a brave new age when he wrote, "To love truth for truth's sake is the principal part of human perfection in this world."

Excluded from the salons of the aristocracy, the middle classes created a culture of their own. Their music making centered on the home, the church, and the university group (known as *collegium musicum*). For them came into being the comic opera which, like the prose novel, was filled with keen and witty observation of life. For them painting forsook its grandiose themes and turned to intimate scenes of bourgeois life. The Dutch school, represented by Vermeer, embodied the vitality of a new burgher art that reached its high point in Rembrandt (see page 25), a master whose insights penetrated the recesses of the soul. Under the leadership of merchant princes and financiers, the culture of the city came to rival that of the palace. These new connoisseurs vied with the court in their love of splendor, responding to the sensuous beauty of brocade and velvet, marble and jewels and precious metals. This aspect of the Baroque finds expression in the painting of Peter Paul Rubens (see page 93), whose canvases exude a driving energy, a reveling in life. His voluptuous nudes established the seventeenth-century ideal of feminine beauty.

The Baroque was an intensely devout period. Religion was a rallying cry on some of the bloodiest battlefields in history. The Protestant camp included

Religion

The art of **Jan Vermeer** (*1632–75*) *turned to intimate scenes of bourgeois life.* The Artist and His Studio. (Kunsthistorisches Museum, Vienna)

England, Scandinavia, Holland, and the north German cities, all citadels of the rising middle class. On the Catholic side were the two powerful dynasties, Hapsburg and Bourbon, who fought one another no less fiercely than they did their Protestant foes. After decades of struggle, France emerged as the leading state on the Continent; Germany was in ruins; England rose to world power. Europe was ready to advance to the stage of modern industrial society.

Protestant culture was rooted in the Bible. John Milton (1608–74) in *Paradise Lost* produced the poetic epic of Protestantism, even as Dante three and a half centuries earlier had produced that of the Catholic in *The Divine Comedy.* The Catholic world tried to retrieve the losses inflicted by Luther's secession. The Counter Reformation mobilized all the forces of the church militant. Its rapturous mysticism found expression in the canvases of El Greco (1541–1614) whose eerie landscapes, bathed in an unearthly light, are creations of a visionary mind that distorts the real in its search for a reality beyond.

Between the conflicting currents of absolute monarchy and rising bourgeois power, Reformation and Counter Reformation, the Baroque fashioned its grandiose art. Alien to its spirit were restraint and detachment. Rather it achieved its ends through violent opposition of forces, lavish creativity, and emotional abandon. With these went the capacity to organize a thousand details into an overpowering whole.

The role of the artist   Artists played a variety of roles in Baroque society. They might be ambassadors and intimates of princes, as were Rubens and Van Dyck; or priests, as was Vivaldi; or political leaders, like Milton. They functioned under royal or princely patronage, as did Corneille and Racine; or, like Bach, were in the employ of a church or a free city. To the aristocrats whom they served they might be little more than purveyors of elegant entertainment. Yet, beneath the obsequious manner and fawning dedications demanded by the age, there was often to be found a spirit that dared to probe all existing knowledge and shape new worlds; a voice addressing itself to those who truly listened—a voice that was indeed "the trumpet of a prophecy."

17

Main Currents in Baroque Music

"The end of all good music is to affect the soul."—CLAUDIO MONTEVERDI

Origins of the Monodic Style

With the transition from Renaissance to Baroque came a momentous change: the shifting of interest from a texture of several independent parts to music in which a single melody predominated; that is, from polyphonic to homophonic texture. The new style, which originated in vocal music, was named *monody*—literally, "one song," music for one singer with instrumental accompaniment. (Monody is not to be confused with monophony, which is an unaccompanied vocal line; see page 17). The year 1600 is associated with the emergence of the monodic style. Like many such milestones, the date merely indicates the coming to light of a process that was long preparing.

Monody

The victory of the monodic style was achieved by a group of Florentine writers, artists, and musicians known as the Camerata, a name derived from the Italian word for salon. Among them were Vincenzo Galilei, father of the astronomer Galileo Galilei, and the composers Jacopo Peri (1561–1633) and Giulio Caccini (c. 1545–1618). The members of the Camerata were aristocratic humanists. Their aim was to resurrect the musical-dramatic art of ancient Greece. Since almost nothing was known of ancient music, the Camerata instead came forth with an idea that was very much alive.

The Camerata

This idea was that music must heighten the emotional power of the text. "I endeavored," wrote Caccini in 1602, "the imitation of the conceit of the words, seeking out the chords more or less passionate according to the meaning." Thus came into being what its inventors regarded as the *stile rappresentativo* (representational style), consisting of a vocal line that moved freely over a foundation of simple chords.

Stile rappresentativo

The Camerata appeared at a time when it became necessary for music to free itself from the complexities of counterpoint. The year 1600, like the year 1900, bristled with discussions about *le nuove musiche*—"the new music"—and what its adherents proudly named "the expressive style." They soon realized that this representational style could be applied not only to a poem but to an entire drama. In this way they were led to what many regard as the single most important achievement of Baroque music—the invention of the opera.

Origins of opera

New Harmonic Structures

The melody-and-chords of the new music was far removed from the intricate interweaving of voices in the old. Since musicians were familiar with the basic harmony, it was unnecessary to write the chords out in full. Instead, the composer put a numeral, indicating the chord required, above or below the bass note. For example, the figure 6 under a bass note indicated a chord whose root lay a sixth above the note. The application of this principle on a large scale resulted in the *figured bass* or *thorough-bass* (from *basso continuo*, a continuous bass, "thorough" being the old form of "through"). The actual filling in and elaboration of the harmony was left to the performer.

Figured bass

So important was this practice for a century and a half that the Baroque is often referred to as the period of thorough-bass. The figured bass required at least two players: one to perform the bass line on a sustaining instrument—cello or bassoon—and the other to fill in or "realize" the chords on an instrument capable of harmony, such as a harpsichord or organ, a guitar or lute. The realization of the thorough-bass would have been impossible if musicians of the period had not been ready to "think with their fingers." A church organist was expected as a matter of course to be able to improvise

Thorough-bass instruments

The thorough-bass instrument looming above the harpsichord testifies to the importance of the basso continuo practice in Baroque performance. A wash drawing by **Giuseppe Zocchi** (*1711–69*), Concerto.

an intricate contrapuntal piece. The ability in this regard of great organists such as Bach and Handel was legendary.

The Baroque witnessed one of the most significant changes in all music history: the transition from the Medieval church modes to major-minor tonality. As music turned from vocal counterpoint to instrumental harmony, it demanded a simplification of the harmonic system. The various church modes gave way to two standard scales: major and minor. With the establishment of major-minor tonality, the thrust to the keynote or tonic became the most powerful force in music.

Major-minor tonality

Now each chord could assume its function in relation to the key center. Composers of the Baroque soon learned to exploit the opposition between the chord of rest, the I (tonic), and the active chord, the V (dominant). So, too, the movement from home key to contrasting key and back became an important element in the shaping of musical structure. Composers developed larger forms of instrumental music than had ever been known before.

Tonic and dominant

Important in this transition was a major technical advance. Due to a curious quirk of nature, keyboard instruments tuned according to the scientific laws of acoustics (first discovered by the ancient Greek philosopher Pythagoras) give a pure sound in some keys but increasingly out-of-tune intervals in others. As instrumental music acquired greater prominence, it became more and more important to be able to play in all the keys; thus a variety of tuning systems were developed. In the seventeenth century, a discovery was made: by slightly mistuning the intervals within the octave—and thereby spreading the discrepancy evenly among all the tones—it became possible to play in every major and minor key without unpleasant results. This tuning adjustment is known as *equal temperament*. It increased the range of harmonic possibilities available to the composer. Although we are uncertain which of the many temperaments or tuning systems was preferred by Johann Sebastian Bach, he demonstrated that he could write in every one of the twelve major and twelve minor keys. The result, *The Well-Tempered Clavier*, is a two-volume collection, each containing twenty-four preludes and fugues, or one in every possible key. Equal temperament eventually transformed the major-minor system, making it a completely flexible medium of expression.

Equal temperament

The growing harmonic sense brought about a freer handling of dissonance. Baroque musicians used dissonant chords for emotional intensity and color. In the setting of poetry the composer heightened the impact of an expressive word through dissonance.

Use of dissonance

Baroque Musical Style

The Baroque, with its fondness for energetic movement, demanded a vigorous rhythm based on the regular recurrence of accent. The bass part became the carrier of the new rhythm. Its relentless beat is an arresting trait in many compositions of the high Baroque. This steady pulsation, once under way, never slackens or deviates until the goal is reached. It imparts to Baroque music its unflagging drive, producing the same effect of turbulent yet controlled motion that animates Baroque painting, sculpture, and architecture. In effect, rhythm pervaded the musical conception of the Baroque and helped it capture the movement and drive of a vibrant era.

Vigorous rhythm

The elaborate scrollwork of Baroque architecture bears witness to an abundance of energy that would not leave an inch of space undecorated. Its musical counterpart is to be found in one of the main elements of Baroque style—the principle of continuous expansion. A movement will start off with a striking musical figure that unfolds through a process of ceaseless spinning out. In vocal music the melody of the Baroque was imbued with the desire always to heighten the impact of the words. Wide leaps and the use of chromatic tones helped create a noble melody whose spacious curves outlined a style of grand expressiveness and pathos.

Continuous melody

Baroque music does not know the constant fluctuation of volume that marks later styles. A passage uniformly loud will be followed by one uniformly soft, creating the effect of light and shade. The shift from one level to the other, known as *terraced dynamics*, is a characteristic feature of the Baroque style. For greater volume of tone, Baroque composers wrote for a larger number of players rather than directing each instrument to play louder; as a means of expression within a passage they found their main source of dynamic expression in the contrast between a soft passage and a loud—that is, between the two terraces of sound rather than in the crescendos of later styles. This conception shapes the structure of the music, endowing it with a monumental simplicity.

Terraced dynamics

It follows that Baroque composers were much more sparing of expression marks than those who came after. The music of the period carries little else than an occasional *forte* or *piano*, leaving it to the player to supply whatever else may be necessary.

The Rise of the Virtuoso Musician

The heightened interest in instruments in the Baroque era went hand in hand with the need to master their technique. There followed a dramatic rise in the standards of playing, which paralleled the design improvements introduced by the great builders of instruments in Italy and Germany. This in turn made it possible for composers to write works that demanded a more advanced playing technique. Out of this development came the challenging harpsichord sonatas of Domenico Scarlatti (1685–1757) and the virtuosic violin works of Archangelo Corelli (1653–1713), to name only two masters of the period.

The emergence of instrumental virtuosity had its counterpart in the vocal sphere. The rise of opera saw the development of a phenomenal vocal technique that has never been surpassed. At this time, too, women began to enter the ranks as professional musicians, both as composers and performers. In Italy, Barbara Strozzi (1619–64) enjoyed a successful career as a singer before turning her efforts to composing, and a trio of women singers from Ferrara in northern Italy were known throughout Europe not only for "the timbre and training of their voices but in the design of exquisite passages of embellishment."

The castrato

The advance in vocal virtuosity was much encouraged by the rise of the *castrato*, the artificial male soprano or alto who dominated the operatic scene of the early eighteenth century. Such singers were castrated during their boyhood in order to preserve the soprano or alto register of their voices for the rest of their lives. What resulted, after years of training, was an incredibly agile voice of enormous range, powered by breath control the like of which singers today cannot even begin to approach. The castrato's voice combined the power of the male with the brilliance of the upper register. Strange as it may seem to us, Baroque audiences associated it with heroic male roles. The era of the French Revolution witnessed the decline and eventual abolition of a custom so incompatible with human dignity. When castrato roles are performed today, they are usually sung in lower register by a tenor or baritone, or in the original register by a woman singer in male costume.

Improvisation

Improvisation played an important role in Baroque music. Singers and players alike added their own embellishments to what was written down (as is the custom today in jazz). This was their creative contribution to the work. The practice was so widespread that Baroque music sounded quite different in performance from what it looked like on paper.

The Doctrine of the Affections

The *doctrine of the affections* related primarily to the union of music and poetry, where the mental and emotional state was made explicit by the text. The Baroque inherited from the Renaissance an impressive technique of word painting, in which the music vividly mirrored the words.

The ultimate supremacy of music over text shows itself in two traits that strike the listener in hearing the vocal literature of the Baroque. We have already encountered both. In the first place, lines, phrases, and individual words are repeated over and over again in order to allow room for the necessary musical expansion. This practice springs from the realization that music communicates more slowly than words and needs more time in which to establish its meaning. In the second place, a single syllable will be extended to accommodate all the notes of an expressive melodic line, so that the word is stretched beyond recognition, or treated melismatically. Thus, the music born of words ends by swallowing up the element that gave it birth.

In instrumental music the practice took root of building a piece on a single mood or "affection." This was established at the outset by a striking musical subject out of which grew the entire composition. In this way composers discovered the imperious gesture that opens a piece of Baroque music, establishing a tension and pathos that pervade the whole movement.

Internationalism in Music

The Baroque was a period of international culture. National styles existed—without nationalism. Jean-Baptiste Lully (1632–87), an Italian, created the French lyric tragedy. Handel, a German, gave England the oratorio. There was free interchange among national cultures. The sensuous beauty of Italian melody, the pointed precision of French dance rhythm, the luxuriance of German counterpoint, the freshness of English choral song—these nourished an all-European art that absorbed the best of each.

Baroque composers were employed by courts, towns, churches, or opera houses. They were in direct contact with their public. Most likely they were their own musical interpreters, which made the contact even closer. They frequently created their compositions for specific occasions—a royal wedding or a religious service, for example—and for immediate use: in a word, for communication. They began by writing for a particular time and place, but they ended by creating for the ages.

UNIT VII

■

Vocal Music of the Baroque

18

Baroque Opera

The Components of Opera

An *opera* is a drama that is sung. It combines the resources of vocal and instrumental music—soloists, ensembles, chorus, orchestra, and sometimes ballet—with poetry and drama, acting and pantomime, scenery and costumes. To weld the diverse elements into a unity is a problem that has exercised some of the best minds in the history of music.

Recitative   Explanations necessary to plot and action are generally presented in a kind of musical declamation known as *recitative*. This disjunct vocal style, which grew out of the earliest monodies of the Florentine Camerata, imitates the natural inflections of speech; its rhythm is curved to the rhythm of the language. Instead of a purely musical line, recitative is often characterized by a rapid patter and "talky" repetition of the same note; also by rapid question-and-answer dialogue that builds dramatic tension in the theater. In time, two styles of recitative became standard: *secco*, which features a sparse accompaniment and moves with great freedom, and *accompagnato*, which is accompanied by various instruments and thus moves more evenly.

Aria   Recitative gives way at the lyric moments to the *aria* (Italian for "air"), which releases through melody the emotional tension accumulated in the course of action. The aria is a song, generally of a highly emotional kind. It is what audiences wait for, what they cheer, what they remember. An aria, because of its beauty, can be effective even when removed from its context. Many arias are familiar to multitudes who have never heard the operas from which they are excerpted. One formal convention that developed early in the genre's history is the *da capo aria*, a ternary or **A-B-A** form that brought back the first section with improvised embellishments by the soloist.

An opera may contain ensemble numbers—trios, quartets, quintets, and so on—in which the characters pour out their respective feelings. The chorus is used in conjunction with solo voices or it may function independently. It may comment and reflect upon the action in the manner of the chorus in Greek tragedy. Or it may be integrated into the action.

Ensembles

The orchestra too supports the action of the opera, setting the appropriate mood for different scenes. An opera usually begins with an instrumental number, known as the *overture*, which may introduce melodies from arias to come. Each act of the opera normally has an orchestral introduction, and interludes may occur between scenes as well.

The opera composer works with a *librettist*, who writes the text of the work, creating characters and plot with some dramatic insight and fashioning situations that justify the use of music. The *libretto*, or text of the opera, must be devised so as to give the composer an opportunity for diverse numbers—arias, recitatives, duets, ensembles, choruses, interludes—that have become the traditional features of this art form.

Libretto

Early Opera in Italy

An outgrowth of Renaissance theatrical traditions and the musical experiments of the Florentine Camerata, early opera lent itself to the lavish spectacles and scenic displays that graced royal weddings and similar ceremonial occasions. *Orfeo* (1607) and *Arianna* (1608) were composed by the first great master of the new genre, Claudio Monteverdi, in whom the dramatic spirit of the Baroque found its true spokesman. It was in his operas that the innovations of the Florentine Camerata reached artistic maturity.

Although the earliest operas derived their plots from Greek mythology, Monteverdi's *The Coronation of Poppea* (1642), a late work from his Venetian period, instead turned to history. By this time the first public opera houses had been opened in Venice. Opera was moving out of the palace to become a widely cultivated form of popular entertainment. In the early court operas Monteverdi used a heterogeneous orchestra consisting of whatever instruments happened to be available. But in writing for a theater whose repertory would include works by other composers, he adhered to—and helped evolve—a more standardized ensemble.

In Monteverdi's late operas, the action calls for a varied cast of characters spread across the social spectrum from Emperor to commoners, with vivid characterization of the main personages and dramatic confrontations between them. They treat powerful emotions that find expression in recitatives and arias, choruses and passages in arioso style (between aria and recitative). With *The Coronation of Poppea*, Monteverdi established the love duet as an essential feature of the opera both in the first act and at the end. From Monteverdi, the heritage descends through two hundred years of Italian opera to Giuseppe Verdi.

Opera in England

The masque

During the reigns of the first two Stuart kings, James I (r. 1603–25) and Charles I (r. 1625–49), the English masque emerged into prominence. This was a type of aristocratic entertainment that combined vocal and instrumental music, with poetry and dance. Many masques were presented privately in the homes of the nobility.

In the period of the Commonwealth that followed (1649–60), stage plays were forbidden; the Puritans regarded the theater as an invention of the devil. However, a play set to music could be passed off as a "concert." The "semi-operas" that flourished during the rule of Oliver Cromwell (1653–58) were essentially plays with a liberal mixture of solo songs, ensembles, and choral numbers interspersed with instrumental pieces. Since the dramatic tradition in England was much stronger than the operatic, it was inevitable that in these works the spoken word took precedence over the sung. However, in the 1680s, an important step toward opera was taken when John Blow presented his *Venus and Adonis*, which was sung throughout. This paved the way for the first great English opera, *Dido and Aeneas*, by Blow's pupil Henry Purcell.

Henry Purcell: His Life and Music

"As Poetry is the harmony of Words, so Musick is that of Notes; and as Poetry is a Rise above Prose and Oratory, so is Musick the exaltation of Poetry."

Henry Purcell

Henry Purcell (1659–95) occupies a special niche in the annals of his country. He was last in the illustrious line that, stretching back to pre-Tudor times, won for England a foremost position among the musically creative nations.

Purcell's brief career unfolded at the court of Charles II (1660–85), extending through the turbulent reign of James II (1685–88) into the period of William and Mary (1689–1702). He held various posts as singer, organist, and composer. Purcell's works cover a wide range, from the massive contrapuntal choruses of the religious anthems and the odes in honor of his royal masters.

Yet this national artist realized that England's music must be part of the European tradition. It was his historic role to assimilate the achievements of the Continent—the dynamic instrumental style, the movement toward major-minor tonality, the recitative and aria of Italian opera, and the pointed rhythms of the French—and to acclimate these to his native land.

Purcell's court odes and religious anthems hit off the tone of solemn ceremonial in an open-air music of great breadth and power. His instrumental music ranks with the finest achievements of the middle Baroque. His songs display the charm of his lyricism no less than his gift for setting the English language. In the domain of the theater he produced, besides a quantity of music for plays, what many of his countrymen still regard as the peak of English opera.

Principal Works

Dramatic music, including *Dido and Aeneas* (1689) and *The Fairy Queen* (1692); incidental music for plays

Sacred vocal music, including a Magnificat, Te Deum, and anthems

Secular vocal music, including court odes and welcome songs

Instrumental music, including fantasias, sonatas, marches, overtures, In nomines; harpsichord suites and dances

Purcell: Dido and Aeneas

Presented in 1689 "at Mr. Josias Priest's boarding school at Chelsy by young Gentlewomen . . . to a select audience of their parents and friends," *Dido and Aeneas* achieved a level of pathos for which there was no precedent in England. A school production imposed obvious limitations, to which Purcell's genius adapted itself in extraordinary fashion. Each character is projected in a few telling strokes. The mood of each scene is established with the utmost economy. As in all school productions, this one had to present ample opportunities for choral singing and dancing. The opera took about an hour. Within that span, Purcell created a work of incredible concentration and power.

He based the work on an episode in Virgil's *Aeneid*, the epic poem that traces the adventures of the hero Aeneas after the fall of Troy. Both Purcell and his librettist, Nahum Tate, could assume that their audience was thoroughly familiar with Virgil's classic. They could therefore compress the plot and suggest rather than fill in the details. Aeneas and his men are shipwrecked on the shores of Carthage. Dido, the Carthagenian Queen, falls in love with him; he returns her affection. But he cannot forget that the gods have commanded him to continue his journey until he reaches Italy; it is his "manifest destiny" to be the founder of Rome. Much as he hates to hurt the Queen, he knows that he must depart; she too ultimately realizes that she must let him go. She prepares to meet her fate in the moving lament that is the culminating point of the opera, "When I am laid in earth." (For the text, see Listening Guide 7.) In Virgil's poem Dido mounts the funeral pyre, whose flames light the way for Aeneas's ships as they sail out of the harbor.

Following the brief recitative "Thy hand, Belinda," Dido's lament unfolds over a five-measure *ground bass* or ostinato that descends along the chromatic scale, always a symbol of grief in Baroque music. The term ground bass refers to a phrase repeated over and over in the lower voice while the upper voices pursue their indepedent course. With each repetition, some aspect of the melody, harmony, or rhythm is changed.

Ground bass

In *Dido and Aeneas* Purcell struck the true tone of lyric drama. This masterpiece earned the composer a unique place in history. His contemporaries called "the British Orpheus."

Listening Guide 7

PURCELL: *Dido and Aeneas*, **end of Act III**

Date: 1689

Genre: opera

28 Recitative: "Thy hand, Belinda," sung by Dido;

Text: Thy hand, Belinda, darkness shades me,
    On thy bosom let me rest,
    More I wou'd but death invades me,
    Death is now a welcome guest.

Introduces lament aria; sung over sparse accompaniment
Aria: "When I am laid in earth," Dido's lament

Basis: ground bass, 5-measure pattern in slow triple meter, descending chromatic scale, repeated eleven times

29 Opening of aria,
with two statements
of ground bass

Statements of Ground Bass	Setting
1	Instrumental introduction
2	When I am laid in earth, may my wrongs
3	create no trouble in thy breast.
4	When I am laid . . .
5	create no trouble . . .
6	Remember me, remember me, but ah
7	forget my fate, remember me, but ah forget my
8	fate. Remember me . . .
9	forget my fate . . .
10	Instrumental closing
11	Instrumental closing

Late Baroque Opera

Opera in the late Baroque found its master in George Frideric Handel, who, although German by birth, dominated the operatic scene in London during the first decades of the eighteenth century. (Handel's life and works are discussed in Chapter 20.) This was the London of the Hanoverian Kings George I (r. 1714–27) and II (r. 1727–60). It was their taste that he managed to please, and their aristocrats whom, as an opera impresario, he had to win over.

Handel's dramatic works were in the new vein of *opera seria*, or serious Italian opera, that projected heroic or tragic subjects. His opera, *Julius Caesar*, written in 1724, is one of his finest. In this work, Cleopatra, eager to conquer Caesar with her beauty, enchants him with her love song, a da capo aria in **A-B-A** form. The repetition of the **A** section gave the soloist an opportunity for embellishing the melody with trills, runs, grave notes, and similar ornaments. The "single affection" on which this aria is based is established by the opening words, "V'adoro" (I adore you).

Julius Caesar has been revived in recent years with great success. Its music rises above the conventions of late Baroque opera to speak to our own time.

19

Bach and the Baroque Cantata

The Baroque inherited the great vocal polyphony of the sixteenth century. At the same time composers pursued a new interest in solo song accompanied by instruments, and in dramatic musical declamation. Out of the fusion of all these came a new Baroque form—the cantata.

The *cantata* (from the Italian *cantare*, "to sing"—that is, a piece to be sung) is a work for vocalists, chorus, and instrumentalists based on a poetic narrative of a lyric or dramatic nature. It is generally short and intimate, consisting of several movements including recitatives, arias, and ensemble numbers.

Cantatas, however, might be based on either secular or sacred themes. In the Lutheran tradition, to which the late Baroque composer Johann Sebastian Bach belonged, the sacred cantata was an integral part of the service, related, along with the sermon and prayers that followed it, to the Gospel for the day. Every Sunday of the church year required its own cantata. With extra works for holidays and special occasions, an annual cycle came to about sixty cantatas. Bach composed four or five such cycles, from which only two hundred works have come down to us. By the second quarter of the eighteenth century, the German cantata had absorbed the recitative, aria, and duet of the opera; the pomp of the French operatic overture; and the dynamic instrumental style of the Italians. These elements were unified by the all-embracing presence of the Lutheran chorale.

The Lutheran Chorale

A *chorale* is a hymn tune, specifically one associated with German Protestantism. The chorales served as the battle hymns of the Reformation. As one of his reforms, Martin Luther required that the congregation participate in the service. To this end, he inaugurated services in German rather than Latin, and allotted an important role to congregational singing. "I wish," he wrote, "to make German psalms for the people, that is to say sacred hymns, so that the word of God may dwell among the people also by means of song."

Luther and his fellow reformers created the first chorales. They adapted a number of tunes from Gregorian chant, others from popular sources and from secular art music. Originally sung in unison, these hymns soon were written in four-part harmony to be sung by the choir. The melody was put in the soprano, where all could hear it and join in singing. In this way, the chorales greatly strengthened the trend to clear-cut melody supported by chords (homophonic texture).

In the elaborate vocal works that appeared in the Protestant church service, the chorale served as a unifying thread. When at the close of an extended work the chorale unfolded in simple four-part harmony, its granitic strength reflected the faith of a nation. One may imagine the impact upon a congregation attuned to its message. The chorale nourished centuries of German music and came to full flower in the art of Bach.

Johann Sebastian Bach: His Life and Music

"The aim and final reason of all music should be nothing else but the Glory of God and the refreshment of the spirit."

Johann Sebastian Bach (1685–1750) was heir to the polyphonic art of the past. He is the culminating figure of Baroque music and one of the titans in the history of the art.

Bach was born at Eisenach in Germany, of a family that had supplied musicians to the churches and town bands of the region for upwards of a century and a half. Left an orphan at the age of ten, he was raised in the town of Ohrdruf by an older brother, an organist who prepared him for the family vocation. From the first he displayed inexhaustible curiosity concerning every aspect of his art. "I had to work hard," he reported in later years, adding with considerably less accuracy, "Anyone who works as hard will get just as far." At twenty-three he received his first important post:

Johann Sebastian Bach

court organist and chamber musician to the Duke of Weimar. The Weimar period (1708-17) saw the rise of his fame as an organ virtuoso and the production of many of his most important works for that instrument.

The Weimar period

Disappointed because the Duke had failed to promote him, Bach decided to accept an offer from the Prince of Anhalt-Cöthen. Here he served a prince partial to chamber music. In his five years there (1717–23) he produced suites, concertos, sonatas for various instruments, and a wealth of keyboard music; also the six concerti grossi dedicated to the Margrave of Brandenburg.

The Cöthen period

Bach was thirty-eight when he was appointed to one of the most important posts in Germany, that of Cantor of St. Thomas's in Leipzig. The cantor taught at the choir school of that name, which trained the choristers of the city's principal churches; and served as music director, composer, choirmaster, and organist of St. Thomas's. His twenty-seven years in Leipzig (1723–50) saw the production of stupendous works. The clue to his inner, spiritual life must be sought in his music. It had no counterpart in an outwardly uneventful existence divided between the cares of a large family, the pleasures of a sober circle of friends, the chores of a busy professional life, and the endless squabbles with a host of officials of town, school, and church who never conceded that they were dealing with anything more than a competent choirmaster.

The Leipzig years

The prodigious labors of a lifetime took their tolls; his eyesight failed. After an apoplectic stroke he was stricken with blindness. He persisted in his final task, the revising of eighteen chorale preludes for the organ. The dying master dictated to a son-in-law the last of these, *Before Thy Throne, My God, I Stand*.

Principal Works

Sacred vocal works, including over 200 church cantatas; 7 motets; Magnificat (1723); *St. John Passion* (1724); *St. Matthew Passion* (1727); *Christmas Oratorio* (1734); Mass in B minor (1749)

Secular vocal works, including over 20 cantatas

Orchestral music, including 4 Orchestral Suites, 6 *Brandenburg Concertos*, concertos for 1 and 2 violins, for 1, 2, 3, and 4 harpsichords

Chamber music, including 6 sonatas and partitas for unaccompanied violin, 6 sonatas for violin and harpsichord, 6 suites for cello, *The Musical Offering* (1747), flute sonatas, viola da gamba sonatas

Keyboard music, including 2 volumes of *Das wohltemperirte Clavier* (The Well-Tempered Clavier, 1722, 1742), 6 *English Suites* (c.1722), 6 *French Suites* (c. 1722), *Chromatic Fantasy and Fugue* (c. 1720), *Italian Concerto* (1735), *Goldberg Variations* (1741–42), *The Art of the Fugue* (c. 1745–50), suites, fugues, capriccios, concertos, inventions, sinfonias

Organ music, including over 150 chorale preludes, toccatas, fantasias, preludes, fugues, passacaglias

Bach epitomized the great religious artist. He considered music to be "a harmonious euphony to the Glory of God." His music issued in the first instance from the Lutheran hymn tunes known as chorales. Through these, the most learned composer of the age was united to the living current of popular melody, to become the spokesman of a faith.

Instrumental music

The prime medium for Bach's talents was the organ. In his own lifetime he was known primarily as a virtuoso organist, only Handel being placed in his class. In the field of keyboard music his most important work is *The Well-Tempered Clavier*. Of the sonatas for various instruments, a special interest is attached to the six for unaccompanied violin. The *Brandenburg Concertos* present various instrumental combinations pitted against one another. The four Suites for Orchestra are appealingly lyrical.

Religious music

The two-hundred-odd cantatas that have come down to us form the centerpiece of Bach's religious music. They constitute a personal document of transcendent spirituality, projecting his vision of life and death. His Passions are epics of the Protestant faith. The monumental Mass in B minor, which occupied Bach for a good part of the Leipzig period, was inappropriate for the Catholic service due to its length; it found its eventual home in the concert hall.

Last works

His last works reveal the master at the height of his contrapuntal wizardry; these include *The Musical Offering*, in which he elaborated on a theme by Frederick the Great, and *The Art of the Fugue*, which constitutes his final summation of the processes of musical thought, left unfinished at his death.

Bach: Cantata No. 80, A Mighty Fortress Is Our God

Bach's cantatas are generally laid out in anywhere from five to eight movements, of which the first, last, and usually one middle movement are choral numbers. These are normally fashioned from a chorale tune in one of various ways, ranging from simple hymnlike settings to elaborate choral fugues. Interspersed with the choruses are solo arias and recitatives, some of which may also be based on a chorale melody or its text. Bach's lyricism found its purest expression in his arias. These are elaborate movements with ornate vocal lines and expressive instrumental accompaniments. Many are in the da capo aria form of Italian opera (**A-B-A**), in which the contrasting middle section is followed by an ornamented repetition of the first part. Others follow less clear-cut patterns. The aria is introduced by a recitative, which may be either *secco* (supported only by an organ or harpsichord) or *accompagnato* (accompanied by the orchestra).

The orchestral accompaniments abound in striking motives that combine contrapuntally with the vocal line to create the proper mood for the text and illustrate its meaning. In many cases the aria is conceived as a kind of duet between the voice and a solo instrument so that a single instrumental color prevails throughout the piece. This accorded with the doctrine of the "single affection."

In the cantata *A Mighty Fortress Is Our God*, Bach was treading on hallowed ground. Martin Luther's chorale of that name, for which the founder

An illustration from **J. G. Walther's** Music Dictionary (*1732*) *showing the disposition of an orchestra in a cantata performance.*

of Lutheranism probably composed the music as well as the words, is a centerpiece of Protestant hymnology. Luther's words and melody are used in the first, second, fifth, and last movements. The rest of the text is by Bach's favorite librettist, Salomo Franck.

Bach took it for granted that the devout congregation of St. Thomas's Church knew Luther's chorale by heart. A majestic melody of imposing directness, it is today a familiar, Protestant hymn tune. Except for an occasional leap, the melody moves stepwise along the scale. It is presented in nine phrases that parallel the nine lines of each stanza of Luther's poem (the first two phrases are repeated for lines three and four of the poem. See Listening Guide 8).

The cantata opens with a choral fugue in D, in which each line of text receives its own fugal treatment. That is, the musical phrase is announced by one voice and imitated in turn by the other three. Each phrase is an embellished version of the original chorale tune. The trumpets and drums we hear in this movement were added after the master's death by his son Wilhelm Friedemann, who strove to enhance the pomp and splendor of the sound.

First movement

Second movement   The second number depicts Christ's struggle against the forces of evil. Strings in unison set up a leaping figure over a running bass. (We say that instruments are playing *in unison* when they are all playing the same notes.) There follows a duet for soprano and bass in D major; the combination of the soprano's variation on the original tune, the florid counterpoint of the bass, and the assured stride of the great chorale makes one of Bach's most vivid musical pictures.

Subsequent movements   The middle movements of the cantata feature freely-composed recitatives and arias grouped around a spanking Allegro which sets Luther's chorale, sung in unison, in the manner of a march. The final number rounds off the cantata with the chorale sung by full chorus and orchestra. We now hear Luther's melody in Bach's four-part harmonization, each vocal line doubled by instruments. The great melody of the chorale stands revealed in all its simplicity and grandeur. We see Bach today not only as a consummate artist who brought new meanings to music, but as one of the giants of Western culture.

Listening Guide 8   🔲 1A/7

BACH: Cantata No. 80, *A Mighty Fortress Is Our God* (*Ein Feste Burg ist unser Gott*)

Date: 1724, Revised for the Feast of the Reformation

Form: Eight movements, for chorus, soloists, and orchestra

Basis: Chorale (hymn) tune by Martin Luther

OVERALL STRUCTURE

Movement	*Medium*	*Use of Chorale Tune*
1. Choral fugue	chorus and orchestra	Embellished chorale
2. Aria, Duet	soprano and bass	Soprano line only
3. Recitative/arioso	bass solo	
4. Aria	soprano solo	
5. Chorale	chorus and orchestra	Unison chorale
6. Recitative/Arioso	tenor solo	
7. Aria, Duet	alto and tenor	
8. Chorale	chorus and orchestra	Four-part chorale

Original chorale tune by Luther

1. Choral fugue, D major, 4/4 meter.

First Sung by	*Text*	*Translation*
Tenors	Ein feste Burg ist unser Gott	A mighty fortress is our God,
Sopranos	ein' gute Wehr und Waffen;	A good defense and weapon;
Tenors	er hilft uns frei aus aller Not,	He helps free us from all the troubles
Sopranos	die uns jetzt hat betroffen.	That have now befallen us.
Basses	Der alte böse Feind,	Our ever evil foe,
Altos	mit Ernst er's jetzt meint,	In earnest plots against us,
Sopranos	gross Macht und viel List	With great strength and cunning
Tenors	sein grausam Rüstung ist,	He prepares his dreadful plans.
Tenors	auf Erd' ist nicht seins gleichen.	Earth holds none like him.

Opening melody in tenors, with notes of chorale marked

Instrumental canon, based on chorale tune in augmentation

11 2. Duet for soprano and bass, D major, 4/4 meter.

Text	*Translation*
	SOPRANO
Mit unsrer Macht ist nichts getan,	With our own strength nothing is achieved,
wir sind gar bald verloren.	we would soon be lost.
Es streit't für uns der rechte Mann,	But on our behalf strives the Mighty One,
den Gott selbst hat erkoren.	whom God himself has chosen.
Fragst du, wer er ist?	Ask you, who is he?
Er heisst Jesus Christ,	He is called Jesus Christ,
der Herre Zebaoth,	Lord of Hosts,
und ist kein andrer Gott,	And there is no other God,
das Feld muss er behalten.	He must remain master of the field.
	BASS
Alles was von Gott geboren,	Everything born of God
ist zum Siegen auserkoren,	has been chosen for victory.
Wer bei Christi Blutpanier	He who holds to Christ's banner,
in der Taufe Treu' geschworen,	Truly sworn in baptism,
siegt im Geiste für and für.	His spirit will conquer forever and ever.

Opening of soprano line with second stanza of chorale (notes of chorale marked with *x*)

17 8. Chorale, D major, 4/4 meter. Full chorus and orchestra.

Das Wort, sie sollen lassen stahn	Now let the Word of God abide
und kein Dank dazu haben.	without further thought.
Er ist bei uns wohl auf dem Plan	He is firmly on our side
mit seinem Geist und Gaben.	with His spirit and strength.
Nehmen sie uns den Leib,	Though they deprive us of life,
Gut, Ehr, Kind und Weib,	Wealth, honor, child and wife,

lass fahren dahin,   we will not complain,
sie habens kein Gewinn;   It will avail them nothing
das Reich muss uns doch bleiben.   For God's kingdom must prevail.

Opening of hymnlike setting
of chorale, in four voices
(instruments doubling
voices) and continuo

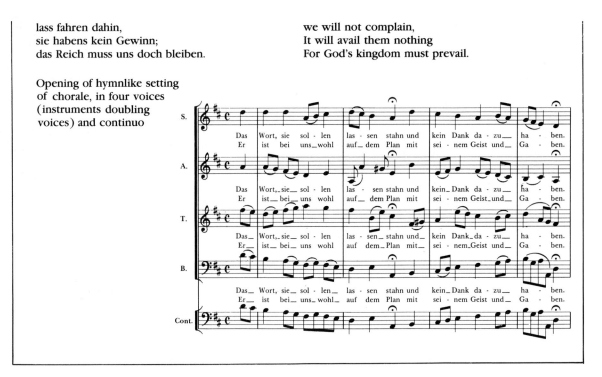

20

Handel and the Baroque Oratorio

The Oratorio

The *oratorio*, one of the great Baroque vocal forms, descended from the religious play-with-music of the Counter-Reformation. It took its name from the Italian word for a place of prayer. The first oratorios were sacred operas, and were produced as opera. However, toward the middle of the seventeenth century, the oratorio shed the trappings of the stage and developed its own characteristics as a large-scale musical work for solo voices, chorus, and orchestra, based as a rule on a biblical story and imbued with religious feeling. It was performed in a church or hall without scenery, costumes, or acting. The action usually unfolded with the help of a narrator, in a series of recitatives and arias, ensemble numbers such as duets and trios, and choruses. The role of the chorus was often emphasized. Bach's Passions represent a special type of oratorio, focusing on the final events of Christ's life. More typical of the genre are the oratorios of George Frideric Handel (1685–1759), perhaps the consummate master of this vocal form.

George Frideric Handel: His Life and Music

"Milord, I should be sorry if I only entertained them. I wished to make them better."

George Frideric Handel

Handel was born in 1685, the same year as Bach, at Halle in Germany, the son of a prosperous barber-surgeon. After a year at the University of Halle the ambitious youth went to Hamburg, where he gravitated to the opera house. There he absorbed the Italian operatic style that was then fashionable. His first opera, *Almira*, was written when he was twenty, and it created a furor. He spent the next three years in Italy, where his operas were received enthusiastically.

At the age of twenty-five Handel was appointed conductor to the Elector of Hanover. He received the equivalent of fifteen hundred dollars a year at a time when Bach at Weimar was paid eighty. A visit to London in the autumn of 1710 brought him for the first time to the city that was to be his home for nearly fifty years. His opera *Rinaldo*, written in a fortnight, conquered the English public with its fresh, tender melodies. A year later Handel obtained another leave and returned to London, this time for good. His opportunity for career advancement came with the founding in 1720 of the Royal Academy of Music. This enterprise, launched for the purpose of presenting Italian opera, was backed by a group of wealthy peers headed by the King. Handel was appointed one of the musical directors and at thirty-five found himself occupying a key position in the artistic life of England. For the next eight years he was active in producing and directing his operas as well as writing them. His pace was feverous, for he worked in bursts of inspiration, turning out a new opera in two to three weeks. To this period belongs *Julius Caesar*, one of his finest works in the new vein of opera seria.

Despite his productivity the Royal Academy failed. The final blow was administered in 1728 by the sensational success of John Gay's *The Beggar's Opera*. Sung in English, its tunes related to the experience of the audience, this humorous ballad opera was the answer of middle-class England to the gods and heroes of the aristocratic opera seria.

Rather than accept failure, Handel turned from opera to oratorio. Among his greatest achievements in this new genre were *Israel in Egypt, Messiah, Judas Maccabaeus*, and *Jeptha*, one of his last works. The British public could not help but respond to the imagery of the Old Testament, set forth in Handel's heroic tone.

There remained to face one final enemy—blindness. But even this blow did not reduce him to inactivity. Like Milton and Bach, he dictated his last works, which were mainly revisions of earlier ones. He continued to appear in public, conducting the oratorios and displaying his legendary powers on the organ until his death. The nation he had served for half a century accorded him its highest honor. "Last night about Eight O'clock the remains of the late great Mr. Handel were deposited at the foot of the Duke of Argyll's Monument in Westminster Abbey. . . . There was almost the greatest Concourse of People of all Ranks ever seen upon such, or indeed upon any other Occasion."

Principal Works

Operas (over 40), including *Almira* (1705), *Rinaldo* (1711), *Giulio Cesare* (Julius Caesar, 1724), *Orlando* (1733)

Oratorios, including *Israel in Egypt* (1739), *Messiah* (1742), *Judas Maccabaeus* (1747), *Solomon* (1749), *Jephtha* (1752); other vocal works include *Acis and Galatea* (masque, 1718), *Ode for St. Cecilia's Day* (1739), anthems, Latin church music

Secular vocal music, including solo and duo cantatas; arias

Orchestral music, including the 12 Concerti Grossi, Op. 6 (1739), *Water Music* (1717), *Royal Fireworks Music* (1749); concertos for oboe, organ, horn

Chamber music, including solo and trio sonatas

Keyboard music, including harpsichord suites, fugues, preludes, airs, dances

Handel was in every sense an international figure. His art united the beautiful vocal melody of the Italian school with the stately gestures of the French style and the contrapuntal genius of the Germans. To these elements he added the majestic chorale tradition of the English.

Handel's rhythm has the powerful drive of the Baroque. He leaned to diatonic harmony even as Bach's more searching idiom favored the chromatic. His melody, rich in mood and feeling, unfolds in great majestic arches. Rooted in the world of the theater, Handel made use of tone color for atmosphere and dramatic expression.

The oratorios of Handel are choral dramas of overpowering vitality and grandeur. Vast murals, they are conceived in epic style. Their soaring arias and dramatic recitatives, stupendous fugues and double choruses consummate the splendor of the Baroque. With the instinct of the born leader he gauged the need of his adopted country, and created in the oratorio an art form steeped in the atmosphere of the Old Testament, ideally suited to the taste of England's middle class.

Handel made the chorus—the people—the center of the drama. Freed from the rapid pace imposed by stage action, he expanded to vast dimensions each scene and emotion. The chorus now touches off the action, now reflects upon it. As in Greek tragedy, it serves both as protagonist and ideal spectator. The characters are drawn larger than life-size. Saul, Joshua, Deborah, Judas Maccabaeus, Samson are archetypes of human nature, creatures of destiny, majestic in defeat as in victory.

Handel: Messiah

In the spring of 1742, the city of Dublin hosted the premier of one of the world's most widely loved works, Handel's *Messiah*. Written down in twenty-four days, this oratorio is the product of Handel working as if possessed. His servant found him, after the completion of the "Hallelujah Chorus," with tears streaming from his eyes. "I did think I did see all Heaven before me, and the Great God Himself!"

The libretto is a compilation of verses from the Old Testament, set in three parts. The first part speaks of the prophecy of the coming of Christ and His birth; the second His suffering, death, and the spread of His doctrine; and the third the redemption of the world through faith. The work, with its massive choruses, moving recitatives, and broadly flowing arias, has come to represent the Handelian oratorio in the public mind.

The climax of the work comes in the second part, the Easter section, with the "Hallelujah Chorus." The musical investiture of the key word (Hallelujah) is one of those strokes of genius that resound through the ages. The drums beat, the trumpets resound. This music sings of a victorious Lord, and His host is an army with banners.

The third part, the Redemption section, opens with "I know that my Redeemer liveth," a serene expression of faith that is one of the great Handel arias. When the soprano voice ascends stepwise on the statement "For now is Christ risen from the dead," reaching the high point on "risen," there is established unassailably the idea of redemption that is the ultimate message of Handel's oratorio. (See Listening Guide 9.)

Listening Guide 9   📼 1A/10

HANDEL: *Messiah*

Date: 1742

Genre: Oratorio (English), in three parts

PART ONE: CHRISTMAS SECTION
PART TWO: EASTER SECTION

3 44. "Hallelujah Chorus," Allegro
    SATB, with homophonic refrain on
    "Hallelujah" alternating with polyphony   Opening of chorus, with refrain in homophonic style

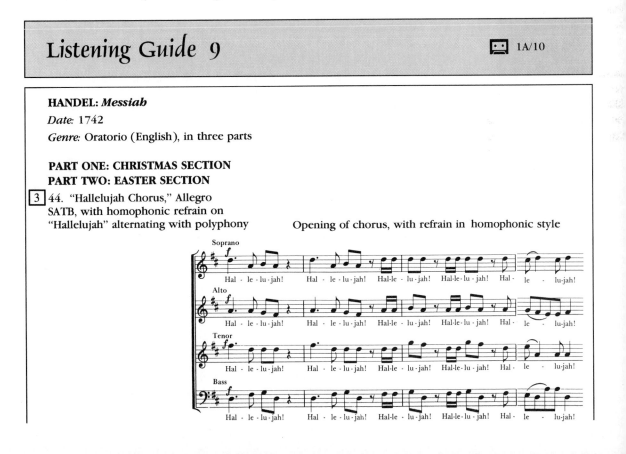

Text

Hallelujah!
For the Lord God Omnipotent reigneth.
The kingdom of this world is become the
Kingdom of our Lord and of His Christ;
and He shall reign for ever and ever.
Hallelujah! King of Kings, and Lord of
   Lords.
Hallelujah!

PART THREE: REDEMPTION SECTION

45. "I know that my Redeemer liveth," soprano aria;
Larghetto; two sections (**A, B**), with
recurring refrain

4 **A:** Orchestra introduces main melody in
E major, repeated by soprano

5 **B:** Opens with refrain in B major; word
painting: rising line depicts Christ's
Ascension

Text

I know that my Redeemer liveth,
and that He shall stand
at the latter day upon the earth.
And though worms destroy this body,
yet in my flesh shall I see God.

I know that my Redeemer liveth.
And though worms destroy this body,
yet in my flesh shall I see God.
I know that my Redeemer liveth.
For now is Christ risen from the dead,
the first fruits of them that sleep.

UNIT VIII

■

Instrumental Music of the Baroque

21

The Baroque Concerto

The Rise of Instrumental Music

The Baroque was the first period in history in which instrumental music was comparable in importance to vocal. The growing interest in this branch of the art stimulated the development of new instruments and the perfection of old. Playing techniques grew more fluent, and great virtuosos appeared— Bach and Handel at the organ, Corelli and Tartini on the violin.

On the whole, composers still thought in terms of line, so that a string instrument, a woodwind, and a brass might be assigned to play the same line in the counterpoint. Besides, since a movement was based upon a single affection, the same instrumental color might be allowed to prevail through-out, as opposed to the practice we will observe in the Classical and Romantic periods, when color was constantly changed. Much music was still performed by whatever instruments happened to be available at a particular time and place. At the same time, composers—especially in the late Baroque—chose instruments more and more for their color. As their specifications became more precise, the art of orchestration was born.

In recent years, a new drive for authenticity has made the original sounds of eighteenth-century music familiar to us even as it has revived Medieval and Renaissance instruments. Recorders and wooden flutes, restored violins with gut strings, the refractory but mellower-toned valveless brass instru-ments are heard again, and the Baroque orchestra has recovered not only its scale, but also its transparent tone quality. The gentler voices of the authentic instruments balance more comfortably in counterpoint. Naturally, they are not completely suitable for our largest concert halls, but they have proved especially effective on recordings.

Concerto Types

No less important than the principle of unity in Baroque music was that of contrast. This found expression in the *concerto*, an instrumental form based on the opposition between two dissimilar masses of sound. (The Latin verb *concertare* means "to contend with," "to view with.")

Solo concerto

Baroque composers produced two types of concerto: the solo concerto and the concerto grosso. That for solo instrument and an accompanying instrumental group became an important medium for experimentation in sonority and instrumental virtuosity, especially in the hands of the Italian master Antonio Vivaldi. The violin concerto was the most important variety of solo concerto. It usually consisted of three movements, in the sequence allegro-adagio-allegro, and prepared the way for the violin concerto of the Classic and Romantic periods.

Concerto grosso

The *concerto grosso* was based on the opposition between a small group of instruments, the *concertino*, and a larger group, the *tutti* or *ripieno* (Italian for full). Bach captured the spirit of the concerto grosso, in which two groups vie with each other in sonorous flights of fancy, in his six *Brandenburg Concertos*. This set was written for presentation to the Margrave Christian of Brandenburg, son of the Great Elector. The second of the set, in F major, has long been a favorite, probably because of the brilliant trumpet part. The solo group consists of trumpet, flute, oboe, and violin, all of them instruments in the high register. The accompanying group includes first and second violins, violas, and double basses. The basso continuo is played by cello and harpsichord.

The concerto embodied what one writer of the time called "the fire and fury of the Italian style." Of the many Italian masters of the concerto, Vivaldi was the greatest and most prolific.

Antonio Vivaldi: His Life and Music

> *"Above all, he was possessed by music."* —MARC PINCHERLE

Antonio Vivaldi

For many years interest in the Baroque centered on Bach and Handel to such an extent that other masters were neglected. None suffered more in this regard than Antonio Vivaldi (1678–1741), who has been rediscovered in the twentieth century.

Antonio Vivaldi was born in Venice, the son of a violinist. He was ordained in the Church in his twenties, and came to be known as "the red priest," an epithet which referred to nothing more than the color of his hair. For the greater part of his career Vivaldi was *maestro de' concerti* at the most important of the four music schools for which Venice was famous. These were attached to charitable institutions of a religious nature that the city maintained for the upbringing of orphaned girls, and they played a vital role in the musical life of the Venetians. Much of Vivaldi's output was written for the concerts at the Conservatorio del'Ospedale della Pietà, which at-

In Concert in a Girl's School, **Francesco Guardi** (*1712–93*) *depicts a Venetian entertainment featuring an orchestra of young ladies* (*upper left*). *The school might well have been the one at which Vivaldi was music master.* (Munich, Alte Pinakothek; Photo Joachim Blauel-Artothek)

tracted visitors from all over Europe. Judging by the music that Vivaldi wrote for them, the young ladies were expert performers.

In addition to his position in Venice, Vivaldi spent time in other Italian cities, especially in conjunction with his work as an opera composer. The end of his life is mysterious; a contemporary Venetian account states that "the Abbé Don Antonio Vivaldi, greatly esteemed for his compositions and concertos, in his day made more than fifty thousand ducats, but as a result of excessive extravagance he died poor in Vienna." He was buried in a pauper's grave, and to save expense his funeral was given "only a small peal of bells."

Vivaldi was active during a period that was of crucial importance in the exploration of the new instrumental style—a style in which the instruments were liberated from their earlier bondage to vocal music. His novel use of rapid scale passages, extended arpeggios, and contrasting registers contributed decisively to the development of violin style and technique. In his love of brilliant color, Vivaldi was a true son of Venice. He also played a leading part in the history of the concerto, exploiting with vast effectiveness the contrast in sonority between large and small groups of players.

Principal Works

Orchestral music, over 230 violin concertos including *Le quattro stagioni* (The Four Seasons, Op. 8, nos. 1–4, c. 1725); other solo concertos (bassoon, cello, oboe, flute, recorder), double concertos, ensemble concertos, sinfonias

Chamber music, including sonatas for violin, cello, flute; trio sonatas

Vocal music, including oratorios, mass movements (Gloria), Magnificat, psalms, hymns, motets; secular vocal music, including solo cantatas and operas

Vivaldi was amazingly prolific, even for that prolific era. Much of his music is still unknown. Only with the publication of his complete works—a project begun in 1947 and still not finished—will it be possible to evaluate fully the achievement of this strikingly original musician.

Vivaldi: "Spring" from The Four Seasons

Perhaps Vivaldi's best-known work is *The Four Seasons*, a group of four violin concertos. We have spoken of the fondness for word painting that shows itself in Baroque vocal works, where the music is meant to portray the action described by the words. In *The Four Seasons*, Vivaldi applies this principle to instrumental music. Each of the concertos is accompanied by a poem describing the joys of that particular season. Each line of the poem is printed above a certain passage in the score; the music at that point mirrors, as graphically as possible, the action described.

Of the four concertos, "Spring" (*La Primavera*) is the least graphic; it evokes mood and atmosphere rather than specific actions. The solo violin is accompanied by an orchestra consisting of first and second violins, violas, and cellos, with the basso continuo realized (improvised from the figured bass) on harpsichord or organ. The poem is a sonnet whose first two quatrains are distributed throughout the first movement, an Allegro in E major. (See Listening Guide 10 for the text.)

First movement

Both poem and music evoke the birds' joyous welcome to spring and the gentle murmur of streams, followed by thunder and lightning. The image of birdcalls takes shape in staccato notes, trills, and running scales; the storm is portrayed by shuddering repeated notes answered by quickly ascending scales. Throughout, an orchestral refrain called a *ritornello* returns again and again in alternation with the solo section. Ultimately, "the little birds return to their melodious warbling" and we return to the home key of E. A florid passage for the soloist leads to the final ritornello.

Ritornello

Second and third movements

In the second movement, a Largo in 3/4, Vivaldi evokes an image of the goatherd who sleeps "in a pleasant field of flowers" with his faithful dog by his side. Over the bass line of the violas, which sound an ostinato rhythm of an eighth note followed by a quarter on the second beat of each measure, he wrote, "The dog who barks." This dog clearly has a sense of rhythm. The solo violin unfolds a tender, melancholy melody in the noblest Baroque style. The Finale, an Allegro, is marked "Rustic Dance." Nymphs and shepherds dance in the fields as the music suggests the drone sound of bagpipes. Ritornelli and solo passages alternate in bringing the work to a happy conclusion.

Vivaldi's art flowered from a noble tradition. His dynamic conceptions pointed to the future. How strange that he had to wait until the middle of the twentieth century to come into his own.

Listening Guide 10   1B/1

VIVALDI: "Spring" from *The Four Seasons* ("La primavera" from *Le quattro stagioni*)

Date: Published 1725

Genre: Programmatic concerto for solo violin from Opus 8 (*The Contest between Harmony and Inspiration*), Nos. 1–4: *The Four Seasons,* each based on an Italian sonnet:

No. 1: "Spring" ("La primavera")
No. 2: "Summer" ("L'estate")
No. 3: "Autumn" ("L'autunno")
No. 4: "Winter" ("L'inverno")

Opus 8, No. 1, "Spring"
Movements: 3
Basis: Italian sonnet, translated below:

I Allegro	Joyful Spring has arrived, The birds greet it with their cheerful song, And the brooks in the gentle breezes flow with a sweet murmur.
	The sky is covered with a black mantle And lightning and thunder announce a storm. When they fall silent, the birds Take up again their melodious song.
II Largo	And in the flower-rich meadow, To the gentle murmur of bushes and trees The goatherd sleeps, with his faithful dog at his side.
III Allegro (Rustic Dance)	To the festive sounds of a rustic bagpipe Nymphs and shepherds dance in their favorite spot When spring appears in its brilliance.

I. First movement: Allegro, in ritornello form, E major

Ritornello theme

	Time	Program	Description
31	0:00	Spring	Ritornello 1, in E major
	0:31	Birds	Solo 1
			Birdlike trills and high running scales
32	1:04	Spring	Ritornello 2
	1:11	Murmuring brooks	Solo 2
			Whispering figures like water flowing
	1:33	Spring	Ritornello 3
	1:41	Thunder and lightning	Solo 3, modulates
			Repeated notes, fast ascending scales
33	2:06	Spring	Ritornello 4, in relative minor (C sharp)
	2:14	Birds	Solo 4
	2:30		Trills and repeated notes
			Ritornello 5, returns to E major
	2:41		Solo 5
			Florid running passage
34	2:54		Ritornello 6, closing tutti

22

Other Baroque Instrumental Forms

Sonata The sonata (from the Italian *suonare,* "to sound," indicating a piece to be sounded on instruments) was widely cultivated throughout the Baroque. In its early stages, it consisted of either a movement in several sections, or several movements that contrasted in tempo and texture. Of the first type, Domenico Scarlatti was the consummate master. His fame rests on his over five hundred solo harpsichord sonatas, called *Exercisi* (exercises) by the composer. Scarlatti's one-movement binary form, with modulations from home to related keys and back again, bear the seed of the sonata-allegro form that was about to come into being.

Chamber and church sonata Of the multi-movement sonata types, a distinction was drawn between the *sonata da camera* or *chamber sonata*, which was usually a suite of stylized dances intended for performance in the home, and the *sonata da chiesa* or *church sonata*, which was more serious in tone and more contrapuntal in texture. Its four movements, arranged in the sequence slow-fast-slow-fast, were supposed to make little use of dance rhythms. In practice the two types somewhat overlapped. Many church sonatas ended with one or more dancelike movements, while many chamber sonatas opened with an impressive introductory movement in the church-sonata style.

Trio sonata Sonatas were written for one to six or eight instruments. The favorite combination for such works was two violins and continuo, called a *trio sonata* because of the three printed staves in the music. Yet the title is misleading, because it refers to the number of parts rather than to the number of players. As we saw, the basso continuo needed two performers—a cellist to play the bass line, and a harpsichordist or organist to realize the harmonies indicated by the figures. Thus it takes four players to perform a trio sonata.

One of the most majestic forms of Baroque music is the *passacaglia*, *Passacaglia* which utilizes the principle of the ground bass. A melody is introduced alone in the bass, usually four or eight bars long, in a stately triple meter. The theme is repeated again and again, serving as the foundation for a set of continuous variations that exploit all the resources of polyphonic art. A related type is the *chaconne*, in which the variations are based not on a *Chaconne* melody but on a succession of harmonies repeated over and over. Passacaglia and chaconne exemplify the Baroque urge toward abundant variation and embellishment of a musical idea, and that desire to make "much out of little" which is the essence of the creative act.

The operatic overture was an important genre of large-scale orchestral music. Two types were popular during this period. The *French overture* *Overtures* generally followed the pattern slow-fast, with its fast section in a loose fugal style. The *Italian overture* consisted of three sections: fast-slow-fast. The opening section was not in fugal style; the middle section was lyrical; there followed a vivacious, dancelike finale. This pattern, expanded into three separate movements, was later adopted by the concerto grosso and the solo concerto. In addition, we shall see that the opera overture of the Baroque was one of the ancestors of the symphony of later eras.

The suite of the Baroque era consisted of a series of varied dance move- *Suite* ments, all in the same key. It was a natural outgrowth of earlier dance traditions that paired dances of contrasting tempos and character. The suite presented an international galaxy of dance types: the German *allemande*, in duple meter at a moderate tempo; the French *courante*, in triple meter at a moderate tempo; the Spanish *sarabande*, a stately dance in triple meter; and the English *jig* (gigue), in a lively 6/8 or 6/4. These had begun as popular dances, but by the time of the late Baroque they had left the ballroom far behind and become abstract types of art music. Between the slow sarabande and fast gigue might be inserted a variety of optional numbers of a graceful song or dance type such as the minuet, the *gavotte*, or the lively *bourrée*. These dances of peasant origin introduced a refreshing earthiness into their more formal surroundings. The suite sometimes also incorporated the operatic overture, as well as a variety of other brief pieces with attractive titles.

Among the most memorable contributions to the genre are the four orchestral suites of Bach and two by Handel, the *Water Music* and the *Royal Fireworks Music*. The essential element of the suite was dance rhythm, with its imagery of physical movement. It offered composers an elegant entertainment based on popular rhythms that could be transmuted into art.

Keyboard Instruments and Forms

The three important keyboard instruments of the Baroque were the organ, *Organ* the harpsichord, and the clavichord. The Baroque organ had a pure, transparent tone. Its stops let the voices stand out clearly so that the ear could follow the counterpoint. The colors of the various stops constrasted sharply; but although the tone was penetrating, it was not harsh because the wind pressure was low. Through the use of two keyboards it was possible to achieve terraced dyanmics, or even levels of soft and loud.

Harpsichord

The *harpsichord* too was capable of producing different sonorities because of its two keyboards. The instrument differed from the piano in two important respects. First, its strings were plucked by quills instead of being struck with hammers. The resultant tone was bright and silvery, but it could not be sustained like the tone of the piano. There had to be continual movement in the sound: trills, embellishments of all kinds, chords broken up into arpeggio patterns, and the like. Second, the pressure of the fingers on the keys varied the tone only slightly on the harpsichord, whereas the piano has a wide range of dynamics. But it was an ideal medium for contrapuntal music, for it brought out the inner voices with luminous clarity. It was immensely popular during the Baroque as a solo instrument. In addition, the harpsichord was indispensable in the realization of the thoroughbass, and was the mainstay of the ensemble in chamber music and at the opera house.

Clavichord

The *clavichord* was a favorite instrument for the home. Its sound is produced by the action of a hammer in contact with a string as long as a note is depressed. This allowed for some unique expressive effects not available on the harpsichord. However, by the end of the eighteenth century

A two-manual harpsichord by Jan Couchet of Antwerp, made in about 1650. (Metropolitan Museum of Art, The Crosby Brown Collection of Musical Instruments, 1889. Photograph by Sheldon Collins)

This German clavichord by Christian Kintzing, dated 1763, offered an amazing range of tonal variety. (Metropolitan Museum of Art)

both clavichord and harpsichord had been supplanted in public favor by the piano. The word *clavier* was used in Germany as the general term for keyboard instruments, including harpsichord, clavichord, and organ. Whether a certain piece was intended for one rather than the other must often be gathered from the style rather than the title.

The Fugue and Its Devices

The keyboard forms of the Baroque fell into two categories: free forms based on harmony, with a strong element of improvisation, such as the prelude; and stricter forms based on counterpoint, the most important of which was the fugue. Bach's keyboard music shows his mastery of both types.

A *prelude* is a fairly short piece based on the continuous expansion of a melodic or rhythmic figure. It originated in improvisation on the lute and keyboard instruments, but in the late Baroque it served to introduce a group of dance pieces or a fugue. Since its texture was for the most part homophonic, it made an effective contrast with the contrapuntal texture of the fugue that followed it. *Prelude*

From the art and science of counterpoint issued one of the most exciting types of Baroque music, the fugue. The name is derived from *fuga*, the Latin for "flight." A *fugue* is a highly-structured contrapuntal composition in which a theme or subject of strongly marked character pervades the entire fabric, entering now in one voice, now in another. The fugue consequently is based on the principle of imitation. The subject constitutes the unifying idea, the focal point of interest in the contrapuntal web.

A fugue may be written for a group of instruments; for a solo instrument; for several solo voices or for full chorus. Whether the fugue is vocal or instrumental, the several lines are called voices, which indicates the origin of the type. In vocal and orchestral fugues each line is articulated by another performer or group of performers. In fugues for keyboard instruments the ten fingers manage the complex interweaving of the voices. *Fugal voices*

The *subject* or theme is stated alone at the outset in one of the voices. It is then imitated in another voice—this is the *answer*—while the first continues with a *countersubject* or countertheme. Depending on the number *Subject* *Answer* *Countersubject* of voices in the fugue, the subject will then appear in a third voice and be answered in the fourth, with the other voices usually weaving a free contrapuntal texture against these. (If a fugue is in three voices there is, naturally, no second answer.) When the theme has been presented in each voice once, *Exposition* the first section of the fugue, the *Exposition,* is at an end. From then on the fugue alternates between sections that feature the entrance of the subject *Episodes* and less weighty interludes known as *episodes*, which serve as areas of relaxation.

The subject of the fugue is stated in the home key, the tonic. The answer is given in a related key, that of the dominant, which lies five tones above the tonic. There may be modulation to foreign keys in the course of the fugue, which builds up tension against the return home. The Baroque fugue thus embodied the contrast between home and contrasting keys that was one of the basic principles of the new major-minor system.

As the fugue unfolds, there must be not only a sustaining of interest but the sense of mounting urgency that is proper to an extended art work. Each recurrence of the theme reveals new facets of its nature. The composer manipulates the subject as pure musical material in the same way that the *Stretto* sculptor molds his clay. Especially effective is *stretto*, in which the theme is imitated in close succession. The effect is one of voices crowding upon each other, creating a heightening of tension that brings the fugue to its climax. The final statement of the subject, generally in a decisive manner, brings the piece to an end.

The fugue, then, is a rather free form based on imitative counterpoint, that combined the composer's technical skill with imagination, feeling, and exuberant ornamentation. There resulted a type of musical art that may well be accounted one of the supreme achievements of the Baroque.

Bach: Prelude and Fugue in C minor, from The Well-Tempered Clavier, Book I

In Chapter 17, we described *The Well-Tempered Clavier* as the celebrated work that circumnavigated the tonal globe, a journey made possible by the new system of equal temperament for tuning keyboard instruments. It was this system, you will remember, that made it possible to play in all the keys. The first volume, completed in 1722 during the years Bach worked in Cöthen, contains a prelude and fugue in each of the twelve major and twelve minor keys. The second volume, also containing twenty-four preludes and fugues, appeared twenty years later.

The Prelude and Fugue in C minor is No. 2 in the first volume of *The Well-Tempered Clavier*. The Prelude is a "perpetual-motion" type of piece based on running sixteenth notes in both hands that never let up, outlining a single chord in each measure. We associate emotion in music with a beautiful melody. This Prelude shows how deeply moving a series of harmonies can be.

The fugue, in three voices, is based on one of those short, incisive themes for which Bach had a special affinity. First presented by the alto voice in the home key of C minor, it is answered by the soprano in G minor, key of the dominant. There are two countersubjects that serve to shed new light on the subject, whose successive entries are separated by episodes woven out of the basic idea. (See Listening Guide 11.) As in the Prelude, the music is pervaded by a total unity of mood powered by unflagging rhythm. When the piece finally reaches the C-major chord at the end, we are left with the sense of a journey completed, an action happily consummated.

Listening Guide 11

📼 1B/2

BACH: Prelude and Fugue in C minor, from *The Well-Tempered Clavier*, Book I

Date: 1722

6 0:00 **Prelude**: Free, improvisatory-style piece
Establishes key of C minor
Begins Allegro with fast repeated sixteenth-note pattern through various harmonies
Ends with cadenza-like passage

Fugue: 3-voiced (SAB), with two-measure subject
Features many episodes with fragments of subject

Subject

Code for line graph:

Subject/Answer: ————————
Countersubject 1: – – – – – – – –
Countersubject 2: –·––·––·––·–
Episode: ~~~~~~~~~~~

7 1:45 EXPOSITION:

		episode 1		episode 2
S				
A				
B				

Measure 1   3   5   7   9
Key   c   G   c

	episode 3		episode 4	
S				
A				
B				

8 2:15

Measure 11   13   15   17   20
Key   E♭   (relative major)   G   c

9 2:49

	episode 5	cadential extension
S		
A		free
B		free

Measure 23   26   29
Key   c   c

■

To the Age of Enlightenment

The Rococo and the Age of Sensibility

As famous as Louis XIV's "I am the State" is his successor's "After me, the deluge." In the reigns of the two Louis, which lasted for more than a hundred years, the old regime passed from high noon to twilight. The gilded minority at the top of the social pyramid exchanged the goal of power for that of pleasure. Art moved from the monumentality of the Baroque to the caprice of the Rococo.

The word derives from the French *rocaille*, a shell, suggesting the decorative scroll-and-shell-work characteristic of the style. The Rococo took shape as a reaction from the grandiose gesture of the Baroque. Out of the disintegrating world of the Baroque came an art of subtle allure centered on the salon and the boudoir—a miniature, ornate art aimed at the enchantment of the senses and predicated upon the attractive doctrine that the first law is to enjoy oneself.

The greatest painter of the French Rococo was Jean Antoine Watteau (1685–1721). To the dream-world of love and gallantry that furnished the themes of his art, Watteau brought the insights and the techniques of his Flemish heritage. His counterpart in music was François Couperin (1668–1733), who—although he spoke the language of the Rococo—was rooted in the illustrious past. He was one of a family of distinguished musicians and the greatest of the French school of clavecinists. (The harpsichord is known in French as *clavecin*.) His art crystallizes the miniature world of the Rococo and the attributes of Gallic genius—wit, refinement, clarity, and precision. Its goal is to charm, to delight, to entertain.

The Rococo witnessed as profound a change in taste as has ever occurred in the history of music. In turning to a polished entertainment music, composers embraced a new ideal of beauty. Elaborate polyphonic texture yielded to a single melody line with a simple chordal accompaniment, much the same way that the contrapuntal complexities of late Renaissance music gave

François Couperin

132

Jean Antoine Watteau (*1684–1721*), *with his dream-world of love and gallantry, was the artistic counterpart of François Couperin.* La Gamme d'Amour (*The Gamut of Lov*e). (The National Gallery, London)

way to the early Baroque ideal of monody. It is surely true that history repeats itself. This age desired its music above all to be simple and not devoid of natural feeling. Thus was born the "sensitive" style of the *Empfindsamkeit* and the Age of Sensibility—an age that saw the first stirrings of that responsiveness to emotion that was to come to full flower with Romanticism.

Empfindsamkeit

The new style reached its apex in Germany in the mid-eighteenth century, a period that saw the activity of Bach's four composer sons—Wilhelm Friedemann, Carl Philipp Emanuel, Johann Christoph, and Johann Christian. They and their contemporaries consummated that revolution in taste which caused Bach's music to be neglected after his death.

This musical revolution saw the expansion of the major instrumental genres of the sonata, the new directions of the concerto, and the enrichment of symphonic styles with elements drawn from the operatic aria and overture, from the tunes and rhythms of Italian comic opera. To the charm of the gallant style they added the emotional urgency of a world in ferment. From all this was born a new thing—the idiom of the Classical sonata cycle, which we will discuss in a later chapter. The new art form was the collective achievement of several generations of musicians who were active in Italy, France, and Germany throughout the pre-Classical period (c. 1730–75).

The Changing Opera

The vast social changes taking shape in the eighteenth century were bound to be reflected in the lyric theater. Baroque opera, geared to an era of absolute monarchy, had no place in the changing scene. Increasingly its pretensions were satirized by men of letters all over Europe. The defeat of opera seria in London by *The Beggar's Opera* in 1728 had its counterpart in Paris a quarter of a century later. In 1752 a troupe of Italian singers in the French capital presented a soon-to-be famous comic opera *La serva padrona* (The *"War of the Buffoons"* Servant Mistress) by Giovanni Battista Pergolesi (1710–36). Immediately there ensued the "War of the Buffoons" between those who favored the traditional French court opera and those who saw in the Italian comic opera, called *opera buffa*, a new realistic art. The former camp was headed by the King, Madame de Pompadour, and the aristocracy; the latter by the Queen and the Encyclopedists—Rousseau, d'Alembert, Diderot—who hailed the comic form for its expressive melody and natural sentiment, and because it had thrown off what they regarded as the outmoded "fetters of counterpoint." In the larger sense, the War of the Buffoons was a contest between the rising bourgeois art and a dying aristocratic art.

It was a German-born composer trained in Italy and writing for the Imperial Court in Vienna who brought lyric tragedy into harmony with the *Gluck* thought and feeling of a new era. Christoph Willibald Gluck (1714–87) found his way to a style that met the new need for dramatic truth and expressiveness. "I have striven to restrict music to its true office of serving poetry by means of expression and by following the situations of the story, without interrupting the action or stifling it with a useless superfluity of ornaments." How well he realized the aesthetic needs of the new age: "Simplicity, truth, and naturalness are the great principles of beauty in all forms of art."

This conviction was embodied in his works written for the Imperial theatre at Vienna, notably *Orpheus and Eurydice* (1762) and *Alceste* (1767), both of which were collaborations with the poet Raniero Calzibigi. There followed the lyric dramas with which he conquered the Paris Opéra, the most important being the two based on Homeric legend—*Iphigenia in Aulos*, (1774) and *Iphigenia in Taurus* (1778). In these works he successfully fused a number of elements: the monumental choral scenes and dances that had always been a feature of French lyric tragedy, the animated ensembles of comic opera, the verve and dynamism of the new instrumental style in Italy and Germany, and the broadly arching vocal line that was part of Europe's operatic heritage. The result was a music drama whose dramatic truth and expressiveness profoundly affected the course of operatic history.

A Comparison of Baroque and Classical Styles

Baroque (c. 1600–1750)	*Classical* (c. 1750–1825)
Monteverdi, Purcell, Scarlatti, Corelli, Vivaldi, Handel, Bach	Haydn, Mozart, Beethoven, Schubert
Continuous melody with wide leaps, chromatic tones for emotional effect	Symmetrical melody in balanced phrases and cadences; tuneful, diatonic, with narrow leaps
Single rhythm dominates; steady energetic pulse; freer in vocal music	Dance rhythms favored; regularly recurring accents
Chromatic harmony for expressive effect; major-minor system established with brief excursions to other keys	Diatonic harmony favored; tonic-dominant relationship expanded, becomes basis for large-scale form
Polyphonic texture predominates, linear-horizontal dimension	Homophonic textures; chordal-vertical dimension
Fugue, concerto grosso, trio sonata, suite, chaconne, prelude, passacaglia	Symphony, solo concerto, solo sonata, string quartet, and other chamber music ensembles
Opera, Mass, oratorio, cantata	Opera, opera buffa, Mass, solo song
Binary form predominant	Ternary form predominant; sonata-allegro form developed
Religious music dominant	Secular music dominant
Terraced (contrasting) dynamics	Continuously changing dynamics through crescendo and decrescendo
Continuous tone color throughout one movement	Changing tone colors from one section to the next
String orchestra, with added woodwinds; organ and harpsichord in use	Orchestra standardized into four choirs. Introduction of clarinet, trombone; rise of piano to prominence
Improvisation expected; harmonies realized from figured bass	Improvisation largely limited to cadenzas in concertos
Single affection; emotional exuberance and theatrical gesture	Emotional balance and restraint

PART FIVE

■

More Materials of Form

"Order is the shape upon which beauty depends."—PEARL S. BUCK

Henri Matisse (*1869–1954*) The Cowboy *from* Jazz. (Paris, Teriade, 1947. Collection, The Museum of Modern Art, New York. Gift of the artist.)

UNIT IX

Focus on Form

23

The Development of Musical Themes

"I alter some things, eliminate and try again until I am satisfied. Then begins the mental working out of this material in its breadth, its narrowness, its height and depth."—LUDWIG VAN BEEETHOVEN

Thinking, whether in words or tones, demands continuity and sequence. Every thought must flow out of the one before and lead logically into the next. In this way is created a sense of steady progression toward a goal. If we were to join the beginning of one sentence to the end of another, it would not make any more sense than if we united the first phrase of one melody and the second of another. On the contrary, an impression of cause and effect, of natural flow and continuity, must pervade the whole musical fabric.

We saw that when a musical idea is used as a building block in the construction of a composition, it is called a *theme*. We also saw that a musical expansion of this theme is known as *thematic development* and that, conversely, a theme can be fragmented by dividing it into its constituent motives, a *motive* being its smallest melodic unit. A motive can grow, as a germ cell multiplies, into an expansive melody, or it can be treated in *sequence*, that is, repeated at a higher or lower level.

Thematic development generally does not take place in short lyric pieces, songs, or dances. In such compositions a simple contrast between sections and a modest expansion within each section supplies the necessary continuity. By the same token, thematic development finds its proper frame in the large forms of music. To those forms it imparts an epic-dramatic quality, along with the clarity, coherence, and logic that are the indispensable attributes of this most advanced type of musical thinking.

An example from the well-known opening of Beethoven's Symphony No. 5, which we shall study later, illustrates the thematic development of a four-note motive that is repeated in sequence one step lower, and that grows into a theme.

Beethoven: Symphony No. 5 in C minor

Opening of first movement:

Theme based on repetitions of motive:

Theme based on extension of motive:

24

The Sonata Cycle

"The history of the sonata is the history of an attempt to cope with one of the most singular problems ever presented to the mind of man, and its solution is one of the most successful achievements of his artistic instincts."—HUBERT PARRY

All music has form, some of it simple, some of it complex. We have already discussed two of the simplest forms: two-part or binary **(A-B)** and three-part or ternary **(A-B-A).**

Form is especially important in *absolute* or *pure* music, where there is no story or text to hold the music together. Here the story is the music itself; its shape, consequently, is of primary concern for both the composer and the listener. Large-scale works have an overall form that shapes the relations of the several movements and the various tempos in which those are cast. In addition, each movement has an internal form that binds its different sections into one artistic whole.

A sonata, as the Classical masters Haydn, Mozart, and their successors understood the term, is an instrumental work consisting of a series of three or four contrasting movements. For the purposes of this study, we refer to such a compositional structure as a *sonata cycle*. The name sonata is used specifically for a chamber piece intended for one or two instruments. However, other types of instrumental works are also examples of the sonata cycle. If more than two players are involved, the work is called, as the case may be, a trio, quartet, quintet, sextet, septet, octet, or nonet. A sonata cycle for solo instrument and orchestra is called a concerto; a sonata cycle for the whole orchestra, a symphony.

The First Movement

The most highly organized and characteristic movement of those making up the sonata cycle is the opening one, which is usually in a fast tempo such as Allegro. This is written in what is variously known as *first-movement form, sonata-allegro form*, or simply, *sonata form* (We will use the term *sonata-allegro* in this text.) A movement in sonata-allegro form is based on two assumptions. The first is that a musical movement takes on direction and goal if, after establishing itself in the home key, it modulates to another area and ultimately returns to the home key. We may therefore regard sonata form as a drama between two contrasting key areas. Second is the assumption that a theme may have its latent energies released through the development of its constitutent motives. Most useful for this purpose is a brief, incisive theme, one that has momentum and tension, and that promises more than it reveals at first sight. The themes will be stated or "exposed" in the first section; developed in the second, and restated or "recapitulated" in the third.

Sonata-allegro form

The opening section of sonata-allegro form, the *Exposition* or Statement, generally sets forth the two opposing keys and their respective themes. (A theme may consist of several related ideas, in which case we speak of it as a *theme group*.) The first theme and its expansion establish the home key or tonic. A transition or *bridge* leads into a contrasting key; in other words, the function of the bridge is to modulate. The second theme and its expansion establish the contrasting key. A closing section or *codetta* rounds off the Exposition in the contasting key. In the Classical sonata form, the Exposition is repeated. The adventurous quality of the Exposition derives in no small measure from the fact that it brings us from the home key to the contrasting key.

Exposition (Statement)

The *Development* wanders further through a series of foreign keys, build-

Development

ing up tension against the inevitable return home. The composer reveals the potentialities of the themes by breaking them into their component motives, recombining them into fresh patterns, and releasing their latent energies, their explosive force. In the Development, conflict erupts and the action reaches maximum intensity. The theme may be modified or varied, expanded or contracted, combined with other motives or with new material. If the sonata is for orchestra—that is, a symphony—a fragment of the theme may be presented by one group of instruments and imitated by another. Now it appears in the upper register, now deep in the bass. Each measure seems to grow out of the preceding by an inescapable law of cause and effect. Each adds to the drive and the momentum.

Recapitulation (Restatement)

When the developmental surge has run its course, the tension abates. A bridge passage leads back to the tonic. The beginning of the third section, the *Recapitulation* or Restatement, is in a sense the psychological climax of sonata form, just as the peak of many a journey is the return home. The first theme appears as we first heard it, in the tonic, proclaiming the victory of unity over variety, of continuity over change.

The Recapitulation follows the general path of the Exposition, restating the first and second themes more or less in their original form. Most important of all, in the Recapitulation the opposing elements are reconciled, the home key emerges triumphant. For this reason, the third section differs in one important detail from the Exposition: the composer now remains in the tonic for the second theme, which was originally in a contrasting key. In other words, although the second theme and its expansion unfold in sub-

Summary of Sonata-Allegro Form

Exposition (*or Statement*)	*Development*	*Recapitulation* (*or Restatement*)
[Slow introduction—optional] First theme (or theme group) and its expansion in tonic ↓	Builds up tension against the return to tonic by:	First theme (or theme group) and its expansion in tonic ↓
Bridge—modulates to a contrasting key ↓	1. Frequent modulation to foreign keys	Bridge (rarely modulates) ↓
Second theme (or theme group) and its expansion in contrasting key ↓	2. Fragmentation and manipulation of themes and motives ↓	Second theme (or theme group) and its expansion transposed to tonic ↓
Codetta. Cadence in contrasting key (Exposition repeated)	Transition back to tonic	Coda. Cadence in tonic

stantially the same way as before, we now hear this material transposed into the home key. There follows the final pronouncement, the *coda*, in the home key. This is fashioned from material previously heard in the codetta, to which new matter is sometimes added. The coda (Italian for "tail") rounds off the movement with a vigorous final cadence.

Coda

A dramatist creates opposing personalities as the chief characters of a work. So, too, the composer achieves a vivid contrast between the musical ideas that form the basis of a movement. The opposition between two themes may be underlined in a number of ways: through a contrast in dynamics—loud against soft; in register—low against high; in timbre—strings against winds, one instrumental combination against another; in rhythm and tempo—an animated pattern against one that is sustained; in tone production—legato against staccato; in type of melody—an active melody line with wide range and leaps against one that moves quietly along the scale; in type of harmony—consonance against dissonance, diatonic chords against chromatic; in type of accompaniment—quietly moving chords against extended arpeggios. Not all of these may appear in a given work. One contrast, however, is required, being the basis of the form: the contrast of key. And the opposition may be further intensified by putting one theme in the major and the other in minor.

The Second Movement

The second is most often the slow movement of the sonata cycle, offering a contrast to the Allegro that preceded it. If so, it will be a songful movement that gives the composer an opportunity to present the purely lyrical aspect of the musical art. It is often an Andante or Adagio in **A-B-A** form or a theme and variations.

We saw that repetition is a basic element of musical structure. This being so, composers devised ways of varying an idea when they restated it. Variation is an important procedure that is to be found in every species of music. But there is one type of piece in which it constitutes the ruling principle—the *theme and variations*, which frequently serves as the second movement of a sonata or symphony. The theme is stated at the outset, so that the audience will know the basic idea that serves as the point of departure. The melody may be of the composer's invention or may be borrowed from another, as in the case of Britten's *Variations and Fugue on a Theme by Purcell* (see page 44). The theme is apt to be a small two- or three-part form, simple in character to allow room for elaboration. There follows a series of variations in which certain features of the original idea are retained while others are altered. Each variation sets forth the idea with some new modification—one might say in a new disguise—through which the listener glimpses something of the original theme.

Theme and variations

Melodic variation

To the process of variation the composer brings all the techniques of musical embellishment. Melodic variation is a favorite procedure in a jazz group, where the solo player embellishes a popular tune with a series of

144

FOCUS ON FORM

Harmonic variation

arabesques. In harmonic variation the chords that accompany a melody are replaced by others, perhaps shifting from major to minor mode. Or the melody may be entirely omitted, the variation being based on the harmonic skeleton. The type of accompaniment may be changed or the melody may be shifted to a lower register with new harmonies sounding above it. So too

Rhythmic variation

the rhythm, meter, and tempo may be varied, with interesting changes in the nature of the tune. This may take on the guise of a waltz, a polka, a minuet, a march. The texture may be enriched by interweaving the melody with new themes. Or the original theme may itself become an accompaniment for a new melody. By combining these methods with changes in dynamics and tone color, the expressive content of the theme may be changed, so that it is presented now as a funeral march, now as a serenade, folk dance, caprice, or boat song.

The Third Movement

Minuet and trio

In the Classical symphony, the third movement almost invariably is a *minuet and trio*. The minuet originated in the French court in the mid-seventeenth century; its stately 3/4 time embodied the ideal of grace of an aristocratic age. In the eighteenth century the minuet was taken over into the sonata cycle, where it served as the third movement.

Since dance music lends itself to symmetrical construction, we often find in a minuet a clear-cut structure based on phrases of four and eight measures. In tempo the minuet ranges from stateliness to a lively pace and whimsical character.

The custom prevailed of presenting two dances as a group, the first being repeated at the end of the second (**A-B-A**). The one in the middle was originally arranged for only three instruments; hence the name trio, which persisted even after the customary setting for three was abandoned. The trio as a rule is lighter in texture and quieter of gait. Frequently woodwind tone figures prominently in this section, creating an out-of-doors atmosphere that lends it a special charm. At the end of the trio we find da capo or D.C. ("from the beginning"), signifying that the first section is to be played over again. Minuet-trio-minuet is a symmetrical three-part structure in which each part in turn is a small two-part or three-part form.

This structure is elaborated through repetition of the subsections, a procedure that the composer indicates with a *repeat sign* (:‖:). However, when the minuet returns after the trio the repeat signs are customarily ignored. A codetta may round off each section.

Minuet (A)	Trio (B)	Minuet (A)
‖:a:‖:b-a:‖	‖:c:‖:d-c:‖	a - b - a
or	or	or
‖:a:‖:b:‖	‖:c:‖:d:‖	a - b

Beethoven substituted the impetuous *scherzo* for the minuet in the nine-   *Scherzo*
teenth-century symphony. This is generally the third movement, occasionally
the second, and is usually in 3/4 time. Like the minuet, it is a three-part form
(scherzo-trio-scherzo), the first section being repeated after the middle part.
But it differs from the minuet in its faster pace and vigorous rhythm. The
scherzo—Italian for "jest'—is marked by abrupt changes of mood ranging
from the humorous or the whimsical to the mysterious and even demonic.

The Fourth Movement

The Classical sonata cycle often ended with a *rondo*, which is a lively   *Rondo*
movement suffused with the spirit of the dance. Its distinguishing characteristic is the recurrence of a central idea—the rondo theme—in alternation
with contrasting elements. Its symmetrical sections create a balanced architecture that is satisfying aesthetically and easy to grasp. In its simplest
form, **A-B-A-B-A,** the rondo is an extension of three-part form. If there are
two contrasting themes the sections may follow an **A-B-A-C-A** or similar
pattern.

The true rondo as developed by the Classical masters was more ambitious
in scope. Typical was the formation **A-B-A-C-A-B-A.** Because the theme is
to be heard over and over again it must be catchy and relaxing. The rondo
figured in eighteenth- and nineteenth-century music both as an independent
piece and as a member of the sonata cycle. While eighteenth-century composers were fond of using a rondo for the fourth movement, we will observe
that symphonists in the nineteenth century as often as not cast the finale in
the shape of a sonata-allegro whose spacious dimensions served to balance
the first movement.

The Sonata Cycle as a Whole

The four-movement cycle of the Classical masters, as found in their symphonies, sonatas, string quartets, and various types of chamber music, became
the vehicle for their most important instrumental music. The following
outline sums up the common practice of the Classic-Romantic era. It will
be helpful provided you remember that it is no more than a general scheme
and does not necessarily apply to all works of this kind.

The Classical masters of the sonata thought of the four movements of the
cycle as self-contained entities connected by key. First, third, and fourth
movements were in the home key, with the second movement in a contrasting key. The nineteenth century sought a more obvious connection
between movements—a thematic connection. This need was met by *cyclical*   *Cyclical structure*
structure in which a theme from the earlier movements appeared in the
later ones as a kind of motto or unifying thread.

The sonata cycle satisfied the composers' need for an extended instrumental work of an abstract nature. With its infusion of emotional and intellectual elements, its intermingling of lyric contemplation and action, the
sonata cycle may justly claim to be one of the most ingenious art forms ever
devised.

Sonata Cycle: General Scheme

Movement	Character	Form	Tempo
First	Epic-dramatic	Sonata-allegro	Allegro
Second	Slow and lyrical	Theme and variations	Andante,
		not in common Sonata-allegro, or **A-B-A**	Adagio, Largo
Third	Dancelike		
	Minuet (18th century)	Minuet and trio *3/4 time*	Allegretto
	Scherzo (19th century) *faster*	Scherzo and trio *sch trio sch*	Allegro
Fourth	Lively, "happy ending"	Sonata-allegro	Allegro, Vivace,
	(18th century)	Rondo	Presto
	Epic-dramatic with	Sonata-rondo	
	triumphal ending	Theme and variations	
	(19th century)		

PART SIX

◼

Eighteenth-Century Classicism

*"When a nation brings its innermost nature to consummate expression in arts and letters we speak of its classic period. Classicism stands for .experience, for spiritual and human maturity which has deep roots in the cultural soil of the nation, for the mastery of the means of expression in technique and form, and for a definite conception of the world and of life; the final compression of the artistic values of a people."—*PAUL HENRY LANG

Francesco Guardi (*1712–93*) Fantastic Landscape. (The Metropolitan Museum of Art, Gift of Julia A. Berwind, 1953)

UNIT X

■

The Classical Spirit

25
Classicism in the Arts

"Tis more to guide, than spur the Muse's steed;
Restrain his fury, than provoke his speed;
The winged courser, like a gen'rous horse,
Shows most true mettle when you check his course."—ALEXANDER POPE

Historians observe that style in art moves between two poles, the classic and the romantic. Both the classic artist and the romantic strive to express significant emotions, and to achieve that expression within beautiful forms. Where they differ is in their point of view. The classical spirit seeks order, poise, and serenity as surely as the romantic longs for strangeness, wonder, and ecstasy. Classic artists are apt to be more objective in their approach to art and to life. They try to view life sanely and "to see it whole." The romantics, on the other hand, are apt to be intensely subjective, and view the world in terms of their personal feelings. Classic and romantic ideals have alternated and even existed side by side from the beginning of time, for they correspond to two basic impulses in human nature: on the one hand, the need for moderation, the desire to have emotion purged and controlled; on the other, the desire for uninhibited emotional expression, the longing for the unknown and the unattainable.

Specifically, the classic and romantic labels are attached to two important periods in European art. The Classical era held the stage in the last half of the eighteenth century and the early decades of the nineteenth.

The dictionary defines Classicism in two ways: in general terms, as pertaining to the highest order of excellence in literature and art; specifically, pertaining to the culture of the ancient Greeks and Romans. Implicit in the Classical attitude is the notion that supreme excellence has been reached in the past and may be attained again through adherence to tradition.

Eighteenth-century Classicism drew its inspiration from the art and culture of ancient Greece. A painting by **Jacques-Louis David** (*1748–1825*), The Death of Socrates. (The Metropolitan Museum of Art. Wolfe Fund, 1931. Catherine Lorillard Wolfe Collection)

Classical artists regard neither their individuality nor their personal experience as the primary material of their art. For them the work of art exists in its own right rather than as an extension of their egos. Where Romantics are inclined to regard art primarily as a means of self-expression, Classicists stress its powers as a means of communication. For the extremely personal utterance of the Romantics, Classicists substitute symbols of universal validity. Classicism upholds the control and the discipline of art. This wholeness of view encourages the qualities of order, stability, and harmonious proportion that we associate with the Classical style.

Enlightened despotism

The art of the eighteenth century bears the imprint of the spacious palaces and formal gardens, with their balanced proportions and finely wrought detail, that formed the setting for enlightened despotism. In the middle of the century, Louis XV presided over the extravagant fetes in Versailles, Frederick the Great ruled in Prussia, Maria Theresa in Austria, Catherine the Great in Russia. In such a society the ruling class enjoyed its power through hereditary right.

Bourgeois revolution

Before the eighteenth century ended, Europe was convulsed by the French Revolution. The Classical era therefore witnessed both the twilight of the old regime and the dawn of a new political-economic alignment in Europe—specifically, the transfer of power from the aristocracy to the middle class, whose wealth was based on a rapidly expanding capitalism, on mines and factories, steam power and railroads. This shift was made possible by the Industrial Revolution, which gathered momentum in the mid-eighteenth century with a series of important inventions, from Watt's steam engine and Hargreaves's spinning jenny in the 1760s to Eli Whitney's cotton gin in 1793.

These decades saw significant advances in science. Benjamin Franklin discovered electricity in 1752, Priestley discovered oxygen in 1774, and Jenner perfected vaccination in 1796. There were important events in intellectual life, such as the publication of the French *Encyclopédie* (1751–72) and the first edition of the *Encyclopaedia Britannica* (1771).

The intellectual climate of the Classical era, consequently, was nourished by two opposing streams. On the one hand Classical art captured the exquisite refinement of a way of life that was drawing to a close. On the other it caught the first intimations of a new way of life that was struggling to be born. The eighteenth century has been called the Age of Reason; but the opponents of the established order, the philosophers who created the French *Encyclopédie* and the Enlightenment—Voltaire, Rousseau, and their comrades—also invoked reason for the purpose of attacking the existing order. Therewith these spokesmen for the rising middle class became the prophets of the approaching upheaval.

Intellectual dualism

Eighteenth-century thinkers idealized the civilization of ancient Greece and Rome. They viewed the Greek temple as a thing of beauty, unity and proportion, lightness and grace. Yet here too the revival of interest in Classical antiquity meant different things to the opposing camps. To the protagonists of the middle class, Greece and Rome represented city-states that had rebelled against tyrants and thrown off despotism. It was in this spirit that the foremost painter of revolutionary France, Jacques Louis David, decked his canvases with the symbols of Athenian and Roman democracy. In this spirit, too, Thomas Jefferson patterned both the Capitol and the University of Virginia after Greek and Roman temples, thereby giving strength to the Classic revival in this country, which made Ionic, Doric, and Corinthian columns an indispensable feature of our public buildings well into the twentieth century.

Classical ideals

Already in the 1760s a number of works had already appeared that clearly indicate the new interest in a romantic point of view. In the same decade Rousseau, the "father of Romanticism," produced some of his most significant

Thomas Jefferson's design for the library of the University of Virginia at Charlottesville reflects his admiration for the pure beauty of the Roman temple form.

writings. His celebrated declaration, "Man is born free and everywhere he is in chains," epitomizes the temper of the time. So too the first outcropping of the Romantic spirit in Germany, the movement known as *Sturm und Drang* (Storm and Stress), took shape in the 1770s, when it produced two characteristic works by its most significant young writers—the *Sorrows of Werther* by Goethe and *The Robbers* by Schiller. (Goethe, we shall see, became a favorite lyric poet of the Romantic composers.) By the end of the century the atmosphere had completely changed. The two most important English poets of the late eighteenth century—Robert Burns and William Blake—stand entirely outside the Classical stream, as does the greatest end-of-the-century painter, the Spaniard Goya, whose passionate realism anticipates a later age. (See page 222.)

Eighteenth-century Classicism, then, mirrored the unique moment in history when the old world was dying and the new was being born. From the meeting of two historic forces emerged an art of noble simplicity whose achievement constitutes one of the pinnacles of Western culture.

The Artist under Patronage

Eighteenth-century artists functioned under a system of aristocratic patronage. The social functions at court created a steady demand for new works that they had to supply. It is true that in point of social status they were little better than servants, but this was not quite as depressing as it sounds, for in that society virtually everybody was a servant of the prince save other princes. The patronage system gave artists economic security and a social framework within which they could function. It offered important advantages to the great artists who successfully adjusted to its requirements, as the career of Haydn richly shows. On the other hand, Mozart's tragic end illustrates how heavy was the penalty exacted from those unable to make that adjustment.

Women too found a place as musicians under the patronage system. In Italy and France, professional female singers achieved prominence in opera and in court ballets. Some found a place within aristocratic circles as singers, instrumentalists, and music teachers, offering private lessons to members of the nobility and bourgeoisie. With the growth of the music trades, especially music printing and publishing, women found more opportunities open to them. Important also was the rise of amateur music making, which allowed women of the middle as well as upper classes an outlet for their talents.

At this time music was beginning to move from palace to public concert hall. The rise of the public concert gave composers a new platform where they could appear as performer or conductor of their works. Haydn and Beethoven conducted their symphonies at concerts, Mozart and Beethoven played their piano concertos. Their audience came to hear their new works, unlike ours, which is mainly interested in the music of the past and generally avoids contemporary works. The eagerness of eighteenth-century audiences for new music could not but stimulate composers to be as productive as possible.

26

Classicism in Music

"Ought not the musician, quite as much as the poet and painter, to study nature? In nature he can study man, its noblest creature."—
JOHANN FRIEDRICH REICHARDT (1774)

The Classical period in music (c. 1750–1825) centers on the achievements of the four masters of the Viennese school—Haydn, Mozart, Beethoven, and Schubert—and their contemporaries. Their art reached its flowering in a time of great musical experimentation and discovery, when musicians were confronted by three challenging problems: first, to explore to the full the possibilities offered by the major-minor system; second, to perfect a large form of absolute instrumental music that would mobilize those possibilities to the fullest degree; and third, having found this ideal form in the sonata cycle, to differentiate between its various types—the solo and duo sonata, trio, quartet, and other kinds of chamber music, the concerto, and the symphony.

The Viennese school

If by Classicism we mean strict adherence to traditional forms we certainly cannot apply the term blanketly to the composers of the Viennese school. They experimented boldly and ceaselessly with the materials at their disposal. It should not surprise us, too, that Romantic elements abound in the music of Haydn, Mozart, and Beethoven, especially in their late works. As for Schubert, although his symphonies and chamber music fall within the Classical orbit, his songs and piano pieces, which we will take up later in this book, stamp him a Romantic.

In consequence, the term Classicism applies to the art of the four Viennese masters in only one—but that one perhaps the most important—of its meanings: "as pertaining to the highest order of excellence." They and their contemporaries solved the problems presented to them so brilliantly that their symphonies and concertos, piano sonatas, duo sonatas, trios, string quartets, and similar works remained as unsurpassable models for all who came after.

Elements of Classical Style

The music of the Viennese masters is notable for its elegant, singable melodies. These were usually based on symmetrical four-bar phrases marked off by clear-cut cadences, so that they were immediately perceptible to the ear. Classical melody sang even when it was intended for instruments. It moved stepwise or by narrow leaps within a narrow range, and it was firmly rooted in the key. Clarity was helped by repetition and the frequent use of sequence—that is, the repetition of a pattern at a higher or lower pitch. These and kindred devices made for symmetrical, balanced structures that were readily accessible to the listener.

Symmetrical melody

Equally clear were the harmonies that sustained these melodies. The chords were firmly rooted in the key, and did not change so rapidly as to be confusing. The chords underlined the balanced symmetry of phrases and cadences; they formed vertical columns of sound over which the melody unfolded freely and easily.

Diatonic harmony

The harmony of the Classical period was based on the seven tones of the major or minor scale; in other words, it was largely *diatonic*. This circumstance gives the music of Haydn, Mozart, and Beethoven its freshness, its resilience, its sense of being rooted in the key.

Rhythmic regularity

Melody and harmony were powered by strong flexible rhythms that moved at a steady tempo, setting up expectations that were sure to be fulfilled. Much of the music was in one of the four basic meters—2/4, 3/4, 4/4, or 6/8. If a piece began in a certain rhythm, it was apt to stay there until it was over. Classical rhythm worked closely with melody and harmony to make clear the symmetrical phrase-and-cadence structure of the piece. Out of the interaction of these three basic elements came musical structures that delighted the ear without mystifying it.

The form unfolded in clearly shaped sections that established the home key, moved to a contrasting but closely related key or keys, and returned to the home key. There resulted the beautifully molded, architectural forms of the Classical style, amply fulfilling the listener's need for both unity and variety.

Folk elements

Despite its aristocratic elegance, Classical music absorbed a variety of folk and popular elements. This influence makes itself felt not only in the German dances and waltzes of the Viennese masters but also in their songs and in the Allegros and rondos of their symphonies, concertos, string quartets, and sonatas. How often the rondo finale of a Haydn or Mozart symphony has all the verve and lightheartedness of a popular dance, and what charm this adds to the movement!

Classicism, to sum up, achieved the final synthesis of the intellectual currents of eighteenth-century life. The Classical masters struck a perfect balance between emotion and intellect, heart and mind. The Classical spirit finds a fit symbol in the god of light, Apollo, whose harmonious proportions so eloquently proclaim the cult of ideal beauty.

UNIT XI

■

Classical Chamber Music

27

Eighteenth-Century Chamber Music Style

"No other form of music can delight our senses with such exquisite beauty of sound, or display so clearly to our intelligence the intricacies and adventures of its design."—SIR WILLIAM HENRY HADOW

Chamber music, as we have seen, is music for small ensembles (two to about ten players) with one player to the part. It is so named for its suitability for performance in a small chamber or salon. In the intimate domain of chamber music, each instrument is expected to assert itself to the full, but the style of playing differs from that of the solo virtuoso. Where the virtuoso is encouraged to exalt one's own personality, the chamber music player functions as part of a team.

The Classical era saw the golden age of chamber music. Haydn, Mozart, Beethoven, and Schubert established the true chamber music style, which is the nature of a friendly conversation among equals. The central position in Classical chamber music was held by the *string quartet*, which, we have seen, consists of two violins (a first and a second), viola, and cello. Other favored combinations were the duo sonata—piano and violin, or piano and cello; the trio—piano, violin, and cello; and the quintet, usually a combination of string or wind instruments, or a string quartet and solo instrument such as the piano or clarinet. The age produced some memorable examples of chamber music for larger groups as well—sextets, septets, and octets.

Also widely cultivated were types of composition that stood midway between chamber music and symphony, their chief purpose being as sociable

Chamber groups

155

By the early 1800s, when **Carl Heinrich Arnold** (*1798–1874*) *made this drawing of* A String Quartet at Spohr's House, *chamber music-making at home was exceedingly popular.*

diversion or entertainment. Most popular among these were the *divertimento* and the *serenade*.

The String Quartet

The string quartet presents a special challenge both to composer and listener. To begin with, a small ensemble of string instruments lacks the contrasting tone colors of woodwinds and brass. This circumstance stimulates the composer to overcome the lack by every means possible. In its general structure the string quartet follows the four-movement scheme of the sonata cycle.

The quartets of Haydn feature dense musical textures based on development of motives, while Mozart's are more lyrical and relaxed. Beethoven and Schubert further expanded the architecture of the quartet, the former through motivic development and the latter through the element of pure song that was his special gift. Folk elements abound in Haydn's quartets, while Mozart's exhude the elegance of court dances. Beethoven's rousing scherzos replaced the graceful minuet and trio of the Classical era.

Because the string quartet was addressed to a small group of cultivated music lovers, composers did not need here the expansive gestures of the great public forms of music such as the symphony or concerto. They could therefore entrust to the string quartet their most private thoughts. In consequence, the final quartets of Haydn, Mozart, and Beethoven contain some of their most profound utterances, and are justly prized as constituting one of the high points of their art.

28

Mozart and Classical Chamber Music

*"People make a mistake who think that my art has come easily to me.
Nobody has devoted so much time and thought to composition as I.
There is not a famous master whose music I have not studied over and
over."*

Something of the miraculous hovers about the music of Mozart (1756–91).
His masterful melodic writing, his elegance of style, and his rich orchestral
colors sound effortless. This deceptive simplicity is indeed the art that con-
ceals art.

Wolfgang Amadeus Mozart: His Life and Music

Mozart was born in Salzburg, Austria, son of Leopold Mozart, an esteemed
composer-violinist attached to the court of the Archbishop of Salzburg. He
began his career as the most extraordinarily gifted child in the history of
music. He first started to compose before he was five, and performed at the
court of the Empress Maria Theresa at the age of six. The following year his
ambitious father organized a grand tour that included Paris, London, and
Munich. By the time he was thirteen the boy had written sonatas, concertos,
symphonies, religious works, and several operas.

He reached manhood having attained a mastery of all forms of his art.
The speed and sureness of his creative power, unrivaled by any other composer, is best described by himself: "Though it be long, the work is complete
and finished in my mind. I take out of the bag of my memory what has
previously been collected into it. For this reason the committing to paper
is done quickly enough."

Mozart's relations with his patron, Hieronymus von Colloredo, Prince-
Archbishop of Salzburg, were most unhappy. The high-spirited young artist
rebelled against the social restrictions imposed by the patronage system. At
length he could endure his position no longer. He quarreled with the Archbishop, was dismissed, and at twenty-five established himself in Vienna to
pursue the career of a free artist, while he sought an official appointment.
Ten years remained to him. These were spent in a tragic struggle to achieve
financial security and to find again the lost serenity of his childhood. Worldly
success depended on the protection of the court. But the Emperor Joseph
II passed him by in favor of lesser men such as Antonio Salieri or, when he
finally took Mozart into his service, assigned him to tasks unworthy of his
genius, such as composing dances for the court balls. Of his remuneration
for this work Mozart remarked with bitterness, "Too much for what I do,
too little for what I could do."

*Wolfgang Amadeus
Mozart*

*From patronage to
free artist*

The da Ponte operas   With the opera *The Marriage of Figaro*, written in 1786 on a libretto by Lorenzo da Ponte, Mozart reached the peak of his career. He was commissioned to do another work for the Prague Opera the following year. With da Ponte again as librettist he produced *Don Giovanni*. But the opera baffled the public. The composer whom we regard as the epitome of clarity and grace was, in the view of the frivolous audience of his time, difficult to understand. His music, it was said, had to be heard several times in order to be grasped.

Final years   His final years were spent in growing want. The frequent appeals to his friends for aid mirror his despair and helplessness. He describes himself as "always hovering between hope and anxiety." In the last year of his life, after a falling off in his production, he nerved himself to the final effort. For the popular Viennese theater he wrote *The Magic Flute*, on a libretto by the actor-impresario-poet Emanuel Schikaneder. With a kind of fevered desperation he turned to his last task, the Requiem. Mozart in his overwrought state became obsessed with the notion that this Mass for the Dead was intended for himself and that he would not live to finish it. His premonition concerning the Requiem came true. He failed rapidly while in the midst of the work. His favorite pupil, Süssmayr, completed the Mass from the master's sketches, with some additions of his own.

Mozart died in 1791, shortly before his thirty-sixth birthday. In view of his debts he was given "the poorest class of funeral." His friends followed to the city gates; but the weather being inclement, they turned back, leaving the hearse to proceed alone. "Thus, without a note of music, forsaken by all he held dear, the remains of this prince of harmony were committed to the earth—not even in a grave of his own but in the common paupers' grave."

Mozart is pre-eminent for the inexhaustible wealth of his melodic ideas. His melodies are simple, elegant, and songful. He had a fondness for moderately chromatic harmonies, especially in the development sections of his sonata forms. A born man of the theater, he infused a sense of drama into his instrumental forms, particularly through contrasts of mood ranging from the ebullient to the tragic. His richly colorful orchestration is notable for its limpid quality as well as for the freedom of the part writing and the careful interweaving of the instrumental lines.

Chamber music   In chamber music Mozart favored the string quartet. His works in this form range in expression from the buoyantly songful to the austerely tragic. The last ten quartets rank with the finest specimens in the literature, among them being the set of six dedicated to Haydn.

Piano works   One of the outstanding pianists of his time, Mozart wrote copiously for his favorite instrument. He led the way in developing one important form: the concerto for piano and orchestra. He wrote more than twenty works for this medium, which established the piano concerto as one of the important types of the Classical era.

Symphonies   The more than forty symphonies—the exact number has not been determined—tend toward ever greater richness of orchestration, freedom of part writing, and depth of emotion. The most important are the six written in the final decade of his life. With these works the symphony achieves its

Principal Works

Orchestral music, including some 40 symphonies (late symphonies: No. 35, *Haffner*, 1782; No. 36, *Linz*, 1783; No. 38, *Prague*, 1786; No. 39, 40, and 41, *Jupiter*, all from 1788); cassations, divertimentos, serenades (K. 525, *Eine kleine Nachtmusik*, 1787), marches and dances

Concertos, including 5 for violin and 27 for piano; concertos for clarinet, oboe, French horn, bassoon, flute, and flute and harp

Operas, including *Idomeneo* (1781), *Die Entführung aus dem Serail* (The Abduction from the Seraglio, 1782), *Le nozze di Figaro* (The Marriage of Figaro, 1786), *Don Giovanni* (1787), *Così fan tutte* (1790), *Die Zauberflöte* (The Magic Flute, 1791).

Choral music, including 18 masses, the Requiem, K. 626 (incomplete, 1791), and other liturgical music

Chamber music, including 23 string quartets; string quintets; clarinet quintet; oboe quartet; flute quartet; piano trios and quartets, violin and piano sonatas; wind serenades and divertimentos

Keyboard music, including 17 piano sonatas, and Fantasia in C minor (K. 475, 1785)

Secular vocal music

position as the most weighty form of abstract music. But the central current in Mozart's art that nourished all the others was opera, to which we will return in a later chapter.

Mozart: Eine kleine Nachtmusik, *K. 525*

Mozartian elegance and delicacy of touch are embodied in this serenade for strings, whose title means "A Little Night Music." Probably the work was intended for a double string quartet supported by a bass. The version we know has four movements—compact, intimate, and beautifully proportioned; originally there were five. (See Listening Guide 12.)

The opening movement is a sonata-allegro form of a marchlike character. The first theme, a rapidly ascending, disjunct melody, contrasts strongly with the graceful downward-curving second theme. Second is the Romanza, an eighteenth-century Andante that is lyrical yet maintains a pleasant reserve. The Minuet and Trio is an Allegretto that begins in a bright assertive manner. The Trio presents a lovely contrast with a soaring curve of truly Mozartean melody, after which the Minuet is presented without repeats. Fourth is a perfect example of the Classical rondo finale, exuberant, jovial, and—a trait inseparable from this master—stamped with an aristocratic refinement.

In the music of Mozart subjective emotion is elevated to the plane of the universal. Mozart is one of the supreme artists of all time; the voice of pure beauty in music, and probably the most sheerly musical composer that ever lived.

Listening Guide 12   2A/1

Mozart: *Eine kleine Nachtmusik*, **K. 525**

Date: 1787

Medium: Double string quartet or chamber orchestra

Movements: 4

I. First movement: Allegro, sonata-allegro form, 4/4 meter, G major

EXPOSITION

1 0:00   Theme 1—aggressive, ascending "rocket" theme, symmetrical phrasing, in G major

2 0:48   Theme 2—graceful, contrasting theme, less hurried, in key of dominant, D major

     1:00   Closing theme—insistent, repetitive character

     (Repeat of Exposition)

3 3:05   DEVELOPMENT
          Short, begins in D major, manipulates Theme 1, modulates, and prepares for Recapitulation in G major

          RECAPITULATION

4 3:38   Theme 1, in G major

5 4:20   Theme 2, in G major

     4:33   Closing theme, leads to

     5:03   Coda

II. Second movement: Romanza, Andante, rondo (A-B-A-C-A) form, duple meter, C major

III. Third movement: Minuet and Trio, Allegretto, 3/4 meter, G major, regular 4-measure phrases

11 0:00   Minuet theme—in accented triple meter, decisive, two sections, each repeated

12 0:57   Trio theme—more lyrical and connected; two sections, each repeated

13 1:45   Minuet returns, with repeats

IV. Fourth movement: Allegro, 4/4 meter, G major Rondo-like form, two main themes in alternation

UNIT XII

The Classical Symphony

29
The Nature of the Symphony

"To write a symphony means, to me, to construct a world."
—GUSTAV MAHLER

Historical Background

The central place in Classical instrumental music was taken by the symphony, a genre that grew in dimension and significance until, with the final works of Mozart and Haydn, it became the most important type of absolute music.

The symphony as it developed in the Classical period had its roots in the Italian opera overture of the earlier part of the century. As we have already noted, this was a piece for orchestra in three sections that followed the pattern fast-slow-fast. Eventually these sections became separate movements, to which the early German symphonists added a number of effects that were later taken over by Haydn and Mozart. Among these was the use of a quick, aggressively rhythmic theme rising from low to high register with such speed that it came to be known as a *rocket theme* (such as we saw in the opening theme of Mozart's *Eine kleine Nachtmusik*), as well as drawn-out crescendos slowly gathering force as they mounted to a climax. Both these effects are generally credited to composers active at Mannheim in eastern Germany; with the addition of the minuet and trio, also a Mannheim contribution, the symphony paralleled the string quartet in following the four-movement sonata cycle.

The Classical Orchestra

The Classical masters established the orchestra as we know it today. They based the ensemble on the blending of the four instrumental groups. The

161

heart of this orchestra was the string choir. Woodwinds, used with great imagination, ably seconded the strings. The brass sustained the harmonies and contributed body to the tone mass, while the timpani supplied rhythmic life and vitality. The eighteenth-century orchestra numbered from thirty to forty players. The volume of sound was still largely considered in relation to the salon rather than the concert hall. (It was toward the end of the Classical period that musical life began to move from the one to the other.) The orchestra of Haydn and Mozart lent itself to delicate nuances in which each timbre stood out radiantly. They created a dynamic style of orchestral writing in which all the instruments participated actively. The interchange and imitation of themes among the various instrumental groups assumed the excitement of a witty conversation. The Classical orchestra brought to absolute music a number of effects long familiar in the opera house. The gradual crescendo and decrescendo established themselves as staples of the new symphonic style. Hardly less conspicuous were the abrupt alterations of soft and loud, sudden accents, dramatic pauses, the use of tremolo and pizzicato. These and similar devices of operatic music added drama and tension to the Classical orchestral style.

The Movements of the Symphony

The first movement is an Allegro in sonata-allegro form, often preceded by a slow introduction, especially in the symphonies of Haydn. The sonata-allegro form, we saw, was based on the opposition of two keys personified by the contrast between two themes. However, Haydn sometimes based a sonata-allegro movement on a single theme, which was first heard in the tonic key and then in the contrasting key. Such a movement is referred to as *monothematic*. Mozart, on the other hand, preferred two themes with maximum contrast between them. This contrast was frequently achieved through varied instrumentation, giving the gently lyrical second theme to the woodwinds.

Monothematic

The slow movement of a symphony is often a three-part form (**A-B-A**), a theme and variations, or a modified sonata-allegro (without a development section). Generally marked Largo, Adagio, or Andante, this movement is in a key other than the tonic, with colorful orchestration that emphasizes the woodwinds. Since the mood is essentially lyrical, there is less development of themes here than in the opening movement.

Third is the Minuet and Trio in triple meter, a graceful **A-B-A** form in the home key. The Trio is gentler in mood, with a moderately flowing melody and the prominence of horn tone that gives it an outdoor sound. Beethoven's scherzo, also in 3/4 time, is taken at a headlong pace.

The fourth movement is normally a vivacious finale, an Allegro molto or Presto that is not only faster but also lighter than the first movement, in rondo or sonata-allegro form, which brings the cycle to a happy ending. It often features themes of a folk-dance character, especially in Haydn's works. With Beethoven's Fifth Symphony the fourth movement was transformed into a triumphal finale in sonata-allegro form.

30

Haydn and the Classical Symphony

"I have only just learned in my old age how to use the wind instruments, and now that I do understand them I must leave the world."

The long career of Joseph Haydn (1732–1809) spanned the decades when the Classical style was being formed. He imprinted upon it the stamp of his personality, and made a contribution to his art—especially the symphony and string quartet—that in scope and significance was second to none.

Joseph Haydn: His Life and Music

He was born in Rahrau, a village in lower Austria, son of a wheelwright. Folksong and dance were his natural heritage. The beauty of his voice secured him a place as chorister in St. Stephen's Cathedral in Vienna, where he remained until he was sixteen. With the breaking of his voice his time at the choir school came to an end. He then established himself in Vienna, and set himself to master his craft. He eked out a living through teaching and accompanying, and often joined the roving bands of musicians who performed in the streets. In this way the popular Viennese idiom entered his style along with the folk idiom he had absorbed in childhood.

Before long, Haydn attracted the notice of the music-loving aristocracy of Vienna. In 1761, when he was twenty-nine, he entered the service of the Esterházys, a family of enormously wealthy Hungarian princes famous for their patronage of the arts. He remained in their service for almost thirty years—that is, for the greater part of his creative career. The palace of the Esterházys was one of the most splendid in Europe, and music played a central part in the constant round of festivities there. Haydn's life is the classic example of the patronage system operating at its best. "My Prince was always satisfied with my works. I not only had the encouragement of constant approval but as conductor of an orchestra I could make experiments, observe what produced an effect and what weakened it, and was thus in a position to improve, alter, make additions or omissions, and be as bold as I pleased."

By the time Haydn reached middle age his music had brought him fame throughout Europe. After the Prince's death he made two visits to England (1791–92, 1794–95), where he conducted his works with phenomenal success. He returned to his native Austria laden with honor, financially well off. He died in 1809, revered by his countrymen and acknowledged throughout Europe as the premier musician of his time.

Joseph Haydn

Esterházy patronage

163

Principal Works

Orchestral music, including over 100 symphonies (6 *Paris Symphonies*, Nos. 82–87, 1785–86; 12 *London* or *Salomon Symphonies*, Nos. 93–104, 1791–95); concertos for violin, cello, harpsichord, and trumpet; divertimentos

Chamber music, including some 68 string quartets, piano trios, and divertimentos

Sacred vocal music, including 14 masses (*Mass in Time of War*, 1796; *Lord Nelson Mass*, 1798); oratorios, including *Die sieben letzten Worte* (The Seven Last Words of Christ, 1796), *Die Schöpfung* (The Creation, 1798), and *Die Jahreszeiten* (The Seasons, 1801)

Dramatic music, including 14 operas

Keyboard music, including about 40 sonatas
Songs, including folksong arrangements; secular choral music

It was Haydn's historic role to help perfect the new instrumental language of the late eighteenth century. His terse, angular themes lent themselves readily to motivic development. Significant too, in his symphonies of the 1790s, was his expansion of the size and resources of the orchestra through greater emphasis on the brass, clarinets, and percussion. It was in his expressive harmony, structural logic, and endlessly varied moods that the mature Classical idiom seemed to be fully realized for the first time.

String quartets

The string quartet occupied a central position in Haydn's art; his works are today an indispensable part of the repertory. Like the quartets, the

Symphonies

symphonies—over a hundred in number—extend across the whole of Haydn's career. Especially popular are the twelve written in the 1790s, in two sets of six, for his appearances in England. Known as the *London* or *Salomon Symphonies*, they abound in effects generally associated with later composers: syncopation, sudden crescendos and accents, dramatic contrasts of soft and loud, daring modulations, and an imaginative use of instruments. Of Haydn's symphonies it may be said, as it has been of his quartets, that they are the spiritual birthplace of Beethoven.

Church music

Haydn was also a prolific composer of church music; his fourteen Masses form the chief item in this category. Among the most frequently performed of these is his Mass in D minor, called the *Lord Nelson Mass* (1798). His two oratorios, *The Creation* and *The Seasons,* follow in the grand tradition of Handel.

Haydn's tonal imagery was basically instrumental in character. Yet he recognized that a good melody must be rooted in the nature of the human voice. "If you want to know whether you have written anything worth preserving," he counseled, "sing it to yourself without any accompaniment." His ceaseless experimenting with form should dispel the notion that the Classicist adheres to tradition. On the contrary, he chafed against the arbitrary restrictions of the theorists. "What is the good of such rules? Art is free and should be fettered by no such mechanical regulations."

Haydn: Symphony No. 104 (London)

Haydn's last symphony is regarded by many as his greatest. The solemn introduction, marked Adagio, opens in D minor with a fanfare-like motive announced in unison by the whole orchestra. The atmosphere is one of "strangeness and wonder." The movement proper, an Allegro in sonata-allegro form, is launched by an irresistible tune that has all the energy and verve of Haydn's mature style. (See Listening Guide 13.) Instead of introducing a lyrical second theme, Haydn repeats his opening theme in the new key. This monothematic technique is a hallmark of Haydn's mature style, and underscores an important point about sonata-allegro form.

The second movement is an Andante that has been well described as a perfect example of Viennese grace and warmth. Third is a Minuet and Trio—that is, an **A-B-A** form—in Haydn's most exuberant manner. The finale is an Allegro spiritoso in duple meter. The theme has the high spirits that Haydn derived from his heritage of Croatian folksong and dance.

Listening Guide 13   1B/3

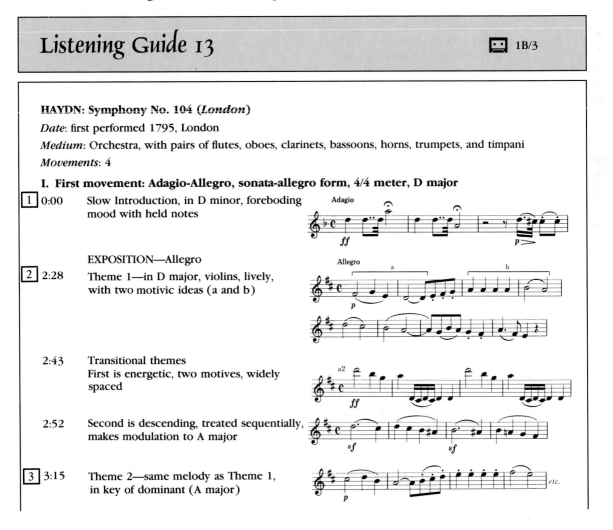

HAYDN: Symphony No. 104 (*London*)

Date: first performed 1795, London

Medium: Orchestra, with pairs of flutes, oboes, clarinets, bassoons, horns, trumpets, and timpani

Movements: 4

I. First movement: Adagio-Allegro, sonata-allegro form, 4/4 meter, D major

	0:00	Slow Introduction, in D minor, foreboding mood with held notes
	2:28	EXPOSITION—Allegro Theme 1—in D major, violins, lively, with two motivic ideas (a and b)
	2:43	Transitional themes First is energetic, two motives, widely spaced
	2:52	Second is descending, treated sequentially, makes modulation to A major
	3:15	Theme 2—same melody as Theme 1, in key of dominant (A major)

3:49   Closing theme—2 motives in counterpoint; lower is light, played staccato

(Repeat of Exposition)

4 6:00   DEVELOPMENT

Manipulates motives, mostly in minor;
expands second motive of Theme 1

Ornamented version of second motive,
Theme 1, in flute

Same motive, transformed into
ascending line to climax

RECAPITULATION

5 7:08   Theme 1—returns in D major in oboe
line, with added countermelody in flute

6 8:04   Theme 2—returns in tonic (same melody in
Theme 1)
    8:20   Closing—builds in rhythmic activity until end

  **II. Second movement: Andante, 2/4 meter, G major. Ternary (A-B-A) form, with free
variations**

**III. Third movement: Menuetto, Allegro, 3/4 meter, D major, three-part form: (Minuet-Trio-
Minuet)**

IV. Fourth movement: Finale, Spiritoso, 2/2 meter, D major, Sonata-allegro form

31

Beethoven and the Symphony in Transition

"Freedom above all!"

Beethoven (1770–1827) belonged to the generation that received the full impact of the French Revolution. He created the music of a heroic age and, in accents never to be forgotten, proclaimed its faith in the power of man to shape his destiny.

Ludwig van Beethoven: His Life and Music

Beethoven was born in Germany, in the city of Bonn in the Rhineland, where his father and grandfather were singers at the court of the local prince, the Elector Max Friedrich. At eleven and a half he was assistant organist in the court chapel and a year later he became harpsichordist in the court orchestra.

Ludwig van Beethoven

Arrangements were made some years later for him to study with Haydn in Vienna at the Elector's expense. His powers as a pianist took the music-loving aristocracy by storm. In an era of revolution, this young genius came to the "princely rabble," as he called them, forcing them to receive him as an equal and friend. "It is good to move among the aristocracy," he observed, "but it is first necessary to make them respect you."

Then, fate struck in a vulnerable spot: he began to lose his hearing. As his deafness closed in—the first symptom appeared when he was in his late twenties—it was borne in on him that art must henceforth give him the happiness life withheld. The will to struggle asserted itself; he fought his way back to health. "I am resolved to rise superior to every obstacle. With whom need I be afraid of measuring my strength? I will take Fate by the throat. It shall not overcome me. Oh how beautiful it is to be alive—would that I could live a thousand times!"

Having conquered the chaos within himself, he came to believe that man could conquer chaos. This became the epic theme of his music: the progression from despair to conflict, from conflict to serenity, from serenity to triumph and joy. The revelation that had come to him through suffering was a welcome message to the world that was struggling to be born. He became the major prophet of the nineteenth century, the architect of its heroic vision of life. A ride in an open carriage in inclement weather brought on an attack of dropsy that proved fatal. He died in his fifty-seventh year, famous and revered.

Beethoven is the supreme architect in music. His genius found expression in the structural type of thinking embodied in the sonata and symphony. His compositional activity fell into three periods. The first reflected the

Principal Works

Orchestral music, including nine symphonies: No. 1 (1800); No. 2 (1802); No. 3, *Eroica* (1803); No. 4 (1806); No. 5 (1808); No. 6, *Pastoral* (1808); No. 7 (1812); No. 8 (1812); No. 9, *Choral* (1824); Overtures, including *Leonore* (Nos. 1, 2, 3) and *Egmont*, and incidental music

Concertos, including five for piano, one for violin (1806), and one triple concerto (piano, violin, and cello, 1804)

Chamber music, including string quartets, piano trios, quartets, one quintet, one septet, violin and cello sonatas; serenades and wind chamber music

32 piano sonatas, including Op. 13, *Pathétique* (1806), Op. 27, No. 2, *Moonlight* (1801), Op. 53, *Waldstein* (1804), Op. 57, *Appassionata* (1805)

1 opera (*Fidelio*, 1805)

Choral music, including *Missa Solemnis* (1823)

Songs, including song cycle *An die ferne Geliebte* (To the Distant Beloved, 1816)

Three periods   Classical elements he inherited from Haydn and Mozart. The middle period saw the appearance of characteristics more closely associated with the nineteenth century: strong dynamic contrasts, explosive accents, and longer movements. He expanded the dimensions of the first movement, especially the coda, and like Haydn and Mozart made the Development section the dynamic center of the form. In his hands the slow movement acquired a hymnic character, the embodiment of Beethovenian pathos. The scherzo became a movement of rhythmic energy. He enlarged the finale into a movement comparable in size and scope to the first, and ended the symphony on a note of triumph. In his third period—the years of the final piano sonatas and string quartets—he found his way to more chromatic harmonies and developed a skeletal language from which all nonessentials were rigidly pared away.

Symphonies   His nine symphonies are spiritual dramas of universal appeal. The first two stand closest to the two classical masters who preceded him; with his Third Symphony, the *Eroica*, Beethoven achieved his mature style. The Fifth Symphony has fixed itself in the popular mind as the archetype of all that a symphony is. The Seventh rivals it in universal appeal. The Ninth, the *Choral Symphony*, strikes the searching tone of Beethoven's last period. Its finale, in which vocal soloists and chorus join with the orchestra in a setting of Schiller's *Ode to Joy*, a ringing affirmation of the time when "all men shall be brothers."

Piano music   Beethoven's five piano concertos went hand in hand with—and in turn encouraged—the rising popularity of the instrument. His thirty-two sonatas are an indispensable part of its literature, whether for the amateur pianist or concert artist. He wrote much chamber music, the string quartet being closest to his heart. The six quartets of Opus 18 are the first in a series that extended throughout the whole of his career. His supreme achievements in this area are the last five quartets.

His creative activity, extending over a span of thirty-five years, bears witness to a ceaseless striving after perfection. "I feel as if I had written scarcely more than a few notes," he remarked at the end of his career.

Beethoven: Symphony No. 5 in C minor

The most popular of all symphonies, Beethoven's Symphony No. 5 in C minor, Opus 67, is also the most concentrated expression of the frame of mind and spirit that we have come to call Beethovenian. The first movement springs out of the rhythmic idea of "three shorts and a long" that dominates the symphony. It is the most compact and commanding gesture in the whole symphonic literature. This sonata-allegro is dramatic, peremptory, compact. (See Listening Guide 14 for analysis.) It ends with an extended coda in which the basic rhythm reveals a new fund of explosive energy.

Beethovenian serenity imbues the second movement, a theme and variations, with two melodic ideas. In the course of the movement Beethoven brings all the procedures of variation—changes in melodic outline, harmony, rhythm, tempo, dynamics, register, key, mode, and type of accompaniment—to bear upon his two themes.

Third in the cycle is the Scherzo, which opens with a rocket theme introduced by cellos and double basses. After the Trio in C major, the Scherzo returns in a modified version, followed by a transitional passage in which the basic rhythm of the first movement is heard.

The fourth movement, a monumental sonata form, once again brings back the "three shorts and a long." This return of material from an earlier movement gives the symphony its cyclical form. Of his own genius, Beethoven proclaimed "I am the Bacchus who presses out the glorious wine for mankind. Whoever truly understands my music is freed thereby from the miseries that others carry about in them."

Listening Guide 14   🔲 2A/3

BEETHOVEN: Symphony No. 5 in C minor, Op. 67

Date: 1807–08

Movements: 4

I. First movement: Allegro con brio, 2/4 meter, C minor. Sonata-allegro form

EXPOSITION

33   0:00   Theme 1—based on famous four-
note motive, in C minor

0:06 Treated sequentially

0:43 Expanded from four-note motive

|34| 0:44 Theme 2—more lyrical, in woodwinds, in E-flat major, heard against rhythm of four-note motive

2:08 Codetta, based on four-note motive

Repeat of Exposition

|35| 2:52 DEVELOPMENT
3:03 Manipulation of four-note motive through a descending sequence

3:13 Melodic variation, interval filled in, and inverted

4:12 Expansion through repetition

RECAPITULATION
|36| Theme 1—in C minor, brief oboe solo
|37| Theme 2—returns in C major

|38| CODA—extended treatment of four-note motive

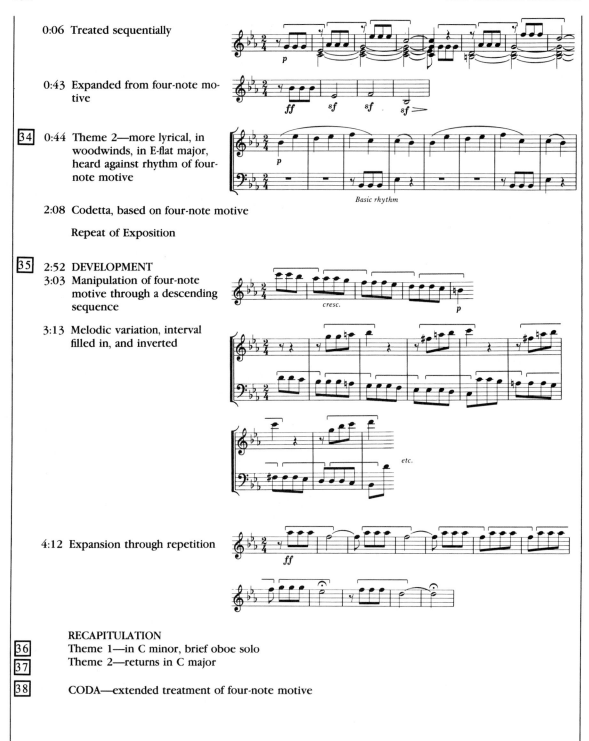

II. Second movement: Andante con moto, 3/8 meter, A-flat major. Theme and variation form, with two themes.

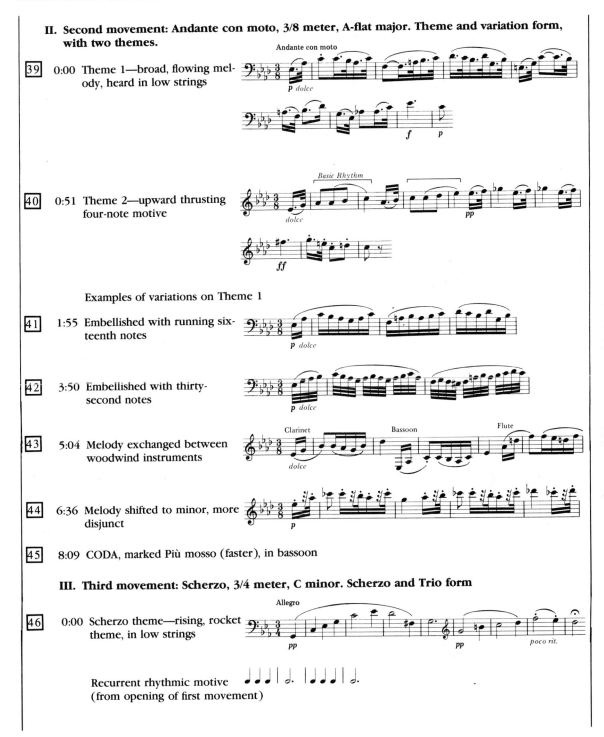

39   0:00   Theme 1—broad, flowing melody, heard in low strings

40   0:51   Theme 2—upward thrusting four-note motive

Examples of variations on Theme 1

41   1:55   Embellished with running sixteenth notes

42   3:50   Embellished with thirty-second notes

43   5:04   Melody exchanged between woodwind instruments

44   6:36   Melody shifted to minor, more disjunct

45   8:09   CODA, marked Più mosso (faster), in bassoon

III. Third movement: Scherzo, 3/4 meter, C minor. Scherzo and Trio form

46   0:00   Scherzo theme—rising, rocket theme, in low strings

Recurrent rhythmic motive
(from opening of first movement)

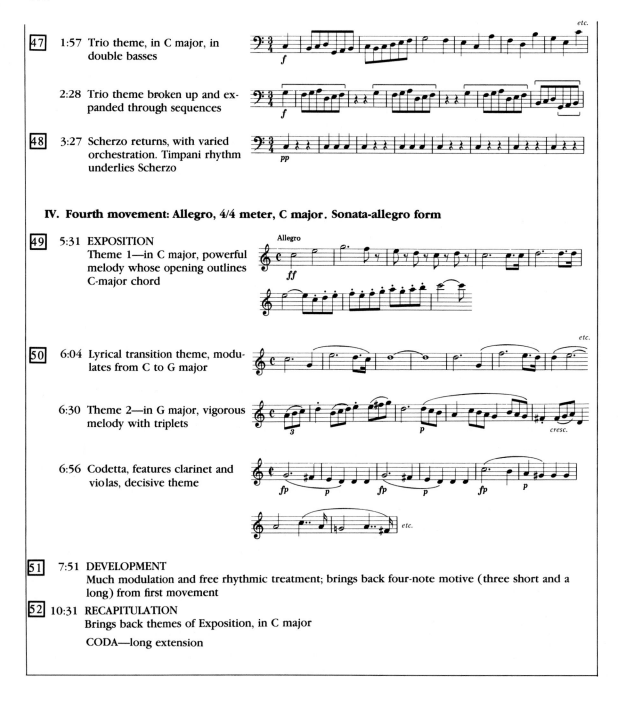

47 1:57 Trio theme, in C major, in double basses

2:28 Trio theme broken up and expanded through sequences

48 3:27 Scherzo returns, with varied orchestration. Timpani rhythm underlies Scherzo

IV. Fourth movement: Allegro, 4/4 meter, C major. Sonata-allegro form

49 5:31 EXPOSITION
Theme 1—in C major, powerful melody whose opening outlines C-major chord

50 6:04 Lyrical transition theme, modulates from C to G major

6:30 Theme 2—in G major, vigorous melody with triplets

6:56 Codetta, features clarinet and violas, decisive theme

51 7:51 DEVELOPMENT
Much modulation and free rhythmic treatment; brings back four-note motive (three short and a long) from first movement

52 10:31 RECAPITULATION
Brings back themes of Exposition, in C major

CODA—long extension

UNIT XIII

■

The Eighteenth-Century Concerto and Sonata

32

The Classical Concerto

The Movements of the Concerto

The concerto remained one of the dominant forms of the Classical era. In the Baroque era, we saw that the word *concerto* implied a mixing together of two disparate elements, such as a soloist and orchestra or a solo group and orchestra. The Classical era shifted the emphasis to the concerto for solo instrument—especially piano or violin—and orchestra.

The three movements of the Classical concerto follow the traditional pattern fast-slow-fast already established. A characteristic feature of the concerto is the *cadenza*, a fanciful solo passage in the manner of an improvisation that is interpolated into the movement. The cadenza came out of a time *Cadenza* when improvisation was an important element in art music, as it still is today in jazz. Taken over into the solo concerto, the cadenza made a dramatic effect: the orchestra fell silent and the soloist launched into a free play of fantasy on one or more themes of the movement.

The concerto begins in sonata-allegro form, the first section being a double *First movement* Exposition. That is, the orchestra announces the two contrasting themes but remains in the tonic key, then the soloist takes over the themes, with modulation to the dominant key for the second theme. The Development section gives the soloist ample opportunity for virtuoso display. The Recapitulation remains in the tonic key, with a cadenza toward the end of the movement in the style of a brilliant improvisation, and a coda brings the movement to a close with a strong affirmation of the home key.

Second is the slow lyrical movement, generally an Andante, Adagio, or *Second movement* Largo, which features the soloist in poetic, songlike melody. This movement

Summary of Concerto Form

First movement:	Double Exposition Form
Exposition 1:	Orchestra, in tonic
	Theme 1
	Theme 2
Exposition 2:	Soloist with orchestra
	Theme 1, in tonic
	Theme 2, in dominant
Development:	Varied treatment by soloist and orchestra
Recapitulation:	Theme 1 and 2, in tonic, orchestra and soloist
Cadenza:	Soloist
Coda:	Orchestra and soloist, in tonic
Second movement:	Slow, lyrical, in **A-B-A** or theme and variations form, in key closely related to tonic
Third movement:	Fast sonata or rondo form, in tonic

is often in a key that lies close to the tonic but contrasts with it, such as the key a fourth above. Thus, if the first movement is in C major, the second might very well be in F major, four steps above.

The finale is generally an Allegro molto (very fast) or Presto, usually shorter than the first movement, often in rondo form or in a rondo that has taken over some developmental features of sonata-allegro form. This movement may contain a cadenza of its own that calls for virtuoso playing and brings the piece to an exciting end.

Mozart: Piano Concerto in C major, K. 467

Mozart, we saw, played a crucial role in the development of the piano concerto. His concertos were written primarily as display pieces for his own public performances. They abound in the brilliant flourishes and ceremonious gestures characteristic of eighteenth-century social music.

The sunny Piano Concerto in C major, K. 467 (1785), belongs to one of Mozart's most productive periods. The first movement is an Allegro maestoso whose opening pages show how richly Mozart's instrumental art was nourished by the opera house; the principal theme could have come straight out of a scene in an opera buffa. More important, its first two measures constitute a motive that is wonderfully capable of growth and development. (See the analysis in Listening Guide 15.) In connection with this movement we may speak of a theme group rather than a single theme.

First movement

Mozart, in his concertos, uses the sonata-allegro form with infinite variety; no two first movements are alike. Since this particular movement is fashioned out of flowing melodies, the result is an unusually spacious form. The orchestra presents the thematic material, which is then repeated by the soloist—in short, a double Exposition. The virtuoso figuration in the piano part is heard against broadly spun phrases in the strings or woodwinds.

The Recapitulation opens with the strings playing the main theme in the home key, followed immediately by the second idea. Where are the subsidiary themes we heard in the Exposition? It turns out that Mozart is saving them for the coda, which rounds out the movement with all the courtly grace of the eighteenth century and prepares the way for the cadenza. We unfortunately do not possess Mozart's cadenza; it is a wise artist who makes his own as short as possible. The basic motive returns in the final measures. One might have expected so bright an Allegro to have a brilliant ending. Mozart surprises us. The movement ends like one of those opera buffa scenes in which the characters tiptoe off stage.

The second movement is a serenely flowing Andante in F. Its gentle poignancy explains why nineteenth-century composers such as Chopin and Tchaikovsky worshiped Mozart above all others. After a middle section that stresses D minor, the melody returns in the remote key of A-flat major—a procedure closer to the Romantic mind than the Classical. Mozart does not repeat the theme literally; he varies it with fanciful embellishments. The movement finds its way back to the home key, and the coda rounds it off with a pianissimo ending. *Second movement*

The gay finale is a rondo in C major, marked Allegro vivace assai (very fast and lively), that opens with a tune straight out of opera buffa. In its vivacity and good humor, this movement typifies the Classical rondo finale. But at this time the rondo was absorbing certain features of sonata-allegro form, especially the dynamic movement from key to key and—most important of all—the development of themes and motives. There resulted a form that may be considered a sonata-rondo, of which this Allegro is an excellent example. *Third movement*

The filigree work on the piano demands nimble fingers. Clearly Mozart enjoyed displaying his prowess as a pianist. There is much lively interplay between piano and orchestra, both of which—after a brief cadenza that ushers in the final appearance of the theme—share in the brilliant C-major ending.

Within a decade, Beethoven, in a remarkable fusion of concerto-style and symphonic form, took the genre into the Romantic era. His works project the tensions between piano and orchestra within a truly imposing architecture. His Piano Concerto No. 5 in E-flat major (1809), dubbed the *Emperor*, is a milestone in the history of the genre. In this work, the piano enters at once, creating a dramatic confrontation between the soloist and the orchestra which continues throughout the spacious form. He further opened a new chapter in the history of the concerto by writing out the cadenza, rather than depending on the performer's ability to improvise in performance. Henceforth, composers, with few exeptions, followed Beethoven's example.

Listening Guide 15

MOZART: Piano Concerto in C major, K. 467

Date: 1785

Movements: 3

I. First movement: Allegro maestoso, 4/4 meter, C major. Double exposition form.

EXPOSITION

20 0:00   Theme group 1—in orchestra (strings), in C major. Disjunct melody, with rests, outlines triads; first in high strings, then in low strings.

0:50   Theme in winds, alternates brass and woodwinds

1:34   Rising and ascending theme, in flutes, then violins

3:30   Theme group 2—introduced by piano, in G minor

21 4:05   Main theme of group 2, lyrical, in G major; first heard in piano, then in woodwinds

4:32   Closing idea—reminiscent of opening of movement; brilliant passagework in piano

DEVELOPMENT

22 6:02   Begins with full orchestra

6:53   New theme introduced in piano, in E minor

	7:09	Figurations in piano, lyrical melodies in strings and woodwinds
		RECAPITULATION
23	8:25	Theme group 1—opening idea, in orchestra, in C major
		Transition, piano figurations
24	9:35	Theme group 2—in piano, in C major
		Closing idea—based on opening theme, in C major
25	12:02	Cadenza—improvised by piano, no accompaniment leads into brief orchestral coda

II. Second movement: Andante, 4/4 meter, F major. Ternary (A-B-A) form

| 26 | 0:00 | A section—underlying rhythmic pulse in triplets; muted middle-range strings, with plucked cellos and basses |

| | | Theme—muted violins, 3-measure phrases |

		Theme repeated in piano statement, against pizzicato strings
27	2:09	**B** section—in D minor, in piano, with strings accompanying more chromatic, disjunct lines
	4:13	**A** section—melody returns in A-flat major, in piano, varied from opening, ends in F major

III. Third movement: Allegro vivace assai, 2/4 meter, C major. Rondo form.

| 29 | 0:00 | A theme—light, bouncy tune, introduced in strings, in C major |

		Theme heard in piano, then in strings and woodwinds, with piano figurations
30	1:37	**B** theme—in G major, in woodwinds and horns, taken over by piano
		Developmental section—more chromatic, piano runs
31	2:47	**A** theme—in piano, then full orchestra, C major; motives exchanged between piano and woodwinds
32	5:10	**B** theme—returns in C major, in piano, light character; piano runs lead to hold on G major chord
33	6:03	Cadenza—solo piano
34	7:01	**A** theme—first in piano, then strings; piano has fast runs to final three closing chords

The Classical Sonata

We saw in an earlier chapter that the sonata, as Haydn, Mozart, and their successors understood the term, was an instrumental work consisting of a series of contrasting movements for one or two instruments. The movements were three or four in number (sometimes two), and followed the basic sonata-cycle we described in our discussion of string quartet, symphony, and concerto.

In the Classical era the sonata became an important genre for amateurs in the home, as well as for composers appearing in concerts as performers of their own music. The late eighteenth century favored the sonata for piano solo as well as sonatas for violin or cello and piano. These at first presented the piano as the major instrument with the string instrument acting as accompaniment. Mozart and Beethoven changed this approach. In their duo sonatas the two instruments are treated as equal partners. The duo sonatas of Mozart are mostly for violin and piano, since he played the violin himself and was partial to it. It is the piano sonatas of Beethoven, however, that stand tallest in the solo literature for that instrument and epitomize the genre in the Classical era.

Beethoven: Piano Sonata in C minor, Op. 13 (Pathétique)

The title of the Piano Sonata in C minor, Opus 13—*Pathétique*—was Beethoven's own. Certainly the quality of Beethovenian pathos is manifest from the first chords of the slow introduction. Marked Grave (solemn), this celebrated opening has something fantasy-like about it, as if Beethoven had captured here the passionate intensity that so affected his listeners when he improvised at the keyboard.

First movement In the movement proper, marked Allegro di molto e con brio (very fast and with vigor), Beethoven uses the resources of the instrument most imaginatively: contrasts in dynamics and register, the brilliance of rapid scale passages, the excitement of tremolo, and the power of a slowly gathering crescendo allied with a gradual climb in pitch.

Second movement The second movement is the famous Adagio cantabile (slow and songful) which shows off the piano's ability to sing. This "hymnic adagio" combines an introspective character with the quality of strength that Beethoven made his own.

Third movement The final movement is a Rondo, to whose principal theme the C-minor tonality imparts a darker coloring that sets it apart from the usually cheerful rondo-finales of Haydn and Mozart. (See Listening Guide 16 for analysis). The frame is spacious; within it, lyric episodes alternate with dramatic.

The *Pathétique* has been a favorite for generations. In the hands of a great artist it stands revealed as one of Beethoven's most personal sonatas.

Listening Guide 16

BEETHOVEN: Piano Sonata in C minor (*Pathétique*), Op. 13

Date: 1798

Movements: 3

I. First movement: Grave-Allegro di molto e con brio, 4/4 meter, C minor. Sonata-allegro form

II. Second movement: Adagio cantabile, 2/4 meter, A-flat major. Rondo form (A-B-A-C-A)

21 0:00 **A** section—lyrical melody, first in middle range, then repeated up an octave

Adagio cantabile

22 1:13 **B** section—contrasting lyrical melody, modulating

23 2:10 **A** section returns in A-flat major

24 2:45 **C** section—more dramatic, with triplet figures, accents, and arpeggios

25 3:30 **A** section—returns in A-flat major

III. Third movement: Allegro, duple meter, C minor. Rondo form (A-B-A-C-A-B-A)

UNIT XIV

■

Vocal Forms of the Classical Era

34

Classical Choral Music and Opera

"I had always placed a certain confidence in opera, hoping that from it will rise . . . tragedy in a nobler form."—JOHANN VON SCHILLER

Classical Choral Forms

Requiem

The late eighteenth century inherited a rich tradition of choral music from the Baroque. Among the principal forms of choral art were the Mass and Requiem. A *Mass* is a musical setting of the most solemn service of the Roman Catholic Church and a *Requiem* is a musical setting of the Mass for the Dead. Its name comes from the opening verse "Requiem aeternam dona eis, Domine" (Rest eternal grant unto them, O Lord). Included are prayers in keeping with the solemnity of the occasion, among them the awesome evocation of the Last Judgment, *Dies irae* (Day of Wrath). Both mass types were originally intended to be performed in the church, a tradition which carried well into the Classical era in the Catholic countries of the Hapsburg domain. By the nineteenth century these choral forms had found a much larger audience in the concert hall. The blending of many voices in a large space such as a church or cathedral could not fail to be an uplifting experience. For this reason both the Catholic and Protestant church were patrons of music throughout the ages. Both Haydn and Mozart made major contributions to the Mass repertory. Haydn's Mass in D minor (*Lord Nelson*) remains one of his most frequently performed works, and Mozart's Requiem, his last composition, quickly established itself as one of the masterpieces of the Classical Viennese School.

Important too was the *oratorio*, which we have encountered as a genre made popular by Handel in such works as *Messiah*. Haydn wrote two oratorios—*The Creation* and *The Seasons*, which attained enormous popularity throughout the nineteenth century and helped build the new mass public.

Classical Opera

The opera house was a center of experimentation in the Classical era. Opera was the most important branch of musical entertainment and the one that reached the widest public. The music was the point of departure and imposed its forms on the drama.

The opera of the eighteenth century accurately reflected the society out of which it sprang. The prevalent form was *opera seria*, "serious" or tragic Italian opera, a highly formalized genre inherited from the Baroque that occupied itself mainly with the affairs of kings and heroes drawn from the legends of Greek antiquity. Its rigid conventions were shaped by the poet Pietro Metastasio (1698–1782), whose librettos were set again and again throughout the century. Opera seria consisted mainly of a series of recitatives and arias that were specifically designed to display the virtuosity of star singers. It spoke to a society dominated by the tastes and needs of the aristocracy.

Opera seria

However, new winds were blowing in the second half of the century. Increasingly the need was felt for simplicity and naturalness, for an opera more realistically attuned to human emotion. One impulse toward reform

Comic opera

In this anonymous eighteenth-century watercolor, Haydn is thought to be at the harpsichord while conducting an opera performance at Esterházy. (Theatermuseum, Munich)

came from the operas of Christoph Willibald Gluck, whose achievement in this regard we have already recounted. Another derived from the popular comic opera that flourished in every country of Europe. Known in England as *ballad opera*, in Germany as *Singspiel*, in France as *opéra comique*, and in Italy as *opera buffa*, comic opera was the answer of the rising middle class to the aristocratic form it would inevitably supplant. It differed from opera seria in several basic respects. It was sung in the language of the audience rather than in Italian, which was the official language of international opera. It presented lively, down-to-earth plots rather than the remote concerns of gods and mythological heroes. It featured exciting ensembles at the end of each act in which all the characters participated instead of the solo arias that were the norm in the older opera. And it abounded in farcical situations, humorous dialogue, popular tunes, and the impertinent remarks of the buffo, the traditional character derived from the theater of buffoons, who spoke to the audience with a wink and a nod, and in a bass voice, which brought a new sound into a theater hitherto dominated by the artificial soprano of the castrato.

As the Age of Revolution approached, comic opera became an important social force whose lively wit delighted even the aristocrats it satirized. From its cradle in Italy, Classical opera buffa spread all over Europe, steadily expanding its scope until it culminated in the works of the greatest musical dramatist of the eighteenth century—Mozart.

Mozart: The Marriage of Figaro

da Ponte

Mozart found his ideal librettist in Lorenzo da Ponte (1749–1838), an Italian-Jewish adventurer and poet whose dramatic vitality was akin to his own. Their collaboration produced, in addition to *The Marriage of Figaro*, *Don Giovanni*, and *Così fan tutte*.

Da Ponte adapted his libretto for *The Marriage of Figaro* from the play by Pierre-Augustin Caron de Beaumarchais (1732–99), which was truly revolutionary in that it satirized the upper classes and allowed Figaro, the clever and impudent valet of Count Almaviva, consistently to outwit his master. When Louis XVI read the manuscript, he pronounced it detestable and unfit to be seen. It was the liberal friends of Marie Antoinette who persuaded the King to revoke his veto and saw to it that the play was produced. Hapsburg Vienna was even more conservative than Bourbon Paris: the play was forbidden there. But what could not be spoken could be sung. Mozart's opera was produced at the Imperial Court Theater in May 1786, and brought him the greatest success of his life.

Da Ponte used all the traditional devices of bedroom farce. Characters are disguised as each other, fall prey to all sorts of misunderstandings, and are caught in compromising situations they barely manage to wriggle out of. He cut some of Beaumarchais's complications and, as court poet to Emperor Joseph II, was clever enough to know that he must soften the political satire sufficiently to make it palatable.

Although *The Marriage of Figaro* came out of the rich tradition of popular

In this scene from a recent performance of The Marriage of Figaro *by the New York City Opera, Susanna and Cherubino are seen just before the Count's entrance.* (Photo © by Martha Swope)

comic opera, Mozart's genius lifted the genre to another dimension. In place of the stereotyped characters of opera buffa he created real human beings who come alive through his music, so that we can identify with their emotions. The Count is a likable philanderer, the Countess is noble in her suffering. Her maid, Susanna, is pert and endlessly resourceful in resisting the advances of her master. Figaro is equally resourceful in foiling the schemes of the Count. And the Countess's page, Cherubino, is irresistible in his boyish ardor and innocence.

In Classical opera the part of a young man was often sung by a soprano or alto wearing trousers. In Mozart's opera the soprano voice is ideally suited to Cherubino's romantic idealism. His aria in Act I, "Non so più," establishes his character as a young man in love with love. "I no longer know who I am or what I'm doing," he sings. "Every woman I see makes me blush and tremble." (For the Italian-English text and analysis of the aria see Listening Guide 17.)

Cherubino's aria is followed by recitative, which we know is the rapid-fire, talky kind of singing whose main function it is to advance the plot. Eighteenth-century audiences accepted this change of texture and orchestration just as we today accept, in a Broadway musical, the change from song to spoken dialogue.

The action moves rapidly, with overtones of farce. Cherubino has sung his love song to the Countess in Susanna's room. When the Count arrives to ask Susanna to meet him that night in the garden, Cherubino hides behind a huge armchair. At this point the music master Basilio, a gossip if ever there was one, arrives looking for the Count, who tries to hide behind the chair. Susanna adroitly places herself between the Count and Cherubino, so that the page is able to slip in front of the chair and curl up in it. Ever resourceful, she manages to cover him with a tablecloth (in some productions, a dressing gown). With both the front and back of the armchair occupied, Susanna berates Basilio as a gossip and panderer. At this point the Count reveals his presence by planting himself in front of the chair.

Susanna is aghast that the Count has been discovered in her room. The Count, having overheard Basilio's statement that Cherubino adores the Countess, is angry with the young man. And Basilio thoroughly enjoys the rumpus he has stirred up. The action stops as the three join in a trio in which each of them expresses his or her emotion. There is quick exchange among the three voices and much repetiton of text. The extended structure of this trio is related to sonata form. No one ever equaled Mozart's ability to reconcile the demands of a dramatic situation with the requirements of absolute musical form.

The Count pulls the tablecloth from the chair and discovers Cherubino. Furious at finding the youth in Susanna's room, he vows to banish him from the castle. At this point Figaro arrives with a group of peasants whom he has told that the Count has decided to abolish the "right of the first night," the hated feudal privilege that gave the lord of the manor the right to deflower every young woman in his domain. In their gratitude the peasants have come to serenade their master, singing, "His great kindness preserves the purity of a bride for the one she loves." Figaro, delighted to have forced the Count's hand, announces his impending marriage to Susanna, and the Count plays along by accepting the tributes of the crowd.

Figaro intercedes for the page with his master, whereupon the Count relents, appoints Cherubino to a captain's post in his regiment, and leaves with Basilio. The complications in the next three acts lead to a happy ending. The Count is reconciled with his wife, and Figaro wins his beloved Susanna.

Two centuries have passed since Mozart's characters first strutted across a stage. They live on in the opera houses of the world, lifted above time and fashion by the genius of their creator.

Listening Guide 17   📼 2B/2

MOZART: *The Marriage of Figaro* (*Le nozze di Figaro*)

Date: 1786

Genre: Opera buffa (comic opera)

Librettist: Lorenzo da Ponte

Basis: Play by Beaumarchais

Principal characters:
  Figaro, servant to Count Almaviva
  Susanna, maid to Countess Almaviva
  Cherubino, page
  Count Almaviva
  Countess Almaviva
  Doctor Bartolo
  Marcellina, his housekeeper

Act I, #6: Aria, Cherubino

Form: **A-B-A-C**, followed by recitative

A—quick rhythms (in E-flat)

B—more lyrical (in B-flat)

A—returns (in E-flat)

C—begins quietly, then builds
   (in E-flat, modulates)

Cherubino

21	Non so più cosa son, cosa faccio,	I don't know what I am, what I'm doing;

Non so più cosa son, cosa faccio,
or di foco, ora sono di ghiaccio,
ogni donna cangiar di colore,
ogni donna mi fa palpitar.
Solo ai nomi d'amor, di diletto,
mi si turba, mi s'altera il petto,
e a parlare mi sforza d'amore
un desio ch'io non posso spiegar.
Parlo d'amor vegliando,
parlo d'amor sognando,
all'acqua, all'ombra, ai monti,
ai fiori, all'erbe, ai fonti,
all'eco, all'aria, ai venti,
che il suon de' vani accenti
portano via con sè.
E se non ho chi m'oda.
parlo d'amor con me!

I don't know what I am, what I'm doing;
first I seem to be burning, then freezing;
every woman makes me change colour,
every woman I see makes me shake.
Just the words 'love' and 'pleasure'
bring confusion; my breast swells in terror
yet am I compelled to speak of love
by a force which I cannot explain.
I speak of love while waking,
I speak of love while dreaming,
to the water, to shadows, to mountains,
to the flowers, the grass and the fountains,
to the echo, to the air, to the winds
which carry the idle words
away with them.
And if there is no one to listen,
I speak of love to myself!

(Seeing the Count in the distance, Cherubino hides behind the chair.)

22	Ah! Son perduto!	I'm done for!

Susanna

Che timor . . . il Conte! Misera me!   I'm afraid . . . the Count! Poor me!
(tries to conceal Cherubino)

Count Almaviva (*entering*)

Susanna, tu mi sembri agitata   Susanna, you seem to be agitated
e confusa.   and confused.

Susanna

Signor, io chiedo scusa,   My lord, I beg your pardon,
ma, se mai qui sorpresa,   but . . . indeed . . . the surprise . . .
per carità, partite.   I implore you, please go.

Count (*sits down on the chair and takes Susanna's hand; she draws it forcibly away*)

Un momento, e ti lascio.	One moment, then I'll leave.
Odi.	Listen.

Susanna

Non odo nulla.	I don't want to hear anything.

Count

Due parole: tu sai che ambasciatore a Londra	Just a couple of words: you know that the king
il re mi dichiarò;	has named me ambassador to London;
e di condur meco Figaro destinai.	I had intended to take Figaro with me.

Susanna

Signor, se osassi—	My lord, if I may dare—

Count (*rising*)

Parla, parla, mia cara,	Speak, speak, my dear,
e con quel dritto ch'oggi prendi su me,	and with that right you have of me today,
finche tu vivi chiedi, imponi, prescrivi.	as long as you live you may ask, demand,
	prescribe.

Susanna

Lasciatemi, signor,	Let me go, my lord,
dritti non prendo,	I have no rights,
non ne vò, non ne intendo.	I do not want them, nor claim them.
Oh me infelice!	Oh what misery!

Count

Ah no, Susanna, io ti vò far felice!	Ah no, Susanna, I want to make you happy!
Tu ben sai quanto io t'amo;	You well know how much I love you;
a te Basilio tutto già disse.	Basilio has told you that already.
Or senti, se per pochi momenti	Now listen, if you would meet me
meco in giardin, sull'imbrunir del giorno,	briefly in the garden at dusk,
ah, per questo favore io pagherei . . .	ah, for this favour I would pay . . .

Basilio (*outside the door*)

È uscito poco fa.	He went out just now.

Count

Chi parla?	Whose voice is that?

Susanna

O Dei!	Oh, heavens!

Count

Esci, ed alcun non entri.	Go, and let no one come in.

Susanna

Ch'io vi lascio qui solo?	And leave you here alone?

Basilio (*outside*)

Da madama sarà, vado a cercarlo.	He'll be with my lady, I'll go and find him.

Count

Qui dietro mi porrò.	I'll get behind here.

(*points to the chair*)

Susanna

Non vi celate.	No, don't hide.

Count

Taci, e cerca ch'ei parta.	Hush, and try to make him go.

Susanna

Ohimè! che fate?	Oh dear! What are you doing?

(*The Count is about to hide behind the chair; Susanna steps between him and the page. The Count pushes her gently away. She draws back; meanwhile the page slips round to the front of the chair and hops in with his feet drawn up. Susanna rearranges the dress to cover him.*)

Susanna, il ciel vi salvi!
Avreste a caso veduto il Conte?

E cosa deve fare meco il Conte?

Animo, uscite.

Aspettate, sentite, Figaro di lui cerca.

Oh cielo!
Ei cera chi, dopo voi, più l'odia.

Vediam come mi serve.

Io non ho mai nella moral sentito,
ch'uno ch'ami la moglie odii il marito.

Per dir che il Conte v'ama.

Sortite, vil ministro dell'altrui sfrenatezza:
io non ho d'uopo della vostra morale,
del Conte, del suo amor!

Non c'è alcun male.
Ha ciascun i suoi gusti.
Io mi credea che preferir
doveste per amante,
come fan tutte quante,
un Signor liberal, prudente e saggio,
a un giovinastro, a un paggio.

A Cherubino?

A Cherubino! Cherubin d'amore,
ch'oggi sul far del giorno
passeggiava qui intorno per entrar.

Uom maligno, un'impostura è
    questa.

E un maligno con voi
chi ha gli occhi in testa?
E quella canzonetta,
ditemi in confidenza,
Io sono amico,
ed altrui nulla dico,
è per voi, per madama?

Chi diavol gliel'ha detto?

Basilio
Heaven bless you, Susanna!
Have you seen his lordship by any chance?

Susanna
And what should his lordship be doing here
    with me?
Come now, be gone!

Basilio
But listen, Figaro is looking for him.

Susanna
(*aside*) Oh dear!
Then he's looking for the one man who,
    after yourself, hates him most!

Count (*aside*)
Now we'll see how he serves me.

Basilio
I have never heard it preached
that one who loves the wife should hate the
    husband.
That's a way of saying that the Count loves you.

Susanna
Get out, vile minister of others' lechery!
I have no need of your preaching,
nor of the Count or his lovemaking!

Basilio
No offence meant.
Everyone to their own taste.
I thought you would have preferred
as your lover,
as all other women would,
a lord who's liberal, prudent, and wise,
to a raw youth, a mere page.

Susanna
To Cherubino?

Basilio
To Cherubino! Love's little cherub,
who early today
was hanging about here waiting to come in.

Susanna
You insinuating wretch, that's a lie.

Basilio
Do you call it an insinuation
to have eyes in one's head?
And that little ditty,
tell me confidentially
as a friend,
and I will tell no one else,
was it written for you or my lady?

Susanna (*aside*)
Who the devil told him about that?

	Basilio
A proposito, figlia, istruitelo meglio.	By the way, my child, you must teach him better,
Egli la guarda a tavola sì spesso,	At table he gazes at her so often
e con tale immodestia,	and so wantonly,
che s'il Conte s'accorge—	that if the Count noticed it—
e sul tal punto, sapete, egli è una bestia—	on that subject, as you know, he's quite wild—
	Susanna
Scellerato! e perchè andate voi	You wretch! Why do you go around
tai menzogne spargendo?	spreading such lies?
	Basilio
Io! che ingiustizia!	I! How unfair!
Quel che compro io vendo,	That which I buy I sell,
a quel che tutti dicono,	and to what is common knowledge
Io non aggiungo un pelo.	I add not a tittle.
	Count (*emerging from his hiding-place*)
Come! che dicon tutti?	Indeed! And what is common knowledge?
	Basilio (*aside*)
Oh bella!	How wonderful!
	Susanna (*aside*)
Oh cielo!	Oh heavens!

Act I, #7: Terzetta (Trio): Count, Basilio, and Susanna

Form: sonata-type structure, with development and recapitulation

Style: quick exchange between voices; much text repetition; each character with own emotional commentary

The Count—angry

Basilio and the Count—comforting Susanna who has fainted

	Count
[23] Cosa sento! Tosto andate,	I heard it all! Go at once
E scacciate il seduttor!	throw the seducer out!
	Basilio
In mal punto son qui giunto;	I have come at an unfortunate moment;
Perdonate, o mio signor.	forgive me, my lord.
	Susanna (*nearly fainting*)
Che ruina! me meschina!	What a catastrophe! I am ruined!
Son'oppressa dal terror!	Terror grips my heart!
	Count
Tosto andate, andate . . .	Go at once, go . . .
	Basilio
In mal punto . . .	I have come . . .
	Susanna
Che ruina!	What a catastrophe!

. . . son qui giunto; . . .

. . . e scacciate . . .
. . . il seduttor.

. . . perdonate, . . .
. . . o mio signor.

Me meschina!

Me meschina!
Son oppressa dal terror,

Ah! già svien la poverina!
Come, oh Dio! le batte il cor.

Pian, pianin, su questo seggio—

Dove sono? Cosa veggio?
Che insolenza! andate fuor.

Siamo qui per aiutarvi, . . .

. . . è sicuro il vostro onor.

. . . non turbarti, o mio tesor.

Ah, del paggio, quel ch'ho detto,
era solo un mio sospetto.

E un'insidia, una perfidia,
non credete all'impostor.

Parta, parta il damerino, . . .

Poverino!

. . . parta, parta il damerino.

Poverino!

Poverino! poverino!
ma da me sorpreso ancor!

Come?

Che?

Che?

Basilio
. . . at an unfortunate moment

Count
. . . and throw . . .
. . . the seducer out.

Basilio
. . . forgive me, . . .
. . . o my lord.

Susanna
I am ruined!

I am ruined!
Terror grips my heart.

Basiiio, Count (*supporting Susanna*)
Ah! The poor girl's fainted!
O God, how her heart is beating.

Basilio
Gently, gently on to the chair—
(*taking her to the chair*)

Susanna (*coming to*)
Where am I? What's this I see?
What insolence! Leave this room.

Basilio, Count
We're here to help you, . . .

Basilio
. . . your virtue is safe.

Count
. . . do not worry, sweetheart.

Basilio
What I was saying about the page
was only my own suspicion.

Susanna
It was a nasty insinuation,
do not believe the liar.

Count
The young fop must go, . . .

Susanna, Basilio
Poor boy!

Count
. . . the young fop must go.

Susanna, Basilio
Poor boy!

Count
Poor boy! Poor boy!
But I caught him yet again!

Susanna
How!

Basilio
What?

Susanna
What?

	Basilio
Come?	How?
	Susanna, Basilio
Come? che?	How? What?
	Count
Da tua cugina,	At your cousin's house
l'uscio ier trovai rinchiuso,	I found the door shut yesterday.
picchio, m'apre Barbarina,	I knocked and Barbarina opened it
paurosa, fuor dell'uso.	much more timidly than usual.
Io, dal muso insospettito,	My suspicions aroused by her expression,
guardo, cerco in ogni sito,	I had a good look around
ed alzando pian, pianino,	and, very gently lifting
il tappeto al tavolino,	the cloth upon the table,
vedo il paggio.	I found the page.

(*imitating his own action with the dress over the chair, he reveals the page*)

Ah, cosa veggio?	Ah, what do I see?
	Susanna
Ah! crude stelle!	Ah! wicked fate!
	Basilio
Ah! meglio ancora!	Ah! Better still!
	Count
24 Onestissima signora, . . .	Most virtuous lady, . . .
	Susanna
Accader non può di peggio.	Nothing worse could happen!
	Count
. . . or capisco come va!	. . . now I see what's happening!
	Susanna
Giusti Dei, che mai sarà!	Merciful heaven, whatever will happen?
	Basilio
Così fan tutte . . .	They're all the same . . .
	Susanna
⌈ Giusti Dei! che mai sarà!	Merciful heaven! Whatever will happen!
│ Accader non può di peggio,	Nothing worse could happen!
⌊ ah no! ah no!	ah no! ah no!
	Basilio
⌈ . . . le belle,	. . . the fair sex,
│ non c'è alcuna novità,	there's nothing new about it,
⌊ così fan tutte.	they're all the same.
	Count
⌈ Or capisco come va,	Now I see what's happening,
│ onestissima signora!	most virtuous lady!
⌊ or capisco	Now I see
	Basilio
Ah, del paggio quel che ho detto,	What I was saying about the page
era solo un mio sospetto.	was only my own suspicion.
	Susanna
⌈ Accader non può di peggio	Nothing worse could happen
│	**Count**
│ Onestissima signora	Most virtuous lady
│	**Basilio**
⌊ Così fan tutte	They're all the same

Tr. by LIONEL SALTER

TRANSITION IV

■

From Classicism to Romanticism

"I am very greatly obliged by the diploma of honorary membership you so kindly sent me. May it be the reward of my devotion to the art of music to be wholly worthy of such a distinction one day. In order to give musical expression to my sincere gratitude as well, I shall take the liberty before long of presenting your honorable Society with one of my symphonies in score."—FRANZ SCHUBERT

Today we speak of the four masters of the Viennese Classical school—Haydn, Mozart, Beethoven, and Schubert—yet their approaches to style and form are completely individual. Two of these masters, Beethoven and Schubert, spanned the eras of Classicism and Romanticism as important transitional figures. Beethoven's middle period works already exhibit elements of nineteenth-century style, and his late works, especially his piano sonatas and string quartets, are moulded in the chromatic harmonies and extended forms of Romanticism.

The symphonies and quartets of Franz Schubert (1797–1828) pronounce him the heir of the Viennese Classical tradition. In his handling of large forms and in his radiant orchestral sonorities, he clearly followed in the line of development from Haydn and Mozart. In his songs and piano music, however, he was truly a Romantic. His sentimental, lyrical melodies sing forth the sounds of a new era.

A Comparison of Classical and Romantic Styles

Classical (c. 1750–1825)	*Romantic* (c. 1820–1900)
Haydn, Mozart, Beethoven, Schubert	Beethoven, Schubert, Mendelssohn, Schumann, Chopin, Liszt, Berlioz, Brahms, Tchaikovsky, Strauss

Classical (c. 1750–1825)	*Romantic (c. 1820–1900)*
Symmetrical melody in balanced phrases and cadences; tuneful; diatonic, with narrow leaps	Expansive, singing melodies; wide ranging; more varied, with chromatic inflections
Clear rhythmically, with regularly recurring accents; dance rhythms favored	Rhythmic diversity and elasticity; tempo rubato
Diatonic harmony favored; tonic-dominant relationships expanded, become basis for large-scale forms	Increasing chromaticism; expanded concepts of tonality
Homophonic textures; horizontal perspective	Homophony, turning to increased polyphony in later years of era
Symphony, solo concerto, solo sonata, string quartet	Same large forms, including one-movement symphonic poem; solo piano works
Opera, mass, solo song	Same vocal forms, adding works for solo voice/orchestra
Ternary form predominant; sonata-allegro form developed; absolute forms preferred	Expansion of forms and interest in continuous forms as well as miniature programmatic forms
Secular music dominant; aristocratic audience	Secular music dominant; middle-class audience
Continuously changing dynamics through crescendo and decrescendo	Widely ranging dynamics for expressive purposes
Changing tone colors between sections of works	Continual change and blend of tone colors; experiments with new instruments and unusual ranges
String orchestra with woodwinds and some brass; 30 to 40-member orchestra; rise of piano to prominence	Introduction of new instruments (tuba, English horn, saxophone); much larger orchestras; piano dominates as solo instrument
Improvisation largely limited to cadenzas in concertos	Increased virtuosity and expression; composers specify more in scores
Emotional restraint and balance	Emotions, mood, atmosphere emphasized; interest in the bizarre and macabre

PART SEVEN

The Nineteenth-Century

"Music is the most romantic of all the arts—one might almost say, the only genuinely romantic one—for its sole subject is the infinite. Music discloses to man an unknown realm, a world in which he leaves behind all definite feelings to surrender himself to an inexpressible longing."—E.T.A. HOFFMANN (1776–1822)

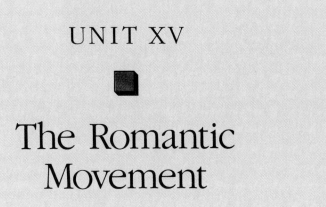

UNIT XV

■

The Romantic Movement

35

The Spirit of Romanticism

"Romanticism is beauty without bounds—the beautiful infinite."—JEAN
PAUL RICHTER (1763–1825)

The Romantic era, stemming out of the social and political upheavals that
followed in the wake of the French Revolution, came to the fore in the
second quarter of the nineteenth century.

The French Revolution was the outcome of momentous social forces. It *French Revolution*
signaled the transfer of power from a hereditary feudal-agricultural aristocracy to the middle class, whose position depended on commerce and industry. As in the case of the American Revolution, this upheaval heralded
a social order shaped by the technological advances of the Industrial Revolution. The new society, based on free enterprise, emphasized the individual
as never before. The slogan "Liberty, Equality, Fraternity" inspired hopes
and visions to which few artists failed to respond. Sympathy for the oppressed,
interest in simple folk and in children, faith in mankind and its destiny—all
these, so intimately associated with the time, point to the democratic character of the Romantic movement.

The Romantic poets rebelled against the conventional form and matter *Romantic poets*
of their Classical predecessors; they leaned toward the fanciful, the picturesque, and the passionate. The revolt against the formalism of the Classical
age numbered among its adherents a line of lyric poets including the German
Heinrich Heine, the Frenchmen Victor Hugo and Alphonse de Lamartine,
and the Englishmen Wordsworth, Coleridge, Byron, Shelley, and Keats. The
new spirit of individualism expressed itself in the Romantic artists' sense of

195

Sympathy for the oppressed underscored the essentially democratic character of the Romantic movement. **Honoré Daumier** (*1808–79*) **The** Third-Class Carriage. (The Metropolitan Museum of Art, Bequest of Mrs. H. O. Havemeyer, 1929. The H. O. Havemeyer Collection)

uniqueness, their heightened awareness of themselves as individuals apart from all others. "I am different from all the men I have seen," proclaimed Jean Jacques Rousseau. "If I am not better, at least I am different." Thus, one of the prime traits of the Romantic arts was their emphasis on an intensely emotional type of expression.

The newly won freedom of the artist proved to be a mixed blessing. Confronted by a philistine world indifferent to artistic and cultural values, artists felt more and more cut off. A new type emerged—the artist as bohemian, the rejected dreamer who starved in an attic and through peculiarities of dress and behavior "shocked the bourgeois." Eternal longing, regret for the lost happiness of childhood, an indefinable discontent that gnawed at the soul—these were the ingredients of the Romantic mood. Yet the artist's pessimism was not without its basis in external reality. It became apparent that the high hopes fostered by the Revolution were not to be realized overnight. Despite the brave slogans, all people were not yet equal or free. Inevitably optimism gave way to doubt and disenchantment—"the illness of the century."

This malaise was reflected in the arts of the time. Hugo dedicated *Les Misérables* "to the unhappy ones of the earth." The nineteenth-century novel found its great theme in the conflict between the individual and society. Jean Valjean and Heathcliff, Madame Bovary and Anna Karenina, Oliver Twist, Tess of the d'Urbervilles, and the Karamazovs—a varied company rises from those impassioned pages to point up the frustrations and guilts of the nineteenth-century world.

Hardly less persuasive was the art of those who sought escape. Some glamorized the past, as did Walter Scott and Alexandre Dumas. Longing for far-off lands inspired the exotic scenes that glow on the canvases of J.M.W.

The nineteenth-century longing for far-off lands inspired such exotic scenes as the painting Femmes d'Alger *by* **Eugène Delacroix** (*1798–1863*). (The Louvre, Paris)

Turner and Eugène Delacroix. The Romantic poets and painters loved the picturesque and the fantastic. Theirs was a world of "strangeness and wonder": the eerie landscape we encounter in the writings of Coleridge, Hawthorne, or Poe.

Romanticism dominated the artistic output of the nineteenth century. It gave its name to a movement and an era, and created a multitude of colorful works that still hold millions in thrall.

36

Romanticism in Music

"Music is the melody whose text is the world."—SCHOPENHAUER

Great changes in the moral, political, and social climate of an epoch seek to be expressed also in the art of that epoch. But they cannot be unless the new age places in the artist's hand the means of giving expression to new ideas. This was precisely the achievement of the Romantic movement in music—that it gave composers the means of expressing what the age demanded of them.

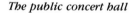

Improved instruments

The Industrial Revolution brought with it not only cheaper and more responsive instruments, but important improvements in wind instruments that strongly influenced the sound of Romantic music. For example, the addition of valves to brass instruments made them much more maneuverable, so that composers like Wagner and Tchaikovsky could assign melodies to the horn that would have been unplayable in the time of Haydn and Mozart. Several new wind instruments were developed as well, including the tuba and the saxophone. So too, as a result of improved manufacturing techniques, the piano acquired a cast-iron frame and thicker strings that gave it a deeper and more brilliant tone. If an impassioned piano work by Liszt sounds different from a sonata of Mozart, it is not only because Liszt's time demanded of him a different kind of expression, but also because it put at his disposal a piano capable of effects that were neither available nor necessary in the earlier period.

Secondly, the gradual democratization of society brought with it a broadening of educational opportunities. New conservatories were established in the chief cities of Europe that trained more and better musicians than formerly. As a result, nineteenth-century composers could count on instrumental performers whose skill was considerably more advanced than in *The public concert hall* former times. As music moved from palace and church to the public concert hall, orchestras increased in size and efficiency, and gave composers a means of expression more varied and colorful than they had ever had before. This naturally had a direct influence upon the sound. For example, where most eighteenth-century music ranged in dynamic level only from piano (soft) to forte (loud), the dynamic range of the orchestra in the nineteenth century

The nineteenth-century orchestra offered the composer new instruments and a larger ensemble. Contemporary woodcut of an orchestral concert at the Covent Garden Theater, London, 1846.

was far greater. Now came into fashion the heaven-storming crescendos, the *Increased expressiveness*
violent contrasts of loud and soft that lend such drama to the music of the
Romantics. As orchestral music became more and more important, the technique of writing for orchestra—that is, orchestration—became almost an
art in itself. At last the musician had a palette comparable to the painter's,
and used it as the painter did—to conjure up sensuous beauty and enchantment, to create mood and atmosphere, to suggest nature scenes and calm
or stormy seascapes.

The desire for direct communication led composers to use a large number
of expressive terms intended to serve as clues to the mood of the music,
with the result that a highly characteristic vocabulary sprang up. Among the
directions frequently encountered in nineteenth-century scores are *dolce*
(sweetly), *cantabile* (songful), *dolente* (weeping), *mesto* (sad), *maestoso*
(majestic), *gioioso* (joyous), *con amore* (with love, tenderly), *con fuoco*
(with fire), *con passione, espressivo, pastorale, agitato, misterioso, lamentoso, trionfale*. These suggest not only the character of the music but
the frame of mind behind it.

The interest in folklore and the rising tide of nationalism impelled Ro- *Use of folklore*
mantic musicians to make use of the folk songs and dances of their native
lands. As a result, a number of national idioms—Hungarian, Polish, Russian,
Bohemian, Scandinavian—came to the fore and opened up new areas to
European music, greatly enriching its melody, harmony, and rhythm.

Exoticism

Nineteenth-century exoticism manifested itself, first, as a longing of the
northern nations for the warmth and color of the south; second, as a longing
of the West for the fairy-tale splendors of the Orient. The former impulse
found expression in the works of German, French, and Russian composers
who turned for inspiration to Italy and Spain. The long list includes Tchaikovsky's *Capriccio italien*, Mendelssohn's *Italian Symphony*, Chabrier's *Es-
paña*; the masterpiece in this category is Bizet's *Carmen*.

The glamour of the East was brought to international prominence by the
Russian national school. The fairy-tale background of Asia pervades Russian
music. Rimsky-Korsakov's orchestrally resplendent *Scheherazade*, Alexander
Borodin's opera *Prince Igor*, and Ippolitov-Ivanov's *Caucasian Sketches* are
among the many Orientally inspired works that found favor throughout the
world. Italian composers also utilized exotic themes: Verdi in *Aïda*, and
Puccini in his operas *Madama Butterfly* and *Turandot*. As we will see later,
it was not until the twentieth century that the musical idioms of these distant
cultures permeated Western styles to any great extent.

Romantic Style Traits

Even when written for instruments, Romantic melody was easy to sing and *Singable melody*
hum. The nineteenth century above all was the period when musicians tried
to make their instruments "sing." It is no accident that the themes from

Romantic symphonies, concertos, and other instrumental works have been transformed into popular songs, for Romantic melody was marked by a lyricism that gave it an immediate emotional appeal, as is evidenced by the enduring popularity of the tunes of Schubert, Chopin, Verdi, among others. Through innumerable songs and operas as well as instrumental pieces, Romantic melody appealed to a wider audience than had ever existed before.

Expressive harmony

Nineteenth-century music strove for a harmony that was highly emotional and expressive. Under the impact of the Romantic movement, composers such as Richard Wagner sought combinations of pitches more dissonant than their forebears had been used to.

Expanded forms

The composers of the nineteenth century gradually expanded the instrumental forms they had inherited from the eighteenth. These musicians needed more time to say what they had to say. A symphony of Haydn or Mozart is apt to take about twenty minutes; one by Tchaikovsky, Brahms, or Dvořák lasts at least twice that long. As public concert life developed, the symphony became the most important form of orchestral music, comparable to the most spacious form in Romantic literature—the novel. As a result, nineteenth-century composers approached the writing of a symphony with greater deliberation than their predecessors. Where Haydn wrote more than a hundred symphonies and Mozart more than forty, Schubert, Bruckner, and Dvořák (following the example of Beethoven) wrote nine; Tchaikovsky, six; Schumann and Brahms, four; César Franck, one. As the Romantics well realized, it was not easy to write a symphony after Beethoven. New orchestral forms emerged as well, including the one-movement symphonic poem, the choral symphony, and works for solo voice with orchestra.

Music in the nineteenth century drew steadily closer to literature and painting—that is, to elements that lay outside the realm of sound. The connection with Romantic poetry and drama is most obvious, of course, in the case of music with words. However, even in their purely orchestral music the Romantic composers responded to the mood of the time and captured with remarkable vividness the emotional atmosphere that surrounded nineteenth-century poetry and painting.

The result of all these tendencies was to make Romanticism as potent a force in music as it was in the other arts. Nineteenth-century music was linked to dreams and passions, to profound meditations on life and death, human destiny, God and nature, pride in one's country, desire for freedom, the political struggles of the age, and the ultimate triumph of good over evil. These intellectual and emotional associations, nurtured by the Romantic movement, enabled music to achieve a commanding position in the nineteenth century as a moral force, a vision of human greatness, and a direct link between the artist's inner life and the outside world.

The Musician in Nineteenth-Century Society

The emergence of a new kind of democratic society could not but affect the conditions governing the lives of composers and performers. Concert life began to center on the public concert hall as well as the salons of the aristocracy and upper middle class. Where eighteenth-century musicians

*An evening of string quartet music at the Berlin house of Bettina von Arnim,
featuring Joseph Joachim as first violinist. Water color by* **Johann Carl Arnold,**
c. 1855. (Freies Deutsches Hochstift, Goethemuseum, Frankfurt [Main] Photo:
Ursula Edelmann)

had functioned under the system of aristocratic patronage and based their
careers upon the favor of royal courts or the nobility, nineteenth-century
musicians were supported by the new middle-class public. Musicians of the
eighteenth century had been a kind of glorified servant class who ministered
to the needs of a public high above them in social rank. In the nineteenth
century, however, musicians met their audience as equals. Indeed, as solo
performers began to dominate the concert hall, whether as pianists, violinists,
or conductors, they were "stars" who were idolized by audiences. Mendelssohn, Liszt, and Paganini were welcomed into the great homes of their
time in quite a different way than had been the case with Haydn and Mozart
half a century earlier.

Ascendancy of the soloist

Music thrived in the private home and in the civic life of most cities and
towns as well. Permanent orchestras and singing societies abounded, printed
music was readily available at a cost affordable to many, and music journals
kept the public informed about musical activities and new works.

With this expansion of musical life, composers and performing artists
were called upon to assume new roles as educators. Felix Mendelssohn,
active as composer, pianist, and conductor, used his immense prestige to
found and direct the Leipzig Conservatory, whose course of training became
a model for music schools all over Europe and America. The Russian com-
poser-pianist Anton Rubinstein performed a similar role as founder of the
St. Petersburg (now Leningrad) Conservatory. Robert Schumann became a
widely read critic. Franz Liszt was not only active as a composer and con-

ductor but was also the greatest pianist of his time. In later life he taught extensively and raised up a generation of great concert pianists. Richard Wagner directed his own theater at Bayreuth and was thus instrumental in educating the new public to understand his music dramas. Composers everywhere were active in organizing concerts and music festivals, and thus played a leading role in educating the new mass public.

Women in Music

Standard histories of music have largely excluded consideration of the role of women as composers and performers; this circumstance results from insufficient attention to social considerations of the time, including the educational opportunities, the hierarchy of the social classes, and the economics of the music professions. Recent scholarship supports the contributions of women to music through the eras—although rarely as leaders in innovative changes of style.

The society of the nineteenth century saw sizable numbers of women make careers as professional musicians. This was possible through the broadening of educational opportunities that included the establishment of public conservatories whose doors were open to women; in such schools, women could receive training as singers, instrumentalists, and even as composers. Likewise, the rise of the piano as the favored chamber instrument—both solo and with voice or instruments—provided women of the middle and upper classes with a performance outlet that was socially acceptable. There was one area in which women's talents received full expression—the lyric theater. As opera singers, they performed major roles in dramatic works for the stage.

Composition, on the other hand, proved to be largely a man's province. The generally accepted view held by men that women lacked creativity in the arts drove some nineteenth-century women to pursue literary careers under male pseudonyms: George Eliot, George Sand, and Daniel Stern, to name three. However, despite the social pressures against them, a few women defied the conventions of their time and made a name for themselves as composers. We shall discuss the work of one of the best known of these pioneers: the pianist-composer Clara Schumann.

Women also exerted an important influence as patrons of music or through their friendships with composers. George Sand played an important part in the career of Chopin, as did Carolyne Sayn-Wittgenstein in that of Liszt. Nadejda von Meck is remembered as the woman who supported Tchaikovsky in the early years of his career and made it possible for him to compose. Also, several women of the upper class became known as the hostesses of musical salons where composers could gather to perform and discuss their music. One such musical center was in the home of the Mendelssohn family, where Fanny Mendelssohn, a respected performer and composer herself, hosted concerts that featured works by her more famous brother, Felix.

All in all, women made steady strides toward professional expertise throughout the nineteenth century, and thereby laid the foundation for their achievements in the twentieth.

UNIT XVI

■

The Nineteenth-Century Art Song

37

The Romantic Song

"Out of my great sorrows I make my little songs."—HEINRICH HEINE

The art song met the nineteenth-century need for intimate personal expression. Coming into prominence in the early decades of the century, it emerged as a particularly attractive example of the new lyricism.

Types of Song Structure

We distinguish between two main types of song structure. The simplest of these is *strophic form*, in which the same melody is repeated with every stanza, or strophe, of the poem. This formation, which occurs very frequently in folk and popular song, permits no real closeness between words and music. Instead it sets up a general atmosphere that accommodates itself equally well to all the stanzas. The first may tell of the lover's expectancy, the second of his joy at seeing his beloved, the third of her father's harshness in separating them, and the fourth of her sad death, all these being sung to the same tune.

Strophic form

The other song type is what the Germans call *durchkomponiert*, or "through-composed"—that is, composed from beginning to end, without repetitions of whole sections. Here the music follows the story line, changing with each stanza according to the text. This makes it possible for the composer to mirror every shade of meaning in the words.

Through-composed form

203

The Lied

Despite the prominence of song throughout the ages, the art song as we know it today was a product of the Romantic era. It was created by the union of poetry and music in the early nineteenth century. Among the great Romantic masters of the art song were Franz Schubert, Robert Schumann, and Johannes Brahms. The new genre thus came to be known throughout Europe by the German word for song—*Lied* (plural, *Lieder*). A Lied is a solo vocal song with piano accompaniment. Some composers wrote groups of Lieder that were unified by some narrative thread or a descriptive theme; such a group is known as a *song cycle*.

Song cycle

The Lied depended for its flowering on the upsurge of lyric poetry that marked the rise of German Romanticism. Goethe (1749–1832) and Heine (1797–1856) are the two leading figures among a group of poets who, like Wordsworth and Byron, Shelley and Keats in English literature, cultivated a subjective mode of expression through the short lyric poem. The Lied brought to flower the desire of the Romantic era for the union of music and poetry, ranging from tender sentiment to dramatic balladry. Its favorite themes were love and longing, the beauty of nature, and the transience of human happiness.

The triumph of the Romantic art song was made possible by the emergence of the piano as the universal household instrument of the nineteenth century. The piano accompaniment translated the poetic images into musical equivalents. Voice and piano together created a short lyric form charged with feeling, suited alike for amateurs and artists, for the home as for the concert room. Within a short time the Lied achieved immense popularity and made a durable contribution to world art.

38

Schubert and the Lied

"When I wished to sing of love it turned to sorrow. And when I wished to sing of sorrow it was transformed for me into love."

In the popular mind Franz Schubert's life has become a romantic symbol of the artist's fate. He suffered poverty and was neglected during his lifetime. He died young. And after his death he was enshrined among the immortals.

Franz Schubert: His Life and Music

Schubert (1797–1828) was born in a suburb of Vienna, the son of a school-master. The boy learned the violin from his father, piano from an elder brother; his beautiful soprano voice gained him admittance to the imperial chapel and school where the court singers were trained. His teachers were fully astonished at the musicality of the shy, dreamy lad. One of them re-marked that Franz seemed to learn "straight from Heaven."

Franz Schubert

His school days over, young Schubert tried to follow in his father's foot-steps, but he was not cut out for the routine of the classroom. He found escape in the solitude of his attic, immersing himself in the lyric poets who were the first voices of German Romanticism. As one of his friends said, "Everything he touched turned to song." The music came to him with miraculous spontaneity. *Erlkönig*, set to a poem by Goethe, was written in a few hours when he was a teenager. It is one of his greatest songs.

Schubert was singularly unable to stand up to the world. Songs that in time sold in the hundreds of thousands he surrendered literally for the price of a meal. As the years passed, the buoyancy of youth gave way to a sense of loneliness, the tragic loneliness of the Romantic artist. "My music is the product of my talent and my misery. And that which I have written in my greatest distress is what the world seems to like best."

He still yielded to flurries of optimism when success appeared to lie within his grasp, but eventually there came to him an intimation that the struggle had been decided against him. "It seems to me at times that I no longer belong to this world." This was the emotional climate of the magnificent song cycle *Winterreise* (Winter Journey). Overcoming his discouragement, he embarked on his last effort. To the earlier masterpieces was added, in that final year, an amazing list that includes the Mass in E flat, the String Quintet in C, the last three piano sonatas, published posthumously, and thirteen of his finest songs.

He was thirty-one years old when he died in 1828. His possessions con-sisted of his clothing, his bedding, and "a pile of old music valued at ten florins": his unpublished manuscripts. In the memorable words of Sir George Grove, "There never has been one like him, and there never will be another."

Principal Works

More than 600 Lieder, including 3 song cycles, among them *Die schöne Müllerin* (The Lovely Maid of the Mill, 1823) and *Winterreise* (Winter's Journey, 1827)

8 symphonies, including the *Unfinished* (No. 8, 1822)

Chamber music, including 15 string quartets; 1 string quintet; 2 piano trios and the *Trout Quintet*; 1 octet; various sonatas

Piano sonatas, dances, and character pieces

Choral music, including 7 masses, other liturgical pieces, and partsongs

Operas and incidental music for dramas

Schubert stood at the confluence of the Classic and Romantic eras. His symphonies are Classical in their clear form, their dramatic momentum, and continuity. But in his Lieder and piano pieces he was wholly the Romantic. The melodies have a tenderness, a quality of longing that match the Romantic quality of the poetry to which they are set. This magical lyricism impelled the composer Franz Liszt to call him "the most poetic musician that ever was."

Chamber music was Schubert's birthright as a Viennese. His string quartets, the *Trout Quintet*, and the Quintet in C bear the true Schubertian stamp. The piano sings the new lyricism in his Impromptus and *Moments musicaux* (Musical Moments), and piano sonatas. Finally there are the songs, more than six hundred of them. Many were written down at white heat, sometimes five, six, seven in a single morning. Certain of his melodies achieve the universality of folksong. Their eloquence and freshness of feeling have never been surpassed. A special place is occupied by two superb song cycles— *Die schöne Müllerin* (The Lovely Maid of the Mill) and *Winterreise*.

Schubert: Erlkönig

This masterpiece of Schubert's youth (1815) captures the Romantic "strangeness and wonder" of Goethe's celebrated ballad. *Erlkönig* (The Erlking) is based on the legend that whoever is touched by the King of the Elves must die.

The eerie atmosphere of the poem is established by the piano part. Galloping triplets are heard against a rumbling figure in the bass. This motive, so Romantic in tone, pervades the song and imparts to it an astonishing unity despite its through-composed form. The poem has four characters: the narrator, the father, the child, and the seductive Elf (see Listening Guide 18). The characters are vividly differentiated through changes in the melody, harmony, rhythm, and type of accompaniment. The song is through-composed; the music follows the unfolding narrative with a steady rise in tension—and pitch—that builds to the climax. Abruptly the obsessive triplet rhythm lets up, getting slower as horse and rider reach home. Created by a marvelous boy of eighteen, it was a milestone in the history of Romanticism.

Listening Guide 18

2A/6

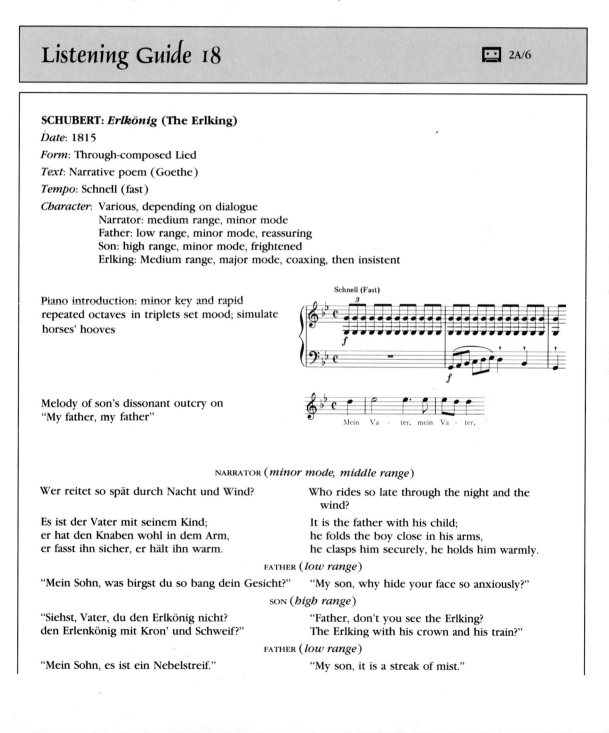

SCHUBERT: *Erlkönig* **(The Erlking)**

Date: 1815

Form: Through-composed Lied

Text: Narrative poem (Goethe)

Tempo: Schnell (fast)

Character: Various, depending on dialogue
      Narrator: medium range, minor mode
      Father: low range, minor mode, reassuring
      Son: high range, minor mode, frightened
      Erlking: Medium range, major mode, coaxing, then insistent

Piano introduction: minor key and rapid repeated octaves in triplets set mood; simulate horses' hooves

Melody of son's dissonant outcry on "My father, my father"

NARRATOR (*minor mode, middle range*)

Wer reitet so spät durch Nacht und Wind?	Who rides so late through the night and the wind?
Es ist der Vater mit seinem Kind;	It is the father with his child;
er hat den Knaben wohl in dem Arm,	he folds the boy close in his arms,
er fasst ihn sicher, er hält ihn warm.	he clasps him securely, he holds him warmly.

FATHER (*low range*)

"Mein Sohn, was birgst du so bang dein Gesicht?"	"My son, why hide your face so anxiously?"

SON (*high range*)

"Siehst, Vater, du den Erlkönig nicht?	"Father, don't you see the Erlking?
den Erlenkönig mit Kron' und Schweif?"	The Erlking with his crown and his train?"

FATHER (*low range*)

"Mein Sohn, es ist ein Nebelstreif."	"My son, it is a streak of mist."

ERLKING (*major mode, melodic*)

"Du liebes Kind, komm, geh mit mir!   "Dear child, come, go with me!
gar schöne Spiele spiel' ich mit dir;   I'll play the prettiest games with you.
manch bunte Blumen sind an dem Strand;   Many colored flowers grow along the shore,
meine Mutter hat manch' gülden Gewand."   My mother has many golden garments."

SON (*high range, frightened*)

"Mein Vater, mein Vater, und hörest du nicht,   "My father, my father, and don't you hear
was Erlenkönig mir leise verspricht?"   The Erlking whispering promises to me?"

FATHER (*low range, calming*)

"Sei ruhig, bleibe ruhig, mein Kind;   "Be quiet, stay quiet, my child;
in dürren Blättern säuselt der Wind."   The wind is rustling in the dead leaves."

ERLKING (*major mode, cajoling*)

"Willst, feiner Knabe, du mit mir gehn?   "My handsome boy, will you come with me?
meine Töchter sollen dich warten schön;   My daughters shall wait upon you;
mein Töchter führen den nächtlichen Reihn   my daughters lead off in the dance every night,
und wiegen und tanzen und singen dich ein."   and cradle and dance and sing you to sleep."

SON (*high range, outcry*)

"Mein Vater, mein Vater, und siehst du nicht dort   "My father, my father, and don't you see there
Erlkönigs Töchter am düstern Ort?   The Erlking's daughters in the shadows?"

FATHER (*low range, reassuring*)

"Mein Sohn, mein Sohn, ich seh' es genau,   "My son, my son, I see it clearly;
es scheinen die alten Weiden so grau."   The old willows look so gray."

ERLKING (*gay, then insistent*)

"Ich liebe dich, mich reizt deine schöne Gestalt,   "I love you, your beautiful figure delights me!
und bist du nicht willig, so brauch' ich Gewalt."   And if you're not willing, then I shall use force!"

SON (*high range, terrified*)

"Mein Vater, mein Vater, jetzt fasst er mich an!   "My father, my father, now he is taking hold of
                                                            me!
Erlkönig hat mir ein Leids gethan!"   The Erlking has hurt me!"

NARRATOR (*middle register, speechlike*)

Dem Vater grauset's, er reitet geschwind,   The father shudders, he rides swiftly on;
er hält in Armen das ächzende Kind,   He holds in his arms the groaning child,
erreicht den Hof mit Müh' und Noth: He reaches the courtyard weary and anxious;
in seinen Armen das Kind war todt.   In his arms the child was dead.

Tr. by PHILIP L. MILLER

Unit XVII

The Nineteenth-Century Piano Piece

39

The Piano in the Romantic Era

"Provided one can feel the music, one can also make the pianoforte sing."—LUDWIG VAN BEETHOVEN

The rise in popularity of the piano was an important factor in shaping the musical culture of the Romantic era. All over Europe and America the instrument became a mainstay of music in the home. It proved especially attractive to the amateur because, unlike the string and wind instruments, it was capable of playing melody and harmony together. The piano thus played a crucial role in the taste and experience of the new mass public.

Hardly less important was the rise of the piano recital. At first the performer was also the composer; Mozart and Beethoven introduced their own piano concertos to the public, Franz Liszt first presented his *Hungarian Rhapsodies* as did Paganini his thrilling violin pieces. With the rise of the concert industry, however, a class of virtuoso performers arose whose only function it was to dazzle audiences by playing music others had written.

At the same time a series of crucial technical improvements led to the development of the modern concert grand. By the opening of the twentieth century the piano recital had come to occupy a central position on the musical scene.

The Short Lyric Piano Piece

The short lyric piano piece was the instrumental equivalent of the song in its projection of lyric and dramatic moods within a compact frame. Among

A rather ornate grand piano made by Johann Georg Groeber of Innsbruck, Austria, in about 1810. (Yale University Collection of Musical Instruments)

the terms most frequently used as titles are *impromptu* ("on the spur of the moment"), *intermezzo* (interlude), *nocturne* (night song), *moment musical, prelude,* and, of larger dimensions, the *rhapsody* and *ballade*. In the dance category are the *waltz, mazurka, écossaise* (Scottish dance), *polonaise* (Polish dance), and *march*. Composers also used titles of a fanciful and descriptive nature. Typical are Robert Schumann's *In the Night, Soaring,* and *Whims*; Liszt's *Forest Murmurs* and *Fireflies*. The nineteenth-century masters of the short piano piece—Schubert, Chopin and Liszt, Mendelssohn, Schumann and Brahms, among others—showed inexhaustible ingenuity in exploring the technical resources of the instrument and its capacities for lyric-dramatic expression.

40

Chopin and Nineteenth-Century Piano Music

"My life . . . an episode without a beginning and with a sad end."

In the annals of his century, Frédéric François Chopin (1810–49) is known as the "poet of the piano." The title is a valid one. His art, issuing from the heart of Romanticism, constitutes the golden age of that instrument.

Frédéric François Chopin: His Life and Music

Chopin, the national composer of Poland, was half French. His father had emigrated to Warsaw, where he married a lady-in-waiting to a countess and taught French to the sons of the nobility. Frédéric, who displayed his musical gift in childhood, was educated at the newly founded Conservatory of Warsaw. At the age of twenty-one, he left for Paris, where he spent the rest of his career. Paris in the 1830s was the center of the new Romanticism. The circle in which Chopin moved included musicians such as Liszt, Berlioz, and Rossini; literary figures such as Victor Hugo, Balzac, Lamartine, George Sand, and Alexandre Dumas. The poet Heinrich Heine was his friend, as was the painter Delacroix. Although Chopin was a man of emotions rather than ideas, he could not but be stimulated by his contact with the leading intellectuals of France.

Frédéric François Chopin

Through the virtuoso pianist Franz Liszt he met Mme. Aurore Dudevant, "the lady with the somber eye," known to the world as the novelist George Sand. She was thirty-four, Chopin twenty-eight when the famous friendship began. Mme. Sand was brilliant and domineering; her need to dominate found its counterpart in Chopin's need to be ruled. She left a memorable account of this fastidious artist at work: "His creative power was spontaneous, miraculous. It came to him without effort or warning. . . . But then began the most heartrending labor I have ever witnessed. It was a series of attempts, of fits of irresolution and impatience to recover certain details. He would shut himself in his room for days, pacing up and down, breaking his pens, repeating and modifying one bar a hundred times. . . ."

For the next eight years Chopin spent his summers at Mme. Sand's chateau at Nohant, where she entertained the cream of France's intelligentsia. These were productive years for him, although his health grew progressively worse and his relationship with Mme. Sand ran its course from love to conflict, from jealousy to hostility. They parted in bitterness.

According to his friend Liszt, "Chopin felt and often repeated that in breaking this long affection, this powerful bond, he had broken his life." The lonely despair of the Romantic artist, pervades his last letters. "What has become of my art?" he writes during a visit to Scotland. "And my heart, where have I wasted it?"

He died of tuberculosis in Paris at the age of thirty-nine. It is not without significance that despite his homesickness he spent the whole of his adult life in Paris. Thus Poland was idealized in his imagination as the symbol of that unappeasable longing which every Romantic artist carries in his heart. Heine, himself an expatiate, divined this when he wrote that Chopin is "neither a Pole, a Frenchman, nor a German. He reveals a higher origin. He comes from the land of Mozart, Raphael, Goethe. His true country is the land of poetry."

Chopin was one of the most original artists of the Romantic era. His idiom is so entirely his own there is no mistaking it for any other. He was the only master of the first rank whose creative life centered about the piano. It is remarkable that so many of his works have remained in the pianist's repertory. His Nocturnes are tinged with varying shades of melancholy. The Preludes

Principal Works

Piano and orchestra, including 2 piano concertos

Piano music, including 4 Ballades, Fantasy in F minor (1841), *Berceuse* (1844), *Barcarolle* (1846), 3 sonatas, preludes, études, mazurkas, nocturnes, waltzes, polonaises, impromptus, scherzos, rondos, marches, and variations

Chamber music, all including piano; songs

are visionary fragments. The Etudes transform piano technique into poetry. The Impromptus are fanciful, capricious, and the Waltzes capture the brilliance and coquetry of the salon. The Mazurkas, derived from a Polish peasant dance, evoke the idealized landscape of his youth. Among the larger forms, the four Ballades are epic poems of spacious structure. while the Fantasy in F minor reveals the composer at the summit of his art.

Chopin: Polonaise in A flat

The Polonaise was a stately processional dance in which Poland's nobles hailed their kings. Chopin's revival of this dance form reveals the heroic side of his art as well as the Polish nationalist. The most popular of his Polonaises is the one in A flat, Opus 53 (1842). The introduction establishes a dramatic mood against which is set the opening theme, a proud and chivalric melody in a stately triple meter. (See outline of the work in Listening Guide 19.)

Tempo rubato   Important here, as in all of Chopin's music, is the *tempo rubato*—the "robbed time" (or, "borrowed time") that is so characteristic of Romantic style. In tempo rubato, certain liberties can be taken with the rhythm without upsetting the basic beat. As Chopin taught it, the accompaniment—say the left hand—was played in strict time while above it the right-hand style might hesitate a little here or hurry forward there. In either case, the "borrowing" had to be repaid before the end of the phrase. Rubato, like any seasoning, has to be used sparingly. But when it is done well it imparts to the music a waywardness, a quality of caprice that can be enchanting. And it remains an essential ingredient of the true Chopin style.

Listening Guide 19

CHOPIN: Polonaise in A flat, Op. 53

Date: 1842

Form: **A-B-A′**, with introduction

Genre: Polonaise, a stately triple-meter Polish dance

Tempo: Alla Polacca e maestoso (like a polonaise and majestic). Use of rubato tempo

30 0:00 INTRODUCTION
Dramatic mood established, fast ascending lines builds into main theme of **A**

31 0:31 SECTION **A**
Stately dancelike theme, in tonic key (A-flat major); repeated in louder statement, in octaves

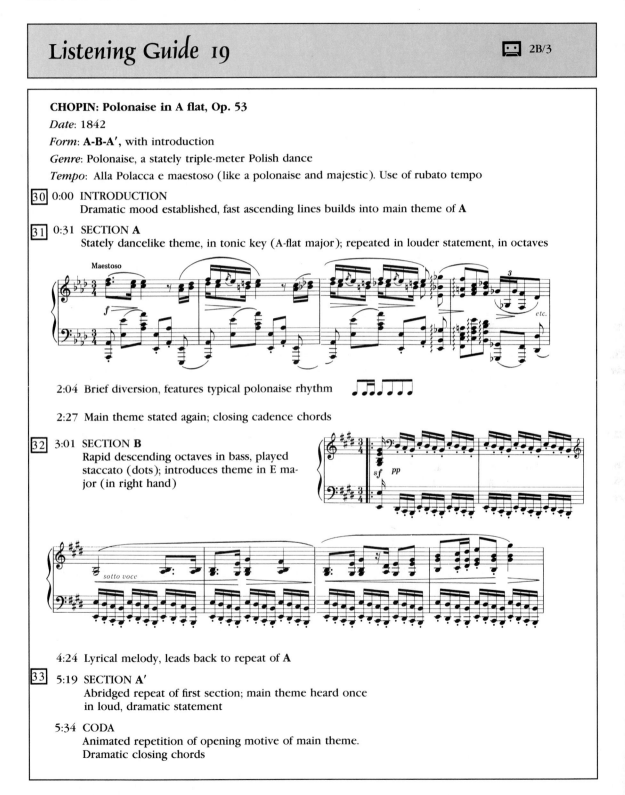

2:04 Brief diversion, features typical polonaise rhythm

2:27 Main theme stated again; closing cadence chords

32 3:01 SECTION **B**
Rapid descending octaves in bass, played staccato (dots); introduces theme in E major (in right hand)

4:24 Lyrical melody, leads back to repeat of **A**

33 5:19 SECTION **A′**
Abridged repeat of first section; main theme heard once in loud, dramatic statement

5:34 CODA
Animated repetition of opening motive of main theme. Dramatic closing chords

41

Clara Schumann: A Nineteenth-Century Woman Musician

"The superiority which characterizes the artist as a pianist is matched by her compositions. A unique mixture of authentic masculine seriousness and intellectual rigor together with feminine emotion and amiability is reflected in the works of Clara Schumann."—ANONYMOUS REVIEWER, Breslauer Zeitung, 23 December, 1877

Clara Schumann

Clara Schumann (1819–96) is universally regarded as one of the most distinguished woman musicians of the nineteenth century. She was admired throughout Europe as a leading pianist of her time, but the world in which she lived was not fully prepared to acknowledge that a woman could be an outstanding composer. Hence her considerable creative gifts were not recognized or encouraged during her lifetime.

Clara Schumann: Her Life and Music

Clara Schumann's close association with two great composers put her in the center of the musical life of her time; these were her husband, Robert Schumann (see Chapter 47), and her life-long friend, Johannes Brahms (see Chapter 49). Under the stern guidance of her father, Friedrich Wieck, Clara studied piano from age five, made her first public appearance as a concert artist in Leipzig at age nine, and took her first extended concert tour several years later, travelling as far as Paris. By 1835, she was acclaimed throughout Europe as a prodigy of exceptional talent. She faced the first great crisis in her life in 1837: the violent opposition of her father to her marriage to Robert. After a three-year battle, the two were married. Clara then faced the problems of a woman torn between the demands of an exacting career and her responsibilities as a wife and mother. She bore eight children, yet she managed throughout those years to maintain her position as one of the outstanding concert artists of Europe. Liszt admired her playing for its "complete technical mastery, depth, and sincerity of feeling." She dedicated her talents to the propagation of her husband's music. She gave the first performance of many of his important works and also became known as a leading interpreter of the music of Brahms and Chopin.

Clara's life was not an easy one. "What will become of my work?" Clara wrote after learning she was expecting a fifth child, "Yet Robert says 'children are blessings' and he is right . . . so I have decided to face the difficult time that is coming as cheerfully as possible. Whether it will always be like this, I don't know." Although Clara enjoyed a loving relationship with her husband, life became increasingly difficult. Robert was given to shifting moods and

214

Principal Works

Solo piano music, including dances, caprices, romances, scherzos, impromptus, character pieces (*Quatre pièces fugitives*, Op. 15, 1845), variations (including one on a theme by Robert Schumann, 1854), cadenzas for Mozart and Beethoven piano concertos

1 piano concerto with orchestra or quintet (1837)

Chamber music, including 1 piano trio (1846) and 3 Romances for violin and piano (1855–56)

Lieder, with texts by Burns, Rückert, Heine, Geibel, Rollet, and Lyser

frequent depressions that eventually led to a complete breakdown. After Robert's death, she concertized in order to support herself and her children. Now she in turn was sustained by Brahms's devotion; but their love was transformed into a lifelong friendship.

Clara had the talent, the training, and the background that many composers would envy, but from the beginning of her career she accepted the attitude of her time toward a woman composer. At twenty she confided to her diary, "I once believed that I possessed creative talent, but I have given up this idea; a woman must not desire to compose—there has never yet been one able to do it. Should I expect to be the one? To believe this would be arrogant. . . ."

Called the "Priestess" by her colleagues, Clara was devoutly serious about her artistic endeavors. Her husband was sympathetic to her creativity, assisting when he could with the publication of her music. But Robert accepted the attitude of the time. "Clara has composed a series of small pieces," he wrote in their joint diary, "which show a musical and tender ingenuity such as she never attained before. But to have children, and a husband who is always living in the realm of imagination, does not go together with composing. She cannot work at it regularly, and I am often disturbed to think how many profound ideas are lost because she cannot work them out."

Her output runs to twenty-three opuses, mostly songs and piano pieces. There are two large-scale works—a piano concerto and a trio for piano and strings, several virtuoso pieces, and a gesture of homage—a set of *Variations on a Theme by Robert Schumann*.

Clara Schumann: Quatre pièces fugitives

These four short pieces (1845) well illustrate Clara's affinity for the short lyric form. As might be expected from a great pianist, she had a natural command of the piano idiom. This set of unrelated works was composed over a period of several years and was dedicated to her half-sister, Marie Wieck, who, at age thirteen, was just embarking on a concert career. The third piece of the group, marked Andante espressivo, follows a clear-cut three-part **(A-B-A)** structure, with marked contrast between the **A** and **B** sections. The opening section presents a slow, heartfelt melody, somber in character. The middle part is more animated and moves with faster notes, after which the music returns to the slow, sad melody of the first part. (For analysis, see Listening Guide 20.) The mood of intimate lyricism falls well within the Romantic style. This is the finely wrought work of one who well deserves the praise the world has at last accorded her.

Listening Guide 20   3A/1

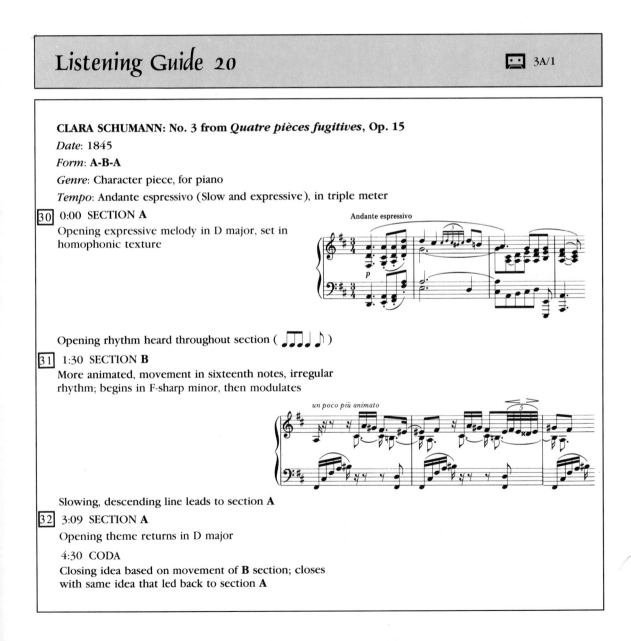

CLARA SCHUMANN: No. 3 from *Quatre pièces fugitives*, Op. 15

Date: 1845

Form: **A-B-A**

Genre: Character piece, for piano

Tempo: Andante espressivo (Slow and expressive), in triple meter

30 0:00 SECTION **A**

Opening expressive melody in D major, set in homophonic texture

Andante espressivo

Opening rhythm heard throughout section (♩♩♩ ♩ ♪)

31 1:30 SECTION **B**

More animated, movement in sixteenth notes, irregular rhythm; begins in F-sharp minor, then modulates

un poco più animato

Slowing, descending line leads to section **A**

32 3:09 SECTION **A**

Opening theme returns in D major

4:30 CODA

Closing idea based on movement of **B** section; closes with same idea that led back to section **A**

UNIT XVIII

◼

Romantic Program Music

42

The Nature of Program Music

". . . The renewal of music through its inner connection with poetry."—FRANZ LISZT

Program music is instrumental music endowed with literary or pictorial associations; the nature of these associations is indicated by the title of the piece or by an explanatory note—the "program"—supplied by the composer. Program music is distinguished from *absolute* or *pure music*, which consists of musical patterns that have no literary or pictorial meanings.

This literary-inspired genre was of special importance in a period like the nineteenth century when musicians became sharply conscious of the connection between their art and the world about them. It helped them to bring music closer to poetry and painting, and to relate their work to the moral and political issues of their time.

Varieties of Program Music

A primary impulse toward program music derived from the opera house, where the overture served as an introduction to an opera (or a play). Many operatic overtures achieved independent popularity as concert pieces. This pointed the way to a new type of overture not associated with an opera: a single-movement piece for orchestra, based on a striking literary idea, such as Tchaikovsky's *Romeo and Juliet*. This type of composition, the *concert overture*, might be descriptive or it could embody a patriotic idea.

The concert overture

Incidental music

Another species of program music, *incidental music* generally consists of an overture and a series of pieces to be performed between the acts of a play and during the important scenes. The most successful pieces of incidental music were generally arranged into suites, a number of which became vastly popular. Mendelssohn's music for Shakespeare's *A Midsummer Night's Dream* is one of the most popular works in this category. Incidental music is still used today, and has spawned two very important offshoots: film music and background music for television drama.

The impulse toward program music was so strong that it invaded even the hallowed form of absolute music—the symphony. Thus came into being the *program symphony*, a multimovement orchestral work. The best-known examples are three program symphonies of Berlioz—*Symphonie fantastique, Harold in Italy, Romeo and Juliet*—and two of Liszt, the *Faust* and *Dante* symphonies.

Program symphony

As the nineteenth century wore on, the need was felt more and more for a large form of orchestral music that would serve the Romantic era as well as the symphony had served the Classical. Toward the middle of the century the long-awaited step was taken with the creation of the *symphonic poem*. This was the nineteenth century's one original contribution to the large forms. It was the achievement of Franz Liszt, who first used the term in 1848. His *Les Préludes* is among the best-known examples of this type of music.

Symphonic poem

A symphonic poem is a piece of program music for orchestra, in one movement, which in the course of contrasting sections develops a poetic idea, suggests a scene, or creates a mood. It differs from the concert overture in one important respect: whereas the concert overture generally retains one of the traditional Classical forms, the symphonic poem is much freer in its structure. The symphonic poem (also called *tone poem*) gave composers the canvas they needed for a big single-movement form. It became the most widely cultivated type of orchestral program music through the second half of the century.

Program music is one of the striking manifestations of nineteenth-century Romanticism. This type of music emphasized the descriptive element; it impelled composers to try to express specific feelings; and it proclaimed the direct relationship of music to life.

43

Berlioz and the Program Symphony

*"To render my works properly requires a combination of extreme
precision and irresistible verve, a regulated vehemence, a dreamy
tenderness, and an almost morbid melancholy."*

Hector Berlioz described the prevailing characteristics of his music as passionate expression, intense ardor, rhythmic animation, and unexpected turns.
The flamboyance of Victor Hugo's poetry and the dramatic intensity of
Eugène Delacroix's painting found their counterpart in Berlioz's music. He
was the first great exponent of musical romanticism in France.

Hector Berlioz: His Life and Music

Hector Berlioz (1803–69) was born in France in a small town near Grenoble.
His father, a well-to-do physician, expected him to follow in his footsteps,
and at eighteen Hector was dispatched to the medical school in Paris. The
Conservatory and the Opéra, however, exercised an infinitely greater at-
traction than the dissecting room. The following year the fiery youth made
a decision that horrified his upper middle-class family: he gave up medicine
for music.

The Romantic revolution was brewing in Paris. Berlioz, along with Victor
Hugo and Delacroix, found himself in the camp of "young France." Having
been cut off by his parents, he gave lessons, sang in a theater chorus, and
turned to various musical chores. He fell under the spell of Beethoven; hardly
less powerful was the impact of Shakespeare, to whose art he was introduced
by a visiting English troupe. For the actress whose Ophelia and Juliet excited
the admiration of the Parisians, young Berlioz conceived an overwhelming
passion. In his *Memoirs*, which read like a Romantic novel, he describes his
infatuation for Harriet Smithson: "I became obsessed by an intense, overpowering sense of sadness. I could not sleep, I could not work, and I spent
my time wandering aimlessly about Paris and its environs."

In 1830 he was awarded the coveted Prix de Rome, which gave him an
opportunity to live and work in the Eternal City. That year also saw the
composition of what has remained his most celebrated work, the *Symphonie
fantastique*. Upon his return from Rome a hectic courtship of Miss Smithson
ensued. There were strenuous objections on the part of both their families
and violent scenes, during one of which the excitable Hector attempted
suicide. He was revived. They were married.

Now that the unattainable ideal had become his wife, his ardor cooled.
It was Shakespeare he had loved rather than Harriet, and in time he sought
the ideal elsewhere. All the same, the first years of his marriage were the
most fruitful of his life. By the time he was forty he had produced most of
the works on which his fame rests.

*Hector Berlioz. Portrait
by* **Gustave Courbet**
(*1819–77*).

219

Principal Works

Orchestral music, including overtures: *Waverley* (1828), *Rob Roy* (1831), *Le roi Lear* (King Lear, 1831), and program symphonies: *Symphonie fantastique* (1830), *Harold en Italie* (Harold in Italy, 1834), and *Roméo et Juliette* (1839)

Choral music, including a Requiem mass (1837), Te Deum (Hymn of Praise, 1849), *La damnation de Faust* (The Damnation of Faust, 1846), and the oratorio *L'enfance du Christ* (The Childhood of Christ, 1854)

3 operas, including *Les Troyens* (The Trojans, 1858) and *Béatrice et Bénédict* (1862)

9 solo vocal works with orchestra

Writings on music, including a treatise on orchestration (1834/55)

In the latter part of his life he conducted his music in all the capitals of Europe. But Paris resisted him to the end. His last major work was the opera *Béatrice et Bénédict*, on his own libretto after Shakespeare's *Much Ado About Nothing*. After this effort the flame was spent, and for the last seven years of his life the embittered master wrote no more. He died at sixty-six, tormented to the end. "Some day," wrote Richard Wagner, "a grateful France will raise a proud monument on his tomb." The prophecy has been fulfilled.

Berlioz was one of the boldest innovators of the nineteenth century. His approach to music was wholly individual, his sense of sound unique. From the start he had an affinity—where orchestral music was concerned—for the vividly dramatic or pictorial program.

His works exemplify the favorite literary influences of the Romantic period. *The Damnation of Faust* was inspired by Goethe; *Harold in Italy*, a program symphony with viola solo and *The Corsair*, an overture, are after Byron. Shakespeare is the source for the overture *King Lear* and for the dramatic symphony *Romeo and Juliet*.

Berlioz's most important opera, *The Trojans*, on his own libretto based on Virgil, has been successfully revived in recent years. His sacred vocal works, including the Requiem and the Te Deum, are conceived on a grandiose scale.

It was in the domain of orchestration that Berlioz's genius asserted itself most fully. His daring originality in handling the instruments opened up a new world of Romantic sonority. His scores, calling for a larger orchestra than had ever been used before, abound in novel effects and discoveries that served as models to all who came after him. Indeed, the conductor Felix Weingartner called Berlioz "the creator of the modern orchestra."

Berlioz: Symphonie fantastique

Berlioz's best-known symphony was written at the height of his infatuation with Harriet Smithson, when he was twenty-seven years old. Extraordinary is the fact that he not only attached a program to a symphony, but that he drew the program from his personal life. "A young musician of morbid sensibility and ardent imagination in a paroxysm of lovesick despair has poisoned himself with opium. The drug, too weak to kill, plunges him into a heavy sleep accompanied by strange visions. . . . The beloved one herself becomes for him a melody, a recurrent theme [*idée fixe*] that haunts him everywhere."

Idée fixe

The "fixed idea" that symbolizes the beloved—the basic theme of the symphony—is subjected to variation in harmony, rhythm, meter, and tempo; dynamics, register, and instrumental color. These transformations take on literary as well as musical significance. Thus the basic motive, recurring by virtue of the literary program, becomes a musical thread unifying five movements that are diverse in mood and character. (See Listening Guide 21 for theme and analysis.)

I. "Reveries, Passions." "He remembers the weariness of soul, the indefinable yearning he knew before meeting his beloved. Then, the volcanic love with which she at once inspired him, his delirious suffering . . . his religious consolation." The Allegro section introduces a soaring melody—the fixed idea. At the climax of the movement the fixed idea is recapitulated fortissimo by full orchestra.

First movement

II. "A Ball." "Amid the tumult and excitement of a brilliant ball he glimpses the loved one again." The dance movement is in ternary or three-part form. In the middle section the fixed idea reappears in waltz time.

Second movement

III. "Scene in the Fields." "On a summer evening in the country he hears two shepherds piping. The pastoral duet, the quiet surroundings . . . all unite to fill his heart with a long absent calm. But *she* appears again. His heart contracts. Painful forebodings fill his soul. . . ." The composer described his aim in the pastoral movement as a mood "of sorrowful loneliness."

Third movement

IV. "March to the Scaffold." "He dreams that he has killed his beloved, that he has been condemned to die and is being led to the scaffold. . . . At the very end the fixed idea reappears for an instant, like a last thought of love interrupted by the fall of the axe." This diabolical march movement exemplifies the nineteenth-century love of the fantastic. The theme of the beloved appears at the very end, on the clarinet, and is cut off by a grim fortissimo chord.

Fourth movement

V. "Dream of a Witches' Sabbath." "He sees himself at a witches' sabbath surrounded by a host of fearsome specters who have gathered for his funeral. Unearthly sounds, groans, shrieks of laughter. . . ." The melody of his beloved is heard, but it has lost its noble and reserved character. It has become a vulgar tune, trivial and grotesque. It is she who comes to the infernal orgy. A howl of joy greets her arrival. She joins the diabolical dance. Bells toll for the dead. A burlesque of the *Dies Irae*. Dance of the witches. The dance and the *Dies Irae* combined."

Fifth movement

This final movement opens with a Larghetto (not quite as slow as largo). Berlioz here exploits an infernal spirit that nourished a century of satanic operas, ballets, and symphonic poems. The infernal mood is heightened with the introduction of the traditional religious chant *Dies irae* (Day of Wrath) from the ancient Mass for the Dead. The movement reaches its climax when

Francisco Goya (*1746–1828*) *anticipated the passionate intensity of Berlioz's music in this painting of the* Witches' Sabbath, *c. 1819–23.* (Museo del Prado, Madrid)

this well-known melody, now in shorter note values, is combined with the Witches' Dance. This passage leads to a rousingly theatrical ending for a theatrical subject.

There is a bigness of line and gesture about the music of Berlioz, an overflow of vitality and inventiveness. He is one of the major prophets of the Romantic era.

Listening Guide 21

2B/4

BERLIOZ: *Symphonie fantastique*

Date: 1830

Genre: Program symphony, 5 movements

Program: A lovesick artist in an opium trance is haunted by a vision of his beloved, which becomes an *idée fixe* (fixed idea).

I. "Reveries, Passions"
Largo, Allegro agitato e appassionato assai (lively, agitated, and very impassioned). Introduces the main theme, the fixed idea

II. "A Ball"
Valse Allegro non troppo (Waltz, not too fast), triple meter dance, **A-B-A** form

III. "Scene in the Fields"
Adagio, in 6/8 meter, **A-B-A** form

IV. "March to the Scaffold"
Allegretto non troppo
Duple meter march in minor mode

V. "Dream of a Witches' Sabbath"

Time	Description
7 0:00	Larghetto—very soft muted strings evoke infernal atmosphere; chromatic scales in strings, low brass, and high woodwinds evoke "unearthly sounds, groans, shrieks of laughter"
8 1:36	Allegro—fixed idea in high clarinet in transformed version with trills and grace notes ("a vulgar tune, trivial and grotesque")
2:46	Dance tune forecast by its opening motive in strings
3:08	Bells chime ("Bells toll for the dead")
9 3:34	Chant tune *Dies irae* sounded in tubas and bassoons, first slow, then twice as fast in the brass
4:05	"Burlesque of the *Dies irae*" in strings and woodwinds in irregular rhythm
10 5:25	"Dance of the Witches" ("Ronde du Sabbat")— begins in low strings with driving rhythm; contrapuntal fabric as tune is passed to other instruments
11 8:12	"The dance and the *Dies irae* combined"

a tune not new

44

The Rise of Musical Nationalism

*"I grew up in a quiet spot and was saturated from earliest childhood
with the wonderful beauty of Russian popular song. I am therefore
passionately devoted to every expression of the Russian spirit. In short,
I am a Russian through and through!"*—PETER ILYICH TCHAIKOVSKY

In nineteenth-century Europe, political conditions encouraged the growth
of nationalism to such a degree that it became a decisive force within the

Romantic movement. National tensions on the Continent—the pride of the conquering nations and the struggle for freedom of the suppressed ones—gave rise to emotions that found an ideal expression in music.

The Romantic composers expressed their nationalism in a number of ways. Several based their music on the songs and dances of their people; a number wrote dramatic works based on folklore or the life of the peasantry; some wrote symphonic poems and operas celebrating the exploits of a national hero, a historic event, or the scenic beauty of their country. Nor were the political implications of musical nationalism lost upon the authorities. Verdi's operas had to be altered again and again to suit the Austrian censor. During World War II the Nazis forbade the playing of Bedřich Smetana's tone poem *The Moldau* in Prague and of Chopin's Polonaises in Warsaw because of the powerful symbolism residing in these works. By associating music with the love of homeland, nationalism enabled composers to give expression to the cherished aspirations of millions of people. The Romantic movement is unthinkable without it.

Schools of Musical Nationalism

National School	Representative Composer	Typical Work
Eastern European School	Bedřich Smetana (1824–84)	*My Country* (including *The Moldau*)
	Antonín Dvořák (1841–1904)	*Slavonic Dances*
	Franz Liszt (1811–86)	*Hungarian Dances*
Scandanavian School	Edvard Grieg (1843–1907)	*Peer Gynt Suite*
	Jean Sibelius (1865–1957)	*Finlandia*
Russian School (including 3 members of The Mighty Five)	Nikolai Rimsky-Korsakov (1844–1908)	*Prince Igor*
	Modest Musorgsky (1839–81)	*Pictures at an Exhibition*
	Alexander Borodin (1833–87)	*From the Steppes of Central Asia*
	Peter Ilyich Tchaikovsky (1840–93)	*1812 Overture*
English School	Frederick Delius (1862–1934)	*A Village Romeo and Juliet*
	Sir Edward Elgar (1857–1934)	*Pomp and Circumstance*
Spanish School	Isaac Albéniz (1860–1909)	*Suite Iberia*
	Manuel de Falla (1876–1946)	*The Three-Cornered Hat*

A Czech Nationalist: Bedřich Smetana

"I try to write only as I feel in myself."

The Czech national school of composers was founded by Bedřich Smetana (1845–84). As in the case of several nationalist composers, Smetana's career unfolded against a background of political agitation. Bohemia stirred restlessly under Austrian rule, caught up in a surge of nationalist fervor that culminated in the uprisings of 1848. Young Smetana aligned himself with the patriotic cause. After the revolution was crushed, the atmosphere in Prague was oppressive for those suspected of sympathy with the nationalists. In 1856 Smetana accepted a post as conductor in Sweden.

On his return to Bohemia five years later, he resumed his career as a national artist and worked for the establishment of a theater in Prague where the performances would be given in the native tongue. Of his eight operas on patriotic themes, several are still performed today. One—*The Bartered Bride*—attained worldwide fame. Hardly less important in the establishing of Smetana's reputation was the cycle of six symphonic poems entitled *My Country*, which occupied him from 1874 to 1879. These works are steeped in the beauty of Bohemia's countryside, the rhythm of her folksongs and dances, the pomp and pageantry of her legends. Best known of the series is the second, *The Moldau*, Smetana's finest achievement in the field of orchestral music.

Bedřich Smetana

Smetana: The Moldau

In this tone poem the famous river becomes a poetic symbol of the beloved homeland. (For the text of Smetana's program, see Listening Guide 22.) The music suggests the rippling streams that flow through the Bohemian forest to form the mighty river. A hunting scene is evoked by French horns and trumpets, and a peasant wedding in the lilting measures of a folk dance. The mood changes to one of enchantment as nymphs emerge from their fairy-tale haunts to hold their nightly revels. Finally, as the Moldau approaches Prague, it flows past castles and fortresses that remind the poet of his country's vanished glory.

Principal Works

8 operas, including *The Bartered Bride* (1866)

Orchestral music, including *Má vlast* (My Country), cycle of 6 symphonic poems (No. 2 is *The Moldau* or *Vltava*, 1874)

Chamber and keyboard works; choral music and songs

The Moldau flows in majestic peace through Prague.

Listening Guide 22

2B/5

SMETANA: *The Moldau*

Date: 1874

Genre: Symphonic poem, from cycle *Má vlast*

Tempo: Allegro commodo non agitato (fast not agitated)

Program: Scenes along the river Moldau in Bohemia

Smetana's program: "Two springs pour forth in the shade of the Bohemian forest, one warm and gushing, the other cold and peaceful. Coming through Bohemia's valleys, it grows into a mighty stream. Through the thick woods it flows as the gay sounds of the hunt and the notes of the hunter's horn are heard ever closer. It flows through grass-grown pastures and lowlands where a wedding feast is being celebrated with song and dance. At night, wood and water nymphs revel in its sparkling waves. Reflected on its surface are fortresses and castles—witnesses of bygone days of knightly splendor and the vanished glory of martial times. The Moldau swirls through the St. John Rapids, finally flowing on in majestic peace toward Prague and welcomed by historic Vysehrad. Then it vanishes far beyond the poet's gaze."

Time	Program	Description
1 0:00	Source of river, two springs	Rippling figures in flute, then added clarinets; plucked string accompaniment
	Stream broadens	Rippling figure moves to low strings
2 1:03	River theme	Stepwise melody in violins, minor mode, rippling in low strings. Repeated

Allegro commodo non agitato

p dolce   < *sf* > *p*   < *dim.*   < > >

3	2:48	Hunting scene	Fanfare in French horns and trumpets. Rippling continues (in strings). Dies down to gently rocking motion

4	3:39	Peasant dance	Repeated notes in strings lead to rustic folk tune, staccato in strings and woodwinds. Closes with repeated single note in strings

5	5:15	Nymphs in moonlight	Mysterious, long notes in double reeds. Rippling figures in flutes; muted string theme with harp, punctuated by French horn. Brass crescendo, fanfare

6	7:59	River theme	Like beginning, strings in minor, then shift to major (raised third scale step)

7	8:50	St. John's Rapids	Brass and woodwinds exchange an agitated dialogue, build to climax, die out

	10:03	River theme	Full orchestra, loudest statement

8	10:32	Ancient castle (near river mouth)	Brass hymnlike tune, slow, then accelerates

	11:24	River dies away	Strings slow down, loose momentum. Two forceful closing chords

Absolute Forms

45
The Romantic Symphony

"A great symphony is a man-made Mississippi down which we irresistibly flow from the instant of our leave-taking to a long foreseen destination."—AARON COPLAND

We saw that during the Classical period the symphony established itself as the most exalted form of absolute orchestral music. The three Viennese masters—Haydn, Mozart, and Beethoven—carried it to its highest level of significance and formal beauty. They bequeathed to the composers of the Romantic era a flexible art form that could be brought into harmony with the emotional needs of the new age.

In the course of its development the symphony steadily gained greater weight and importance. By now music had moved from palace to public concert hall, and the orchestra had very much increased in size, as had the symphony. The nineteenth-century symphonists were not as prolific as their forbears had been. The Romantic masters—Mendelssohn, Schumann, Brahms, and Tchaikovsky—each wrote fewer than seven symphonies. All of these were in the domain of absolute music, while Liszt and Berlioz cultivated the program symphony.

The Nature of the Symphony

We know well the standard four-movement symphony form that was the legacy of the Classical masters. In the hands of Romantic composers, the symphony takes on new proportions. The number and tempo scheme of the movements is not religiously followed; Tchaikovsky, for example, closes his Sixth Symphony, the *Pathétique*, with a long and expressive slow movement and Beethoven pushed the cycle to five movements in his Sixth Symphony, the *Pastoral*.

First movements generally retain the basic elements of sonata-allegro form. *First movement*
The most dramatic movement of the Romantic cycle, the first, might draw
out the slow introduction and oftens features a long and expressive Development section that ventures into distant keys and transforms themes
into something the ear hears as entirely new.

The second movement of the Romantic symphony may retain its slow *Second movement*
and lyrical nature; the range of moods presented, however, spans the emotional spectrum from whimsical and playful to tragic and passionate. This
movement is frequently in a loose three-part form, but may also fall into
the theme and variations mold.

Third in the cycle is the strongly rhythmic and impetuous scherzo, with *Third movement*
overtones of humor, surprise, whimsy, or folk dance. In mood it may be
anything from elfin lightness to demonic energy. The tempo marking—
generally Allegro, Allegro molto, or Vivace—indicates a lively pace. Scherzo
form generally follows the **A-B-A** structure of the minuet and trio. In some
symphonies, such as Beethoven's Ninth, the scherzo comes second in the
cycle.

The fourth and last member of the Romantic symphony cycle is of a *Fourth movement*
dimension and character designed to balance the first movement. The work
may draw to a close on a note of triumph or pathos. Frequently, this movement is a spirited Allegro in sonata-allegro form. We shall see, however, that
some composers experimented with fourth movement forms. Brahms's
Fourth Symphony, for example, turns to the noble Baroque passacaglia (a
work based on a melodic or harmonic ostinato) for its closing movement.

Mendelssohn's *Italian* (1833): An Early Romantic Symphony

I. First movement Exposition	Allegro vivace, sonata form, 6/8 meter, A major Theme 1—dancelike, energetic theme in A major Theme 2—lyrical, gracious melody in woodwinds Codetta or Closing theme, based on Theme 1
Development	Expansion of Theme 1; introduction of new motive, then ex- panded; combination of Theme 1 and new motive; crescendo leads to Recapitulation
Recapitulation	(Abridged) Theme 1, in tonic key (A major) Theme 2, in tonic key (A major)
Coda	Più animato poco a poco (more animated, little by little)
II. Second movement	Andante con moto, modified sonata-allegro form, 4/4 meter, D minor. Lyrical, elegiac mood
III. Third movement	Con moto moderato, Scherzo and Trio, 3/4 meter, A major. Quick triple meter, dance movement
IV. Fourth movement	Saltarello, Presto, 4/4 meter, A minor. Light, dancelike themes based on two popular Italian dances, the *saltarello* and the *tar- antella*

The nineteenth-century symphony occupies a place of honor in the output of the Romantic era. It retains its hold on the public, and remains one of the striking manifestations of the spirit of musical Romanticism.

A Typical Early Romantic Symphony

Felix Mendelssohn   Felix Mendelssohn (1809–47) stands out among the early Romantic symphonists. As one dedicated to the preservation of Classical forms in an age that was turning from them, Mendelssohn was not untouched by Romanticism. Of his four symphonies the best known is the Fourth, the *Italian*, which dates from the "grand tour" that the young Mendelssohn undertook in the course of which he visited England, Scotland, Italy, and France. He recorded some of his impressions in one of his most widely loved works.

46

The Romantic Concerto

"We are so made that we can derive intense enjoyment only from a contrast."—SIGMUND FREUD

The Nature of the Concerto

The Romantic concerto is, in its dimensions, comparable to the symphony. Retaining its three-movement structure, the Romantic cycle presents a dramatic Allegro, usually in sonata form, followed by a lyrical slow movement and a vigorous finale.

Double exposition   The elaborate structure of the Classical double exposition is treated with more freedom by Romantic composers. The solo instrument may not wait for an orchestral exposition to make its first statement, and the cadenza, normally played at the close of the Recapitulation and before the Coda, may occur earlier as a part of the Development.

Second movements continue to deliver lyrical melodies, often in a loosely structured three-part form. The brilliant finales of the Romantic concerto bring the dramatic tension between soloist and orchestra, analogous to that between protagonist and chorus in Greek tragedy, to a head. The soloist is often featured again in a flashy cadenza that closes the concerto cycle.

Virtuosity in the Nineteenth Century

The roots of the Romantic concerto stretched back to the late eighteenth century. Mozart and Beethoven, both formidable pianists, performed their concertos in public; these works delighted and dazzled their audiences. The

In this contemporary woodcut from the 1870s, the noted virtuoso Hans von Bülow is seen performing a piano concerto with orchestra in New York City.

concerto thus had to be a "grateful" vehicle that enabled performing artists to exhibit their gifts as well as the capacities of the instrument. This element of technical display, combined with appealing melodies, has helped to make the concerto one of the most widely appreciated types of concert music.

As the concert industry developed, ever greater emphasis was placed upon the virtuoso soloist. Technical brilliance became a more and more important element of concerto style. Nineteenth-century performers carried virtuosity to new heights. This development kept pace with the increase in the size and resources of the symphony orchestra. The Romantic concerto took shape as one of the most favored genres of the age. Mendelssohn, Chopin, Liszt, Schumann, Brahms, and Tchaikovsky all contributed to its literature. Their concertos continue to delight audiences all over the world, alongside those of Haydn, Mozart, and Beethoven.

Among the most important nineteenth-century virtuosi were the sensational violinist Nicolo Paganini (1782–1840) and the great pianist and showman Franz Liszt (1811–86). An actor to his fingertips, Liszt possessed the personal magnetism of which legends are made. Instead of sitting with his back to the audience or facing it, as had been the custom hiterto, he introduced the more effective arrangement that prevails today, displaying his handsome profile to best advantage. His music was as impassioned as his playing. Liszt was one of the creators of modern piano technique. Fascinated with the instrument's capabilities, he was drawn, like Chopin, to the étude or study piece. Typical is his étude, *Wilde Jagd* (Wild Hunt; 1838, revised 1851), which shows off his reckless virtuosity.

Franz Liszt

47

Robert Schumann
and the Romantic Concerto

"Music is to me the perfect expression of the soul."

The turbulence of German Romanticism, its fantasy and subjective emotion, found their voice in Robert Schumann. His music is German to the core, yet he is no local figure. He rose above the national to make his contribution to world culture.

Robert Schumann: His Life and Music

Robert Schumann

Schumann (1810–56) was born in Zwickau, a town in northwestern Germany, son of a bookseller whose love of literature was reflected in the boy. At his mother's insistence he undertook the study of law, first at the University of Leipzig, then at Heidelberg. The youth daydreamed at the piano, steeped himself in Goethe and Byron, and attended an occasional lecture. His aversion to the law kept pace with his passion for music; it was his ambition to become a pianist. At last he won his mother's consent and returned to Leipzig to study with Friedrich Wieck, one of the foremost pedagogues of the day.

The young man practiced intensively to make up for his late start. Sadly, physical difficulties with the fingers of his right hand ended his hopes as a pianist. He then turned his interest to composing, and in a burst of creative energy produced, while still in his twenties, his most important works for piano.

He was engaged concurrently in an important literary venture. With a group of like-minded enthusiasts he founded the journal *Die Neue Zeitschrift für Musik* (The New Journal for Music). Under his direction the periodical became one of the most important music journals in Europe.

The hectic quality of this decade was intensified by his courtship of the gifted pianist and composer Clara Wieck (See Chapter 41). The marriage took place in 1840, when Clara was twenty-one and Robert thirty. This was his "year of song," when he produced over a hundred of the Lieder that represent his lyric gift at its purest.

The two artists settled in Leipzig, pursuing their careers side by side. Yet neither her love nor that of their children could ward off his increasing withdrawal from the world. In 1850 Schumann was appointed music director at Düsseldorf. But he was ill-suited for public life and was forced to relinquish the post. He fell prey to auditory hallucinations. Once he rose in the middle of the night to write down a theme that he imagined had been brought him by the spirits of Schubert and Mendelssohn. It was his last melody. A week later, in a fit of melancholia, he threw himself into the Rhine River. He was rescued by fishermen and placed in a private asylum near Bonn. He died two years later at the age of forty-six.

Principal Works

More than 300 Lieder, including song cycles *Frauenliebe und Leben* (A Woman's Love and Life, 1840) and *Dichterliebe* (A Poet's Love, 1840)

Orchestral music, including 4 symphonies and 1 piano concerto (A minor, 1841–45)

Chamber music, including 3 string quartets, 1 piano quintet, 1 piano quartet; piano trios; sonatas

Piano music including 3 sonatas; numerous miniatures and collections including *Papillons* (Butterflies, 1831), *Carnaval* (1835), and *Kinderszenen* (Scenes from Childhood, 1838); large works including *Symphonic Etudes* (1835–37), and Fantasy in C (1836–38)

1 opera; incidental music

Choral music

In the emotional exuberance, fantasy, and whimsy of his music Schumann is the true Romantic. His piano pieces brim over with impassioned melody, novel changes of harmony, and vigorous rhythms. As a composer of Lieder he ranks second only to Schubert. His favorite theme is love, particularly from a woman's point of view. Notable are several song cycles, the best known of which are *Dichterliebe* on poems of Heine, and *Frauenliebe und Leben* on poems of Chamisso.

Thoroughly Romantic in feeling are the four symphonies. These works, especially the first and fourth, communicate a lyric freshness that has kept them alive. Typical of the essence of German Romanticism is the opening of the *Spring Symphony*, his first. "Could you infuse into the orchestra," he wrote the conductor, "a kind of longing for spring? At the entrance of the trumpets I should like them to sound as from on high, like a call to awakening."

Schumann: Piano Concerto in A minor

In 1841 Schumann composed a *Phantasie for Piano and Orchestra* which ultimately became the first movement of his celebrated Piano Concerto. He added the second and third movements in 1845.

The first movement, a spacious Allegro affetuoso (fast and with feeling) opens with a brief but dramatic Introduction, followed by the main theme, a haunting melody of great tenderness and an inward quality typical of Schumann. The second theme of the movement is not a new idea at all, but an imaginative transformation of the first theme. A Development section features some interesting transformations of the theme, which lead to the Recapitulation. The cadenza, Schumann's own, is both emotional and introspective. This Allegro achieves a nice balance between lyrical and virtuoso elements.

Listening Guide 23

SCHUMANN: Piano Concerto in A minor

Date: 1841/45

Movements: 3

I. First movement: Allegro affettuoso, 4/4 meter, A minor

EXPOSITION

2	0:00	Orchestral introduction: Fast
		Theme 1—lyrical melody, in minor
	0:04	Orchestral statement (oboe)
3	0:24	Solo piano statement

4		Theme 2—derived from first theme, marked Animato (animated)
	2:00	Solo piano introduces theme
	2:25	Orchestra (clarinet)—in animated statement
		Closing—triumphal orchestral statement

DEVELOPMENT

| 5 | 4:20 | Marked Andante espressivo. Features dialogue between piano and clarinet. Modulates, returns to A minor for Recapitulation |

RECAPITULATION

6	7:17	Theme 1—orchestra (oboe), in A minor; solo piano
7	9:12	Theme 2—solo piano orchestra (clarinet)
8	11:20	CADENZA: Solo piano, unaccompanied, in improvised style
9	13:06	CODA: Marked Allegro molto Marchlike melody, based on Theme 1

II. Second movement: Intermezzo (Interlude), Andantino grazioso. Ternary (A-B-A) form, 2/4 meter, in F major

III. Third movement: Allegro vivace. Sonata form, triple meter, A major

Second is an Intermezzo (Interlude) marked Andantino grazioso (a little faster than Andante, with grace), an intimate dialogue between piano and strings whose main idea is derived from a motive of the opening theme of the first movement. The finale is an Allegro vivace (fast and lively) in 6/8 time, which creates a sense of vigorous movement that conjures up the outdoors.

In this concerto Schumann achieved the perfect fusion of dramatic and lyric elements. The work is universally regarded as his masterpiece.

UNIT XX

■

Choral and Dramatic Music in the Nineteenth Century

48

The Nature of Romantic Choral Music

"In a sense no one is ignorant of the material from which choral music springs. For this material is, in large measure, the epitomized thought, feeling, aspiration of a community rather than an individual."—PERCY M. YOUNG: *THE CHORAL TRADITION*

The nineteenth century, we found, witnessed a broadening of the democratic ideal and an enormous expansion of the musical public. This climate was uniquely favorable to choral music, which flowered as an enjoyable group activity involving increasing numbers of music lovers. As a result, choral music came to play an important part in the musical life of the Romantic era.

Singing in a chorus required less skill than playing in an orchestra. It attracted many music lovers who had never learned to play an instrument, or who could not afford to buy one. With a modest amount of rehearsal (and a modest amount of voice), they could learn to take part in the performance of great choral works. The music they sang, being allied to words, was somewhat easier to understand than absolute music, both for the performers and the listeners. The members of the chorus not only enjoyed a pleasant social evening once or twice a week but also, if their group was good enough, became a source of pride to their community.

Choral music offered the masses an ideal outlet for their artistic energies. It served to alleviate the drabness of life in the English factory towns of the

In the nineteenth century, enormous choral and orchestral forces were the order of the day. A contemporary engraving depicting the opening concert at St. Martin's Hall, London, 1850.

early Victorian period. And it had the solid support of the authorities, who felt that an interest in music would protect the lower orders from dangerous new ideas that were floating around. This aspect of the situation is amusingly illustrated in the constitution of the Huddersfield Choral Society (1836), which stipulated that "No person shall be a member of this Society who frequents the 'Hall of Science' or any of the 'Socialist Meetings,' nor shall the Librarian be allowed to lend any copies of music (knowingly) belonging to this society to any Socialist, upon pain of expulsion." England was approaching the ferment of the Chartist uprisings over social and political reforms, and one had to be careful.

The repertory centered about the great choral heritage of the past. Nevertheless, if choral music was to remain a vital force, its literature had to be enriched by new works that would reflect the spirit of the time. The list of composers active in this area includes some of the most important names of the nineteenth century: Schubert, Berlioz, Mendelssohn, Schumann, Liszt, Verdi, Brahms, Dvořák. Out of their efforts came a body of choral music that forms a delightful enclave in the output of the Romantic period.

Among the main forms of choral music in the nineteenth century were the Mass, Requiem, and oratorio. We have seen that all three forms were originally intended to be performed in church, but by the nineteenth century they had found a wider audience in the concert hall. In addition, a vast literature sprang up of secular choral pieces. These were settings for chorus of lyric poems in a variety of moods and styles. They were known, we saw,

Choral forms

Partsongs   as *partsongs*—that is, songs in three or four voice parts. Most of them were short melodious works, not too difficult for amateurs. They gave pleasure both to the singers and their listeners, and played an important role in developing the new mass audience of the nineteenth century.

It is important to remember that in choral music the text is related to the music in a different way than in solo song. The words are not as easy to grasp when a multitude of voices project them. In addition, the four groups in the chorus may be singing different words at the same time. Most important of all, music needs more time to establish a mood than words do. For these reasons the practice arose of repeating a line, a phrase, or an individual word over and over again instead of introducing new words all the time. This principle is well illustrated by the choral work discussed in the next chapter.

49

Brahms and Choral Music

"It is not hard to compose, but it is wonderfully hard to let the superfluous notes fall under the table."

An austere, high-minded musician, Johannes Brahms created an art dedicated to the purity of the Classical style. His veneration for the past and his mastery of musical architecture brought him closer to the spirit of Beethoven than any of his contemporaries.

Johannes Brahms: His Life and Music

Johannes Brahms

Brahms (1833–97) was born in Hamburg, son of a double-bass player whose love of music was greater than his attainments. His first compositions made an impression on Joseph Joachim, leading violinist of the day, who made it possible for Brahms to visit Robert and Clara Schumann at Düsseldorf. The friendship with the Schumanns opened up new horizons for him. Five months later came the tragedy of Schumann's mental collapse. With a tenderness and strength he had not suspected in himself, he tided Clara over the ordeal of Robert's illness.

Robert lingered for two years while Johannes was shaken by the great love of his life. Fourteen years his senior and the mother of seven children, Clara Schumann appeared to young Brahms as the ideal of womanly and artistic achievement. (See discussion of Clara Schumann in Chapter 41). He

Principal Works

Orchestral music, including 4 symphonies (1876, 1877, 1883, 1884–85), *Variations on a Theme by Haydn* (1873), 2 overtures (*Academic Festival*, 1880; *Tragic*, 1886), and 4 concertos (2 for piano, 1858, 1881; 1 for violin, 1878; 1 double concerto for violin and cello, 1887)

Chamber music, including string quartets, quintets, sextets; piano trios, quartets, and 1 quintet; clarinet quintet; and sonatas (violin, cello, clarinet/viola)

Piano music, including sonatas, character pieces, dances, and variation sets (on a theme by Handel, 1861; on a theme by Paganini, 1862–3)

Choral music, including *A German Requiem* (1868), *Alto Rhapsody* (1869), and partsongs

Lieder, including *Four Serious Songs* (1896) and folksong arrangements

was torn by feelings of guilt, for he loved and revered Robert Schumann, his friend and benefactor. He thought of suicide and spoke of himself, as one may at twenty-two, as "a man for whom nothing is left."

This conflict was resolved the following year by Schumann's death, but another conflict took its place. Now that Clara was no longer the unattainable ideal, Brahms was faced with the choice between love and freedom. His ardor subsided into a lifelong friendship. Two decades later he could still write her, "I love you more than myself and more than anybody and anything on earth."

Ultimately, he settled in Vienna, which remained the center of his activities for the next thirty-five years. In the stronghold of the Classical masters he found a favorable soil for his art, his northern seriousness refined by the grace and congeniality of the South. The time was ripe for him. His fame filled the world and he became the acknowledged heir of the Viennese masters.

Just as in early manhood his mother's death had impelled him to complete *A German Requiem*, so the final illness of Clara Schumann in 1896 gave rise to the *Four Serious Songs*. Her death profoundly affected the composer, already ill with cancer. He died ten months later, at the age of sixty-four.

Brahms was a traditionalist whose aim was to show that new and important things could still be said in the language of the Classical masters. His four symphonies are unsurpassed in the late Romantic period for breadth of conception and design, while in the two piano concertos and the violin concerto, the solo instrument is integrated into a full-scale symphonic structure.

In greater degree than any of his contemporaries Brahms captured the tone of intimate communion that is the essence of chamber-music style. As a song writer Brahms stands in the direct line of succession to Schubert and

Schumann. We will study his finest choral work, *A German Requiem*, written to texts from the Bible he selected himself. A song of acceptance of death, this work more than any other spread his fame during his lifetime.

Brahms: A German Requiem

A German Requiem was rooted in the Protestant tradition into which Brahms was born. Its aim was to console the living and lead them to a serene acceptance of death as an inevitable part of life. Hence its gentle lyricism. Brahms chose his text from the Old as well as New Testament, from the Psalms, Proverbs, Isaiah, and Ecclesiastes as well as from Paul, Matthew, Peter, John, and Revelation. He was not a religious man in the conventional sense, nor was he affiliated with any particular church; significantly, Christ's name is never mentioned. He was impelled to compose his requiem by the death, first of his benefactor and friend Robert Schumann, then of his mother, whom he idolized; but the piece transcends the personal and endures as a song of mourning for all mankind.

Written for soloists, four-part chorus, and orchestra, *A German Requiem* is in seven movements arranged in a formation resembling an arch. There are connections between the first and last movements, between the second and sixth, and between the third and fifth; this leaves the fourth movement, the widely sung chorus "How Lovely Is Thy Dwelling Place," as the centerpiece of the arch.

Based on a verse from Psalm 84, "How Lovely Is Thy Dwelling Place," is in **A-B-A-C-A** form. That is, the first two lines of the Psalm are heard three times, separated by the two contrasting sections that present the other lines. The first two sections for the most part move at a slow pace, but the third section (**C**) moves more quickly in a vigorous rhythm, as befits the line "that praise Thee evermore," with much expansion on "evermore." With the final reappearance of the **A** section the slower rhythm returns. Marked piano and dolce (soft, sweet), this passage serves as a coda that brings the piece to its gentle close.

Listening Guide 24   🖭 3A/3

BRAHMS: *A German Requiem*

Date: 1868

Genre: Requiem, for Protestant church

Medium: 4-part chorus, soloists, and orchestra

Movements: 7

Language: German

10 **Fourth movement: Mässig bewegt**

Text: Psalm 84

Form: Rondo (**A-B-A-C-A**)

Character: Lilting triple meter, marked Dolce (sweetly)

Opening melody: clarinets and flutes
begin in inversion of beginning phrase in
chorus:

Form	Text	Translation	Description
A	Wie lieblich sind deine Wohnungen Herr Zebaoth!	How lovely is Thy dwelling place, O Lord of hosts!	flowing arch-shaped melody; sopranos begin; homophonic texture
B	Meine Seele verlanget und sehnet sich nach den Vorhöfen des Herrn: sein Lieb und Seele freuen sich in dem lebendigen Gott.	My soul longs and even faints for the courts of the Lord; my flesh and soul rejoice in the living God.	builds up through word repetition to "sehnet"; climax on "lebendigen"
A	Wie lieblich . . .	How lovely . . .	
C	Wohl denen, die in deinem Hause wohnen, die loben dich immerdar!	Blessed are they that live in Thy house, that praise Thee evermore!	martial quality; faster note movement in strings; more vitality
A	Wie lieblich . . .	How lovely . . .	coda-like; soft, gentle closing

50

Romantic Opera

"It is better to invent reality than to copy it." —GIUSEPPE VERDI

For well over three hundred years the opera has been one of the most alluring forms of musical entertainment. A special glamour is attached to everything connected with it—its arias, singers, and roles, not to mention its opening nights.

At first glance opera would seem to make impossible demands on the credulity of the spectator. It presents us with human beings caught up in dramatic situations, who sing to each other instead of speaking. The reasonable question is (and it was asked most pointedly throughout the history of opera by literary men): how can an art form based on so unnatural a procedure be convincing? The question ignores what must always remain

Some of the allure of an opera performance may be glimpsed in this photograph of the interior of the Cuvilliés Theater in Munich, one of the world's most beautiful opera houses, during a performance of Wagner's Das Rheingold.

the fundamental aspiration of art: not to copy nature but to heighten our awareness of it.

True enough, people in real life do not sing to each other. Neither do they converse in blank verse, as Shakespeare's characters do; nor live in rooms of which one wall is conveniently missing so that the audience may look in. All the arts employ conventions that are accepted both by the artist and the audience. The conventions of opera are more in evidence than those of poetry, painting, drama, or film, but they are not different in kind. Once we have accepted the fact that the carpet can fly, how simple to believe that it can also carry the prince's luggage.

Opera functions in the domain of poetic drama. It uses the human voice to impinge upon the spectator the basic emotions—love, hate, jealousy, joy, grief—with an elemental force possible only to itself. The logic of reality gives way on the operatic stage to the logic of art, and to the power of music over the imagination.

The Development of National Styles

Opera, as one of the most important and best loved musical genres of the nineteenth century, fostered different national styles in the three leading countries of musical Europe—France, Germany, and Italy.

France

Grand opera

Paris was the opera center of all Europe in the late eighteenth and early nineteenth centuries. Nourished by the propagandist purposes of France's new leaders, *grand opera* rose to the fore. Focusing on serious, historical themes, this new genre suited the bourgeoisie's taste for the big and the spectacular very well. Fitted out with huge choruses, crowd scenes, elaborate dance episodes, ornate costumes and scenery, grand opera was as much a spectacle as a musical event. Giacomo Meyerbeer (1791–1864), a German composer who studied in Italy, was primarily responsible for bringing grand opera to Paris. His best-known works in the style are *Robert le diable* (Robert the Devil, 1831) and *Les Huguenots* (1836), both of which reveal scrupulous attention to the drama as a whole—a blend of social statement, history, and spectacle with memorable melodies and intricate orchestration. Less pretentious than French grand opera was *opéra comique*, which required smaller performance forces, was written in a simpler style, and featured spoken dialogue rather than recitatives. One of the lighter works that delighted Parisian audiences was Jacques Offenbach's (1819–80) *Orphée aux enfers* (Orpheus in the Underworld, 1858), which blended wit and satire into the popular model. These two genres merged—the spectacle of grand opera and the simplicity of opéra comique—to produce *lyric opera*. This hybrid featured appealing melodies and romantic drama, and found its greatest proponent in Georges Bizet (1838–75), whose *Carmen* is one of the masterpieces of the French lyric stage.

Opéra comique

Lyric opera

Nineteenth-century Germany did not have the long-established opera tradition of France and Italy. The immediate predecessor of Romantic German opera was *Singspiel*, a light or comic drama with spoken dialogue. The first spokesman for the German Romantic spirit in opera was Carl Maria von Weber (1786–1826), whose best-known work is *Der Freischütz* (1821). Supernatural beings and mysterious forces of nature intertwined with the fate of heros and heroines to produce drama featuring simple and direct melodies, almost folklike, accompanied by expressive timbres and harmonies. The greatest figure in German opera—and one of the most significant in the history of the Romantic era—was Richard Wagner, who created the music drama, a genre that integrated theater and music completely.

Germany

Italy, in the early nineteenth century, still recognized the opposing styles of *opera seria* (serious opera) and *opera buffa* (the Italian version of comic opera) that were legacies of an earlier period. Important exponents of these styles include Gioacchino Rossini (1792–1868), whose masterpiece was *Il Barbiere di Siviglia* (The Barber of Seville, 1816), Gaetano Donizetti (1797–1848), composer of some seventy operas including *Lucia di Lammermoor* (1835), and Vincenzo Bellini (1801–35), whose *Norma* (1831) is in the more serious style of the time. These operas were all written in the *bel canto* (literally, beautiful singing) style, characterized by florid melodic lines, and delivered by voices of great agility and purity of tone. The consummate master of the bel canto style was Giuseppe Verdi, who sought to develop a uniquely national Italian operatic style.

Italy

Bel canto style

51

Verdi and Italian Opera

"Success is impossible for me if I cannot write as my heart dictates!"

Giuseppe Verdi

In the case of Giuseppe Verdi (1813–1901), the most widely loved of operatic composers, time, place, and personality were happily met. He inherited a rich musical tradition, his capacity for growth was matched by masterful energy and will, and he was granted a long span of life in which his gifts attained their full flower.

Giuseppe Verdi: His Life and Music

Born in a hamlet in northern Italy where his father kept a little inn, Verdi grew up amid the poverty of village life. His talent attracted the attention of a prosperous merchant in the neighboring town of Busseto, a music lover who made it possible for the youth to pursue his studies. After two years in Milan he returned to Busseto to fill a post as organist. When he fell in love with his benefactor's daughter, the merchant in wholly untraditional fashion accepted the penniless young musician as his son-in-law. Verdi was twenty-three, Margherita sixteen.

Three years later he returned to the conquest of Milan with the manuscript of an opera, which was produced at La Scala in 1839 with fair success. The work brought him a commission to write others. Shortly after, Verdi faced the first crisis of his career. He had lost his first child, a daughter, before coming to Milan. The second, a baby boy, was carried off by fever, a catastrophe followed several weeks later by the death of his young wife. "In a sudden moment of despondency I despaired of finding any comfort in my art and resolved to give up composing."

The months passed; the distraught young composer adhered to his decision. One night he happened to meet the impresario of La Scala, who forced him to take home the libretto of *Nabucco* (Nebuchadnezzar, King of Babylon). With this work the musician was restored to his art. *Nabucco*, presented at La Scala in 1842, was a triumph for the twenty-nine-year-old composer and launched him on a spectacular career.

Italy at this time was in the process of birth as a nation. The patriotic party aimed at liberation from the Hapsburg yoke and the establishment of a united kingdom under the House of Savoy. Verdi from the beginning identified himself with the national cause. "I am first of all an Italian!" In this charged atmosphere his works took on special meaning for his countrymen. No matter in what time or place the opera was laid, they interpreted it as an allegory of their plight. The chorus of exiled Jews from *Nabucco*, "Va pensiero,' 'became a patriotic song, which still endures today.

Although he was now a world-renowned figure, Verdi retained the simplicity that was at the core both of the artist and man. The outer activities of this upright man framed an inner life of extraordinary richness. It was

Principal Works

28 operas, including *Macbeth* (1847), *Rigoletto* (1851), *Il trovatore* (The Troubadour, 1853), *La traviata* (The Lost One, 1853), *Un ballo in maschera* (A Masked Ball, 1859), *La forza del destino* (The Force of Destiny, 1862), *Don Carlos* (1867), *Aïda* (1871), *Otello* (1887), *Falstaff* (1893)

Vocal music, including a Requiem Mass (1874)

Chamber music, including 1 string quartet and piano works

this that enabled him to move with unflagging creativity from one master-piece to the next. He was fifty-seven when he wrote *Aïda*. At seventy-three he completed *Otello*, his greatest lyric tragedy. In 1893, on the threshold of eighty, he astonished the world with *Falstaff*.

True Italian that he was, Verdi based his art on melody, which to him was the most immediate expression of human feeling. "Art without spon-taneity, naturalness, and simplicity," he maintained, "is no art."

Of his first fifteen operas the most important are *Rigoletto*, based on Victor Hugo's drama *Le Roi s'amuse* (The King Is Amused); *Il trovatore*, derived from a fanciful Spanish play; and *La traviata*, which we will discuss. The operas of the middle period are on a more ambitious scale, showing Verdi's attempt to assimilate elements of the French grand opera. The three most important are *Un ballo in maschera, La forza del destino,* and *Don Carlos.* Verdi's artistic aims came to fruition in *Aïda*, the work that ushers in his final period (1870–93). In 1874 came the Requiem, in memory of Alessandro Manzoni, the novelist and patriot whom Verdi revered as a national artist.

Verdi found his ideal librettist in Arrigo Boito (1842–1918). For their first collaboration they turned to Shakespeare's *Otello*, the apex of three hundred years of Italian lyric tragedy. After its opening night the seventy-four-year-old composer declared, "I feel as if I had fired my last cartridge. Music needs youthfulness of the senses, impetuous blood, fullness of life." He disproved his words when six years later, again with Boito, he completed *Falstaff* in 1893, a fitting crown to the labors of a lifetime.

Verdi: La traviata

La dame aux camélias—The Lady of the Camellias—by the younger Al-exandre Dumas, was a revolutionary play in its time, for it contrasted the noble character of a courtesan—a so-called fallen woman—with the rigidly bourgeois code of morals that ends by destroying her. With a libretto by Francesco Piave based on Dumas' play, the opera—under the title of *La traviata* (The Lost One)—quickly won a worldwide audience.

The heroine is Violetta Valéry, one of the reigning beauties of Paris, who already is suffering from the first ravages of consumption when Alfredo Germont, a young man of good Provençal family, falls in love with her. They go off to a country villa; but their idyllic existence is interrupted by Alfredo's

Act II, Scene 2 in the Opera Theatre of Saint Louis production of La traviata *with Sheri Greenawald as Violetta and Jon Frederic West as Alfredo.* (Photo by Ken Howard)

father, a dignified gentleman who appeals to Violetta not to lead his son to ruin and disgrace the family name. Violetta makes the agonizing decision to leave Alfredo and returns to Baron Douphol, whose mistress she has been.

Unaware of his father's intervention, Alfredo breaks into a festive party at the home of Violetta's friend Flora. Mad with jealousy and rage, he accuses Violetta of having betrayed him, insults her in the presence of her friends, and is challenged to a duel by the Baron. The last act takes place in Violetta's bedroom. Violetta reads a letter from the elder Germont informing her that the duel has taken place. He has told his son of her great sacrifice; both are coming to ask for her forgiveness. Alfredo arrives. He is followed by his father who realizes how blind he has been and, filled with admiration for Violetta, welcomes her as his daughter. It is too late. Violetta dies in Alfredo's arms.

We hear the finale of the second act, at Flora's party. Alfredo, at the gambling table, has played for huge stakes against the Baron and won a great deal of money. When the guests go to the next room for supper, Violetta remains behind to wait for him. Their scene unfolds against a tense, repetitive rhythm in the orchestra that betrays their agitation. (See Listening Guide 25 for the Italian-English text.)

The act ends with a great ensemble in which the voices of the principal characters intermingle as each expresses his feelings. Such an ensemble depends upon an outstanding melody that will guide the ear through the intricate maze of vocal lines. Verdi's great theme soars in a broad curve that imprints itself indelibly upon the mind and—more important—the heart.

Listening Guide 25

 3A/4

VERDI: *La traviata,* Act II, Finale

First performance: 1853, Venice

Librettist: Francesco Maria Piave

Major characters: Violetta Valery, a courtesan
Alfredo Germont, Violetta's lover
Giorgio Germont, Alfredo's father
Gastone, Viscount de Letorieres
Baron Douphol, a rival of Alfredo
Flora Bervoix, friend of Violetta

Act II, scene 2: A party at Flora's house, in Paris

(returns in a state of great agitation, followed by Alfredo)

26 VIOLETTA	Invitato a qui seguirmi,	I've asked him to follow me.
	Verrà desso? Vorrà udirmi?	Will he come? Will he heed me?
	Ei verrà. Ché l'odio atroce	I think he'll come, for his terrible hatred
	Puote in lui più di mia voce . . .	Moves him more than my words . . .

Opening of Violetta's recitative

ALFREDO	Mi chiamaste? Che bramate?	You called me? What do you want?
VIOLETTA	Questi luoghi abbandonate;	You must go,
	Un periglio vi sovrasta!	You're in danger!
ALFREDO	Ah, comprendo. Basta, basta,	Ah, I see, but that's enough,
	E sì vile mi credete?	So you think I'm a coward?
VIOLETTA	Ah no, no, mai!	No, never!
ALFREDO	Ma che temete?	What are you afraid of?
VIOLETTA	Tremo sempre del barone.	The Baron frightens me.
ALFREDO	È fra noi mortal quistione.	It's a question of life and death between us.
	S'ei cadrà per mano mia,	If I kill him,
	Un sol colpo vi torria	You'll lose lover and protector
	Coll'amante il protettore.	At a single blow.
	V'atterrisce tal sciagura?	Doesn't such a fate terrify you?
VIOLETTA	Ma s'ei fosse l'uccisore!	But if he should be the killer?
	Ecco l'unica sventura	That's the only thought
	Ch'io pavento a me fatale.	That puts the fear of death into me.
ALFREDO	La mia morte! Che ven cale?	My death? What do you care about that?
VIOLETTA	Deh, partite, e sull'istante!	Please, go, go at once!
ALFREDO	Partirò, ma giura innante	I'll go if you will swear
	Che dovunque seguirai,	That wherever I go,
	Seguirai i passi miei . . .	You'll follow me . . .
VIOLETTA	Ah! No, giammai!	No, never!
ALFREDO	No! Giammai!	No, never!

VIOLETTA	Va, sciagurato!	Go, you are wicked!
	Scorda un nome ch'è infamato!	Forget a name that's without honour!
	Va, mi lascia sul momento	Go, leave me this minute.
	Di fuggirti un giuramento	I've made a solemn vow
	Sacro io feci.	To fly from you.
ALFREDO	A chi? Dillo, chi potea?	Who to? Tell me, who could make you?
VIOLETTA	A chi dritto pien n'avea.	One who had every right.
ALFREDO	Fua Douphol?	Was it Douphol?
	(*with great force*)	
VIOLETTA	Si.	Yes.
ALFREDO	Dunque l'ami?	Then you love him?
VIOLETTA	Ebben . . . l'amo . . .	Yes . . . I love him . . .
	(*running to the door and shouting*)	
ALFREDO	Or tutti a me.	Come here, all of you!
	(*The rest of the company rush in.*)	
ALL	Ne appellaste? Che volete?	You called us? What do you want?
	(*pointing to Violetta, who leans feebly against a table*)	
ALFREDO	Questa donna conoscete?	You know this lady?
ALL	Chi? Violetta?	You mean Violetta?
ALFREDO	Che facesse non sapete?	But you don't know what she's done.
VIOLETTA	Ah! taci!	Oh, don't!
ALL	No.	No.
[27] ALFREDO	Ogni suo aver tal femmina	For me this woman lost all she possessed.
	Per amor mio sperdea.	I was blind.
	Io cieco, vile, misero,	A wretched coward,
	Tutto accettar potea.	I accepted it all.
	Ma è tempo ancora!	But it's time now for me
	Tergermi da tanta macchia bramo.	To clear myself from debt.
	Qui testimon vi chiamo,	I call you all to witness here
	Che qui pagata io l'ho.	That I've paid her back!

Opening of Alfredo's solo,
expressing anger and
bitterness

(*Contemptuously, he throws his winnings at Violetta's feet. She swoons in Flora's arms. Alfredo's father arrives suddenly.*)

ALL	O, infamia orribile	What you have done is shameful!
	Tu commettesti!	So to strike down a tender heart!
	Un cor sensibile	You have insulted a woman!
	Così uccidesti!	Get out of here!
	Di donne ignobile insultatore,	We've no use for you!
	Di qua allontanati,	We've no use for such as you!
	Ne desti orror! Va!	Go!

Choral response to
Alfredo's charges against
Violetta, sung in unison,
delivered forcefully

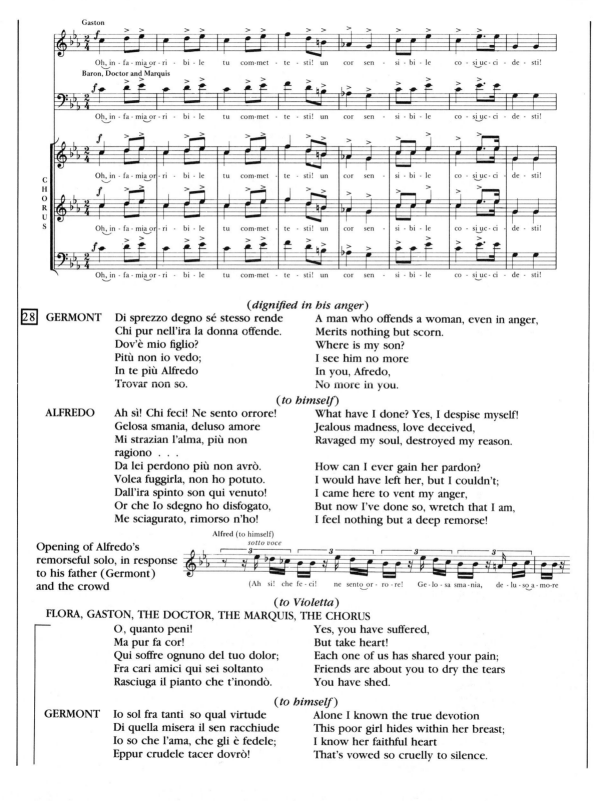

(dignified in his anger)

28	GERMONT	Di sprezzo degno sé stesso rende	A man who offends a woman, even in anger,
		Chi pur nell'ira la donna offende.	Merits nothing but scorn.
		Dov'è mio figlio?	Where is my son?
		Pitù non io vedo;	I see him no more
		In te più Alfredo	In you, Afredo,
		Trovar non so.	No more in you.

(to himself)

ALFREDO	Ah sì! Chi feci! Ne sento orrore!	What have I done? Yes, I despise myself!
	Gelosa smania, deluso amore	Jealous madness, love deceived,
	Mi strazian l'alma, più non ragiono . . .	Ravaged my soul, destroyed my reason.
	Da lei perdono più non avrò.	How can I ever gain her pardon?
	Volea fuggirla, non ho potuto.	I would have left her, but I couldn't;
	Dall'ira spinto son qui venuto!	I came here to vent my anger,
	Or che Io sdegno ho disfogato,	But now I've done so, wretch that I am,
	Me sciagurato, rimorso n'ho!	I feel nothing but a deep remorse!

Opening of Alfredo's remorseful solo, in response to his father (Germont) and the crowd

(to Violetta)

FLORA, GASTON, THE DOCTOR, THE MARQUIS, THE CHORUS

	O, quanto peni!	Yes, you have suffered,
	Ma pur fa cor!	But take heart!
	Qui soffre ognuno del tuo dolor;	Each one of us has shared your pain;
	Fra cari amici qui sei soltanto	Friends are about you to dry the tears
	Rasciuga il pianto che t'inondò.	You have shed.

(to himself)

GERMONT	Io sol fra tanti so qual virtude	Alone I known the true devotion
	Di quella misera il sen racchiude	This poor girl hides within her breast;
	Io so che l'ama, che gli è fedele;	I know her faithful heart
	Eppur crudele tacer dovrò!	That's vowed so cruelly to silence.

		(*softly to Alfredo*)	
BARON	A questa donna l'atroce insulto	Your deadly insult to this lady
	Qui tutti offese, ma non inulto	Offends us all, but such an outrage
	Fia tanto oltraggio, provar vi voglio.	Shall not go unavenged!
	Che il vostro orgoglio fiaccar saprò.	I shall find a way to humble your pride!
ALFREDO	Che feci! Ohimè!	Alas, what have I done?
	Ohimè, che feci!	What have I done?
	Ne sento orrore!	How can I ever
	Da lei perdono più non avrò.	Gain her pardon?

(*coming to herself*)

VIOLETTA	Alfredo, Alfredo, di questo core	Alfredo, how should you understand
	Non puoi comprendere tutto l'amore,	All the love that's in my heart?
	Tu non conosci che fino a prezzo	How should you known that I have proved it,
	Del tuo disprezzo provato io l'ho.	Even at the price of your contempt?
	Ma verrà tempo, in che il saprai	But the time will come when you will know,
	Come t'amassi, confesserai . . .	When you'll admit how much I loved you.
	Dio dai rimorsi ti salvi allora!	God save you then from all remorse!
	Ah! Io spenta ancora t'amerò.	Even after death I shall still love you.

(*Germont leads his son away with him; the Baron follows. Flora and the Doctor take Violetta into the other room as the rest of the company disperses.*)

Violetta's melody, vowing
her love to Alfredo

Al-fre-do, Al-fre - do,   di que-sto co - re   non puoi com-pren-de-re   tut-to l'a - mo - re,

52

Wagner and the Music Drama

"The error in the art genre of opera consists in the fact that a means of expression—music—has been made the object, while the object of expression—the drama—has been made the means."

Richard Wagner (1813–83) looms as probably the single most important phenomenon in the artistic life of the latter half of the nineteenth century. Historians, not without justice, divide the period into "Before" and "After" Wagner. The course of post-Romantic music is unthinkable without the impact of this complex and fascinating figure.

Richard Wagner: His Life and Music

Richard Wagner

Wagner was born in Leipzig, son of a minor police official who died when Richard was still an infant. The future composer was almost entirely self-taught; he had in all about six months of instruction in music theory. At twenty he abandoned his academic studies at the University of Leipzig and obtained a post as chorus master in a small opera house. His career took off when his grand opera, *Rienzi,* won a huge success in Dresden. As a result, its composer in his thirtieth year found himself appointed conductor to the King of Saxony. With his next three works, *The Flying Dutchman, Tannhäuser*, and *Lohengrin* Wagner had taken an important step from the drama of historical intrigue, which was very popular at that time, to the idealized folk legend. He chose subjects derived from medieval German epics, displayed a profound feeling for nature, employed the supernatural as an element of the drama, and glorified the German land and people. But the Dresden public was not prepared for *Tannhäuser*. They had come to see another *Rienzi* and were disappointed.

The revolution broke out in Dresden in 1849, and with it Wagner escaped to his friend Liszt at Weimar, where he learned that a warrant had been issued for his arrest. With the aid of Liszt he was spirited across the border and found refuge in Switzerland. He settled in Zurich and entered on the most productive period of his career. For four years he wrote no music, producing instead his most important literary works, *Art and Revolution, The Art Work of the Future*, and the two-volume *Opera and Drama*, which sets forth his theories of the *music drama*, as he named his type of opera. He next proceeded to put theory into practice in the cycle of four music dramas called *The Ring of the Nibelung*. When he reached the second act of *Siegfried* (the third opera in the cycle), he grew tired, "of heaping one silent score upon the other," and laid aside the gigantic task. There followed two of his finest works—*Tristan und Isolde* and *Die Meistersinger von Nürnberg*.

The Ring

The years following the completion of *Tristan* were the darkest of his life. The mighty scores accumulated in his drawer without hope of performance: Europe contained neither theater nor singers capable of presenting them. At this juncture intervened a miraculous turn of events. An eighteen-year-old boy who was a passionate admirer of his music ascended the throne of Bavaria as Ludwig II. One of the young monarch's first acts was to summon the composer to Munich, where *Tristan* and *Meistersinger* were performed at last. The King commissioned him to complete the *Ring*, and Wagner took up the second act of *Siegfried* where he had left off a number of years before. A theater was planned especially for the presentation of his music dramas, which ultimately resulted in the festival playhouse at Bayreuth. And to crown his happiness he found, to share his empire, a woman equal to him in will and courage—Cosima, the daughter of his old friend Liszt.

Bayreuth

The Wagnerian gospel spread across Europe, a new art-religion. Wagner societies throughout the world gathered funds to raise the temple at Bayreuth. The radical of 1848 found himself, after the Franco-Prussian War, the national artist of Bismarck's German Empire. The *Ring* cycle was completed in 1874, and the four dramas were presented to worshipful audiences at the first Bayreuth festival in 1876.

One task remained. To make good the financial deficit of the festival the master undertook his last work, *Parsifal* a "consecrational festival drama"

Principal Works

13 music dramas (operas), including *Rienzi* (1842), *Der fliegende Holländer* (The Flying Dutchman, 1843), *Tannhäuser* (1845), *Lohengrin* (1850), *Tristan und Isolde* (1865), *Die Meistersinger von Nürnberg* (The Mastersingers of Nuremberg, 1868), *Der Ring des Nibelungen* (The Ring of the Nibelung, 1869–76) consisting of *Das Rheingold* (The Rhine Gold, 1869), (*Die Walküre*) (The Valkyrie, 1856), *Siegfried* (1876), and *Götterdämmerung* (The Twilight of the Gods, 1876); and *Parsifal* (1882)

Orchestral music, including *Siegfried Idyll* (1870)

Piano music; vocal music; choral music

based on the legend of the Holy Grail. He finished it as he approached seventy. He died shortly after, in every sense a conqueror, and was buried at Bayreuth.

Endless melody

Wagner did away with the old "number" opera with its arias, duets, ensembles, choruses, and ballets. His aim was a continuous tissue of melody that would never allow the emotions to cool—what he called "endless melody." The focal point of Wagnerian music drama is the orchestra. He developed a type of symphonic opera as native to the German genius as vocal opera is to the Italian. The orchestra is the unifying principle of his music drama. It floods the action, the characters, and the audience in a torrent of sound that incarnates the sensuous ideal of the Romantic era.

Leitmotifs

The orchestral tissue is fashioned out of concise themes, the *leitmotifs*, or "leading motives"—Wagner called them basic themes—that recur throughout the work, undergoing variation and development even as the themes and motives of a symphony. They have an uncanny power of suggesting in a few strokes a person, an emotion, or an idea; an object—the gold, the ring, the sword; or a landscape—the Rhine, Valhalla, the lonely shore of Tristan's home.

Harmonic innovations

Wagner's musical language was based on chromatic harmony, which he pushed to its then farthermost limits. Chromatic dissonance imparts to Wagner's music its restless, intensely emotional quality. The active chord (the dominant, built on the fifth scale degree) seeking resolution in the chord of rest (the tonic, on the first scale degree) became in Wagner's hands the most romantic of symbols: the lonely man—Flying Dutchman, Lohengrin, Siegmund, Tristan—seeking redemption through the love of the ideal woman, whether Senta or Elsa, Sieglinde or Isolde.

Wagner: Die Walküre

The Ring of the Nibelung centers on the treasure of gold that lies hidden in the depths of the Rhine, guarded by three Rhine Maidens. From this treasure is fashioned the ring that confers unlimited power upon its owner.

But there is a terrible curse on the ring. It will destroy the peace of mind of all who gain possession of it, and ultimately bring them misfortune and death. Thus begins the cycle of four dramas—the Tetrology, as it is known—that ends only when the ring is returned to the Rhine Maidens. Gods and heroes, mortals and dwarfs intermingle freely in this tale of betrayed love, broken promises, magic spells, and general corruption engendered by the lust for power. Wagner freely adapted the story from the myths of the Norse sagas and the legends associated with a medieval German epic, the *Nibelungenlied*.

He wrote the four librettos in reverse order. First came his poem on the death of the hero Siegfried, which became the final opera, *Götterdämmerung*. Siegfried, now possessor of the ring, betrays Brünnhilde, to whom he has sworn his love, and is in turn betrayed by her. Next came the poem of *Siegfried* in which the forces that shaped the young hero were explained. Wagner then wrote the poem about Siegfried's parents, Siegmund and Sieglinde, the basis of *Die Walküre*. Finally, this trilogy was prefaced by *Das Rheingold*, the drama that unleashed the workings of fate and the curse of gold out of which the entire action stemmed.

First performed in Munich in 1870, *Die Walküre* revolves around the twin brother and sister who are the offspring of Wotan by a mortal. (In Norse as in Greek-Roman mythology, kings and heroes were the children of gods.) The ill-fated love of Siegmund and Sieglinde is not only incestuous but also adulterous, for she has been forced into a loveless marriage with the grim chieftain Hunding, who challenges Siegmund to battle. Wotan, father of the gods, is eager for his son to win. But Wotan's wife, Fricka, the stern goddess of marriage and the sacredness of the home, insists that Siegmund has violated the holiest law of the universe, and in the ensuing combat he must die. Although he argues with her, Wotan sadly realizes that even he must obey the law. He summons his favorite daughter, Brünnhilde, and tells her that, in the battle between Siegmund and Hunding, she must see to it that Hunding is the victor. (She is one of the Valkyries, the nine daughters of Wotan whose task it is to circle the battlefield on their winged horses, swooping down to gather up the fallen heroes, whom they bear away to Valhalla, where they will sit forever feasting with the gods. She is the one for whom the opera is named.) When Brünnhilde comes to Siegmund to reveal to him his fate, she yields to pity and decides to disobey her father. The two heroes fight, and Brünnhilde tries to shield Siegmund. At the decisive moment Wotan appears and holds out his spear, upon which Siegmund's sword is shattered. Hunding buries his sword in Siegmund's breast. Wotan, overcome by his son's death, looks ferociously at Hunding, who falls dead. Then the god rouses himself and hurries off in pursuit of the daughter who dared to defy his command.

Brünnhilde's punishment is severe. She is to be deprived of her godhood, Wotan tells her, and become a mortal woman. No more will she sit with the gods, no more bear heroes to Valhalla. He will put her to sleep on the rock and she will fall prey to the first one who finds her. Brünnhilde defends herself. In trying to protect Siegmund was she not carrying out her father's

Flames leap up around the rock, as Wotan, sung by James Morris in this Metropolitan Opera production of Die Walküre, *is silhouetted against the sky.* (Photograph courtesy Winnie Klotz)

innermost desire? She begs him to mitigate her punishment. Let him at least surround the rock with flames, so that only a fearless hero will be able to penetrate the wall of fire. Wotan relents and grants her request.

The opera ends with Wotan's Farewell and the famous Fire Scene. He kisses her on both eyes, which at once close. Then he stalks with solemn determination to the center of the stage and turns the point of his spear toward a mighty rock. Striking the rock three times, he invokes Loge, the god of fire. Flames spring up around the rock—and in the music, as the tall figure of the god in his black cloak is silhouetted against the red sky, "He who fears the point of my spear shall never step through the fire," he intones as the orchestra announces the theme of Siegfried, the fearless hero who in the next music drama will force his way through the flames and awaken Brünnhilde with a kiss. (See Listening Guide 26 for text and analysis.) The curtain falls on as poetic a version of the sleeping-beauty legend as any artist ever penned.

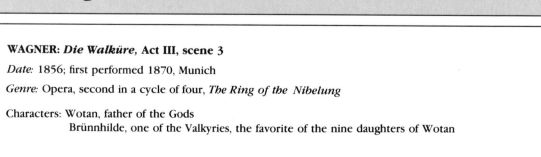

Listening Guide 26

⌨ 3B/1

WAGNER: *Die Walküre,* **Act III, scene 3**

Date: 1856; first performed 1870, Munich

Genre: Opera, second in a cycle of four, *The Ring of the Nibelung*

Characters: Wotan, father of the Gods
Brünnhilde, one of the Valkyries, the favorite of the nine daughters of Wotan

Orchestra, with "slumber" motive

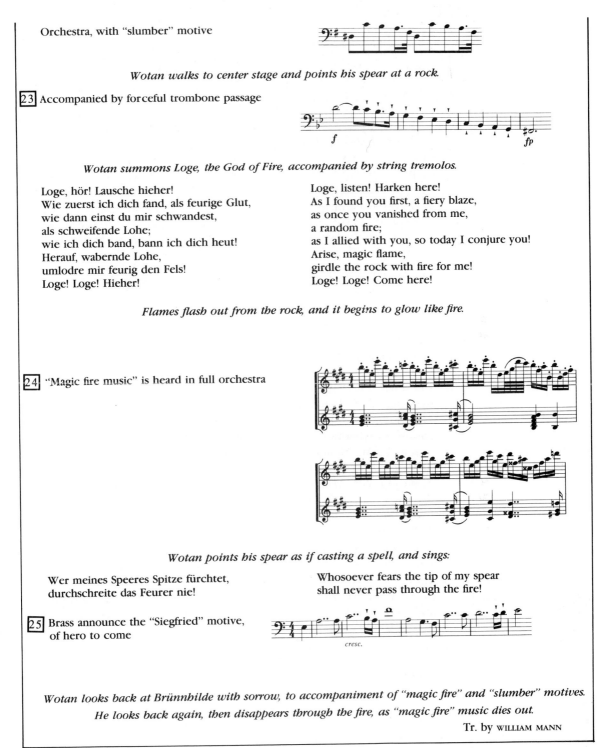

Wotan walks to center stage and points his spear at a rock.

23 Accompanied by forceful trombone passage

Wotan summons Loge, the God of Fire, accompanied by string tremolos.

Loge, hör! Lausche hieher!
Wie zuerst ich dich fand, als feurige Glut,
wie dann einst du mir schwandest,
als schweifende Lohe;
wie ich dich band, bann ich dich heut!
Herauf, wabernde Lohe,
umlodre mir feurig den Fels!
Loge! Loge! Hieher!

Loge, listen! Harken here!
As I found you first, a fiery blaze,
as once you vanished from me,
a random fire;
as I allied with you, so today I conjure you!
Arise, magic flame,
girdle the rock with fire for me!
Loge! Loge! Come here!

Flames flash out from the rock, and it begins to glow like fire.

24 "Magic fire music" is heard in full orchestra

Wotan points his spear as if casting a spell, and sings:

Wer meines Speeres Spitze fürchtet,
durchschreite das Feurer nie!

Whosoever fears the tip of my spear
shall never pass through the fire!

25 Brass announce the "Siegfried" motive,
of hero to come

Wotan looks back at Brünnhilde with sorrow, to accompaniment of "magic fire" and "slumber" motives.
He looks back again, then disappears through the fire, as "magic fire" music dies out.

Tr. by WILLIAM MANN

53

Tchaikovsky and the Ballet

Truly there would be reason to go mad were it not for music."

Ballet has been an adornment of European culture for centuries. It is the most physical of the arts depending as it does upon the leaps and turns of the human body. Out of this material it weaves an enchantment all its own. It is the combination of physical and emotional factors that marks the distinctive power of ballet. The dancer transforms the body into a work of art, and it is this transformation that the world eagerly witnesses.

Few composers typify the end-of-the-century mood as does Peter Ilyich Tchaikovsky (1840–93). None had such a natural affinity for the ballet.

Peter Ilyich Tchaikovsky: His Life and Music

Tchaikovsky was born at Votkinsk in a distant province of Russia, son of a government official. His family intended him for a career in the government. He graduated at nineteen from the aristocratic School of Jurisprudence in St. Petersburg and obtained a minor post in the Ministry of Justice. Not until he was twenty-three did he reach the decision to resign his post and enter the newly founded Conservatory of St. Petersburg. He completed the course in three years and took on a teaching post in the new Conservatory of Moscow. His twelve years there saw the production of some of his most successful works.

Extremely sensitive by nature, Tchaikovsky was subject to attacks of depression aggravated by his guilt over his homosexuality. In the hope of achieving some degree of stability, he married with a student of the Conservatory, Antonina Miliukov, who was hopelessly in love with him. His sympathy for Antonina soon turned into uncontrollable aversion, and he fled, on the verge of a serious breakdown, to his brothers in St. Petersburg.

In this desperate hour, there appeared the kind benefactress who enabled him to go abroad until he had recovered his health, freed him from the demands of a teaching post, and launched him on the most productive period of his career. Nadezhda von Meck, widow of an industrialist, was an imperious and emotional woman whose passion was music, especially Tchaikovsky's. Bound by the rigid conventions of her time and her class, she had to be certain that her enthusiasm was for the artist, not the man; hence she stipulated that she was never to meet the recipient of her bounty. For the next thirteen years Mme. von Meck made Tchaikovsky's career the focal point of her life, providing for his needs with exquisite devotion and tact.

These years saw the spread of Tchaikovsky's fame. He was the first Russian whose music appealed to Western tastes, and in 1891 he was invited to come to America to participate in the ceremonies that marked the opening

Principal Works

8 operas, including *Eugene Onegin* (1879) and *Pique Dame* (The Queen of Spades, 1890)

3 ballets: *Swan Lake* (1877), *The Sleeping Beauty* (1890), and *The Nutcracker* (1892)

Orchestral music, including 7 symphonies (No. 6, *Pathétique*, 1893); 3 piano concertos, 1 violin concerto; symphonic poems and overtures (*Romeo and Juliet*, 1870)

Chamber and keyboard music; choral music and songs

of Carnegie Hall. In 1893, immediately after finishing his Sixth Symphony, the *Pathétique*, he went to St. Petersburg to conduct it. The work met with a lukewarm reception, due in part to the fact that Tchaikovsky, painfully shy in public, conducted his music without any semblance of conviction. Some days later, although he had been warned of the prevalence of cholera in the capital, he carelessly drank a glass of unboiled water and contracted the disease. He died within the week, at the age of fifty-three. The suddenness of his death and the tragic tone of his last work led to rumors that he had committed suicide.

Tchaikovsky: The Nutcracker

Among the best loved works in the ballet literature are Tchaikovsky's three ballets—*Swan Lake, Sleeping Beauty,* and *The Nutcracker.* Although revolutionary in their rhythm and thus difficult to dance, these three works soon established themselves as basic works of the Russian repertory.

The Nutcracker was based on a fanciful story by E. T. A. Hoffmann. An expanded version by Alexandre Dumas père served as the basis for Petipa's scenario, which was offered to Tchaikovsky when he returned from his visit to the United States in 1891. Act I takes place at a Christmas party during which two children, Clara and Fritz, help decorate the tree. Their godfather arrives with gifts, among which is a nutcracker. Russian nutcrackers are often shaped like a human head or a whole person, which makes it quite logical for little Clara to dream that this one was transformed into a handsome prince who takes Clara away with him.

Act II takes place in Confiturembourg, the land of sweets, that is ruled by the Sugar Plum Fairy. The prince presents Clara to his family and a celebration follows, with a series of dances that reveal all the attractions of this magic realm.

The mood is set by the Overture, whose light, airy effect Tchaikovsky achieved by omitting most of the brass instruments. The March is played as the guests arrive for the party, and a snappy little march it is. He introduces a new instrument, the *celesta*, whose ethereal timbre perfectly suits the Sugar Plum Fairy and her veils. In the "Trepak" or "Russian Dance," the

Mikhail Baryshnikov in an American Ballet Theater production of The Nutcracker. *(© Martha Swope)*

orchestral sound is enlivened by a tambourine. Coffee dances the muted "Arab Dance," while Tea responds with the "Chinese Dance," in which bassoons set up an ostinato that bobs up and down against the shrill melody of flute and piccolo. The "Dance of the Toy Flutes" is extraordinarily graceful, which is as it should be. And the climax of the ballet comes with the "Waltz of the Flowers," which has delighted audiences for a century.

PART EIGHT

The
Twentieth Century

"The century of aeroplanes has a right to its own music. As there are no precedents, I must create anew."—CLAUDE DEBUSSY

Nicolas de Stael (*1914–55*) Le Grand concert (*The Big Concert*) (Musée Picasso, Antibes)

TRANSITION V

■

The Post-Romantic Era

"I came into a very young world in a very old time."—ERIK SATIE

The post-Romantic era, overlapping the Romantic period, extended from around 1890 to 1910. This generation of composers included radicals, conservatives, and those in between. Some continued in the traditional path; others struck out in new directions; still others tried to steer a middle course between the old and the new.

The Italian operatic tradition was carried on in the post-Romantic era by a group of composers led by Giacomo Puccini (1858–1924). His mixture of lyricism and late Romantic harmony produced some of the most loved operas of the early twentieth century, including *La bohème* (1896), *Tosca* (1900), and *Madama Butterfly* (1904). His final work, *Turandot* (1926) reflects his consummate mastery of the post-Romantic style.

Giacomo Puccini

Puccini's generation included Ruggiero Leoncavallo, remembered for *I pagliacci* (The Clowns, 1892), and Pietro Mascagni, whose reputation likewise rests on a single success, *Cavalleria rusticana* (Rustic Chivalry, 1890). These Italians were associated with the movement known as *verismo* (realism), which tried to bring into the lyric theater the naturalism of writers Zola, Ibsen, and their contemporaries. Instead of choosing historical or mythological themes, they picked subjects from everyday life and treated them in down-to-earth fashion.

Leoncavallo and Mascagni

The Viennese symphonic tradition extended into the twentieth century through the works of Gustav Mahler (1860–1911), following in the illustrious line from Haydn, Mozart, Beethoven, and Schubert to Brahms and Schumann. Mahler held several prominent conducting posts during his career, including director of the Viennese opera from 1897 to 1907 and conductor of the New York Philharmonic Orchestra from 1909 to 1911.

Gustav Mahler

The spirit of song permeates Mahler's art. He followed Schubert and Schumann in cultivating the song cycle. *Songs of a Wayfarer*, composed in 1885, is a set of four songs suffused with Schubertian longing. The peak of

Gustav Klimt (*1862–1918*), *like Mahler a product of the post-Romantic era in Vienna, has created in* The Kiss (*1907–08*), *an illusion of rich beauty and deeply-felt emotion.* (Osterreichische Gallerie, Vienna)

his achievement in this direction is the cycle of six songs with orchestra that make up *The Song of the Earth*.

In his symphonic works, his tonal imagery was permeated by the jovial spirit of Austrian popular song and dance. His nine symphonies abound in lyricism, with melodies long of line and richly expressive harmonies. (The Tenth Symphony was left unfinished at his death, but recently has been edited and made available for performance.) In his sense of color Mahler ranks with the great masters of the art of orchestration. He contrasts solo instruments in the manner of chamber music, achieving his color effects through clarity of line rather than massed sonorities. It was in the matter of texture that Mahler made his most important contribution to contemporary technique. Basing his orchestral style on counterpoint, he caused two or more melodies to unfold simultaneously, each setting off the other. Mahler never abandoned the principle of tonality; he needed the key as a framework for his vast design. His Fourth Symphony, completed in 1900, is one of his least problematic works, featuring melodies of folklike simplicity. Mahler's intensely personal vision of life and art, evident in all his works, has made him one of the major prophets of the twentieth century.

Among the composers who inherited the symphonic poem of the Romantic era, Richard Strauss (1865–1949) occupied a leading place. Although his first works were in Classical forms, he soon found his true style in the writing of vivid program music, setting himself to develop what he called "the poetic, the expressive in music." *Macbeth*, his first symphonic poem, was followed by *Don Juan*, an extraordinary achievement for a young man of twenty-four. Then came the series of symphonic poems that blazed his name throughout the civilized world: *Death and Transfiguration, Till Eulenspiegel's Merry Pranks, Thus Spake Zarathustra, Don Quixote, A Hero's Life*.

Richard Strauss

Strauss carried to its extreme limit the nineteenth-century appetite for story-and-picture music. His symphonic poems are a treasury of orchestral discoveries. In some he anticipates modern sound effects—the clatter of pots and pans, the bleating of sheep, the gabble of geese, hoofbeats, wind, thunder, storm. Much more important, these works are packed with movement and gesture, with the sound and fury of an imperious temperament.

Strauss's operas continue to be widely performed. *Salome*, to Oscar Wilde's famous play, and *Elektra*, based on Hofmannsthal's version of the Greek tragedy, are long one-act operas. Swiftly paced, moving relentlessly to their climaxes, they are superb theater. *Der Rosenkavalier* has a wealth of sensuous lyricism and some entrancing waltzes. A world figure, Strauss dominated his era as few artists have done.

Alongside these masters who felt strongly the influence the Wagner was a new generation that reacted vigorously against the extremes of Romantic harmony. And with them emerged the movement that more than any other ushered in the twentieth century—Impressionism.

UNIT XXI

■

Turn–of–the–Century Trends

54

Debussy and Impressionism

"For we desire above all—nuance,
Not color but half-shades!
Ah! nuance alone unites
Dream with dream and flute with horn."—PAUL VERLAINE

The Impressionist Painters

In 1867 Claude Monet, rebuffed by the academic salons, exhibited under less conventional auspices a painting called *Impression: Sun Rising*. Before long "impressionism" had become a term of derision to describe the hazy, luminous paintings of this artist (1840–1926) and his school. A distinctly Parisian style, Impressionism counted among its exponents Camille Pissarro (1830–1903), Edouard Manet (1832–83), Edgar Degas (1834–1917), and Auguste Renoir (1841–1919). They strove to retain on canvas the freshness of their first impressions. They took painting out of the studio into the open air. Instead of mixing their pigments on the palette, they juxtaposed brush-strokes of pure color on the canvas, leaving it to the eye of the beholder to do the mixing. An iridescent sheen bathes their pictures. Outlines shimmer and melt in a luminous haze.

The Impressionists abandoned the grandiose subjects of Romanticism. The hero of their painting is not man but light. They preferred "unimportant" material: still life, dancing girls, nudes; everyday scenes of middle-class life, picnics, boating and café scenes; nature in all her aspects, Paris in all her

The Impressionists took painting out of the studio into the open air; their subject was light. **Claude Monet** (*1840–1926*), Impression: Sun Rising (Musée Marmottan, Paris.)

moods. Ridiculed at first—"Whoever saw grass that's pink and yellow and blue?"—they ended by imposing their vision upon the age.

The Symbolist Poets

A parallel revolt against traditional modes of expression took place in poetry under the leadership of the Symbolists, who strove for direct poetic experience unspoiled by intellectual elements. They sought to suggest rather than describe, to present the symbol rather than state the thing. Symbolism as a literary movement came to the fore in the work of Charles Baudelaire (1821–67), Stéphane Mallarmé (1842–98), Paul Verlaine (1844–96), and Arthur Rimbaud (1854–91). These poets were strongly influenced by Edgar Allan Poe (1809–49), whose writings were introduced into France by his admirer, Baudelaire. They experimented in free verse forms that opened new territories to their art, achieving a language indefiniteness that had hitherto been the privilege of music alone.

Turning from the grandiose subjects of Romanticism, the Impressionists derived their themes from the events of everyday life. **Pierre Auguste Renoir** (*1841–1919*), Lady at the Piano (The Art Institute of Chicago, Mr. and Mrs. Martin A. Ryerson Collection)

Impressionism in Music

Impressionism came to the fore at a crucial moment in the history of European music. The major-minor system had served the art since the seventeenth century. Composers were beginning to feel that its possibilities had been exhausted. Debussy and his followers were attracted to other scales, such as the church modes of the Middle Ages, which imparted an archaic flavor to their music. They began to emphasize the primary intervals—octaves, fourths, fifths, and the parallel movement of chords in the manner of Medieval organum. They were sympathetic to the novel scales introduced by nationalists such as the Russian composers Borodin and Musorgsky, or the Norwegian nationalist Edvard Grieg. Especially they responded to the influence of non-Western music: the Moorish strain in the songs and dances of Spain, and the Javanese and Chinese orchestras that were heard in Paris during the World Exposition of 1889. Here they found a new world of sonority: rhythms, scales, and color that offered a bewitching contrast to the traditional forms of Western music.

The *whole-tone scale* that figures prominently in Impressionist music derives from non-Western sources. This is a pattern built entirely of whole-tone intervals. It cannot be formed from the white or black keys alone on a piano keyboard, but by a combination of both (the sequence C-D-E-F♯-G♯-A♯-C provides an example). This scale does not have the pull of the seventh tone to the eighth, the tonic that is a major force in Western music, as the interval is not the usual half step but a whole step instead. There results a fluid scale pattern whose charm can be gauged only from hearing it played.

Whole-tone scale

Also associated with Impressionist music are the use of parallel or "gliding" chords, a writing style prohibited in the Classical system of harmony, and of five-tone combinations known as *ninth chords* (from the interval of a ninth between the lowest and highest tones of the chord). As a result of these, Impressionist music wavered between major and minor without adhering to either. It floated in a borderland between keys, creating elusive effects that might be compared to the misty outlines of Impressionist painting.

Parallel chords

Ninth chords

These evanescent harmonies demanded colors no less subtle. No room here for the thunderous climaxes of the Romantic orchestra. Instead, one instrumental color flows into another close to it, as from oboe to clarinet to flute, in the same way that Impressionist painting flows from one color to another close to it in the spectrum, as from yellow to green to blue.

Orchestral color

Impressionist rhythm, too, shows the influence of non-Western music. The metrical patterns of the Classic-Romantic era frequently give way to music that glides from one measure to the next in a floating rhythm with a veiled pulse, creating a dreamlike effect.

An iridescent sheen bathes this late Impressionist painting as outlines shimmer and melt in a luminous haze. Dated thirty years after Impression: Sun Rising, *but also by* **Claude Monet,** Water Lilies. (Photograph by Lee Boltin)

Musical Impressionism

1. Whole-tone scale (beginning on C)

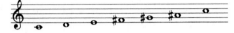

2. Example from Debussy's *Pelléas et Mélisande*, illustrating use of whole-tone scales

3. Parallel movement of chords (octaves and open fifths) in example of ninth- century organum

4. Parallel movement of chords (fifths and octaves), from Debussy's *The Sunken Cathedral*

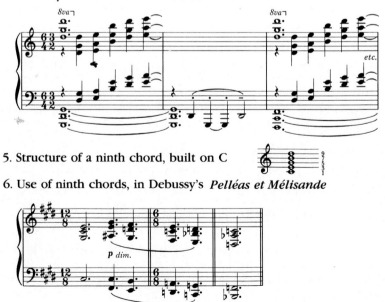

5. Structure of a ninth chord, built on C

6. Use of ninth chords, in Debussy's *Pelléas et Mélisande*

The Impressionists turned away from the large forms of the Austro-German tradition, such as symphony and concerto. They preferred short lyric forms—preludes, nocturnes, arabesques—whose titles suggested intimate lyricism or Impressionist painting. Characteristic are Debussy's *Clair de lune* (Moonlight), *Nuages* (Clouds), *Jardins sous la pluie* (Gardens in the Rain). The question arises: Was Impressionism a revolt against the Romantic tradition or simply its final manifestation? Actually, the Impressionists substituted a French brand of Romanticism for the Austro-German variety.

Claude Debussy: His Life and Music

"I love music passionately. And because I love it I try to free it from barren traditions that stifle it. It is a free art gushing forth, an open-air art boundless as the elements, the wind, the sky, the sea. It must never be shut in and become an academic art."

Claude Debussy

The most important French composer of the early twentieth century, Claude Debussy (1862–1918) was born near Paris in the town of St. Germain-en-Laye, where his parents kept a china shop. He entered the Paris Conservatoire when he was eleven. Within a few years he shocked his professors with bizarre harmonies that defied the sacred rules. "What rules then do you observe?" inquired one of his teachers. "None—only my own pleasure!" "That's all very well," retorted the professor, "provided you're a genius." It became increasingly apparent that the daring young man was.

He was twenty-two when his cantata *L'enfant prodigue* (The Prodigal Son) won the Prix de Rome. Already, he discerned his future bent. "The music I desire," he wrote a friend, "must be supple enough to adapt itself to the lyrical effusions of the soul and the fantasy of dreams."

The 1890s, the most productive decade of Debussy's career, culminated in the writing of *Pelléas et Mélisande*. Based on the symbolist drama by the Belgian poet Maurice Maeterlinck, this opera occupied him for the better part of ten years. After *Pelléas* Debussy was famous. He appeared in the capitals of Europe as conductor of his works and wrote the articles that established his reputation as one of the wittiest critics of his time. The outbreak of war in 1914 rendered him for a time incapable of all interest in music. After a year of silence he realized that he must contribute to the struggle in the only way he could, "by creating to the best of my ability a little of that beauty which the enemy is attacking with such fury." His energies sapped by the ravages of cancer, he worked on with remarkable fortitude.

Debussy died in March 1918 during the bombardment of Paris. It was just eight months before the victory of the nation whose culture found in him one of its most distinguished representatives.

For Debussy, as for Monet and Verlaine, art was primarily a sensuous experience. The epic themes of Romanticism were distasteful to his temperament both as man and artist. "French music," he declared, "is clearness, elegance, simple and natural declamation. French music aims first of all to give pleasure."

Principal Works

Orchestral music, including *Prélude à "L'après-midi d'un faune"* (Prelude to "The Afternoon of a Faun," 1894), Nocturnes (1899), *La mer* (The Sea, 1905), *Images* (1912), incidental music

Dramatic works, including the opera *Pelléas et Mélisande* (1902) and the ballet *Jeux* (Games, 1913)

Chamber music, including a string quartet (1893) and various sonatas (cello, 1915; violin, 1917; flute, viola, and harp, 1915)

Piano music, including *Pour le piano* (Suite, For the Piano, 1901), *Estampes* (1903), and 2 books of Préludes (1909–10, 1912–13)

Songs and choral music, including cantatas

From the Romantic exuberance that left nothing unsaid Debussy sought refuge in an art of understatement, subtle and discreet. He substituted for the sonata structure those short flexible forms that he handled with such distinction. Mood pieces, they evoked the favorite images of Impressionist painting: gardens in the rain, sunlight through the leaves, clouds, moonlight, sea, mist.

Among his orchestral compositions the *Prelude to "The Afternoon of a Faun"* is firmly established in public favor, as are the three Nocturnes (*Clouds, Festivals, Sirens*) and *La mer*. His piano pieces form an essential part of the modern repertory. Among the best known are *Clair de lune* (Moonlight), the most popular piece he ever wrote; *Evening in Granada*, *Reflections in the Water*, and *The Sunken Cathedral*. He was one of the most influential among the group of composers who established the French song as a national art form independent of the Lied. His settings of Baudelaire, Verlaine, and Mallarmé—to mention three poets for whom he had a particular fondness—are marked by exquisite refinement.

Debussy: Prelude to "The Afternoon of a Faun"

Debussy's famous orchestral work was inspired by a poem of Stéphane Mallarmé that evokes the landscape of pagan antiquity. The poem centers on the mythological creature of the forest, half man, half goat. The faun awakes in the woods and tries to remember: was he visited by three lovely nymphs or was this but a dream? He will never know. The sun is warm, the earth fragrant. He curls himself up and falls into a wine-drugged sleep.

The piece opens with a flute solo in the velvety lower register. (See Listening Guide 27 for themes and an excerpt from the poem.) The melody glides along the chromatic scale, narrow in range, languorous. Glissandos on the harp usher in a brief dialogue of the horns. The work is in sections that follow the familiar pattern of statement-departure-return. Characteristic is the relaxed rhythm which flows across the barline in a continuous stream. By weakening and even wiping out the accent Debussy achieved that dream-like fluidity which is a prime trait of Impressionist music.

A more decisive motive emerges, marked *en animant* (growing lively). The third theme, marked *même movement et très soutenu* (same tempo and very sustained), is an ardent melody that carries the composition to an emotional crest. The first melody returns in an altered guise. At the close, "blue" chords sound on the muted horns and violins, infinitely remote. The work dissolves in silence.

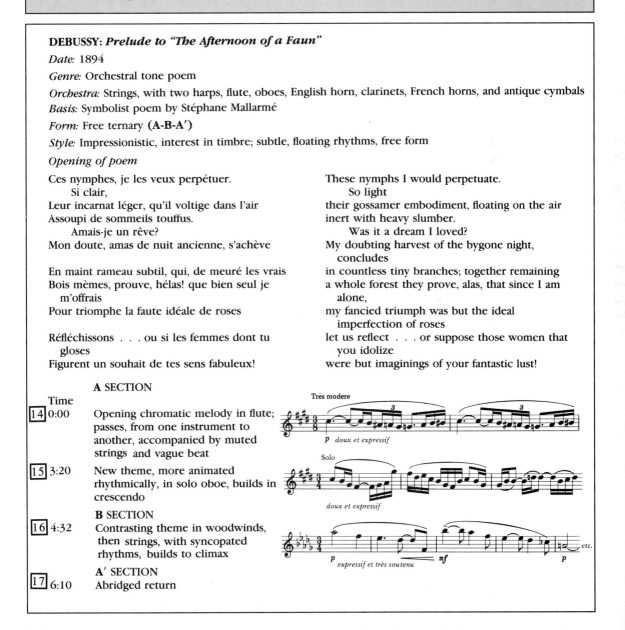

Listening Guide 27   ▭ 3A/5

DEBUSSY: *Prelude to "The Afternoon of a Faun"*

Date: 1894

Genre: Orchestral tone poem

Orchestra: Strings, with two harps, flute, oboes, English horn, clarinets, French horns, and antique cymbals

Basis: Symbolist poem by Stéphane Mallarmé

Form: Free ternary (**A-B-A′**)

Style: Impressionistic, interest in timbre; subtle, floating rhythms, free form

Opening of poem

Ces nymphes, je les veux perpétuer. Si clair,	These nymphs I would perpetuate. So light
Leur incarnat léger, qu'il voltige dans l'air	their gossamer embodiment, floating on the air
Assoupi de sommeils touffus.	inert with heavy slumber.
Amais-je un rêve?	Was it a dream I loved?
Mon doute, amas de nuit ancienne, s'achève	My doubting harvest of the bygone night, concludes
En maint rameau subtil, qui, de meuré les vrais	in countless tiny branches; together remaining
Bois mèmes, prouve, hélas! que bien seul je m'offrais	a whole forest they prove, alas, that since I am alone,
Pour triomphe la faute idéale de roses	my fancied triumph was but the ideal imperfection of roses
Réfléchissons . . . ou si les femmes dont tu gloses	let us reflect . . . or suppose those women that you idolize
Figurent un souhait de tes sens fabuleux!	were but imaginings of your fantastic lust!

A SECTION

Time

14 0:00   Opening chromatic melody in flute; passes, from one instrument to another, accompanied by muted strings and vague beat

15 3:20   New theme, more animated rhythmically, in solo oboe, builds in crescendo

B SECTION

16 4:32   Contrasting theme in woodwinds, then strings, with syncopated rhythms, builds to climax

A′ SECTION

17 6:10   Abridged return

Ravel and Post-Impressionism

Maurice Ravel (1875–1937) stands to Debussy somewhat as Matisse does to Monet: he was a post-Impressionist. His instinctive need for order and clarity of organization impelled him to return—as did the painter—to basic conceptions of form. (See illustrations on pages 5 and 137.) Thus, his art unfolded between the twin goals of Impressionism and neo-Classicism.

Like Debussy, Ravel was drawn to the images that fascinated the Impressionist painters: daybreak, the sea, the interplay of water and light. He too exploited Spanish dance rhythms, worshiped the old French harpsichordists, and was attracted to the scales of Medieval as well as exotic music.

But the differences between him and Debussy were as pronounced as the similarities. His music has an enameled brightness that contrasts with the twilight softness of Debussy's. His rhythms are more incisive and have a drive that Debussy rarely strives for. His sense of key is firmer, his harmony is more dissonant, and his melodies are broader in span. His orchestration derives, as Debussy's did not, from the nineteenth-century masters: he stands in the line of descent from Berlioz, Rimsky-Korsakov, and Richard Strauss. Where Debussy aimed to "decongest" sound, Ravel handled the huge orchestra of the post-Romantic period with brilliant virtuosity. And he was drawn to the Classical forms much earlier in his career than Debussy, who turned to them only toward the end. Ravel won the international public through his orchestral works, including the two concert suites from the ballet *Daphnis and Chloé*, *La Valse*, and the ever popular *Boléro*.

Ravel held up an ideal of sonorous beauty that incarnated the sensibility, elegance, and esprit of French art. And he was one of the composers who opened wide the door to the twentieth century.

UNIT XXII

■

The Early Twentieth Century

55

Main Currents in Early Twentieth-Century Music

"The entire history of modern music may be said to be a history of the gradual pull-away from the German musical tradition of the past century."—AARON COPLAND

The Reaction Against Romanticism

As the quotation from Aaron Copland makes clear, the first quarter of the twentieth century was impelled before all else to throw off the oppressive heritage of the nineteenth. The new attitudes took shape just before the First World War. European art sought to escape its overrefinement. Music turned to the dynamism of non-Western rhythm even as the fine arts discovered the abstraction of African sculpture and the monumental simplicity that shaped the exotic paintings of Henri Rousseau. Out of the vigorous folk music of various cultures came powerful rhythms of an elemental fury, as in Bartók's *Allegro barbaro* (1911) and Stravinsky's *The Rite of Spring* (1913).

Non-Western influences

Expressionism

Expressionism was the German answer to French Impressionism. Whereas the French genius rejoiced in luminous impressions of the outer world, the Germanic temperament preferred digging down to the subterranean regions of the soul. As with Impressionism, the impulse for the movement came

The images on the canvases of Expressionist painters issued from the realm of the unconscious: hallucinated visions that defied the traditional notions of beauty in order to express the artist's inner self. **Wassily Kandinsky** (*1886–1944*), Painting No. 199. 1914. (The Museum of Modern Art, New York. Nelson A. Rockefeller Fund)

from painting. Wassily Kandinsky (1866–1944), Paul Klee (1879–1940), and Oskar Kokoschka (1886–1980) influenced Schoenberg and his disciples even as the Impressionist painters influenced Debussy. Expressionism in music triumphed first in the central European area that lies within the orbit of Germanic culture. It is familiar to Americans through the paintings of Kandinsky and Klee, and the writings of Franz Kafka (1883–1924). Expressionist tendencies reached their full tide in the dramatic works of Schoenberg and his disciple Alban Berg.

The musical language of Expressionism favored a hyperexpressive harmonic language linked to inordinately wide leaps in the melody and to the use of instruments in their extreme registers. Expressionist music soon reached the boundaries of what was possible within the major-minor system. Inevitably, it had to push beyond.

The New Classicism

One way of rejecting the nineteenth century was to return to the eighteenth. The movement "back to Bach" assumed impressive proportions in the early 1920s. Instead of worshiping at the shrine of Beethoven and Wagner, as the Romantics had done, composers began to emulate the great musicians of the eighteenth century—Bach, Handel, Vivaldi—and the detached, objective style that was supposed to characterize their music.

Neoclassicism tried to rid the art of the story-and-picture meanings with which the nineteenth century had endowed it. The new Classicists turned away from the symphonic poem and the Romantic attempt to bring music closer to poetry and painting. They preferred absolute to program music and focused attention on craftsmanship, elegance, and taste, a positive affirmation of the Classical virtues of objectivity and control.

56

New Elements of Musical Style

"I consider rhythm the prime and perhaps the essential part of music."—OLIVIER MESSIAEN

The New Rhythmic Complexity

Twentieth-century music turned away from the standard patterns of duple, triple, and quadruple meter to increasingly complex rhythms. Composers explored the possibilities of nonsymmetrical patterns based on odd numbers: five, seven, eleven, thirteen beats to the measure. In nineteenth-century music a single meter customarily prevailed through an entire movement or section. Now the metrical flow shifted constantly, sometimes with each measure, as we shall see in Stravinsky's *The Rite of Spring*. Formerly, music presented to the ear one rhythmic pattern at a time, sometimes two. Now composers turned to *polyrhythm*—the use of several rhythmic patterns simultaneously. As a result of these innovations, Western music achieved something of the complexity and suppleness of Asiatic and African rhythms.

Polyrhythm

The New Melody

Nineteenth-century melody was fundamentally vocal in character; composers tried to make the instruments "sing." Twentieth-century melody is neither unvocal nor antivocal; it is simply not conceived in relation to the voice. It abounds in wide leaps and dissonant intervals. Besides, much twentieth century music lacks a melodic orientation. Sometimes no melody is to be found because the composer had other goals in mind. Twentieth-century composers have enormously expanded our notion of what is a melody. As a result, many a pattern is accepted as a melody today that would hardly have been considered one a century ago.

The New Harmony

No single factor sets off the music of our time more decisively from that of the past than the new conceptions of harmony that emerged in the twentieth century. The triads of traditional harmony, we saw, were formed by combining three tones, on every other degree of the scale, or in thirds: 1–3–5 (for example, C–E–G), 2–4–6 (D–F–A), and so on. Traditional harmony also employed four-note combinations, with another third piled on top of the triad, known as *seventh chords* (steps 1–3–5–7), and, as we saw in the music of the Impressionists, five-note combinations known as *ninth chords* (steps 1–3–5–7–9). Twentieth-century composers added more "stories" to such chords, forming highly dissonant combinations of six and seven tones. These complex "skyscraper" chords brought greater tension to music than had existed before, and allowed the composer to play two or more streams of *Polyharmony*   harmony against each other, creating *polyharmony.*

The widespread use of chromatic harmony in the late nineteenth century led, in the early twentieth century, to the free use of all twelve tones around a center. Although this approach retained the basic principle of traditional tonality—gravitation to the tonic—it wiped out the distinction between diatonic and chromatic and between major and minor modes. We will see that the expansion of tonality was encouraged by an increased interest in the music of non-Western cultures as well as in the Medieval church modes.

From the development of polyharmony, a further step followed logically: to heighten the contrast of two keys by presenting them simultaneously. *Polytonality*   *Polytonality*—the use of two or more keys together—came to the fore in the music of Stravinsky, among others, whence it entered the vocabulary of the age. Toward the end of a piece, one key was generally permitted to assert itself over the others. In this way the impression was restored of orderly progression toward a central point.

The concept of total abandonment of tonality is associated with the composer Arnold Schoenberg, whom we shall discuss later. He advocated doing away with the tonic by treating the twelve tones as of equal importance—*Atonality*   thus achieving *atonal music*. Atonality was much more of an innovation than polytonality, for it entirely rejected the framework of key. Consonance, according to Schoenberg, was no longer capable of making an impression; atonal music moved from one level of dissonance to another, functioning always at maximum tension, without areas of relaxation.

Having accepted the necessity of moving beyond the existing tonal system, Schoenberg sought a unifying principle that would take the place of the system of tonality. He found this in a strict technique that he had worked out by the early 1920s. He referred to it as "the method of composing with twelve tones"—that is, with twelve equal tones, no one of which is more important than any other. Each composition that uses Schoenberg's method is based on an arrangement of the twelve chromatic tones called a *tone row*. This row is the unifying idea for that particular composition, and serves as the source of all the musical events that take place in it. (The term *dodecaphonic*, the Greek equivalent of *twelve-tone*, is sometimes also used for

Schoenberg's method, while *serial music*, an allusion to the series of twelve tones, has come to refer, in more recent decades, to postwar extensions of the technique.)

    A tone row thus establishes a series of pitches from which a composer builds themes, harmonies, and counterpoints. Schoenberg provided flexibility and variety in this seemingly confining system through alternative forms of the tone row, based on its *transposition* (beginning on other notes), its *inversion* (with the intervals moving in the opposite direction), its *retrograde* (or pitches in reverse order), or even the combination of the last two, in *retrograde inversion*. (You will remember we saw these same techniques or contrapuntal devices in earlier music, especially in the Baroque fugue.)

Serial music

Tone row

Forms of the row

The Emancipation of Dissonance

The history of music, we have seen, has been the history of a steadily increasing tolerance on the part of listeners. Throughout this long evolution, one factor remained constant: a clear distinction was drawn between dissonance, the element of tension, and consonance, the element of rest. Consonance was the norm, dissonance the temporary disturbance. In many contemporary works, however, tension becomes the norm. Therefore, a dissonance can serve even as a final cadence, provided it is less dissonant than the chord that came before. In relation to the greater dissonance, it is judged to be consonant. Twentieth-century composers emancipated the dissonance by freeing it from the obligation to resolve to consonance. Their music taught listeners to accept tone combinations whose like had never been heard before.

Texture: Dissonant Counterpoint

The nineteenth century was preoccupied with harmony; the early twentieth emphasized counterpoint. The new style swept away both the Romantic cloudburst and Impressionistic haze. In their stead was installed an airy linear texture that fit the Neoclassical ideal of craftsmanship, order, and detachment.

    Consonance unites the constituent tones of harmony or counterpoint; dissonance separates them and makes them stand out against each other. Composers began to use dissonance to set off one line against another. Instead of basing their counterpoint on the euphonious intervals of the third and sixth, they turned to astringent seconds and sevenths. Or the independence of the voices might be heightened by putting them in different keys.

Orchestration

The rich sonorities of nineteenth-century orchestration were alien to the temper of the 1920s and '30s. The trend was toward a smaller orchestra and a leaner sound, one that was hard, bright, sober. The decisive factor in the handling of the orchestra was the change to a linear texture. Color came to be used in the new music not so much for atmosphere or enchantment as for bringing out the lines of counterpoint and of form. The string section lost its traditional role as the heart of the orchestra. Its tone was felt to be too personal. Attention was focused on the more objective winds. There was a movement away from brilliancy of sound. The darker instruments came to the fore—viola, bassoon, trombone. The emphasis on rhythm brought the percussion group into greater prominence than ever before and the piano, which in the Romantic era was preeminently a solo instrument, found a place for itself in the orchestral ensemble.

New Conceptions of Form

The first quarter of the century saw the final expansion of traditional form in the gigantic symphonies of Mahler. Music could hardly go farther in this direction. A reaction took shape as composers began to move toward the Classical ideals of tight organization and succinctness. In addition, they revived a number of older forms: fugue, passacaglia and chaconne, concerto grosso, theme and variations, and suite. The tendency to elevate formal *Formalism* above expressive values is known as *formalism*. The New Classicism, like the old, strove for purity of line and proportion.

Composers also vitalized their music through materials drawn from popular styles. The ragtime piano style, with its sprightly syncopations, traveled across the Atlantic to Europe. The rhythmic freedom of jazz captured the ears of many composers, who strove to achieve something of the spontaneity of the popular style. (We will look into the origins of jazz and its influence on other styles in a later chapter.)

57

Stravinsky and the Revitalization of Rhythm

"I hold that it was a mistake to consider me a revolutionary. If one only need break habit in order to be labeled a revolutionary, then every artist who has something to say and who in order to say it steps outside the bounds of established convention could be considered revolutionary."

It is granted to certain artists to embody the most significant impulses of their time and to affect its artistic life in the most powerful fashion. Such an artist was Igor Stravinsky (1882–1971), the Russian composer who for half a century gave impetus to the main currents in twentieth-century music.

Igor Stravinsky

Igor Stravinsky: His Life and Music

Stravinsky was born in Oranienbaum, a summer resort not far from St. Petersburg (now Leningrad), where his parents lived. He grew up in a musical environment; his father was the leading bass at the Imperial Opera. He matriculated at the University of St. Petersburg and embarked on a legal career, meanwhile continuing his musical studies. At twenty he submitted his work to Rimsky-Korsakov, with whom he subsequently worked for three years.

Success came early to Stravinsky. His music attracted the notice of Serge Diaghilev, the legendary impresario of the Paris-based Russian Ballet, who commissioned Stravinsky to write the score for *The Firebird*, which was produced in 1910. It was followed a year later by *Petrushka*. In the spring of 1913 was presented the third and most spectacular of the ballets Stravinsky wrote for Diaghilev, *The Rite of Spring*. The opening night was one of the most scandalous in modern musical history; the revolutionary score touched off a near riot. A year later the composer was vindicated when the work, presented at a symphony concert under Pierre Monteux, was received with enthusiasm and established itself as a masterpiece of the new music.

Diaghilev

The Russian Revolution had severed Stravinsky's ties with his homeland. In 1920 he settled in France, where he remained until 1939. During these years Stravinsky concertized extensively throughout Europe, performing his own music as pianist and conductor. He also paid two visits to the United States. In 1939 he was invited to deliver the Charles Eliot Norton lectures at Harvard University. He was there when the Second World War broke out, and decided to live in this country. He settled in California, outside Los Angeles, and in 1945 became an American citizen. In his later years, Stravinsky's worldwide concert tours made him the most celebrated figure in twentieth-century music. He died in New York on April 6, 1971.

Principal Works

Orchestral music, including Symphonies of Wind Instruments (1920), Concerto for Piano and Winds (1924), *Dumbarton Oaks Concerto* (1938), Symphony in C (1940), Symphony in Three Movements (1945), *Ebony Concerto* (1945)

Ballets, including *L'oiseau de feu* (The Firebird, 1910), *Petrushka* (1911), *Le sacre du printemps* (The Rite of Spring, 1913), *Les noces* (The Wedding, 1923), *Agon* (1957)

Operas, including *Oedipus rex* (1927) and *The Rake's Progress* (1951)

Choral music, including *Symphony of Psalms* (1930), *Canticum sacrum* (1955), *Threni* (1958), and *Requiem Canticles* (1966)

Chamber music; piano music (solo and for two pianos); songs

Stravinsky showed a continuous development throughout his career. This evolution led from the post-Impressionism of *The Firebird* and the audacities of *The Rite of Spring* to the austerely controlled classicism of his maturity.

Early works

Stravinsky was a leader in the revitalization of European rhythm. His was a rhythm of unparalleled dynamic power, furious yet controlled. The national element predominates in his early works, as in *The Firebird* and *Petrushka*, in which he found his personal style. *The Rite of Spring* recreates the rites of pagan Russia. *The Soldier's Tale*, a dance-drama for four characters, is an intimate theater work accompanied by a seven-piece band. The most important work of the years that followed is *The Wedding*, a stylization of a Russian peasant wedding.

Neoclassical period

Stravinsky's Neoclassical period culminated in several major compositions. *Oedipus Rex* is an "opera-oratorio"; the text is a translation into Latin of Cocteau's adaptation of the Greek tragedy. The *Symphony of Psalms*, for chorus and orchestra, is regarded by many as the chief work of Stravinsky's maturity. Equally admired is *The Rake's Progress*, an opera on a libretto by W. H. Auden and Chester Kallman, after Hogarth's celebrated series of engravings. This radiantly melodious score, which uses the set forms of the Mozartean opera, is the quintessence of Neoclassicism.

Twelve-tone works

In the works written after he was seventy, Stravinsky showed himself increasingly receptive to the serial procedures of the twelve-tone style, which in earlier years he had opposed. This preoccupation came to the fore in a number of works dating from the middle 1950s, of which the most important is the ballet *Agon* and *Threni: Lamentations of the Prophet Jeremiah*.

Stravinsky: The Rite of Spring

The Rite of Spring—"Scenes of Pagan Russia"—not only embodies the cult of primitivism that so startled its first-night audience; it also sets forth the lineaments of a new tonal language—the percussive use of dissonance, po-

Valentine Hugo's *sketches of the* Danse Sacrale *for the original production of the ballet* Le Sacre du Printemps (*1913*)*, choreographed by Nijinsky.*

Listening Guide 28

 3B/2

STRAVINSKY: *The Rite of Spring*

Date: 1913

Genre: Ballet (also concert work for orchestra)

Basis: Scenes of Pagan Russia; use of folksongs

OVERALL STRUCTURE:

PART I: THE ADORATION OF THE EARTH

Introduction
Dance of the Youths and Maidens
Game of Abduction
Spring Rounds
Games of the Rival Tribes
Procession of the Sage
Adoration of the Earth
Dance of the Earth

PART II: THE SACRIFICE

Introduction
Mystical Circle of the Adolescents
Glorification of the Chosen One
Evocation of the Ancestors
Sacrifical Dance of the Chosen One

PART I *Introduction (Evocation of Spring)*

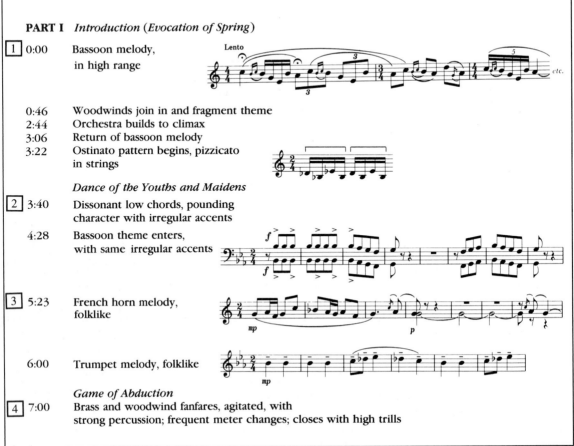

1	0:00	Bassoon melody, in high range
	0:46	Woodwinds join in and fragment theme
	2:44	Orchestra builds to climax
	3:06	Return of bassoon melody
	3:22	Ostinato pattern begins, pizzicato in strings

Dance of the Youths and Maidens

| 2 | 3:40 | Dissonant low chords, pounding character with irregular accents |
| | 4:28 | Bassoon theme enters, with same irregular accents |

| 3 | 5:23 | French horn melody, folklike |
| | 6:00 | Trumpet melody, folklike |

Game of Abduction

| 4 | 7:00 | Brass and woodwind fanfares, agitated, with strong percussion; frequent meter changes; closes with high trills |

lyrhythms, and polytonality. The work is scored for a large orchestra, including an exceptionally varied percussion group.

Part I: "The Adoration of the Earth." The Introduction is intended to evoke the birth of spring. A long-limbed melody is introduced by the bassoon, taking on a curious remoteness from the circumstance that it lies in the instrument's uppermost register. (See Listening Guide 28.) In "Dance of the Youths and Maidens" and "Game of Abduction" we hear Stravinsky's "elemental pounding," projected by dissonant chords in the lower register, polytonal harmonies, and continual dislocation of the accent. The first part ends with the "Dance of the Earth," which is performed to music of enormous physical energy.

In Part II, "The Sacrifice," the Sage must choose the Elect One who will be sacrificed to ensure the fertility of the earth. The climax of the ballet comes with the final number, the "Sacrificial Dance of the Chosen One." The music mounts in fury as the chosen maiden dances until she falls dead. The men in wild excitement bear her body to the foot of the mound. With an ascending run on flutes and piccolos and a fortissimo growl in the orchestra, this vibrant score comes to an end.

58
Schoenberg and the Second Viennese School

"I personally hate to be called a revolutionist, which I am not. What I did was neither revolution nor anarchy."—ARNOLD SCHOENBERG

The German Expressionist movement was manifested in music by the Viennese composer Arnold Schoenberg (1874–1951) and his disciples. Schoenberg's pioneering efforts in the breakdown of the traditional tonal system and the development of the twelve-tone method revolutionized musical composition. His innovations were further developed by his most gifted students, Alban Berg (1885–1935) and Anton Webern (1883–1945). These composers are often referred to as the Second Viennese School (the first being Haydn, Mozart, and Beethoven).

Arnold Schoenberg: His Life and Music

Schoenberg was born in Vienna. He began to study the violin at the age of eight, and soon afterward made his initial attempts at composing. Some time

Arnold Schoenberg

Principal Works

Orchestral music, including *Five Pieces for Orchestra* (1909), *Verklärte Nacht* (Transfigured Night, 1917), Variations for Orchestra (1928), concertos for violin (1936) and piano (1942)

Operas, including *Die glückliche Hand* (The Blessed Hand, 1913), *Moses und Aron* (incomplete, 1932)

Choral music, including *Gurrelieder* (1911), *Die Jacobsleiter* (Jacob's Ladder, 1922), *A Survivor from Warsaw* (1941); smaller choral works, including *Friede auf Erden* (Peace on Earth, 1907)

Chamber music, including 4 string quartets, serenade, wind quintet, string trio

Vocal music, including *Pierrot Lunaire* (1912)

Piano music, including Three Piano Pieces, Op. 11 (1909)

later he became acquainted with a young musician, Alexander von Zemlinsky, who for a few months gave him lessons in counterpoint. This was the only musical instruction he ever had.

Through Zemlinsky young Schoenberg was introduced to the musical elite of Vienna, who at that time were under the spell of Wagner's *Tristan*. In 1899, when he was twenty-five, Schoenberg wrote the string sextet *Transfigured Night*, which he later orchestrated. The following year several of Schoenberg's songs were performed in Vienna and precipitated a scene. "And ever since that day," he once remarked with a smile, "the scandal has never ceased."

With each new work Schoenberg moved closer to as bold a step as any artist has ever taken—the rejection of tonality. The First World War interrupted Schoenberg's creative activity; he was called up for military service. Between 1915 and 1923, he wrote no music, but rather clarified his theories and evolved a set of structural procedures to replace tonality. His "method of composing with twelve tones" soon established him as a leader of contemporary musical thought. In 1925, he was appointed to succeed Ferruccio Busoni as professor of composition at the Berlin Academy of Arts.

This period in Schoenberg's life ended with the coming to power of Hitler in 1933. Like many Austrian-Jewish intellectuals of his generation, he had grown away from his Jewish origins and had converted to Catholicism. After he left Germany, however, he found it spiritually necessary to return to the Hebrew faith. He arrived in the United States in the fall of 1933 and was ultimately appointed to the faculty of the University of California in Los Angeles. He continued his teaching and writing until his death in 1951.

Post-Wagnerian romanticism

Schoenberg's first period may be described as one of post-Wagnerian Romanticism; he still used key signatures and remained within the boundaries of tonality. The best-known work of this period is *Transfigured Night*, Opus 4. Schoenberg's second period was characterized by atonal-Expressionism, in which he abolished the distinction between consonance and dissonance

Atonal expressionism

as well as the sense of a home key. The high points of this period are the Five Pieces for Orchestra, Opus 16, and *Pierrot lunaire*, Opus 21, which we shall discuss.

Schoenberg's third period, that of the twelve-tone method, reached its climax in the Variations for Orchestra, Opus 31. In the fourth and last period of his career—the American phase—he carried the twelve-tone technique to further stages of refinement. Among the late works are the brilliant Piano Concerto and the cantata *A Survivor from Warsaw*.

Twelve-tone period

American period

Schoenberg: Pierrot lunaire

One of Schoenberg's preoccupations was the attempt to bring spoken word and music as close together as possible. He solved the problem through *Sprechstimme* (spoken voice), a new style in which the vocal melody is spoken rather than sung on exact pitches and in strict rhythm. The result was a weird, strangely effective vocal line which he brought to perfection in his most celebrated work, *Pierrot lunaire*.

Sprechstimme

In 1884 the Belgian poet Albert Giraud published a cycle of fifty short poems under the title that Schoenberg later adopted. His Pierrot was the poet-rascal-clown whose chalk-white face enlivened every puppet show and pantomime in Europe. The poems, with their abrupt changes of mood from guilt to playfulness, fired Schoenberg's imagination. He picked twenty-one and set them for a female reciter and a chamber-music ensemble of five players using eight instruments: piano, flute–piccolo, clarinet–bass clarinet, violin–viola, and cello.

Schoenberg conducting a performance of Pierrot lunaire *with soprano Erica Stiedry-Wagner at Town Hall, New York on November 17, 1940. A sketch by* **Benedict Fred Dolbin** (*1883–1971*).

In No. 18, "Der Mondfleck" (The Moonfleck; see Listening Guide 29 for the text), Pierrot, out for fun, is disturbed by a white spot—a patch of moonlight—on the collar of his jet-black jacket. He rubs and rubs but cannot get rid of it. His predicament inspired Schoenberg to contrapuntal complexities of a spectacular kind. The piano presents a three-voice fugue while the other instruments unfold such devices as strict canons in diminution (smaller note values) and retrograde (backwards).

The last poem, No. 21, is "O alter Duft" (O Scent of Fabled Yesteryear), in which Schoenberg brings in all eight instruments. Pierrot revels in the fragrant memories of old times, looking out serenely on a world bathed in sunlight. This return to an earlier, more innocent time leads Schoenberg to sound the gentle thirds and consonant triads of the harmonic system he had abandoned. Pierrot's *Sprechstimme* dies away in a pianissimo. Rarely has an artist captured the mood of their time and place so completely.

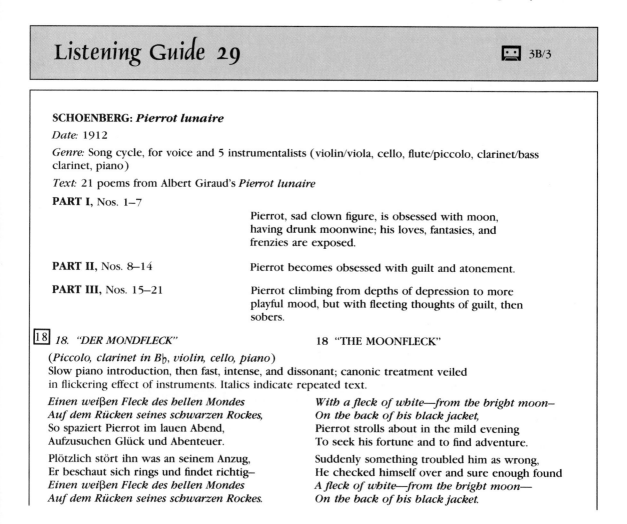

Listening Guide 29   🖭 3B/3

SCHOENBERG: *Pierrot lunaire*

Date: 1912

Genre: Song cycle, for voice and 5 instrumentalists (violin/viola, cello, flute/piccolo, clarinet/bass clarinet, piano)

Text: 21 poems from Albert Giraud's *Pierrot lunaire*

PART I, Nos. 1–7

Pierrot, sad clown figure, is obsessed with moon, having drunk moonwine; his loves, fantasies, and frenzies are exposed.

PART II, Nos. 8–14

Pierrot becomes obsessed with guilt and atonement.

PART III, Nos. 15–21

Pierrot climbing from depths of depression to more playful mood, but with fleeting thoughts of guilt, then sobers.

18 *18. "DER MONDFLECK"*   18 "THE MOONFLECK"

(Piccolo, clarinet in B♭, violin, cello, piano)
Slow piano introduction, then fast, intense, and dissonant; canonic treatment veiled in flickering effect of instruments. Italics indicate repeated text.

Einen weißen Fleck des hellen Mondes	*With a fleck of white—from the bright moon—*
Auf dem Rücken seines schwarzen Rockes,	*On the back of his black jacket,*
So spaziert Pierrot im lauen Abend,	Pierrot strolls about in the mild evening
Aufzusuchen Glück und Abenteuer.	To seek his fortune and to find adventure.
Plötzlich stört ihn was an seinem Anzug,	Suddenly something troubled him as wrong,
Er beschaut sich rings und findet richtig–	He checked himself over and sure enough found
Einen weißen Fleck des hellen Mondes	*A fleck of white—from the bright moon—*
Auf dem Rücken seines schwarzen Rockes.	*On the back of his black jacket.*

Warte! denkt er: das ist so ein Gipsfleck!	Damn! he thinks: there's a spot of plaster!
Wischt und wischt, doch—	Rubs and rubs, but—he can't get it off.
bringt ihn nicht herunter!	
Und so gent er, giftgeschwollen, weiter,	And so goes on his way, his pleasure poisoned,
Reibt und reibt bis an den frühen Morgen—	Rubs and rubs till the early morning—
Einen weißen Fleck des hellen Mondes.	*A fleck from the bright moon.*

19 *21. "O ALTER DUFT"*   21. "O SCENT OF FABLED YESTERYEAR"

(*Flute, piccolo, clarinet in A, bass clarinet in B♭, violin, viola, cello, piano*)
Melancholy mood in simpler setting, dissonant, with musical refrain on words "O alter Duft aus Märchenzeit" (O scent of fabled yesteryear).

O alter Duft aus Märchenzeit.	*O scent of fabled yesteryear,*
Berauschest wieder meine Sinne:	*Intoxicating my senses once again!*
Ein närrisch Heer von Scheimerein	*A foolish swarm of idle fancies*
Durchschwirrt die leichte Luft.	*Pervades the gentle air.*
Ein glückhaft Wunschen macht mich froh	*A happy desire makes me yearn for*
Nach Freuden, die ich lang verachtet:	*Joys that I have long scorned:*
O alter Duft aus Märchenzeit,	*O scent of fabled yesteryear,*
Berauschest wieder mich!	*Intoxicating me again!*
All meinen Unmut gab ich preis:	*All my ill humor is dispelled:*
Aus meinem sonnumrahmten Fenster	*From my sundrenched window*
Beschau ich frei die liebe Welt	*I look out freely on the lovely world*
Und träum hinaus in seige Weiten . . .	*And dream of beyond the horizon . . .*
O alter Duft—aus Märchenzeit!	*O scent of fabled yesteryear!*

Opening, for piano and voice in Sprechstimme

Berg and Webern

Following his teacher's footsteps, Alban Berg's art issued from the world of German Romanticism. His most widely known composition is *Wozzeck* (1925), an opera based on a play by Georg Büchner set in an atonal-Expressionist idiom. Anton Webern, on the other hand, carried the philosophy of brevity of statement to the extreme in musical fabrics characterized by unusual instrumentation. He employed Schoenberg's twelve-tone method with unprecedented strictness, moving toward complete control of the sonorous material or total serialism, thus establishing dodecaphonic thinking as a major influence in twentieth-century composition.

■

The Nationalism of the Twentieth Century

59

Bartók and the European Scene

"What is the best way for a composer to reap the full benefits of his studies in peasant music? It is to assimilate the idiom of peasant so completely that he is able to forget all about it and use it as his musical mother tongue."

Béla Bartók

Twentieth-century nationalism differed from its nineteenth-century counterpart in one important respect. It approached the old folksongs in a scientific spirit, prizing the ancient tunes precisely because they departed from the conventional mold. By this time the phonograph had been invented. The new students of folklore took recording equipment into the field in order to preserve the songs exactly as the village folk sang them, and the composers who used them in their works respected and tried to retain their antique flavor.

This was the mission of Béla Bartók (1881-1945), who attempted to reconcile the folk melody of his native Hungary with the main currents of European music. In the process, he created an entirely personal language and revealed himself as one of the major artists of our century.

Béla Bartók: His Life and Music

Bartók was born in a small Hungarian town where his father was director of an agricultural school. He studied at the Royal Academy in Budapest, where he came in contact with the nationalist movement aimed at shaking off the domination of German musical culture. Early in his career he realized that the true Hungarian folk idiom was to be found only among the peasants.

Principal Works

Orchestral works, including *Music for Strings, Percussion, and Celesta* (1936), Concerto for Orchestra (1943); 2 violin concertos (1908, 1938), 3 piano concertos (1926, 1931, 1945)

1 opera: *Bluebeard's Castle* (1918)

2 ballets: *The Wooden Prince* (1917) and *The Miraculous Mandarin* (1926)

Chamber music, including 6 string quartets (1908–39); *Contrasts* (for violin, clarinet, and piano, 1938); sonatas, duos

Piano music, including *Allegro barbaro* (1911) and *Mikrokosmos* (6 books, 1926–39)

Choral music, including *Cantata profana* (1930); folksong arrangements

Songs, including folksong arrangements

In company with his fellow composer Zoltán Kodály he toured the remote villages of the country, determined to collect the native songs before they died out forever.

With the performance at the Budapest Opera of his ballet *The Wooden Prince*, Bartók came into his own. The fall of the Hapsburg monarchy in 1918 released a surge of national fervor that created a favorable climate for his music. In the ensuing decade Bartók became a leading figure in the musical life of his country.

The alliance between Admiral Horthy's regime and Nazi Germany on the eve of the Second World War confronted the composer with issues that he faced squarely. He protested the performances of his music on the Berlin radio and at every opportunity took an anti-Fascist stand. To go into exile meant surrendering the position he enjoyed in Hungary. But he would not compromise. He came to the United States in 1940 and settled in New York City.

The last five years of his life yielded little in the way of happiness. Sensitive and retiring, he felt uprooted, isolated in his new surroundings. In his last years he suffered from leukemia and was no longer able to appear in public. Friends appealed for aid to ASCAP (American Society of Composers, Authors, and Publishers). Funds were made available that provided the composer with proper care in nursing homes and enabled him to continue writing. A series of commissions spurred him to the composition of his last works. They rank among his finest. He died in the West Side Hospital in New York City.

Bartók found Hungarian peasant music to be based on ancient modes, unfamiliar scales, and nonsymmetrical rhythms. These freed him from what he called "the tyrannical rule of the major and minor keys," and led him to new concepts of melody, harmony, and rhythm.

Bartók's Classicism shows itself in his emphasis on construction. His har-

Béla Bartók as a young man recording folksongs in a Transylvanian mountain village. (The photograph was taken in the 1900s by fellow-composer Zoltán Kodály. (Collection of G. D. Hackett)

mony can be bitingly dissonant. Polytonality abounds in his work; but he never wholly abandoned the principle of key. Like Stravinsky, he is fond of syncopation and repeated patterns (ostinatos). He played a major role in the revitalization of European rhythm, infusing it with earthy vitality and tension. His orchestration ranges from brilliant mixtures to threads of pure color that bring out the intertwining melody lines; from a hard, bright glitter to a luminous haze. A virtuoso pianist himself, Bartók is one of the masters of modern piano writing. He typifies the twentieth-century use of the piano as an instrument of percussion and rhythm. His six string quartets rank among the finest achievements of our century. Bartók is best known to the public by the three major works of his last period, the *Music for Strings, Percussion, and Celesta*, the Concerto for Orchestra, and the master's final statement, the Third Piano Concerto.

Bartók: Music for Strings, Percussion, and Celesta

This work was a landmark in the twentieth-century cultivation of chamber music textures. Bartók's conception called for two string groups and percussion, one including piano and celesta, the other with harp and xylophone.

We hear the fourth movement, an Allegro molto in rondo form, that combines the passionate abandon of Magyar folk dance and contrapuntal processes tossed off with true virtuosity. The assymetrical dance-like rhythm of the central idea alternates with the propulsive, jazzy animation in the contrasting sections. Each recurrence of the rondo theme brings fresh variation. (See Listening Guide 30 for analysis.)

Bartók's prime characteristic both as musician and man was the uncompromising integrity that informed his every act—what a compatriot of his has called "the proud morality of the mind." He was one of the great spirits of our time.

Listening Guide 30

🎦 3B/5

BARTÓK: *Music for Strings, Percussion, and Celesta*

Date: 1936

Medium: double string orchestra, percussion, piano, and celesta

I. Andante tranquillo: Fugue

II. Allegro: Sonata form

III. Adagio: "Night Music"

IV. Allegro molto

Form: Rondo

Basis: folk dance tunes, the first a transformed version of the opening movement fugue subject

Pizzicato chords in strings, resembling folk instruments, and timpani

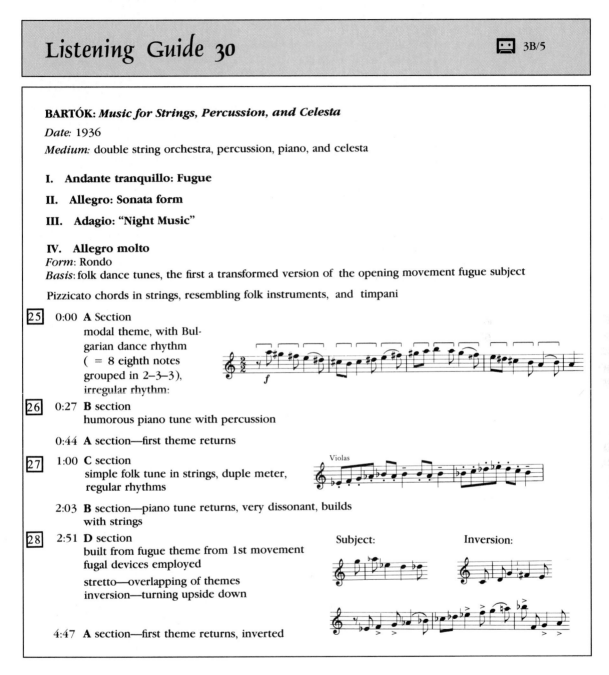

25	0:00	**A Section** modal theme, with Bulgarian dance rhythm (= 8 eighth notes grouped in 2–3–3), irregular rhythm:
26	0:27	**B section** humorous piano tune with percussion
	0:44	**A section**—first theme returns
27	1:00	**C section** simple folk tune in strings, duple meter, regular rhythms
	2:03	**B section**—piano tune returns, very dissonant, builds with strings
28	2:51	**D section** built from fugue theme from 1st movement fugal devices employed
		stretto—overlapping of themes inversion—turning upside down
	4:47	**A section**—first theme returns, inverted

Subject: Inversion:

Twentieth-Century National Schools

French composers in the generation after Debussy and Ravel tried to recapture the wit and *esprit* that are part of their national heritage. They were followers of Erik Satie (1866–1925) in their attempt to develop a style that

French school

combined the composer's objectivity and understatement with Neoclassicism and new concepts of tonality. Among the most important composers of this era was a group known as *Les Six* that included Darius Milhaud (1892–1975), Arthur Honegger (1892–1955), Francis Poulenc (1899–1962), and Germaine Tailleferre (1892–1983), the sole woman in the group. Another important voice was that of Olivier Messiaen (1908–), who imbued his music with much religious symbolism, non-Western rhythms and instrumental colors, and with bird songs, reflecting his fascination of nature.

Russian school   In the post-Romantic period the Russian school produced two composers of international fame. Alexander Scriabin (1872–1915), a visionary artist whose music is wreathed in a subtle lyricism, was one of the leaders in the twentieth-century search for a new harmonic language. The piano works of Sergei Rachmaninoff (1873–1953) are enormously popular with the American public, especially his Second Piano Concerto and Variations on a Theme of Paganini. In the next generation we find two important figures in Sergei Prokofiev (1891–1953), and Dmitri Shostakovitch (1906–1975). Prokofiev strove to recapture the heroic affirmation of the Beethovenian symphony and brought the full power of his resources to the creation of film music. Outstanding among these are *Lieutenant Kijé* (1933) and *Alexander Nevsky* (1938). The first Russian composer of international repute who was wholly a product of Soviet musical culture was Shostakovitch, who was trained at the Leningrad Conservatory. His fifteen symphonies occupy a significant place in the twentieth-century orchestral repertory.

English school   England had produced no major composer for two hundred years until Sir Edward Elgar (1857–1934) appeared upon the scene. He and Frederick Delius (1862–1934) marked their country's return to the concert of nations. They were followed by two figures who were of prime importance in establishing the modern English school—Ralph Vaughan Williams (1872–1958) and Benjamin Britten (1913–76), whose works for the stage have established his reputation as one of the foremost opera composers of our time. Among them are *Peter Grimes* (1945) and *Billy Budd* (1952), after Herman Melville's story. Widely admired too are the lovely Serenade for tenor solo, horn, and string orchestra (1953) and the deeply moving *War Requiem* (1961). You will recall that we discussed Britten's *Young Person's Guide to the Orchestra* earlier in the book.

German school   Among the composers who came into prominence in Germany in the years after the First World War, Paul Hindemith (1895–1963) was the most notable figure. He left Germany when Hitler came to power—his music was banned from the Third Reich as "cultural Bolshevism"—and he spent two decades in the United States, during which he taught at Yale University and at Tanglewood, Massachusetts, where many young Americans came under his influence.

Carl Orff (1895–1982) took his point of departure from the clear-cut melodies and vigorous rhythms of Bavarian folk song. He is best known in this country for his "dramatic cantata" *Carmina burana* (1936). Kurt Weill (1900–50) was one of the most arresting figures to emerge in Germany in the 1920s. For the international public his name is indissolubly linked with

The Three-Penny Opera (1928) which he and the poet Berthold Brecht adapted from John Gay's *The Beggar's Opera*. Frequent revivals have made this one of the century's best known theater pieces.

Hungarian nationalism found another major representative in Zoltán Kodály (1882–1967), who was associated with Bartók in the collection and study of peasant songs. The folklore element is also prominent in his music. Czechoslovakia is well represented by Leoš Janáček (1855–1928), whose operas *Jenufa* (1916) and *The Cunning Little Vixen* (1926) have found great favor with the American public. Spain contributed two attractive nationalists of the post-Romantic era—Isaac Albéniz (1860–1919) and Enrique Granados (1867–1916), who paved the way for the major figure of the modern Spanish school, Manuel de Falla (1876–1936).

Other nationalists

Finland's Jean Sibelius (1865–1957) cut an important figure during the 20s and '30s, especially in England and the United States. His Second Symphony, Violin Concerto, and symphonic poem *Finlandia* retain their popularity. Carl Nielsen (1865–1931) is a Danish composer whose six symphonies have slowly established themselves in our concert life. Ernest Bloch (1880–1959), a native of Switzerland, was one of the few composers of Jewish background to consciously identify himself with his heritage. In *Schelomo*—the Biblical name of King Solomon—he produced a "Hebrew Rhapsody" for cello and orchestra that gave eloquent expression to his nationalism.

60

The American Scene: Art Music

"Music. . . the favorite passion of my soul"—THOMAS JEFFERSON

The American quality in music is not a single thing. It is the great achievement of our nation to have created, out of elements inherited from the past, entirely new and fresh kinds of music.

The Development of an American Style

Until the end of the nineteenth century, the music of the native American Indians remained an isolated oral tradition, ignored by those who arrived here later. Immigrant groups—the Spanish who came to seek gold and preach Catholicism, the Dutch who came to trade, the British and French and Germans who came to escape religious or political persecution, and the Africans who were brought as slaves—carried their own music with them

Early history

from their homelands. This was the mélange that provided the initial ingredients for America's musical melting pot.

In the Atlantic colonies, English music dominated. The Puritans of New England sang psalms from their Protestant tradition, and their *Bay Psalm Book* (1638) was the first book printed in the British colonies of North America. As cities became more populous in the eighteenth century, theatrical entertainments—primarily ballad operas from London—flourished.

The beginnings of American nationalism

The roots of a national style can be seen, however, in the works of several American composers. William Billings (1746–1800) of New England wrote highly individual hymns, anthems, and "fuguing tunes" quite unlike his English forebears, and, in another style came Stephen Foster (1825-64), whose universally loved songs drew on diverse sources including Italian opera, English ballads, and the music of minstrel shows (a theatrical entertainment performed by whites in blackface). African slaves, taught to sing Protestant hymns when they converted to Christianity, absorbed this idiom into the tradition which they had brought from Africa, developing into what came to be known as the "spiritual." All of these were new kinds of music, unique to America.

By 1850, a substantial concert life had grown up in our major cities, but it continued to be dominated by Europe. German music and musicians ruled the concert halls, while opera was principally supplied by the Italians. Young Americans who were attracted to a musical career, whether as composers or performers, went abroad to complete their studies. When they returned home they brought the European traditions with them. One of the first to use native song and dance as a source of inspiration was Louis Gottschalk (1829–69), a pianist and composer born in New Orleans and trained in Paris. Some of Gottschalk's original piano pieces, such as *The Banjo* and *Bamboula*, incorporated features of an Afro-American musical idiom. It was only gradually that American musicians shook off the influence of German music. This development was consummated with Charles Tomlinson Griffes (1884–1920), who turned for inspiration to France and the music of the Impressionists rather than to Germany, where he was trained.

Charles Ives

Meanwhile an unknown New Englander was working in isolation to find a vital way of expressing the American spirit in music—Charles Ives (1874–1954), who stands revealed as the first major prophet of our musical coming of age.

Knowing the musical world was not yet ready for his music, Charles Ives decided against a career in music; rather he entered the business world, composing at night and on weekends. He was rooted in the New England heritage. The sources of his tonal imagery are to be found in the living music of his childhood: hymn tunes and popular songs, the town band at holiday parades, the fiddlers at Saturday night dances, patriotic songs, and the melodies of Stephen Foster. His keen ear caught the the dissonant blend of untutored voices singing a hymn together, the pungent clash of dissonance when two bands, playing different tunes in different keys, were close enough to overlap. These, he realized, were not departures from the norm; they

Ives's music was as firmly rooted in uniquely American traditions as the cowboy bronzes of **Frederic Remington** (*1861–1909*), *such as* The Bronco Buster (Amon Carter Museum, Fort Worth, Texas)

were the norm of American musical speech. Thus he found the way to such conceptions as polytonality, atonlity, polyharmony, and polyrhythms before Schoenberg, Stravinsky, or Bartók did. Typical of his style is the Second Symphony, which was given its first performance in 1951, fifty-four years after Ives wrote it. The work quotes snatches of the American tunes Ives loved in his youth, such as *Turkey in the Straw, Old Black Joe, Columbia the Gem of the Ocean,* and *America the Beautiful.* Charles Ives' works are now firmly established in our concert life. Like the writers he admired—Emerson, Hawthorne, Thoreau—he has become an American classic.

American composers of art music, like Ives, have found their own voices, drawing upon the youthful traditions of which, as Americans, they are the inheritors. The extraordinary emigration of composers from Europe on the eve of the Second World War added a further element to the mix, and their teaching has been assimilated as well. Since World War II, the United States has been the birthplace of many of the most significant new developments in art music. After a long period in search of "American music," we have discovered that there is no such thing, but many different American musics—every one of them impossible to imagine as the product of any other culture.

Aaron Copland (1900–90) successfully integrated a number of American musical idioms, making him a representative figure among twentieth-century American composers. He manifested the serenity, clarity, and sense of balance that we regard as the essence of the Classical temperament.

Aaron Copland: His Life and Music

*"I no longer feel the need of seeking out conscious Americanism.
Because we live here and work here, we can be certain that when our
music is mature it will also be American in quality."*

Aaron Copland

Copland was born "on a street in Brooklyn that can only be described as drab. . . . Music was the last thing anyone would have connected with it." During his early twenties he studied in Paris with Nadia Boulanger, her first full-time American pupil. When Boulanger was invited to give concerts in America, she asked Copland to write a work for her. This was the Symphony for Organ and Orchestra. Contemporary American music was still an exotic dish to New York audiences. After the first performance (1925) Walter Damrosch found it necessary to assuage the feelings of his subscribers. "If a young man at the age of twenty-five," he announced from the stage of Carnegie Hall, "can write a symphony like that, in five years he will be ready to commit murder." Damrosch's prophecy, as far as is known, has not been fulfilled.

In his growth as a composer Copland mirrored the dominant trends of his time. After his return from Paris he turned to the jazz idiom, a phase that culminated in his brilliant Piano Concerto. There followed a period during which the Neoclassicist experimented with the abstract materials of his art. Copland realized that a new public for contemporary music was being created by the radio, phonograph, and film scores. "It made no sense to ignore them and to continue writing as if they did not exist. I felt that it was worth the effort to see if I couldn't say what I had to say in the simplest possible terms." In this fashion Copland was led to what became a most significant development after the 1930s: the attempt to simplify the new music so that it would communicate to a large public. The decade that followed saw the production of the scores that established Copland's pop-

Principal Works

Orchestral music, including 3 symphonies, Piano Concerto (1927), *Short Symphony* (1933), *Statements for Orchestra* (1933–35), *El Salon México* (1936), *A Lincoln Portrait* (1942), *Fanfare for the Common Man* (1942), and *Connotations for Orchestra* (1962)

3 ballets: *Billy the Kid* (1938), *Rodeo* (1942), and *Appalachian Spring* (1944)

Film scores, including *The Quiet City* (1939), *Of Mice and Men* (1939), *Our Town* (1940), *The Red Pony* (1948), and *The Heiress* (1949)

Piano music, including Piano Variations (1930)

Chamber music; choral music and songs

*A scene from the
American Ballet Theater
production of* Rodeo.
(Photo © 1983 by
Martha Swope)

ularity. His music —especially the three ballets, *Billy the Kid, Rodeo*, and
Appalachian Spring— continues to delight an international audience.

Copland: "Hoe-Down" from Rodeo

The second of Copland's American ballets, *Rodeo*, boasts one of his freshest
scores. The choreographer was Agnes de Mille, whose innovations opened
a new era in the American dance theater. The action of the ballet is a cowboy
version of the Cinderella/Ugly Duckling story. The Cowgirl, awkward and
tomboyish, is in love with the Head Wrangler and tries to impress him by
competing with the cowboys; but she makes no headway with the object
of her affections, for he has eyes only for the Rancher's daughter. Later, at
the Saturday night dance, still dressed in her mannish outfit of pants and
shirt, she is very much the wallflower. The sight of the Head Wrangler dancing
cheek to cheek with her rival is too much for her. She runs off, disconsolate.
When she returns she is completely transformed: the trousers have been
replaced by a pretty dress, the boots by slippers, she has a bow in her hair,
is the epitome of feminine allure, and quickly becomes the belle of the ball.

The concert suite that Copland arranged from the ballet consists of four
"dance episodes." (See Listening Guide 31 for titles and analysis.) We hear
the fourth, "Hoe-Down," a sprightly Allegro for which Copland borrowed
two square-dance tunes, *Bonyparte* and *McLeod's Reel*. The music vividly
suggests the traditional stance—head up, chest out, elbows raised, knees
bobbing up and down—that we associate with the more vigorous forms of
square dancing, thus conveying the boundless energy and zest for life that
animated the generations who built our country.

Listening Guide 31   📼 3B/6

COPLAND: *Rodeo*

Date: 1942

Genre: Ballet, arranged as orchestral suite

I. "Buckaroo Holiday"
2 cowboy songs: *Sis Joe* and *If He'd Be a Buckaroo*

II. "Corral Nocturne"

III. "Saturday Night Waltz"

IV. "Hoe-Down"
2 square-dance tunes

Bonyparte

McLeod's Reel

20   0:00   Opening: animated, fast triplet pattern.

        Strings sound as if they are tuning up. Piano and woodblock set up syncopated rhythms with pizzicato strings

     0:40   Tune 1: *Bonyparte*—fast, in strings and xylophone. Brass with syncopated rhythm

21   1:40   Tune 2: *McLeod's Reel*—lighter, sprightly dance heard first in trumpet, passed to various instruments, violins, oboes

     2:38   Piano and pizzicato string rhythm, as above. Slows down and comes to stop on long chord with celesta (bells)

     2:57   Tune 1 returns—interspersed with short references to Tune 2

61

The American Scene: Popular Styles

"Jazz I regard as an American folk music; not the only one, but a very powerful one, which is probably in the blood and feeling of the American people more than any other style of folk music. I believe that it can be made the basis of serious symphonic works of lasting value."—GEORGE GERSHWIN

Music in American Popular Culture

We saw that a diversity of cultures met in the great melting pot that is America. Out of those developed distinctive musical styles quite outside the classical idiom. The marches of John Philip Sousa (1855–1932) came to be internationally recognized as a peculiarly American contribution. So too jazz, rooted in spirituals, blues, and ragtime, which were part and parcel of the American scene, captured the imagination of the world. Around the turn of the nineteenth century the insistent rhythms of Afro-American music began to infuse new life into our popular musical theater. The songs of Jerome Kern, Irving Berlin, and George Gershwin transformed Broadway, and later Hollywood, into world musical centers of popular music. In the ensuing decades American folk and popular idioms came to be loved everywhere.

Ragtime, so called for its "ragged" rhythm, was originally a piano style marked by highly syncopated melodies. Scott Joplin (1868–1917), known as the "King of Ragtime," was one of the first black Americans to become an important composer. He is best remembered for his approximately fifty piano rags, including *The Maple Leaf Rag* (1899) and *The Entertainer*, and for his opera *Treemonisha* (1911), which incorporates black American dance idioms. Joplin was not alone in his attempt to merge ragtime with classical styles. Stravinsky, fascinated with the piano rag, incorporated its rhythmic vitality and syncopations in his *Ragtime for Eleven Instruments* (1918), his *Piano-Rag-Music* (1919), and in one dance number from *The Soldier's Tale* (1918).

Scott Joplin

Jazz and Blues

By *jazz* we mean a music created mainly by black Americans in the early twentieth century as they blended elements drawn from African musics with the popular and art traditions of the West. By examining the basics of jazz and blues we come to appreciate the impact these styles have had on our art music.

Blues is a truly American form of folk music based on a simple, repetitive poetic-musical structure. A blues text typically has a three-line stanza of

Blue note

which the first two are identical. The vocal style of blues was derived from the work songs of Southern blacks. The term *blues* refers to a mood as well as a harmonic progression, usually twelve or sixteen bars (measures) in length. Characteristic is the *blue note*, which represents a slight drop in pitch on the third, fifth, or seventh tone of the scale. One of the greatest of blues singers was Bessie Smith, whose performances were profoundly emotional and expressive.

Blues was a fundamental form in jazz. The music we call jazz was born in New Orleans through the fusion of such black elements as ragtime and blues with other traditional styles—spirituals, work songs, and shouts. Basic to these elements was the art of improvisation. Performers made up their parts as they went along, often with a number of them improvising at once. They were able to do this because all the players knew the basic conditions— the tempo, the form, the harmonic progression, and the order in which instruments were to be featured. A twelve-bar blues progression followed the standard pattern given below.

New Orleans jazz

New Orleans jazz depended upon multiple improvisations by the players, which created a polyphonic texture. Each instrument had its role. The trumpet or cornet played the melody proper or an embellished version of it; the clarinet was often featured in a countermelody above the main tune; the trombone improvised below the trumpet and signaled the chord changes; and the rhythm section—consisting of string bass or tuba, guitar or banjo, and drums—provided rhythmic and harmonic support. Among the "greats" of New Orleans jazz were Joseph "King" Oliver on cornet, Sidney Bechet on soprano saxophone, Ferdinand "Jelly Roll" Morton on piano, and Louis "Satchmo" Armstrong on trumpet.

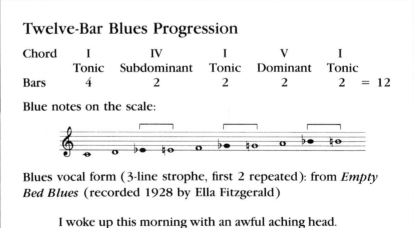

Twelve-Bar Blues Progression

Chord	I	IV	I	V	I	
	Tonic	Subdominant	Tonic	Dominant	Tonic	
Bars	4	2	2	2	2	= 12

Blue notes on the scale:

Blues vocal form (3-line strophe, first 2 repeated): from *Empty Bed Blues* (recorded 1928 by Ella Fitzgerald)

> I woke up this morning with an awful aching head.
> I woke up this morning with an awful aching head.
> My new man had left me, just a room and an empty bed.

King Oliver's Jazz Band in 1923. The young Louis Armstrong may be seen kneeling in front playing a slide trumpet. (William Ransom Hogan Jazz Archive, Tulane University)

Louis Armstrong: West End Blues

In the early 1920s, many New Orleans musicians went up the Mississippi River to Chicago, where "King" Oliver had a New Orleans style ensemble. Louis "Satchmo" Armstrong (c. 1898–1971), a native of New Orleans, joined this band in 1922, at a time when King Oliver's Creole Jazz Band had ten players. The young Armstrong, playing cornet, made his first recordings in 1923 with this ensemble, and went on to revolutionize jazz.

Armstrong was unquestionably the most important single force in the development of early jazz styles. He was a great improviser who expanded the capacities of his instrument in range and tone colors through the use of various mutes. His was a unique melodic-rhythmic style of performance for which his admirers coined the term "swing," which became a standard description of jazz. His 1926 recording of *Heebie Jeebies* introduced *scat singing*, a jazz style that sets nonsense syllables (vocables) to an improvised vocal line. Ella Fitzgerald later brought this technique to a truly virtuosic level.

Swing

Scat singing

Armstrong's style of jazz introduced a number of new features: stop-time choruses (solos accompanied by spaced staccato chords); double-time choruses in which each beat of each measure was subdivided; a flat two- or four-beat meter based on evenly accented pulses; and solo rather than ensemble choruses. Through these innovations, jazz was transformed into a solo art that presented fantasias on chord changes rather than on a repeated melody.

West End Blues is a twelve-bar blues recorded in 1922 by Armstrong and the Savoy Ballroom Five. The number opens with an unaccompanied trumpet solo by Armstrong in double time. There follow five choruses on the tune over the repeating twelve-bar progression we mentioned earlier. (See analysis in Listening Guide 32.) In the first chorus, we hear a solo trumpet melody set to a fairly simple chordal accompaniment. The second chorus brings in the mellow voice of the trombone, supported by a percussive accompaniment. The third chorus features clarinet against Satchmo's scat singing in a call-and-response pattern, while the fourth highlights the piano. The last chorus, a trumpet and clarinet duet, is extended with a brief tag (the jazz term for a short coda). Throughout the selection, we hear many "blue" or bent notes.

Louis Armstrong's sound summed up an era. It has remained one of the high points of the American jazz style.

Duke Ellington

From the inspired, improvisational style of Louis Armstrong, arose the brilliantly composed jazz of Duke Ellington (1899–1974) and the big-band era. With the advent of the big bands, the need was greater for music to be arranged or written down. Ellington played a major role in this development. Himself a fine pianist, he was even better as an orchestrator. His orchestral palette, richer than that of the New Orleans band, included two trumpets, one cornet, three trombones, four saxophones (some doubling on clarinet), two string basses, guitar, drum, vibraphone, and piano. One of Ellington's best-known and most unpretentious works is *Ko-ko,* a twelve-bar blues, expressively set in a minor key. In this work, Ellington drew inspiration from the drum ceremonies based on African religious rites that used to take place in New Orleans's Congo Square.

Ellington made a many-faceted contribution to the world of jazz. As a composer, he brought his art to new heights and a new-found legitimacy; as an arranger, he left a rich legacy of works for a wide range of jazz groups; as a band leader, he served as teacher and model to a whole generation of jazz musicians. He occupies a special place in our cultural heritage.

Bop and bebop

By the end of the 1940s, musicians had become disenchanted with big-band jazz and its limited possibilities. Their rebellion took shape in bop, bebop, and cool-style jazz. *Bop* was a contraction of *bebop*, an invented word whose two syllables suggest the two-note phrase that was the trademark of this style. Dizzie Gillespie, Charlie Parker, Bud Powell, and Thelonius Monk developed bebop in the 1940s. In the next two decades the term came to include a number of substyles such as cool jazz (the "cool" suggesting its restrained, unemotional manner), West Coast jazz, hard bop, and soul jazz.

Third stream

In 1957 the composer Gunther Schuller, in a lecture delivered at Brandeis University, coined the term *third stream*, holding that classical music was the first stream, jazz the second, and the third combined the other two. Although the designation referred mainly to the instruments used, it was soon extended to include other elements as well: the adoption of classical forms and tonal devices.

Listening Guide 32

3B/7

West End Blues, 1928, Louis Armstrong and the Savoy Ballroom Five

Louis "Satchmo" Armstrong, trumpet and vocal

Fred Robinson, trombone   Zutty Singleton, drums

Jimmy Strong, clarinet   Earl "Fatha" Hines, piano

Mancy Cara, banjo

Form: 12–bar blues (Introduction and 5 choruses)

14   0:00   Introduction (9 bars—double time)

Trumpet solo: rhythmically complex and varied; opens with descending, then ascending line

15   0:15   Chorus 1: Trumpet solo over chords; simple, homophonic setting (12 bars)

16   0:49   Chorus 2: Trombone solo over chords, with percussion accompaniment (12 bars)

17   1:22   Chorus 3: Clarinet and vocal solos (scat singing); motives exchanged in imitation (12 bars)

18   1:57   Chorus 4: Piano solo; simple chordal accompaniment (12 bars)

19   2:29   Chorus 5: Trumpet and Clarinet duet (8 bars); polyphonic texture; begins with high note held for 4 bars, then trumpet with double time movement

Piano solo (4 bars)

Tag (2-bar coda): full ensemble

Modern jazz quartet

Schuller's idea was taken over by a number of jazz musicians, among them John Lewis, who formed his Modern Jazz Quartet in answer to the growing demand for jazz on college campuses across the country. The ensemble played concerts that "swung" but also featured serious, composed works. One such work is Lewis's *Sketch* (recorded in 1959), which combined the foursome of his jazz ensemble—piano, vibraphone, drums and string bass—with the Beaux Arts Quartet, one of the finest string quartets in the country.

Influence of jazz

Although classical European composers did not adopt the improvisational procedures that are basic to jazz, they did capture something of its spontaneity and rhythmic freedom. Stravinsky wrote his *Ebony Concerto* (1945) for jazz clarinetist Woody Herman. Ernst Krenek's opera *Jonny spielt auf* (Johnny Plays, 1926), with a jazz violinist as hero, won an international success. The dry textures and snappy rhythms of jazz also resonate through such typically European works as Maurice Ravel's Piano Concerto in G, and Darius Milhaud's ballet *La création du monde* (The Creation of the World, 1923), the operas of Kurt Weill—*The Three-Penny Opera* (1928) and *Mahagonny* (1929)—as well as Alban Berg's *Lulu*.

The American Musical Theater

The American musical theater of today developed from the European *operetta* tradition. It was acclimated to the American taste through a number of composers, chief among them Victor Herbert (1850–1924) and later Jerome Kern (1885–1945), whose musical *Show Boat* (1927) was based on an Edna Ferber novel. In the ensuing decades, the musical established itself as America's unique contribution to world theater.

The genre was dependent on romantic plots in picturesque settings enlivened by comedy, appealing melodies, choruses, and dances. Within the framework of a thoroughly commercial theater a group of talented composers and writers created a body of works that not only enchanted their time but lasted well beyond it. Many of these derived their plots from sophisticated literary sources. Among these may be mentioned Cole Porter's *Kiss Me, Kate* (1948), Frank Loesser's *Guys and Dolls* (1950), Harold Rome's *Fanny* (1954), and Lerner and Loewe's *My Fair Lady* (1956).

This new seriousness led to one of the most enduring work of our lyric theater, George Gershwin's masterpiece *Porgy and Bess* (1935), an "American folk opera" derived from Afro-American folk idioms. This work paved the way for such musicals as Leonard Bernstein's *West Side Story* (1957), one of the first to have a tragic ending, and Jerry Bock's *Fiddler on the Roof* (1964), with lyrics by Sheldon Harnick.

In this climate the collaboration of Richard Rodgers and Oscar Hammerstein II produced a series of memorable works: *Oklahoma!* (1943), *South Pacific* (1949), *The King and I* (1951), and *The Sound of Music* (1959); these too drew their inspiration from literary sources.

In the '70s and '80s Stephen Sondheim brought the genre to new levels of sophistication in a series of works that included *A Little Night Music* (1973), *Sunday in the Park with George* (1983), and *Into the Woods*

(1988). A new era opened with two rock musicals—Gale MacDermot's *Hair* (1968) and Andrew Lloyd Webber's *Jesus Christ Superstar* (1971). Suddenly the romantic show tunes to which millions of young Americans had learned to dance and to flirt went completely out of fashion. After a while, however, melody returned. The British Webber conquered the international stage with *Evita* (1978), *Cats* (1981), and *The Phantom of the Opera* (1986)— works in which, as in the court operas of the Baroque, song and dance were combined with dazzling scenic effects. Together with Claude-Michel Schönberg's *Les Misérables* (1987), these pieces represented a new phenomenon. What had been almost exclusively an American product was now taken over by Europeans.

Leonard Bernstein: His Life and Music

As a composer, conductor, educator, pianist, and television personality, Leonard Bernstein (1918–90) had one of the most spectacular careers of our time. He was born in Lawrence, Massachusetts, the son of Russian-Jewish immigrants. He studied at Harvard and Curtis Institute in Philadelphia, then became one of the band of disciples whom the conductor Serge Koussevitzky gathered around him in Tanglewood. In 1943, when he was twenty-five, Bernstein was appointed Artur Rodzinski's assistant at the New York Philharmonic. A few weeks later, Bruno Walter, the guest conductor, was suddenly taken ill; Rodzinski was out of town. Bernstein, at a few hours' notice, took over the Sunday afternoon concert and coast-to-coast broadcast, and gave an extraordinary performance. Overnight he was famous. Thereafter his career proceeded apace until, in 1958, at the age of forty, he was appointed director of the New York Philharmonic, the first American-born conductor (and the youngest) to occupy the post.

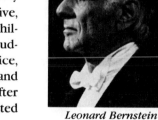

Leonard Bernstein

In his compositions, Bernstein straddled the worlds of serious and popular music. He had a genuine flair for orchestration; the balance and spacing of

Principal Works

Orchestral works, including the *Jeremiah Symphony* (1942), Symphony No. 2, *The Age of Anxiety* (piano and orchestra, 1949), Serenade (violin, strings, and percussion, 1954), Symphony No. 3, *Kaddish* (1963)

Works for chorus and orchestra, including *Chichester Psalms* (1965) and *Songfest* (1977)

Operas, including *A Quiet Place* (1983)

Musicals, including *On the Town* (1944), *Wonderful Town* (1953), *Candide* (1956), and *West Side Story* (1957)

Other dramatic music, including the ballet *Fancy Free* (1944), the film score *On the Waterfront* (1954), and Mass (1971)

Chamber and instrumental music; solo vocal music

sonorities, the use of the brass in the high register, the idiomatic writing that shows off each instrument to its best advantage—all these bespeak a master. His harmonic idiom was spicily dissonant, his jazzy rhythms had great vitality, and he had the gift of melody.

Bernstein's feeling for the urban scene—specifically the New York scene—is vividly projected in his theater music. In *On the Town* (1944), a full-length version of his ballet *Fancy Free* (1944), *Wonderful Town* (1953), and *West Side Story* (1957), he achieved a sophisticated kind of musical theater that explodes with movement, energy, and sentiment. His death in October 1990 aroused universal mourning. He was truly a world figure.

Bernstein: Symphonic Dances, from West Side Story

West Side Story, with book and lyrics by Stephen Sondheim, updated the Romeo and Juliet saga to a modern-day setting of rival gangs of youths on the streets of New York. The hostility between the Jets and the Sharks becomes the modern counterpart of the feud of the Capulets and the Montagues in Shakespeare's play. Tony, one of the Jets, falls in love with Maria, whose brother leads the Sharks. The tale of the star-crossed lovers unfolds in scenes of great tenderness, whence come memorable songs like "Tonight" and "Maria," alternating with electrifying dances choreographed by Jerome Robbins, as the tale mounts inexorably to Tony's tragic death. Bernstein subsequently adapted their music in a set of Symphonic Dances in eight episodes. (See Listening Guide 33.) The score displays the composer's colorful orchestration as well as his imaginative handling of jazz and Latin American rhythms. It calls for an expanded woodwind and percussion section, including the piano. The music of the "Cool" Fugue builds to several climaxes with fugal textures that become increasingly dense and polyphonic

Riff (center) leads the Jets in the "Cool" fugue from West Side Story, *one of the highlights of the 1989 stage hit,* Jerome Robbins' Broadway. (Photo © 1989 Martha Swope)

before they grow gentle and relaxed. This section of the score is from a dance sequence by the Jets, prior to the final fight, or Rumble, with the Sharks. Fleeting references to the lyrical ballads of the play resonate through the score, which demands much of our ears, especially our tolerance of high levels of dissonance.

Listening Guide 33

3B/8

BERNSTEIN: Symphonic Dances from *West Side Story*

Date: 1961

Basis: Dance sequences from musical *West Side Story* (1957)

OVERVIEW OF SYMPHONIC DANCES

Prologue (Allegro moderato)
The growing rivalry between the two teen-age gangs, the Jets and the Sharks.

"Somewhere" (Adagio)
In a visionary dance sequence, the two gangs are united in friendship.

Scherzo (Vivace leggiero)
In the same dream, they break through the city walls, and suddenly find themselves in a world of space, air, and sun.

Mambo (Presto)
Reality again; competitive dance between the two gangs.

Cha-cha (Andantino con grazia)
The star-crossed lovers see each other for the first time and dance together.

"Cool," Fugue (Allegretto)
An elaborate dance sequence in which the Jets practice controlling their hostility.

Rumble (Molto allegro)
Climactic gang battle during which the two gang leaders are killed.

Finale (Adagio)
Love music developing into a procession, which recalls, in tragic reality, the vision of "Somewhere"

"Cool," Fugue

Based largely on several short rhythmic motives

Melody of above drawn from opening of "Maria" (rising augmented fourth, music going to a fifth)

23 0:00   Allegretto: grows out of rhythmic patterns above, adding instruments and increasingly syncopated; alternating woodwinds and strings

0:41   Muted trumpet solo, with regular brush
pattern on cymbals, punctuated by 3-note
motive (vibraphone, piano)

| 24 | 1:00   Fugue subject, with dotted rhythms, begins
in flute, against constant brush in cymbals;
then heard in clarinet and piano, marked
"with jazz feel"

1:30   3-note dotted pattern returns and builds,
against long notes in string

2:12   Solo percussion break followed by
homophonic syncopated chords

Second solo percussion break followed by
unison section based on 3-note motive

| 25 | 2:38   Brass featured in syncopated jazz section,
with shakes on high notes, accompanied by
syncopated patterns in strings and
woodwinds

3:03   Rhythmic pattern from opening returns,
builds to climax

Rumble, Molto allegro

| 26 | 3:42   Synocopations, rhythmic vitality, and complexity build to loud, homophonic
chords in orchestra, irregularly spaced

4:28   Fugal section grows out of 3-note pattern, instruments added, building to regular
pulse on eighth notes; marked crescendo on rising chromatic pattern leads to
final glissando and closing chords.

UNIT XXIV

The New Music

62

New Directions

"From Schoenberg I learned that tradition is a home we must love and forgo."—LUKAS FOSS

We have seen that the term "new music" has been used throughout history. Has not every generation of creative musicians produced sounds and styles that had never been heard before? All the same, the years since World War II have seen such far-reaching innovations in the art that we are perhaps more justified than any previous generation in applying the label to the music of the present. In effect, we have witnessed nothing less than the birth of a new world of sound.

New Trends in the Arts

Only rarely does an important movement in art come into being without precursors. It should therefore not surprise us that several elements of avant-garde art can be traced back to earlier developments. For example, the Dada movement grew up in Zurich during the war and after 1918 spread to other major art centers. The Dadaists, in reaction to the horrors of the blood bath that engulfed Europe, rejected the concept of Art with a capital A—that is, something to be put on a pedestal and reverently admired. To make their point, they produced works of manifest absurdity. They also reacted against the excessive complexity of Western art and tried to recapture the simple, unfettered way in which a child views the world. Erik Satie led the way toward a simple, "everyday" music, and exerted an important influence in the 1920s—along with the writer Jean Cocteau—on the generation of Milhaud, Honegger, and Poulenc. Several decades later this influence came to the fore in the work of the American composer John Cage, who we shall

Dadaism

309

310

Marcel Duchamp (*1887–1968*), *in his* Nude Descending a Staircase, No. 2, *organized the indiscipline of Dada into a visionary art.* (The Philadelphia Museum of Art. Louise and Walter Arensberg Collection 50-134-59)

Surrealism

discuss in a later chapter. The Dada group, which included artists like Hans Arp and Marcel Duchamp, subsequently merged into the school of Surrealists, as exemplified by Salvador Dali, who exploited the symbolism of dreams. Other elements entering into the family tree of contemporary art were Cubism, the Paris-based style of painting embodied in the work of Pablo Picasso, Georges Braque, and Juan Gris, which encouraged the painter to construct a visual world in terms of geometric patterns; and Expressionism, which we discussed in Chapter 55 (See illustrations on pages 274).

Art since the Second World War has unfolded against a background of unceasing social turmoil. This restlessness of spirit is inevitably reflected in the arts, which are passing through a period of violent experimentation with new media, new materials, new techniques. Artists are freeing themselves from every vestige of the past in order to explore new areas of thought and feeling.

Abstract expressionism

The trend away from objective painting guaranteed the supremacy of Abstract Expressionism in this country during the 1950s and '60s. In the canvases of such men as Robert Motherwell and Jackson Pollock, space, mass, and color are freed from the need to imitate objects in the real world. The urge toward abstraction has been felt equally in contemporary sculpture, as is evident in the work of such artists as Henry Moore and Isamu Noguchi. (See illustration on page xxx.)

Theater of the Absurd

At the same time, a new kind of realism has come into being in the art of Jasper Johns, Robert Rauschenberg, and their fellows, who owe some of their inspiration to the Dadaists of four decades earlier. Rauschenberg's aim, as he put it, was to work "in the gap between life and art." This trend culminated in Pop Art, which draws its themes and techniques from modern urban life: machines, advertisements, comic strips, movies, commercial photography, and familiar objects connected with everyday living. The desire to function "in the gap between life and art" motivated Andy Warhol's *Four Campbell's Soup Cans,* Jim Dine's *A Nice Pair of Boots,* and Rauschenberg's own *First Landing Jump* (see page 313).

Pop art

In the field of literature, poetry has been the most experimental genre. Contemporary American poetry ranges over a wide gamut from intellectualism to the Whitmanesque exuberance of the "Beat Generation." Freedom of verse form and a sardonic wit tinged with betterness characterize many of the younger poets. Although the forms of drama and novel are by their very nature based on an imitation of life, they have not remained indifferent to the new trends. The theater has moved away from the social and psychological concerns that permeated the work of Arthur Miller and Tennessee

Poetry

In Abstract Expressionism, space and mass become independent values, liberated from the need to express reality. Elegy to the Spanish Republic, 108. 1965–67, *by* **Robert Motherwell** (*b. 1915*). (The Museum of Modern Art, New York. Charles Mergentime Fund)

The urge toward abstraction has been felt by sculptors such as **Henry Moore** (*b. 1898*) *in his* Lincoln Center Reclining Figure *located in the reflecting pool on New York's Lincoln Center Plaza North.* (Photo © Susanne Faulkner Stavens)

Williams in the 1950s. It has turned instead to the "theater of the absurd," whose leading European proponents—Samuel Beckett, Eugene Ionesco, and Jean Genêt—view the world with a vast disillusionment. The spirit of the absurd has also penetrated the novel—witness such works as John Barth's *Goat-Boy*.

Finally, the cinema—of all the arts the one most securely chained to storytelling of a popular kind—has also responded to the twin impulses of experimentation and abstraction. Among the "new wave" directors may be mentioned Michelangelo Antonioni, Jean-Luc Godard, and Federico Fellini. In films like Alain Resnais' *Last Year at Marienbad* and Ingmar Bergman's *Persona*, the Abstract Expressionist urge found perhaps its most successful cinematic realization to date.

New wave cinema

We have mentioned only a few landmarks on the contemporary scene, but these are enough to indicate that art today has become increasingly intellectual, experimental, and abstract.

Toward Greater Organization in Music

When Schoenberg based his twelve-tone method on the use of tone rows, he was obviously moving toward a much stricter organization of the sound material. It remained for later generations to extend the implications of the tone-row principle to the elements of music other than pitch. The arrangement of the twelve tones in a series might be paralleled by similar groupings of twelve durations (time values), twelve dynamic values (degrees of loudness), or twelve timbres. Other factors, too, might be brought under serial organization. This move toward *total serialism* resulted, in the decades after the war, in an extremely complex, ultrarational music. The composers who

Total serialism

embraced total serialism, such as Pierre Boulez and Karlheinz Stockhausen, pushed to the farthermost limits some of the new ways of hearing and experiencing music.

Toward Greater Freedom in Music

The urge toward a totally controlled music had its counterpart in the desire for greater—even total—freedom from all predetermined forms and procedures. Music of this type emphasizes the antirational element in artistic experience: intuition, chance, the spur of the moment. Composers may rely on the element of chance and allow, let us say, a throw of dice to determine the selection of their material; they may perhaps build their pieces around a series of random numbers generated by a computer; they may indicate the general course of events in regard to pitches, durations, registers, but leave it up to the performer to fill in the details. The performance thus becomes a musical "happening" in the course of which the piece is recreated afresh each time it is played.

Such indeterminate music is known as *aleatory* (from *alea*, the Latin word for "dice," which from ancient times have symbolized the whims of chance). In aleatory music the overall form may be clearly indicated but

Aleatory music

The themes and techniques of Pop Art are drawn from modern urban life while incorporating incongruities into each work. A construction by **Robert Rauschenberg** (*b. 1925*), First Landing Jump. 1961. (*The Museum of Modern Art, New York. Gift of Philip Johnson*)

The mobiles of **Alexander Calder** (*1898–1976*) *achieve an ideal of ever-changing form.* Black Sickles, Black Commas. (Photograph by Lee Boltin)

the details are left to choice or chance. On the other hand, some composers, among them John Cage, will indicate the details of a composition clearly enough, but leave its overall shape to choice or chance; this type of flexible structure is known as *open form*. Related to these tendencies is the increased reliance on improvisation. Taken to its extreme, no criteria are imposed; anything that happens is acceptable.

Lukas Foss

A representative figure of this new freedom is Lukas Foss (1922–), whose *Time Cycle* (1960) and *Echoi* (1961–63) established his place in the forefront of those who were experimenting with indeterminacy, group improvisation, and fresh approaches to sound. In the ensuing decades he consistently maintained his position as one of the leaders of the avant-garde, the compositions of his later period for the most part employing aleatoric procedures.

Contemporary attitudes have liberated not only form but all the elements of music from the restrictions of the past. The concept of a music based on the twelve pitches of the chromatic scale has been left far behind. Electronic instruments make possible the use of sounds that lie "in the cracks of the piano keys"—the *microtonal* intervals, such as quarter tones, that are smaller than the tradition semitones—and very skilled instrumentalists and vocalists have now mastered these novel scales.

Microtonal intervals

The Internationalism of the New Music

World War II and the events leading up to it disrupted musical life on the Continent much more than in this country, with the result that the United States forged ahead in certain areas. For example, the first composer to apply serial organization to dimensions other than pitch was the American Milton Babbitt. The experiments of John Cage anticipated and influenced similar attempts abroad. Earle Brown was the first to use open form; Morton Feldman was the first to write works that gave the performer a choice. Once the war was over the Europeans quickly made up for lost time. Intense experimentation went on in Italy, Germany, France, England, Holland, and Scandinavia. Serial and electronic music have also taken root in Japan, while the music of the East has in turn influenced Western composers.

A number of Europeans have achieved international reputations. Pierre Boulez (1925–), the most important French composer of the avant-garde, is widely known because of his activities as a conductor. For five years he was music director of the New York Philharmonic. At the head of IRCAM (the French government's institute of composition and acoustics), he is the official leader of French musical life today. Luciano Berio (1925–) is a leading figure among the radicals of the post-Webern generation in Italy. He was one of the founders of the electronic studio in Milan that became a center of avant-garde activity, and for several years taught composition at the Juilliard School in New York. The Greek composer Iannis Xenakis (1922–) exemplifies the close ties between music and science characteristic of our time; he was trained as an engineer. Xenakis's music derives its very special sound from massed sonorities, prominent use of glissandos, and a texture woven out of individual parts for each instrument in the orchestra. Krzysztof Penderecki (1933–) is the foremost composer of Poland. His search for new sonorities and new ways of producing them has impelled him to include in his scores such noises as the sawing of wood and the clicking of typewriters. His choral music includes special effects such as hissing, shouting, whistling, articulating rapid consonants, and the like. In this area he has been much influenced by Iannis Xenakis.

Pierre Boulez

Luciano Berio

Iannis Xenakis

Krzysztof Penderecki

Other Aspects of the New Music

Several composers have tried to reconcile serial procedures with tonality. None has played a more important role in this area than George Perle (1915–). In a language based on the twelve-tone scale he has retained the concept of tonal centers. Perle had to wait until his seventies to be recognized as one of the important composers of his generation. In 1986 he won the Pulitzer Prize for his *Wind Quintet IV* and one of the "genius fellowships" of the MacArthur Foundation. Before that he was known chiefly for his books, including *Serial Composition and Atonality* (1962) and *Twelve-Tone Tonality* (1978). Charles Wuorinen (1938–) started out from the sound world of Stravinsky, Schoenberg, and Varèse, and found his way to the twelve-tone system in the 1960s. He freely adapts the procedures of the twelve-tone "system" to the needs of the particular piece he is writing. A prolific composer, he has received his share of awards and honors, among them a Pulitzer Prize and a MacArthur Fellowship. Ralph Shapey (1921–) directs the Contemporary Chamber Players at the University of Chicago. The disciple of Varèse speaks in Shapey's definition of music as "an object in Time and Space: aggregate sounds structured into concrete sculptural forms." His output is mostly instrumental; but he was one of the first American composers to view the voice as an instrument "using syllables in organized sound-structures."

George Perle

Charles Wuorinen

Ralph Shapey

Women in Contemporary Music

Women have played a much more prominent role in the contemporary music scene than they did in the past. They have distinguished themselves not only as performers, a role in which they always excelled, but also as composers, teachers, and conductors. The Paris Conservatoire, for example, has long been recognized for the caliber of the women musicians it has produced. Many composers of our generation studied there under the tutelage of Nadia Boulanger. In the chart on the facing page you will find mention of a few of the most notable women musicians of our time.

63

Non-Western Music and the Contemporary Scene

Unlike Europe, the continents of Asia and Africa do not constitute single cultural units. On the contrary, their societies represent the utmost diversity, from ancient civilizations such as China and India, whose artistic instincts have been refined through thousands of years, to societies like the Pygmies of Africa or the Aborigines of Australia, whose development has not kept pace with the modern world. All these societies have music, but their musical languages differ from one another as much as they differ from the language of Beethoven or Chopin.

But this barrier between musical languages is not an impassable one. Until recently, the Western public had little opportunity to hear music of other cultures. The Second World War brought these disparate worlds closer. The success in the West of such artists as Ravi Shankar introduced European and American audiences to the exquisitely subtle art of India. Authentic recordings of Asian and African music have become increasingly available, making it possible for Western listeners to expand their ears by hearing musics based on totally different assumptions, and performing groups from all over the world are much in demand by Western audiences.

Conversely, Western music has begun to make inroads in Japan, Korea, Indonesia, China, and other countries of Asia. Today symphony orchestras perform works of Beethoven in Beijing and Tokyo, Delhi and Seoul. Their conservatories are teaching Western music, and students from the Far East are coming to study music at the Juilliard School and similar institutions. In addition, artists such as the conductors Zubin Mehta and Seiji Ozawa, the cellist Yo Yo Ma, composers like Toru Takemitsu and Chou Wen-Chung are

Nadia Boulanger (1887–1979)	French conductor and teacher; students include Copland, Carter, Musgrave and Glass, advocate of neo-Classical aesthetic and the performance of French Renaissance and Baroque music
Germaine Tailleferre (1892–1983)	French composer; only woman member of Les Six; trained at Paris Conservatory; neo-Classicist; notable works include ballet *Marchand d'oiseaux* (1923) and Ouverture (1932) for orchestra
Ruth Crawford (1901–53)	American avant-garde composer of the 1920s; first woman awarded a Guggenheim Fellowship to study composition in Europe; String Quartet (1931) exemplifies total organization in music
Louise Talma (1906–)	American composer; studied with Nadia Boulanger; favors serial techniques; works for piano, solo voice and chorus, orchestra; opera *The Alcestiade* (1962) on libretto by Thornton Wilder
Jean Eichelberger Ivey (1923–)	American composer; interest in synthesis of tape and live performers, as in *Sea-Change* (1979) for large orchestra and tape; monodrama *Testament of Eve* (1976) sets her own text
Cathy Berberian (1925–83)	American vocalist of international repute; highly virtuosic, specialized in contemporary music; premiered works by Stravinsky and Berio; married to Berio; wrote works for solo voice and piano
Betsy Jolas (1926–)	French composer; disciple of Messiaen; turned from serial to aleatory procedures; experiments with spatial effects; lyrical style; works for small ensembles, including Quatuor II (1964), for soprano and three strings
Bethany Beardslee (1927–)	American soprano; specialist in contemporary music; presented American premieres of works by Schoenberg, Stravinsky, and Berg; noted for wide vocal range and impressive virtuosity; commissioned Babbitt's *Philomel* (1964) under auspices of Ford Foundation
Thea Musgrave (1929–)	Scottish-born composer; studied with Nadia Boulanger; advocate of New Romanticism; noted for her operas, including *Mary, Queen of Scots* (1977, see p. 329)
Jan DeGaetani (1933–89)	American virtuoso singer; specialized in contemporary music; sang early music with New York Pro Musica; premiered works by Carter and Crumb, including *Ancient Voices of Children* (1970); wrote *The Complete Sightsinger* (1980)
Joan Tower (1938–)	American composer; interest in twelve-tone technique in '60s gave way to more accessible style; chamber works include *Breakfast Rhythms I* and *II* (1975) for clarinet and five instruments
Ellen Taaffe Zwilich (1939–)	American composer; first woman awarded a Pulitzer Prize in composition recognizing her Symphony No. 1 (1983); chamber works for varied instrumental combinations include *Passages* (1981), for soprano and chamber group with poems by A. B. Ammons
Barbara Kolb (1939–)	American composer; first woman to win Prix de Rome; eclectic style; interest in complex metrical patterns; chamber works include *Solitaire* (1972) for piano, vibraphone, and tape; and *Yet That Things Go Round* (1987) for chamber orchestra
Ursula Oppens (1944–)	American pianist; studied at Juilliard; awarded the Avery Fischer Prize in 1976; founding member of Speculum Musicae, highly praised contemporary music ensemble; compositions written for her by Carter and Wuorinen

The internationally renowned Ravi Shankar playing the sitar.

playing an ever more important part in Western musical life. But perhaps the greatest impact that Western music has had worldwide is through the immense popularity of rock music with the world's youth. Thus, in spite of Rudyard Kipling's famous poem—"Oh, East is East, and West is West, and never the twain shall meet,"— East and West are steadily drawing closer.

Music in Society

In every culture, music is intricately woven into the lives and beliefs of its people. Just as in the West, the "classical" exists alongside the "popular," both nourished from the unbelievably rich store of folk music that is intimately interwoven with daily living. Music serves different functions in different societies, though some basic roles are universal: accompanying ceremonial acts, religious or civic; accompanying work to pass the time; entertaining through singing and dancing. The social organization of any particular culture has much to do with the resulting music of its people. In some cultures, only a few people are involved with the actual performance of music, while in others, such as that of the African Pygmies, cooperative work is so much a part of their society that they sing as a group, with each person weaving a separate part to build a complex whole. Music exists for every conceivable type of occasion, but the specific occasions celebrated vary from culture to culture. Thus, musical genres, or categories of repertory, do not transfer from one culture to the next.

Not all music is written down and learned from books or formal lessons. In some cultures, music is transmitted through a master-apprentice relationship that lasts many years, while in others there is no formal instruction; rather, the aspiring musician must learn from watching and listening. Music of most cultures of the world, including some styles of Western popular music, is transmitted by example or imitation and is performed from memory. This music is said to exist in *oral tradition*.

The Languages of Non-Western Musics

We have seen that Western music is largely a melody-oriented art based on a particular musical system from which underlying harmonies are also built. Relatively speaking, rhythm and meter in Western music are based on simpler principles than are melody and harmony. Musics of other cultures sound completely foreign to our ears, sometimes "out of tune," because they are based on entirely different musical systems. Strange as it may seem to Westerners, the music of many cultures does not involve harmony to any great extent. Rather, the construction of melody and the organization of musical time are central to their differing musical languages.

One important factor in these differing languages of music is the way in which the octave is divided. We have seen that in Western music the octave is divided into twelve semitones, from which seven are chosen to form the major scale while a slightly different group of seven comprises the minor scale. These two scales have constituted the basis of the Western musical language for nearly four hundred years.

But the musical languages of other cultures divide the octave differently, producing different scale patterns. Among the most common is the *pentatonic*, or five-note, scale, used in some African, Far Eastern, and American Indian musics. There are a number of different patterns possible in fashioning a pentatonic scale, each with its own unique quality of sound. Thus the scales heard in Japan and China, although both pentatonic, sound quite different. Other scale types include *tritonic*, a three-note pattern found in the music of some South African cultures, and *heptatonic*, or seven-note scales fashioned from a different combination of intervals than major and minor scales.

Some scales are not playable on Western instruments because they employ microtonal intervals that sound "off-key" to Western ears. One manner of producing microtonal music involves an inflection of a pitch, or a brief microtonal dip from the original pitch; this technique, similar to that of the *blue note* in jazz discussed earlier, makes possible a host of subtle inflections unknown in the melody of the West.

We have seen that rhythm is the element that organizes music through time. Since all sounds and silences have duration, all musics have a rhythmic basis. But the regular pulse of Western music, and the organization of these beats into patterns of two, three, and four, are not universal features of music. Indeed, the music of many cultures is far more varied and complex, using patterns and combinations of patterns that are unknown in Western music. Repetitive patterns, often with an obsessive insistence, are a feature of some African musics; these patterns unfold in a web of cross-rhythms and polyrhythms that amaze and confuse the Western ear. Some musics are based on

In their tribal rituals, African dancers may create their own rhythmic accompaniment with gourd rattles strapped to their legs.

Tala

changing meters. On the other hand, a musical selection from southern India depends on a fixed time cycle known as a *tala*, built from uneven groupings of beats (such as $4 + 2 + 2$). In the latter music, a drum first marks the cycle, then divides the tala into smaller and smaller rhythmic cells, building a complex arabesque of sound.

Musical performance practices vary radically from one culture to the next. In musics where a single melodic line is prevalent, instruments may accompany the line with elaborations on it, so that the result remains basically monophonic in texture. Many musics depend on the simple accompaniment of one or several repeated tones for harmonic support. This device, known

Drone

as a *drone*, is heard in Western music as well. The *bagpipe,* for example, is a drone instrument that has been popular for centuries both in Eastern and Western Europe. It has several tubes, one of which plays the melody while the others sound the drones, or sustained notes.

Simple harmonies and polyphonic textures are typical of some musics of Central and Western Africa. Polyphony can arise from the singing or playing of parallel intervals, such as thirds, fourths, or fifths, much as we described in medieval organum. It can take the form of a simple round with a leader and chorus singing the same melody at different times, or it may result from the use of an ostinato, or repeated pattern, sounded in accompaniment to a melody. One formal practice that can be found throughout much of the world is *call-and-response* or *responsorial* singing. Heard in the musics of the Pan-Islamic region of North Africa, the North American Indians, and the New World Negro, to mention only a few, this style of performance is based on a social structure that recognizes a singing leader who is imitated by a chorus of followers. This simple procedure is fundamental to much folk music and to jazz performance as well.

Responsorial singing

Musical Instruments of the World

The diversity of musical instruments from around the world defies the imagination. Every conceivable method of sound production is used, every possible raw material employed. It would be impossible to list or catalog them here. Nor do they all conveniently fit into the standard families of Western instruments (strings, woodwinds, brass, percussion). Thus, specialists have devised an alternate method for classifying instruments, one based solely on the manner in which they generate sounds. There are four categories in this classification system. *Aerophones* produce sound by using air as the primary vibrating means. Common instruments in this grouping are flutes, whistles, and horns. *Chordophones* are instruments that produce sound from a vibrating string stretched between two points. The string may be set in motion by bowing or plucking. *Idiophones* produce the sound from the substance of the instrument itself. They may be struck, blown, shaken, scraped, or rubbed. Examples of idiophones are bells, rattles, xylophones, and cymbals. The fourth category is *membranophones*, referring to any instrument sounded from tightly streched membranes. These drum-type instruments can be struck, plucked, rubbed, or even sung into, thus setting the skin in vibration.

Aerophones

Chordophones

Idiophones

Membranophones

Cross-Cultural Exchanges of Music

Throughout the course of history, the West has felt the influence of other cultures. We have already noted the nineteenth-century fascination with exoticism that spurred interest in the Orient and its arts. Composers of the Russian school were particularly intrigued with the East. The music of Spanish Gypsies is suggested in Bizet's opera *Carmen*, the splendor of ancient Egypt is captured in Verdi's *Aïda*, and the spirit of the so-called "dark continent" is evinced in Saint-Saën's fantasy for piano and orchestra *Afrique* (Africa). Since these composers were writing works based on Western harmonies to be played on Western instruments, they naturally made no attempt to use the authentic scales of Asia or Africa. They contented themselves with writing works which to their imaginations resembled the sound of musics of distant lands. We have also discussed the more sustained efforts at exoticism of the Post-Romantics, especially Debussy who, we saw, fell under the spell of the Javanese gamelan and the whole-tone scale.

Twentieth-century composers, we noted earlier, found inspiration not only in African music but also in the strong rhythmic features of the songs

In this performance of a Balinese Topeng (Masked Dance), part of the gamelan—a double-headed drum and three metallophones—may be seen behind the dancer. (Photograph by Thomas Haar, courtesy of The Asia Society)

Primitivism

and dances of the borderlands of Western culture—southeastern Europe, Asiatic Russia, and the Near East. Notable among these were Bartók, Stravinsky, and Prokofiev. We have also encountered the strong impetus toward primitivism that came from the Afro-American styles developed by black American musicians, which combined the powerful rhythmic impulse of their heritage with the major-minor tonality of their new home. Out of this amalgam grew the rich literature of Negro spirituals, work songs and shouts, and ultimately ragtime, blues and jazz, swing and rock.

The musics of Africa and Asia constitute a rich literature that has had a profound influence on contemporary composers. A number of them have responded to the philosophy of the Far East, especially Zen Buddhism and Indian thought. Among them are three Californians whose work has attracted much notice: Henry Cowell, Harry Partch, and especially John Cage, whose name has been associated with the avant-garde scene for over fifty years.

John Cage

John Cage (1912–) represents the type of eternally questing artist who no sooner solves one problem than he presses forward to another. He exhibited an early interest in non-Western scales, which he learned from his mentor Henry Cowell. Cage's abiding interest in rhythm led him to explore the possibilities of percussion instruments. He soon realized that the traditional dichotomy between consonance and dissonance had given way to a new opposition between music and noise, as a result of which the boundaries of the one were extended to include more of the other. Cage's exploration of percussive rhythm led him to invent what he christened the "prepared piano." The preparation consisted of inserting nails, bolts, nuts, screws, and bits of rubber, wood, or leather at crucial points between the strings of an ordinary grand piano. There resulted a myriad of sounds whose overall effect resembled that of a Javanese gamelan (an ensemble made up of various kinds of gongs, xylophones, drums, bowed and plucked strings, cymbals, and sometimes singers). Cage wrote a number of works for the prepared piano, notably the set of *Sonatas and Interludes* (1946–48). Cage's interest in indeterminacy led to compositions with choices made by throwing dice. He has also relied on the *I Ching* (Book of Changes), an ancient Chinese method of throwing coins or marked sticks for chance numbers, from which he derived a system of charts and graphs governing the series of events that could happen within a given structural space. One final frontier conquered by Cage was the transfer of indeterminacy to tape. This problem he solved in his *Fontana Mix* (1958), which became the first taped work to establish conditions whose outcome could not be foreseen. These experiments established John Cage as a seminal force in the artistic life of our time.

The infusion of non-Western sounds into Western music was not reserved for the classical idiom. In jazz and rock, too, Eastern influences were felt. The saxophonist John Coltrane wrote music that was freed of the rhythmic and harmonic traditions of jazz; rather it employed drones and unusual scales reflecting his interest in Indian and Arabian music. The popularity of meditation drew many jazz performers to Far Eastern ways, as it did Beatles George Harrison and John Lennon in the 1960s. In all these endeavors, we find a fusion of Eastern and Western music that cannot fail to enrich us.

64

New Sounds

Musical styles so different from all that went before need a new breed of instrumentalists and vocalists to cope with their technical difficulties. One has only to attend a concert of avant-garde music to realize how far the art of piano playing or singing has moved from the world of Chopin or Verdi. The piano keyboard may be brushed or slammed or the player may reach inside to pluck the strings directly. A violinist may tap, stroke, and even slap the instrument. Vocal music runs the gamut from whispering to shouting. Wind players have learned to produce a variety of sounds and the percussion section has been enriched by an astonishing variety of noisemakers and special effects. In each of the important musical centers groups of players and singers are springing up who have a genuine affinity with the new music. They are performing an invaluable service for the new music, and it is an encouraging sign that their numbers are growing. Several of the more notable women performers of our time are listed in Chapter 62.

The new virtuosity

Some Contemporary Masters

Elliott Carter

Of the composers who have come into prominence in recent years, none is more widely admired by musicians than Elliott Carter (1908–). His works are not of the kind that achieve easy popularity; but their profundity of thought and maturity of workmanship bespeak a musical intellect of the first order. Carter started out with a musical idiom rooted in diatonic-modal harmony, but gradually assimilated a dissonant chromaticism that places him (if one must attach a label) among the Abstract Expressionists. His impeccable craftsmanship is manifest in Eight Etudes and a Fantasy (1950), which explores the possibilities of a woodwind chamber group in imaginative ways. Carter's works, such as the Double Concerto for Harpsichord and Piano (1961) and the Symphony of Three Orchestras (1976), are oriented toward the most serious aspects of musical art and offer a continual challenge to the listener.

György Ligeti

György Ligeti (1923–) a native Hungarian who established himself first in Vienna, then in Stockholm, belongs to the circle of composers who have tried to broaden the heritage of Schoenberg by making it responsive to more recent currents. He found ways to achieve with traditional instruments the finer gradations of sound made familiar by electronic music. *Atmosphères* (1961), "for large orchestra without percussion," established Ligeti's position as a leader of the European avant-garde. Together with his choral work *Lux aeterna* (1966), it was included in the sound track of the film *2001: A Space Odyssey*, making the composer's name familiar to an international public.

Witold Lutosławski

The Polish composer Witold Lutosławski (1913–) has established himself as one of the most interesting personalities on the contemporary scene. Under the influence of John Cage, Lutosławski coined the term "aleatoric counterpoint" to indicate a type of music in which the pitches for all the parts are written out but the rhythms are improvised within given rules. His works—typical are the three symphonies as well as *Venetian Games* of 1961—show how avant-garde elements can be combined with more traditional styles.

George Crumb: Ancient Voices of Children

In recent years George Crumb (1929–) has forged ahead to a notable position among the composers of his generation. He owes this pre-eminence partly to the emotional character of his music, allied to a highly developed sense of the dramatic. Crumb uses contemporary techniques for expressive ends that make an enormous impact in the concert hall. He has won numerous honors and awards, and is currently professor of composition at the University of Pennsylvania.

Crumb has shown an extraordinary affinity for the poetry of Federico García Lorca, the great poet who was killed by the Fascists during the Spanish Civil War. Besides his *Ancient Voices of Children* (1970), his Lorca cycle includes four other works: *Night Music I* (1963); four books of madrigals (1965-69); *Songs, Drones and Refrains of Death* (1968); and *Night of the Four Moons* (1969).

George Crumb

Ancient Voices of Children is a cycle of songs for mezzo-soprano, boy soprano, oboe, mandolin, harp, electric piano, and percussion. Crumb tirelessly explores new ways of using voice and instruments. Like many contemporary composers he uses the voice like an instrument, in a vocal style which he describes as ranging "from the virtuosic to the intimately lyrical." He found his ideal interpreter in the late mezzo-soprano Jan DeGaetani, whose recording of the work remains as an example for all other interpreters. The score abounds with unusual effects. The soprano opens with a fanciful *vocalise* (a wordless melody, in this case based on purely phonetic sounds) which she directs at the strings of an electrically amplified piano, arousing a shimmering cloud of sympathetic vibrations. The pitch is "bent" to produce quarter tones. Included in the score are a toy piano, harmonica, musical saw, and a wide variety of percussion instruments. The first song from this cycle, *El niño busca su voz* (The little boy is looking for his voice), is very free and fantastic in character. The soprano part offers a virtuoso exhibition of what the voice can do in the way of cries, sighs, whispers, buzzings, trills, and percussive clicks. There are even passages marked "fluttertongue"—an effect we have hitherto associated only with instruments. Throughout Crumb captures the rapturous, improvisational spirit of flamenco song. The passion is here—but in a thoroughly twentieth-century setting.

Vocalise

Listening Guide 34

🖭 3B/9

CRUMB: *Ancient Voices of Children*

Date: 1970

Genre: Song cycle (5 songs and 2 instrumental interludes), based on poetry of Federico García Lorca

1. *El niño busca su voz* (The little boy is looking for his voice)

Text	Translation	Description
		Opens with elaborate vocalise for soprano—cries, trills, other vocal gymnastics
		Sings into piano with pedal down for resonance
32 El niño busca su voz.	The little boy is looking for his voice.	Strophe 1—sung by soprano alone with turns, trills, hisses
(La tenia el rey de los grillos	(The king of the crickets had it.)	Continues with low-pitched recitation
En una gota de agua buscaba su voz el niño.	In a drop of water the little boy was looking for his voice.	
33 No la quiero para hablar; me hare con ella un anillo que llevará mi silencio en su dedo penqueñito.	I do not want it to speak with; I will make a ring of it so that he may wear my silence on his little finger.	Strophe 2—overlaps Strophe 1 Boy soprano sings offstage through cardboard tube Folklike character to melody
	Tr. by W. S. MERWIN	

Electronic Music and the Technological Revolution

"I have been waiting a long time for electronics to free music from the tempered scale and the limitations of musical instruments. Electronic instruments are the portentous first step toward the liberation of music."—EDGARD VARÈSE

Perhaps the single most important musical development of the 1950s and '60s was the emergence of electronic music. This was foreshadowed, during the earlier part of the century, by the invention of a variety of electronic instruments of limited scope, which pointed to a future that was quickly realized by the booming revolution of technology.

The postwar emergence of electronic music falls into three stages. The first stage came with the use of magnetic tape recording. Around 1947 a group of technicians at a Paris radio station, led by Peter Schaeffer, had *Musique concrète*   already begun to experiment with what they called *musique concrète*, a music made up of natural sounds and sound effects that were recorded and then altered by changing the speed of the records. Their activities took on a new impetus when they began to use tape, which gave them a vastly wider range of possibilities in altering the sounds they used as source material, and also enabled them to cut and splice the sounds into new combinations.

The possibility of using not only natural but also artificially generated sounds soon presented itself. With the raw sound (either naturally or electronically produced) as a starting point, the composer could isolate its components, alter its pitch, volume, or other dimensions, play it backward, add reverberation (echo), filter out some of the overtones, or add additional components by splicing and overdubbing. Even though all these operations were laborious and time-consuming—it might take many hours to process only a minute of finished music—composers hastened to avail themselves of the new medium.

The second step in the technological revolution came with the devel-*Synthesizers*   opment of *synthesizers*, which are essentially devices combining sound generators and sound modifiers in one package with a unified control system. The first and most elaborate of these devices was the RCA Electronic Music Synthesizer, first unveiled in 1955; a more sophisticated model was installed four years later at the Columbia-Princeton studio in New York City. This immense and elaborate machine is capable of generating any imaginable sound or combination of sounds, with an infinite variety of pitches, durations, timbres, dynamics, and rhythmic patterns far beyond the capabilities of conventional instruments. The synthesizer represented an enormous step forward, since the composer was now able to control all the characteristics beforehand, and thus could bypass some of the time-consuming manual techniques associated with tape-recorder music.

Karlheinz Stockhausen   Among the pioneers in this new idiom was the German composer Karlheinz Stockhausen (1928–), who wrote two *Electronic Studies* (1953–54), built entirely from electronic sounds devoid of overtones. Later he produced his electronic masterpiece *Gesang der Jünglinge* (Song of the Youths, 1956) for vocal and synthesized sounds on tape.

The Philips Pavilion at the 1958 Brussels World Fair, designed by architect Le Corbusier, had music written for it by Edgard Varèse.

One of the truly original spirits of the music of our time was the French composer Edgard Varèse (1883–1965). The greater part of his music was written in the 1920s and 30s and reflects his rejection of many traditional elements of the art. He later turned to the electronic idiom, in which he wrote *Déserts* (for orchestra and tape, 1954) and *Poème électronique* (1958), an entirely electronic work written for performance in a pavilion designed by the architect Le Corbusier at the Brussels World Fair. This work combines the sounds of the human voice, treated electronically, with taped percussion and synthetic sounds.

Edgard Varèse

Because of its size and cost the RCA machine at Columbia has remained unique; but various smaller synthesizers have been devised that bring most of the resources of electronic music within the reach of a small studio. The best known of these were the Moog, Buchla, and ARP. Today, the Synclavier is the standard machine in many electronic studios. One advantage of these smaller machines is that they can be played directly, thus making "live" electronic performance a possibility.

The third stage of electronic development involves the use of the electronic computer as a sound generator. The basic principle here is the fact that the shape of any sound wave can be represented by a graph, and this graph can in turn be described by a series of numbers, each of which will represent a point on the graph. Such a series of numbers can be translated, by a device known as a digital-to-analog converter, into a sound tape that can be played on a tape recorder. It was further necessary to devise a computer program that would translate musical specifications—pitches, durations, timbres, dynamics, and the like—into numbers. There are now many

Computer-generated music

such programs, and the wide availability of home computers has made them readily accessible. Computer sound-generation is the most flexible of all electronic media, and is likely to dominate the field in years to come.

The combination of electronic sounds with live music has also proved to be a fertile field, especially since many younger composers have been working in both media. Works for soloist and recorded tape have become common, even "concertos" for tape recorder (or live-performance synthesizer) and orchestra. Milton Babbitt (1916–) was one of the first to evaluate the possibilities of electronic music, not because of the new sonorities it made possible, but because it offered the composer complete control of the final result. Babbitt has been especially partial to the combination of soprano voice and tape. *Phonemena* (1969–70), written as an encore number for the singer Bethany Beardslee, explores this idiom while pointing up the interest of contemporary composers in words as pure sound materials quite apart from their meaning.

Milton Babbitt

Another important composer working in this mixed medium is Mario Davidovsky (1934–   ), a professor of composition at Columbia University and director of the Columbia-Princeton Electronic Center. Among his works for tape and live performer is a series known as *Synchronisms* (1963–74). These are dialogues for solo instruments and prerecorded tape.

Mario Davidovsky

Electronic music has permeated the commercial world of music making in a big way. Much of the music we hear today as movie and TV sound tracks is electronically generated, although some effects are so like conventional instruments that we are not always aware of the new technology. Popular music groups have been "electrified" for some years, but now regularly feature synthesizers which simulate conventional rock band instruments as well as altogether new sounds.

65

Recent Trends

"Music can be renewed by regaining contact with the tradition and means of the past, to re-emerge as a spiritual force with reactivated powers of melodic thought, rhythmic pulse, and large-scale structure."—GEORGE ROCHBERG

The New Romanticism

Serial or twelve-tone music, with its emphasis on the intellectual and constructivist aspects of art, has lost some momentum in recent decades in favor of a more eclectic synthesis of styles known as the New Romanticism.

A number of composers began to feel that the time had come to close the gap between themselves and the public and to restore music to its former position as "the language of the emotions," complete with its appealing sweeping melodies, regular rhythms, lush harmonies, and rich orchestral colors.

The New Romanticism had an important precursor in Samuel Barber (1910–81). His music, suffused with feeling, was receptive to the grand gestures of nineteenth-century tradition. Several of his works achieved enormous popularity, among them the light-hearted Overture to *The School for Scandal* (1932) and his elegiac *Adagio for Strings* (1936).

Samuel Barber

Ned Rorem (1923–) is one of the distinguished composers of his generation. He has written widely in all genres, from chamber and orchestral music to opera. His songs are in the great line of descent from those of Ravel, Satie, and Poulenc. His works are stamped with an aristocratic refinement. A gifted writer as well, his memoirs in the form of diaries and collections of criticism have established themselves on the literary scene.

Ned Rorem

The Scottish-born Thea Musgrave (1929–), who is now active in the United States, has focused her attention on opera, an art form that lends itself ideally to the expression of emotion. Among her best-known works are the operas *The Voice of Ariadne* (1973, after Henry James), *Mary, Queen of Scots* (1977), *A Christmas Carol* (1979, after Dickens), and *Harriet, the Woman called Moses* (1985, based on the life of Harriet Tubman, the black Civil War heroine). As a leading exponent of the New Romanticism, Musgrave was particularly attracted to the sad tale of the legendary Mary of Scotland, her best-known work. Besides, a composer born in Scotland cannot but view

Thea Musgrave

Act III, scene 1 of the Virginia Opera production of Mary, Queen of Scots *in 1977. Ashley Putnam sang the leading role.*

Mary's tangled career as a nationalistic theme. Her output also includes two full-length ballets and a number of orchestral, chamber, and choral works.

David Del Tredici

Of a younger generation of composers interested in the New Romanticism, David Del Tredici (1937–) stands out for the broad lyric appeal of his music. In recent years, he has focused on large works for soprano and orchestra inspired by Lewis Carroll's writings. These have found favor with the public, especially *Final Alice* (1976) and *In Memory of a Summer Day* (1980). Among the most accessible works of the New Romantic idiom are those of John Corigliano (1938–), whose music displays an imaginative use of contemporary techniques. His major works include *The Naked Carmen* (1970), an "eclectic rock opera" fashioned after Bizet, and *A Figaro for Antonio* (1985), commissioned by the Metropolitan Opera House.

John Corigliano

Minimalism

Independently of the New Romantics, a group of young composers found their way to simplification of the musical language. They stripped their compositions down to the barest essentials in order to concentrate the listener's attention on a few basic details. This urge toward a minimal art first found expression in painting and sculpture. It became a significant force in contemporary music during the 1970s.

The salient feature of *minimalist music*, as it has come to be known, is the repetition of melodic, rhythmic, and harmonic patterns with very little variation. The music changes so slowly that the listener is forced to focus a maximum of attention on a minimum of detail. Such concentration can have a hypnotic effect, and indeed the term "trance music" has attached itself to some works of the minimalists. But it is a label they reject because, as they point out, their material is selected most carefully and worked out in highly disciplined procedures.

Terry Riley

There are several kinds of minimalist music. In some works the pulse is repeated with numbing regularity. Others are very busy on the surface, though the harmonies and timbres change very slowly. Terry Riley (1935–) introduced the element of pulse and the concept of tiny motivic cells that repeat in his ninety-minute work entitled *In C* (1964). Influenced by the music of the Far East, by ragtime and jazz, and by the theories of John Cage, Riley has incorporated elements of performer choice into electronic music, along with improvisation. The music of Steve Reich (1936–) moves so slowly that it seems to come out of a time sense all his own; this is particularly true of his works on tape. Reich describes his sense of time as "a musical process happening so gradually that listening resembles watching the minute hand of a watch—you perceive it moving only after you stay with it for a while." This contemplative quality is his answer to the pace of our overly competitive society.

Steve Reich

Philip Glass

The most widely known minimalist is Philip Glass (1937–), whose career began at the University of Chicago and the Juilliard School, after which he went off to Paris on a Fulbright scholarship to study with Nadia Boulanger. It was she who imparted to him, as he put it, "the skills that make music go." Even more decisive was his contact with the Indian sitar player Ravi Shankar. Glass was fascinated with non-Western music. "And, of course, I was also hearing the music of Miles Davis, of John Coltrane, and the Beatles." When he returned to New York he became convinced that "modern music had become truly decadent, stagnant, uncommunicative. Composers were writing for each other and the public didn't seem to care." It was out of this conviction that he evolved his own style, drawing upon the musical traditions of India and Africa as well as the techniques of rock and progressive jazz.

John Adams: Short Ride in a Fast Machine

Although both minimalism and the New Romanticism sought above all to escape the overly intellectual world of serialism, they did so by completely different paths. There was bound to appear a composer who, by seeking to expand the expressive gamut of minimalist music, would respond to the emotional impulses emanating from the New Romantics. Such a one was John Adams (1947–), the best known among the second generation of minimalists, who was educated at Harvard and in 1972 began teaching at the San Francisco Conservatory of Music. Strongly influenced by Steve Reich, Adams's is a subtle music marked by warm sonorities and much energy. At the same time he presents a more personal approach to music than do either Glass or Reich.

Adams attracted much attention with his opera *Nixon in China* (1987), which takes place in Beijing during the three days of former President Nixon's visit. The works that followed show Adams increasingly receptive to the sumptuous orchestral palette and expressive harmonies of the New Romanticism. They fully justify his description of himself as "a very emotional composer, one who experiences music on a very physical level. My music is erotic and Dionysian, and I never try to obscure those feelings when I compose."

Short Ride in a Fast Machine is an exuberant work for large orchestra and two synthesizers that stems from the extrovert side of Adams's personality. When asked about the title, Adams replied, "You know how it is when someone asks you to ride in a terrific sports car, and then you wish you hadn't." *Short Ride in a Fast Machine* features a persistent ostinato that with repetition takes on an almost hypnotic power. The steady pulse in the woodblock is so insistent as to be, in the composer's words, "almost sadistic." (See Listening Guide 35 on page 332 for analysis.) Although Adams was almost forty when he wrote it, this is youthful music in its physical vitality and devil-may-care optimism. It serves as a fine introduction to a composer whose work encompasses a variety of moods.

Listening Guide 35   [cassette] 3B/10

ADAMS: *Short Ride in a Fast Machine*

Date: 1986, for the Great Woods Festival in Mansfield, Mass., first performed by the Pittsburgh Symphony.

Medium: Orchestra and two synthesizers

Genre: Fanfare

Basis: Repetition of rhythmic motives

34	0:00	Delirando (frenzied), in 3/2 meter
		Insistent rhythm in woodblock
		Synthesizers and woodwinds join with faster pattern
		Brass enter with highly syncopated pattern that continually evolves
		Woodwinds punctuate activity with fast figure
	0:35	Brass pattern now even, then grows uneven and builds into dissonance again
	1:05	Strings enter, with uneven rhythmic pattern punctuated by bass drum
	1:45	Secco section, spaced notes in strings and woodwinds; lighter texture, builds again
35	3:00	Trumpet solo emerges in section marked "slightly slower"; half-note movement in brass against faster rhythms in other parts
	4:03	Tempo I, fast, syncopated nonmelodious pattern, until end

Coda

We have included in these pages a variety of facts—historical, biographical, and technical—that have entered into the making of music and that must enter into an intelligent listening to music. But books belong to the domain of words, and words have no power over the domain of sound. They are helpful only insofar as they lead us to enjoy the music.

The enjoyment of music depends upon perceptive listening. And perceptive listening (like perceptive anything) is something that we achieve gradually, with practice and effort. By acquiring a knowledge of the circumstances out of which a musical work issued, we prepare ourselves for its multiple meanings; we lay ourselves open to that exercise of mind and heart, sensibility and imagination that makes listening to music so unique an experience. But in the building up of our musical perceptions—that is, of our listening enjoyment—let us always remember that the ultimate wisdom resides neither in dates nor in facts. It is to be found in one place only—the sounds themselves.

Appendix I

Musical Notation

Our musical notation is the result of an evolution that reaches back to antiquity. It has adapted itself to successive systems of musical thought, and continues to do so. It is by no means a perfect tool, but it has proved adequate to the constantly new demands made upon it.

The Notation of Pitch

Musical notation presents a kind of graph of the sounds with regard to their duration and pitch. These are indicated by symbols called *notes,* which are written on the *staff,* a series of five parallel lines with four spaces between:

Staff

The position of the notes on the staff indicates the pitches, each line and space representing a different degree of pitch.

A symbol known as a *clef* is placed at the left end of the staff, and determines the group of pitches to which that staff refers. The *treble clef* ($\frac{\ }{\ }$) is used for pitches within the range of the female singing voices, and the *bass clef* ($\mathcal{9}$) for a lower group of pitches, within the range of the male singing voices.

Clefs

Pitches are named after the first seven letters of the alphabet, from A to G; the lines and spaces are named accordingly. (From one note named A to the next is the interval of an octave, which—as we have seen—is the distance from one *do* to the next in the *do-re-mi-fa-sol-la-ti-do* scale). The pitches on the treble staff are named as follows:

Pitch names

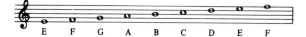

| E | F | G | A | B | C | D | E | F |

And those on the bass staff:

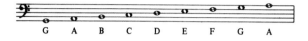

| G | A | B | C | D | E | F | G | A |

For pitches above and below these, short extra lines called *ledger lines* can be added:

| A | B | C | D | G | A | B | C | C | D | E | F | B | C | D | E |

Middle C—the C that, on the piano, is situated approximately in the center of the keyboard—comes between the treble and bass staffs. It is represented by either the first ledger line above the bass staff or the first ledger line below the treble staff, as the following example makes clear. This combination of the two staffs is called the *great staff* or *grand staff*:

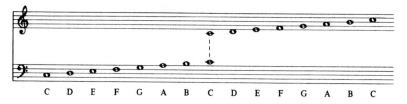

C D E F G A B C D E F G A B C

Accidentals   There are also signs known as *accidentals,* which are used to alter the pitch of a written note. A *sharp* (♯) before the note indicates the pitch a semitone above; a *flat* (♭) indicates the pitch a semitone below. A *natural* (♮) cancels a sharp or flat. Also used are the *double sharp* (×) and *double flat* (♭♭), which respectively raise and lower the pitch by two half-tones—that is, a whole tone.

In many pieces of music, where certain sharped or flatted notes are used consistently throughout the piece, the necessary sharps or flats are written at the beginning of each line of music, in order to save repetition. This may be seen in the following example of piano music. Notice that piano music is written on the great staff, with the right hand usually playing the notes written on the upper staff and the left hand usually playing the notes written on the lower:

etc.

The Notation of Rhythm

Note values   The duration of tones is indicated by the appearance of the notes placed on the staff. These use a system of relative values. For example, in the following table each note represents a duration half as long as the preceding one:

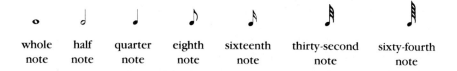

| whole note | half note | quarter note | eighth note | sixteenth note | thirty-second note | sixty-fourth note |

In any particular piece of music, these note values are related to the beat of the music. If the quarter note represents one beat, then a half note lasts for two beats, a whole note for four, with two eighth notes on one beat, or four sixteenths. The following chart makes this clear:

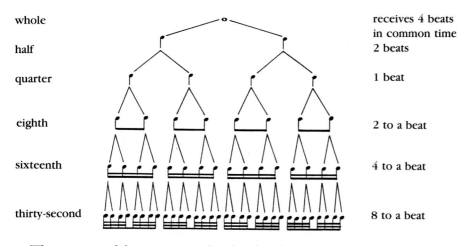

whole		receives 4 beats in common time
half		2 beats
quarter		1 beat
eighth		2 to a beat
sixteenth		4 to a beat
thirty-second		8 to a beat

When a group of three notes is to be played in the time normally taken up by only two of the same kind, we have a *triplet:*

Triplet

It is possible to combine successive notes of the same pitch, using a curved line known as a *tie:*

Tie

beats: 4 + 4 = 8   2 + 4 = 6   1 + ½ = 1½

A *dot* after a note extends its value by half:

Augmentation dot

beats: 4 + 2 = 6   2 + 1 = 3   1 + ½ = 1½   ½ + ¼ = ¾

Time never stops in music, even when there is no sound. Silence is indicated by symbols known as *rests,* which correspond in time value to the notes:

Rests

| whole rest | half rest | quarter rest | eighth rest | sixteenth rest | thirty-second rest | sixty-fourth rest |

The metrical organization of a piece of music is indicated by the *time signature,* which specifies the meter. This consists of two numbers, written one above the other. The upper numeral indicates the number of beats within the measure; the lower one shows which unit of value equals one beat. Thus, the time signature $\frac{3}{4}$ means that there are three beats to a measure, with the quarter note equal to one beat. In $\frac{6}{8}$ time there are six beats in the measure, each eighth note receiving one beat. Following are the most frequently encountered time signatures:

Time signature

duple meter	$\frac{2}{2}$	$\frac{2}{4}$	
triple meter	$\frac{3}{2}$	$\frac{3}{4}$	$\frac{3}{8}$
quadruple meter		$\frac{4}{4}$	
sextuple meter		$\frac{6}{4}$	$\frac{6}{8}$

The following examples show how the system works. It will be noticed that the measures are separated by a vertical line known as a *barline;* hence a measure is sometimes referred to as a *bar.* As a rule, the barline is followed by the most strongly accented beat, the ONE.

Choose your part - ners, skip to my Lou, Choose your part - ners, skip to my Lou,

Choose your part - ners, skip to my Lou, Skip to my Lou, my dar - lin'.

Down in the val - ley, val - ley so low, —— Hang your head o - ver, hear the wind blow. ——

Should auld ac-quaint - ance be for - got, and —— nev - er brought to mind, Should

auld ac - quaint - ance be for - got and —— days of auld lang syne.

Drink to me on - ly with — thine eyes, — And I —— will pledge with mine.

Glossary

absolute music Music that has no literary, dramatic, or pictorial program. Also *pure music.*

a cappella Choral music performed without instrumental accompaniment.

accelerando Quickening or getting faster.

accent The emphasis on a beat resulting in one louder or longer than another in a measure.

accompagnato Accompanied; also a recitative which is accompanied by orchestra.

adagio Quite slow.

aerophone Instrument that produces sound by using air as the primary vibrating means, such as flute, whistle, and horn.

agitato Agitated or restless.

aleatory Indeterminate music in which certain elements of performance (such as pitch, rhythm, or form) are left to choice or chance.

allegro Fast, cheerful.

allemande German dance in moderate duple time, popular during the Renaissance and Baroque periods; often the first movement of a Baroque suite.

alto Up until the 18th century, a high vocal part; thereafter the lowest of the female voices. Also *contralto.*

andante Moderately slow or walking pace.

answer Second entry of the subject in a fugue, usually pitched a 4th below or a 5th above the subject.

anthem Choral setting of a religious text in English, similar to the motet.

antiphonal Performance style in which an ensemble is divided into two or more groups, performing in alternation and then together.

antique cymbals Small disks of brass, held by the player one in each hand, that are struck together gently and allowed to vibrate.

aria Lyric song for solo voice with orchestral accompaniment, generally expressing intense emotion; found in opera, cantata, and oratorio.

arioso Short, aria-like passage.

arpeggio Broken chord in which the individual tones are sounded one after another instead of simultaneously.

Ars Antiqua French sacred polyphonic musical style from the period c. 1160–1320.

Ars Nova 14th-century French polyphonic musical style that transformed the art increasingly from religious to secular themes.

a tempo Return to the previous tempo.

atonality Total abandonment of tonality (centering in a key). Atonal music moves from one level of dissonance to another, without areas of relaxation.

augmentation Statement of a melody in longer note values, often twice as slow as the original.

bagpipe Wind instrument popular in Eastern and Western Europe that has several tubes, one of which plays the melody while the others sound the drones, or sustained notes.

ballade French poetic form and chanson type of the Middle Ages and Renaissance with courtly love texts. Also a Romantic genre, especially a lyric piano piece.

ballad opera English comic opera, usually featuring spoken dialogue alternating with songs set to popular tunes.

ballet A dance form featuring a staged presentation of group or solo dancing with music, costumes, and scenery.

baritone Male voice of moderately low range.

bass Male voice of low range.

bass clarinet Woodwind instrument of the clarinet family with the lowest range.

bass drum Percussion instrument that is played with a large soft-headed stick; the largest orchestral drum.

basse danse Graceful court dance of the early Renaissance; an older version of the pavane.

basso continuo Italian for "continuous bass." See *figured bass.* Also refers to performance group playing the bass, consisting of one chordal instrument (harpsichord, organ) and one bass melody instrument (cello, bassoon).

bassoon Double-reed woodwind instrument with a low range.

bass viol See *double bass.*

beat Regular pulsation; a basic unit of length in musical time.

bebop Complex jazz style developed in the 1940s. Also *bop.*

bel canto "Beautiful singing"; elegant Italian vocal style characterized by florid melodic lines delivered by voices of great agility, smoothness, and purity of tone.

bent pitch See *blue note.*

binary form Two-part (**A-B**) form with each section normally repeated. Also *two-part form.*

blue note A slight drop of pitch on the third, fifth, or seventh tone of the scale, common in blues and jazz. Also *bent pitch.*

blues American form of secular black folk music, related to jazz, that is based on a simple, repetitive poetic-musical structure.

bop See *bebop.*

bourrée Lively French Baroque dance type in duple meter.

branle Quick French group dance of the Renaissance, related to the *ronde.*

brass instrument Wind instrument with a cup-shaped mouthpiece, a tube that flares into a bell, and slides or valves to vary the pitch. Most often made of brass or silver.

bridge Transitional passage connecting two sections of a composition.

bugle Brass instrument that evolved from the earlier military or field trumpet.

Burgundian chanson Fifteenth-century French composition, usually for three voices, some or all of which may be played by instruments. Also *chanson.*

cadence Resting place in a musical phrase; music punctuation.

cadenza Virtuosic solo passage in the manner of an improvisation, performed near the end of an aria or a movement of a concerto.

call and response Performance style with a singing leader who is imitated by a chorus of followers. Also *responsorial singing.*

canon Type of polyphonic composition in which one musical line imitates another at a fixed distance throughout.

cantabile Songful, in a singing style.

cantata Vocal genre for solo singers, chorus, and instrumentalists based on a lyric or dramatic poetic narrative. It generally consists of several movements including recitatives, arias, and ensemble numbers.

cantus firmus "Fixed melody," usually of very long notes and based on a fragment of Gregorian chant that served as the structural basis for a polyphonic composition, particularly in the Renaissance.

capriccio Short lyric piece of a free nature, often for piano.

carol English medieval strophic song with a refrain (burden) repeated after each stanza; now associated with Christmas.

cassation Classical instrumental genre related to the serenade or divertimento and often performed outdoors.

castanets Percussion instruments consisting of small wooden clappers that are struck together. They are widely used to accompany Spanish dancing.

castrato Male singer who was castrated during boyhood to preserve the soprano or alto vocal register, prominent in seventeenth- and early eighteenth-century opera.

celesta Percussion instrument resembling a miniature upright piano, with metal plates struck by hammers that are operated by a keyboard.

cello See *violoncello.*

chaconne Baroque form similar to the *passacaglia,* in which the variations are based on a repeated chord progression.

chamber choir Small group of up to about twenty-four singers, who usually perform *a cappella* or with piano accompaniment.

chamber music Ensemble music for up to about ten players, with one player to a part.

chamber sonata See *sonata da camera.*

chanson French polyphonic song of the Middle Ages and Renaissance, set both to courtly and popular poetry. See also *Burgundian chanson.*

chimes Percussion instrument of definite pitch that consists of a set of tuned metal tubes of various lengths suspended from a frame and struck with a hammer. Also *tubular bells.*

choir A group of singers who perform together, usually in parts, with several on each part; often associated with a church.

chorale Baroque congregational hymn of the German Lutheran church.

chorale prelude Short Baroque organ piece in which a traditional chorale melody is embellished.

chorale variations Baroque organ piece in which a chorale is the basis for a set of variations.

chord Simultaneous combination of two or more typically three tones that constitutes a single block of harmony.

chordophone Instrument that produces sound from a vibrating string stretched between two points; the string may be set in motion by bowing, striking, or plucking.

chorus Fairly large group of singers who perform together, usually in parts with several on each part.

chromatic Melody or harmony built from many if not all twelve semitones of the octave. A *chromatic scale* consists of an ascending or descending sequence of semitones.

church sonata See *sonata da chiesa.*

clarinet Single-reed woodwind instrument with a wide range of sizes.

clausula Short medieval composition in discant style, sung to one or two words or a single syllable, based on a fragment of Gregorian chant.

clavecin French word for harpsichord. See *harpsichord.*

clavichord Stringed keyboard instrument popular in the Renaissance and Baroque that is capable of unique expressive devices not possible on the harpsichord.

clavier Generic word for keyboard instruments, including harpsichord, clavichord, piano, and organ.

coda The last part of a piece, usually added to a standard form to bring it to a close.

codetta In sonata form, the concluding section of the Exposition.

collegium musicum An association of amateur musicians, popular in the Baroque era. A modern University ensemble dedicated to the performance of early music.

comic opera See *opéra comique.*

common time See *quadruple meter.*

compound meter Meter in which each beat is divisible by three, rather than two.

con amore With love, tenderly.

concertante Style based on the principle of opposition between two dissimilar masses of sound; concerto-like.

concert band Instrumental ensemble ranging from forty to eighty members or more, consisting of wind and percussion instruments.

concertino Solo group of instruments in the Baroque *concerto grosso.*

concerto Instrumental genre in several movements for solo instrument (or instrumental group) and orchestra.

concerto grosso Baroque concerto type based on the opposition between a small group of solo instruments (the concertino) and orchestra (the ripieno).

concert overture Single-movement concert piece for orchestra, typically from the Romantic period and often based on a literary program.

conductor Person who, by means of gestures, leads performances of musical ensembles, especially orchestras, bands, or choruses.

con fuoco With fire.

conjunct Smooth, connected melody that moves principally in stepwise motion.

con passione   With passion.

consonance   Concordant or harmonious combination of tones that provides a sense of relaxation and stability in music.

continuous imitation   Renaissance polyphonic style in which the motives move from line to line within the texture, often overlapping one another.

contrabass   See *double bass*.

contrabassoon   Double-reed woodwind instrument with the lowest range in the woodwind family. Also *double bassoon*.

contralto   See *alto*.

cornet   Valved brass instrument similar to the trumpet but more mellow in sound.

cornetto   Early instrument of the brass family with woodwind-like fingerholes. It developed from the cow horn, but was made of wood.

counterpoint   The art of combining in a single texture two or more melodic lines.

countersubject   In a fugue, a secondary theme heard against the subject; a countertheme.

courante   French Baroque dance, a standard movement of the suite, in triple meter at a moderate tempo.

crescendo   Growing louder.

crumhorn   Early woodwind instrument, whose sound is produced by blowing into a capped double reed and whose lower body is curved.

cymbals   Percussion instruments consisting of two large circular brass plates of equal size that are struck sidewise against each other.

da capo   An indication to return to the beginning of a piece.

da capo aria   Lyric song in ternary or **A-B-A** form, commonly found in operas, cantatas, and oratorios.

decrescendo   Growing softer.

Development   Structural reshaping of thematic material; second section of sonata-allegro form that moves through a series of foreign keys while themes from the exposition are manipulated.

diatonic   Melody or harmony built from the seven tones of a major or minor scale. A *diatonic scale* encompasses patterns of seven whole tones and semitones.

diminuendo   Growing softer.

diminution   Statement of a melody in shorter note intervals, often twice as fast as the original.

discant   Medieval polyphony in which all voices move at approximately the same speed; the movement of the lower part (the chant) parallels the movement of the newly composed upper voice.

disjunct   Disjointed or disconnected melody with many leaps.

dissonance   Combination of tones that sounds discordant and unstable.

divertimento   Classical instrumental genre for chamber ensemble or soloist, often performed as light entertainment. Related to *serenade* and *cassation*.

doctrine of the affections   Belief during the Baroque period that the aim of music is to excite or move the passions.

dodecaphonic   Greek for twelve-tone; see *twelve-tone music*.

dolce   Sweetly.

dolente   Sad, weeping.

dominant   The fifth scale step, *sol*.

dominant chord   Chord built on the fifth scale step, the V chord.

double bass   Largest and lowest pitched member of the bowed string family. Also called *contrabass* or *bass viol*.

double bassoon   See *contrabassoon*.

double exposition   In the concerto, twofold statement of the themes, once by the orchestra and once by the soloist.

double-stop   Playing two notes simultaneously on a string instrument.

downbeat   First beat of the measure, the strongest in any meter.

drone   Sustained sounding of one or several tones for harmonic support, a common feature of folk music.

dulcimer   Early folk instrument that resembles the psaltery; its strings are struck with hammers instead of being plucked.

duple meter   Basic metrical pattern of two beats to a measure.

duplum   Second voice of a polyphonic work, especially the Medieval motet.

duration   Length of time something lasts, e.g. the vibration of a musical sound.

dynamics   Element of musical expression relating to the degree of loudness or softness or volume of a sound.

embellishment   Melodic decoration, either impovised or indicated through *ornamentation* signs in the music.

embouchure   The placement of the lips, lower facial muscles, and jaws in playing a wind instrument.

English horn   Tenor-range double-reed woodwind instrument, larger and lower in range than the oboe.

episode   Interlude or intermediate section in the Baroque fugue, which serves as an area of relaxation between statements of the subject.

espressivo   Expressively.

euphonium   Tenor-range brass instrument resembling the tuba.

exoticism   Romantic musical style in which rhythms, melodies, or instruments evoke the color and atmosphere of far-off lands.

Exposition   Opening section; in the fugue, the first section in which the voices enter in turn with the subject; in sonata-allegro form, the first section in which the major thematic material is stated. Also *Statement*.

fantasia   Free instrumental piece of fairly large dimensions in an improvisational style; in the Baroque, it often served as introductory piece to a fugue.

figured bass   Baroque practice consisting of an independent bass line, which continues throughout a piece and often includes numerals indicating the harmony required of the performer. Also *thorough-bass*.

first-movement form   See **sonata-allegro form**.

flat sign   Musical symbol (♭) which indicates lowering a pitch by a semitone.

fluegelhorn   Valved brass instrument resembling a bugle with a wide bell, used in jazz and commercial music.

flute   Soprano-range woodwind instrument, usually made of metal and held horizontally.

form   Structure and design in music, based on repetition, contrast, and variation; the organizing principle of music.

formalism   Tendency to elevate formal above expressive value in music, as in Neoclassical music.

forte (f)   Loud.

fortissimo (ff) Very loud.

French horn Medium-range valved brass instrument that can be played "stopped" with the hand as well as open. Also *horn.*

French overture Baroque instrumental introduction to an opera, ballet, or suite, in two sections: a slow opening followed by an Allegro, often with a brief return to the opening.

fugato A fugal passage in a nonfugal piece, such as in the Development section of a sonata-allegro form.

fugue Polyphonic form popular in the Baroque era in which one or more themes are developed by imitative counterpoint.

full anthem Anglican devotional work similar to the motet of the Catholic Church, performed by choir throughout.

galliard Lively, triple-meter French court dance.

gavotte Duple-meter Baroque dance type of a pastoral character.

gigue Popular English Baroque dance type, a standard movement of the Baroque suite, in a lively compound meter.

gioioso Joyous.

glee club Specialized vocal ensemble that performs popular music, college songs, and more serious works.

glissando Rapid slide through pitches of a scale.

glockenspiel Percussion instrument with horizontal tuned steel bars of various sizes that are struck with mallets and produce a bright metallic sound.

gong Percussion instrument consisting of a broad circular disk of metal, suspended in a frame and struck with a heavy drumstick. Also *tam-tam.*

Gradual Fourth item of the Proper of the Mass, sung in a melismatic style, and performed in a responsorial manner in which soloists alternate with a choir.

grand opera Style of Romantic opera developed in Paris, focusing on serious, historical plots with huge choruses, crowd scenes, elaborate dance episodes, ornate costumes, and spectacular scenery.

grave Solemn; very, very slow.

Gregorian chant Monophonic melody with a freely flowing, unmeasured vocal line; liturgical chant of the Roman Catholic church. Also *plainchant* or *plainsong.*

ground bass A repeating melody, usually in the bass, throughout a vocal or instrumental composition.

guitar Plucked string instrument originally made of wood with a hollow resonating body and a fretted fingerboard.

harmonics Individual pure sounds that are part of any musical tone; in string instruments, crystalline tones in the very high register, produced by lightly touching a vibrating string at a certain point.

harmony The simultaneous combination of notes and the ensuing relationships of intervals and chords.

harp Plucked string instrument, triangular in shape with strings perpendicular to the soundboard.

harpsichord Early Baroque keyboard instrument in which the strings are plucked by quills instead of being struck with hammers like the piano.

heptatonic scale Seven-note scale; in non-Western musics, often fashioned from a different combination of intervals than major and minor scales.

homophonic Texture with principal melody and accompanying harmony, as distinct from *polyphony.*

horn See *French horn.*

idiophone Instrument that produces sound from the substance of the instrument itself by being struck, blown, shaken, scraped, or rubbed. Examples include bells, rattles, xylophones, and cymbals.

imitation Subject or motive presented in one voice and then restated in another, each part continuing as others enter.

improvisation Creation of a musical composition while it is being performed, seen in Baroque ornamentation, cadenzas of concertos, jazz, and non-Western music. See also *embellishment.*

incidental music Music written to accompany dramatic works.

instrument Mechanism that generates musical vibrations and transmits them into the air.

intermezzo Short, lyric piece or movement, often for piano; also a comic interlude performed between acts of an eighteenth-century *opera seria.*

interval Distance and relationship between two pitches.

inversion Mirror image of a melody or pattern, found in fugues and twelve-tone composition.

isorhythmic motet Medieval and early Renaissance motet based on a repeating rhythmic pattern throughout one or more voices.

Italian overture Baroque overture consisting of three sections: fast-slow-fast.

jazz A musical style created mainly by black Americans in the early twentieth century that blended elements drawn from African musics with the popular and art traditions of the West.

jazz band Instrumental ensemble made up of reed (saxophones and clarinets), brass (trumpets and trombones), and rhythm sections (percussion, piano, double bass, and sometimes guitar).

jig Vigorous English Renaissance dance that may be the predecessor of the Baroque *gigue.*

jongleurs Medieval wandering entertainers who played instruments, sang and danced, juggled, and performed plays.

kettledrums See *timpani.*

key Defines the relationship of tones with a common center or tonic; also a lever on a keyboard or woodwind instrument.

keyboard instrument Instrument sounded by means of a keyboard (a series of keys played with the fingers).

keynote See *tonic.*

key signature Sharps or flats placed at the beginning of a piece to show the key of a work.

Klangfarbenmelodie Twentieth-century technique in which the notes of a melody are distributed among different instruments, giving a pointillistic texture.

lamentoso Like a lament.

largo Broad; very slow.

legato Smooth and connected; opposite of staccato.

leitmotif "Leading motive" or basic recurring theme representing a person, object, or idea, commonly used in Richard Wagner's operas.

libretto Text of an opera.

lied German for "song"; most commonly associated with the solo art song of the nineteenth century, usually accompanied by piano.

lute Plucked string instrument, of Middle Eastern origin, popular in Western Europe from the late Middle Ages to the eighteenth century.

lyric opera   Hybrid form combining elements of *grand opera* and *opéra comique,* and featuring appealing melodies and romantic drama.

madrigal   Renaissance secular work originating in Italy for voices, with or without instruments, set to a short, lyric love poem; also popular in England.

madrigal choir   Small vocal ensemble that specializes in *a cappella* secular works.

maestoso   Majestic.

Magnificat   Biblical text on the words of the Virgin Mary, sung polyphonically in church from the Renaissance on.

major scale   Scale consisting of seven different tones that comprises a specific pattern of whole and half steps. It differs from a minor scale primarily in that its third degree is raised half a step.

march   A style incorporating characteristics of military music, including strongly accented duple meter in simple, repetitive rhythmic patterns.

marching band   Instrumental ensemble of American origin; a popular group for entertainment at sports events and parades, consisting of wind and percussion instruments, drum majors/majorettes, and baton twirlers.

marimba   Percussion instrument that is a mellower version of the xylophone; of African and Latin American origins.

masque   English genre of aristocratic entertainment that combined vocal and instrumental music with poetry and dance, developed during the sixteenth and seventeenth centuries.

Mass   Central service of the Roman Catholic Church.

mazurka   Type of Polish folk dance in triple meter.

measure   Rhythmic group or metrical unit that contains a fixed number of beats, divided on the musical staff by barlines.

melismatic   Melodic style characterized by many notes sung to a single text syllable.

melody   Succession of single tones or pitches perceived by the mind as a unity.

membranophone   Any instrument that produces sound from tightly stretched membranes that can be struck, plucked, rubbed, or sung into (setting the skin in vibration).

meno   Less.

mesto   Sad.

metallophone   Percussion instrument consisting of tuned metal bars, usually struck with a mallet.

meter   Organization of rhythm in time; the grouping of beats into larger, regular patterns, notated as *measures.*

mezzo forte (mf)   Moderately loud.

mezzo piano (mp)   Moderately soft.

mezzo-soprano   Female voice of middle range.

micropolyphony   Twentieth-century technique encompassing the complex interweaving of all musical elements.

microtone   Musical interval that is smaller than a semitone, prevalent in non-Western music and in some twentieth-century music.

minimalist music   Contemporary musical style featuring the repetition of short melodic, rhythmic, and harmonic patterns with little variation.

minnesingers   Late Medieval German poet-musicians.

minor scale   Scale consisting of seven different tones that comprises a specific pattern of whole and half steps. It differs from the major scale primarily in that its third degree is lowered half a step.

minuet and trio   An A-B-A form (A = minuet; B = trio) in a moderate triple meter that is often the third movement of the Classical sonata cycle.

misterioso   Mysteriously.

modal   Characterizes music that is based on modes other than major and minor, especially the early church modes.

mode   Scale or sequence of notes used as the basis for a composition; major and minor are modes.

moderato   Moderate.

modulation   The process of changing from one key to another.

molto   Very.

monody   Vocal type, established in the Baroque, in which a single melody predominates.

monophonic   Single line or melody without accompaniment.

monothematic   Work or movement based on a single theme.

motet   Polyphonic vocal genre, secular in the Middle Ages, but sacred or devotional thereafter.

motive   Short melodic or rhythmic idea; the smallest fragment of a theme that forms a melodic-harmonic-rhythmic unit.

movement   Complete, self-contained part within a larger musical work.

music drama   Wagner's term for his operas.

musique concrète   Music made up of natural sounds and sound effects that are recorded and then manipulated electronically.

mute   Mechanical device used to muffle the sound of an instrument.

nakers   Medieval percussion instruments resembling small kettledrums.

neumatic   Plainchant melodic style with two to four notes set to each syllable.

neumes   Early musical notation signs; square notes on a four-line staff.

ninth chord   Five-tone chord spanning a ninth between its lowest and highest tones.

non troppo   Not too much.

notturno   "Night piece"; a serenade-type composition that combines elements of chamber music and symphony.

oboe   Soprano-range double-reed woodwind instrument.

oboe da caccia   Alto-range Baroque oboe.

oboe d'amore   Mezzo-soprano range Baroque oboe, pitched somewhat below the ordinary oboe.

octave   Interval between two tones seven diatonic pitches apart; the lower note vibrates half as fast as the upper and sounds an octave lower.

offbeat   A weak beat or any pulse between the beats in a measured rhythmic pattern.

ondes Martenot   Electronic instrument that produces sounds by means of an oscillator.

open form   Indeterminate contemporary music in which some details of a composition are clearly indicated, but the overall structure is left to choice or chance.

opera   Music drama that is generally sung throughout, combining the resources of vocal and instrumental music with poetry and drama, acting and pantomime, scenery and costumes.

opera buffa Italian comic opera, sung throughout.

opéra comique French comic opera, with some spoken dialogue.

opera seria Tragic Italian opera.

oral tradition Music that is transmitted by example or imitation and performed from memory.

oratorio Large-scale dramatic genre originating in the Baroque, based on a text of religious or serious character, performed by solo voices, chorus, and orchestra; it is similar to opera but without scenery, costumes, or action.

Ordinary Chants from the Roman Catholic Mass and other services that remain the same from day to day throughout the church year.

organ Wind instrument in which air is fed to the pipes by mechanical means; the pipes are controlled by two or more keyboards and a set of pedals.

organal style Organum in which the tenor sings the melody (original chant) in very long notes while the upper voices move freely and rapidly above it.

organum Earliest kind of polyphonic music that developed from the custom of adding voices above a plainchant; they first ran parallel to it at the interval of a fifth or fourth, and later moved more freely.

ornamentation See *embellishment.*

ostinato A short melodic, rhythmic, or harmonic pattern that is repeated throughout a work or a section of one.

overture An introductory movement for orchestra, as in an opera or oratorio, often presenting melodies from arias to come; also orchestral work for concert performance.

part song Vocal secular composition, unaccompanied, in three, four, or more parts.

pas de deux In ballet, a dance for two that is an established feature of classical ballet.

passacaglia Baroque form in moderately slow triple meter, based on a short, repeated bass-line melody that serves as the basis for continuous variation in the other voices.

passepied French Baroque court dance type; a faster version of the minuet.

pastorale Pastoral, country-like.

pavane Stately Renaissance court dance in duple meter.

pentatonic scale Five-note pattern used in some African, Far Eastern, and American Indian musics; can also be found in Western music as examples of exoticism.

percussion instrument Instrument made of metal, wood, stretched skin, or other material that is made to sound by striking, shaking, scraping, or plucking.

phrase Musical unit; often a component of a melody.

pianissimo (pp) Very soft.

piano (p) Soft.

piano Keyboard instrument whose strings are struck with hammers controlled by a keyboard mechanism; pedals control dampers in the strings that stop the sound when the finger releases the key.

pianoforte Original name for the piano.

piccolo Smallest woodwind instrument, similar to the flute, but sounding an octave higher.

pitch Location of a tone in relation to highness or lowness.

pizzicato Performance direction to pluck a string of a bowed instrument with the finger.

plainchant See *Gregorian chant.*

plainsong See *Gregorian chant.*

poco A little.

polka Lively Bohemian dance; also a short, lyric piano piece.

polonaise Stately Polish processional dance in triple meter.

polychoral Performance style developed in the late sixteenth century involving the use of two or more choirs that answer each other or sing together.

polyharmony Two or more streams of harmony played against each other, common in twentieth-century music.

polyphonic Two or more melodic lines combined into a multi-voiced texture, as distinct from *monophonic.*

polyrhythm The use of several rhythmic patterns or meters simultaneously, common in twentieth-century music.

polytonality The use of two or more keys simultaneously, common in twentieth-century music.

portative organ Medieval organ small enough to be carried or set on a table, usually with only one set of pipes.

positive organ Small single-manual organ, popular in the Renaissance and Baroque eras.

prelude Instrumental work intended to precede a larger work.

presto Very fast.

program music Instrumental music endowed with literary or pictorial associations, especially popular in the nineteenth century.

program symphony Multi-movement programmatic orchestral work, typically from the nineteenth century.

Proper Chants from the mass and other services that vary from day to day throughout the church year according to the particular liturgical occasion, as distinct from the *Ordinary,* which remain the same.

psaltery Medieval plucked string instrument similar to the modern zither, consisting of a soundbox over which strings were stretched.

pure music See *absolute music.*

quadruple meter Basic metrical pattern of four beats to a measure. Also *common time.*

quadruple stop Playing four notes simultaneously on a string instrument.

Quadruplum Fourth part of a polyphonic work.

quartal harmony Harmony that is based on the interval of the fourth as opposed to a third; used in twentieth-century music.

range Distance between the lowest and highest tones of a melody, an instrument, or a voice.

rebec Medieval bowed, string instrument, often with a pear-shaped body.

Recapitulation Third section of sonata-allegro form in which the thematic material of the Exposition is restated, generally in the tonic. Also *Restatement.*

recitative Solo vocal declamation which follows the inflections of the text, often resulting in a disjunct vocal style; found in the opera, cantata, and oratorio.

recorder End-blown woodwind instrument with a whistle mouthpiece, generally associated with early music.

regal Small Medieval reed organ.

register Specific area in the range of an instrument or voice.

relative key The major or minor key that shares the same key signature; for example, D minor is the relative minor of F major, both having one flat.

repeat sign   Musical symbol (:‖) that indicates repetition of a passage in a composition.

Requiem Mass   Roman Catholic Mass for the Dead.

resolution   Conclusion of a musical idea, as in the progression from an active chord to a rest chord.

response   Short choral answer to a solo verse; an element of liturgical dialogue.

responsorial singing   Singing, especially in Gregorian chant, in which a soloist or a group of soloists alternates with the choir. See also *call and response.*

Restatement   See *Recapitulation.*

retrograde   Backward statement of melody.

retrograde inversion   Mirror image and backward statement of a melody.

rhythm   The controlled movement of music in time.

ripieno   The larger of the two ensembles in the Baroque concerto grosso. Also *tutti.*

ritardando   Holding back, getting slower.

ritornello   Short recurring instrumental passage found both in the aria and the Baroque concerto.

romance   Originally a ballad; in the Romantic era, a lyric, instrumental work.

ronde   Lively Renaissance "round dance," associated with the outdoors, in which the participants danced in a circle or a line.

rondeau   Medieval and Renaissance poetic form and chanson type with courtly love texts.

rondo   Musical form in which the first section recurs, usually in the tonic. In the Classical sonata cycle, it appears as the last movement in various forms, including **A-B-A-B-A, A-B-A-C-A,** and **A-B-A-C-A-B-A.**

round   Perpetual canon at the unison in which each voice enters in succession with the same melody (for example, *Row, Row, Row Your Boat*).

rubato   "Borrowed time," common in Romantic music, in which the performer hesitates here or hurries forward there, imparting flexibility to the written note values. Also *tempo rubato.*

sackbut   Early brass instrument, ancestor of the trombone.

saltarello   Italian "jumping dance" characterized by triplets in a rapid 4/4 time.

sarabande   Stately Spanish Baroque dance type in triple meter, a standard movement of the Baroque suite.

saxophone   Family of single-reed woodwind instruments commonly used in the concert and jazz band.

scale   Series of tones in ascending or descending order that presents the notes of a key.

scat singing   A jazz style that sets nonsense syllables (vocables) to an improvised vocal line.

scherzo   Composition in **A-B-A** form, usually in triple meter.

secco   Operatic recitative which features a sparse accompaniment and moves with great freedom.

semitone   Also known as a half step, the smallest interval of the Western musical system.

sequence   Restatement of an idea or motive at a different pitch level.

serenade   Classical instrumental genre that combines ele-

ments of chamber music and symphony, often performed in the evening or at social functions. Related to *divertimento* and *cassation.*

serialism   Method of composition in which various musical elements (pitch, rhythm, dynamics, tone color) may be ordered in a fixed series. See also *total serialism.*

service   Anglican church term that denoted music for the unchanging Morning and Evening Prayers and for Communion.

seventh chord   Four-note combination consisting of a triad with another third added on top.

sextuple meter   Compound metrical pattern of six beats to a measure.

sforzando (sf)   Sudden stress or accent on a single note or chord.

sharp sign   Musical symbol (♯) which indicates raising a pitch by a semitone.

shawm   Medieval wind instrument that was the ancestor of the oboe.

side drum   See *snare drum.*

sinfonia   Short instrumental work, found in Baroque opera, to facilitate scene changes.

Singspiel   Comic German drama with spoken dialogue; the immediate predecessor of Romantic German opera.

slide trumpet   Medieval brass instrument of the trumpet family.

snare drum   Small cylindrical drum with two heads stretched over a metal shell, the lower head having strings across it; it is played with two drumsticks. Also *side drum.*

sonata   Instrumental genre in several movements for soloist or small ensemble.

sonata-allegro form   The opening movement of the sonata cycle, consisting of themes that are stated in the first section (Exposition), developed in the second section (Development), and restated in the third section (Recapitulation). Also *sonata form* or *first-movement form.*

sonata cycle   General term describing the multi-movement structure found in sonatas, string quartets, symphonies, concertos, and large-scale works of the eighteenth and nineteenth centuries.

sonata da camera   Baroque chamber sonata, usually a suite of stylized dances. Also *chamber sonata.*

sonata da chiesa   Baroque instrumental work intended for performance in church; in four movements frequently arranged slow-fast-slow-fast. Also *church sonata.*

sonata form   See *sonata-allegro form.*

sonatina   Short, modified sonata form, often consisting of an Exposition and Recapitulation without a Development.

soprano   Highest-ranged voice, normally possessed by women or boys.

sousaphone   Brass instrument adapted from the tuba with a forward bell that is coiled to rest over the player's shoulder for ease of carrying while marching.

Sprechstimme   A vocal style in which the melody is spoken at approximate pitches rather than sung on exact pitches; developed by Arnold Schoenberg.

staccato   Short, detached notes, marked with a dot.

Statement   See *Exposition.*

stile concitato   Baroque style developed by Monteverdi, which introduced novel effects such as rapid repeated notes as symbols of passion.

stile rappresentativo A dramatic recitative style of the Baroque period in which melodies moved freely over a foundation of simple chords.

stopping On a string instrument, altering the string length by pressing it on the fingerboard; on a horn, playing with the bell closed by the hand or a mute.

string instruments Bowed and plucked instruments whose sound is produced by the vibration of one or more strings; also *chordophone.*

string quartet Chamber music ensemble consisting of two violins, viola, and cello. Also, a multi-movement composition for this ensemble.

strophic form Song structure in which the same music is repeated with every stanza (strophe) of the poem.

style Characteristic manner of presentation of musical elements (melody, rhythm, harmony, dynamics, form, etc.).

subdominant Fourth scale step, *fa.*

subdominant chord Chord built on the fourth scale step, the IV chord.

subject Main idea or theme of a work, as in a fugue.

syllabic Plainchant melodic style with one note to each syllable of text.

symphonic poem One-movement orchestral form which develops a poetic idea, suggests a scene, or creates a mood, generally associated with the Romantic era. Also *tone poem.*

symphony Large work for orchestra, generally in three or four movements.

syncopation Deliberate upsetting of the meter or pulse through a temporary shifting of the accent to a weak beat or an offbeat.

synthesizer Electronic instrument that produces a wide variety of sounds by combining sound generators and sound modifiers in one package with a unified control system.

tabor Cylindrical Medieval drum.

taille French term for "tenor," as in a Baroque tenor oboe.

tala Fixed time cycle or meter in Indian music, built from uneven groupings of beats.

tambourine Percussion instrument consisting of a small round drum with metal plates inserted in its rim; it is played by striking or shaking.

tam-tam See *gong.*

tempo Rate of speed or pace of music.

tempo rubato See *rubato.*

tenor Male voice of high range; also, a part, often structural, in polyphony.

tenor drum Percussion instrument that is a larger version of the snare drum with a wooden shell.

ternary form Three-part (**A-B-A**) form based on a statement (**A**), a contrast or departure (**B**), and repetition (**A**). Also *three-part form.*

terraced dynamics Expressive style typical of Baroque music in which volume levels shift abruptly from soft to loud and back without gradual crescendos or decrescendos.

tertian harmony Harmony based on the interval of the third, particularly predominant from the Baroque through the nineteenth century.

texture The threads of melodic lines that make up the vertical aspect of the musical fabric.

thematic development Musical expansion of a theme by varying its melodic outline, harmony, or rhythm. Also *thematic transformation.*

thematic transformation See *thematic development.*

theme Melodic idea used as a basic building block in the construction of a composition; also *subject.*

theme and variations Compositional procedure in which a theme is stated and then altered in successive statements; occurs as an independent piece or as a movement of a sonata cycle.

theme group Several themes in the same key that function as a unit within a section of a form, particularly in sonata-allegro form.

third Interval between two notes that are two diatonic scale degrees apart.

third stream Jazz style that synthesizes characteristics and techniques of classical music and jazz; term coined by Gunther Schuller.

thorough-bass See *figured bass.*

three-part form See *ternary form.*

through-composed Song structure that is composed from beginning to end, without repetitions of large sections.

timbre The quality of a sound that distinguishes one voice or instrument from another. Also *tone color.*

timpani Percussion instrument consisting of a hemispheric copper shell with a head of plastic or calfskin, held in place by a metal ring and played with soft or hard padded sticks. A pedal mechanism changes the tension of the head, and with it the pitch. Also *kettledrums.*

toccata Virtuoso composition, generally for organ or harpsichord, in a free and rhapsodic style; in the Baroque, it often served as introduction to a fugue.

tombeau An instrumental piece or group of pieces that commemorate someone's death.

tom-tom Cylindrical drum without snares.

tonal Based on principles of major-minor tonality, as distinct from *modal.*

tonality Principle of organization around a tonic or home pitch, based on a major or minor scale.

tone color See *timbre.*

tone poem See *symphonic poem.*

tone row An arrangement of the twelve chromatic tones that serves as the basis of a twelve-tone composition.

tonic The first note of the scale or key, *do.* Also *keynote.*

tonic chord Triad built on the first scale tone, the I chord.

total serialism Extremely complex, totally controlled music in which the twelve-tone principle is extended to elements of music other than pitch.

transposition Shifting a piece of music to a different pitch level.

tremolo Rapid repetition of a tone; can be achieved instrumentally or vocally.

triad Common chord type, consisting of three pitches built on alternate tones of the scale (e.g. steps 1–3–5 or *do-mi-sol*).

triangle Percussion instrument consisting of a slender rod of steel bent in the shape of a triangle that is struck with a steel beater.

trill Ornament consisting of the rapid alternation between one tone and the next above it.

trio sonata Baroque chamber sonata type written in three parts: two melody lines and the *basso continuo,* requiring four players to perform.

triple meter Basic metrical pattern of three beats to a measure.

triple-stop Playing three notes simultaneously on a string instrument.

triplum Third part in early polyphony.

tritonic Three-note scale pattern, used in the music of some Southern African cultures.

trombone Tenor-range brass instrument that changes pitch by means of a moveable double slide. There is also a bass version.

troubadour Medieval poet-musicians in southern France.

trouvère Medieval poet-musicians in northern France.

trumpet Highest-pitched brass instrument that changes pitch through valves.

tuba Bass-range brass instrument that changes pitch by means of valves.

tubular bells See *chimes.*

tutti "All"; the opposite of solo. See also *ripieno.*

twelve-tone music Compositional procedure of the twentieth century based on a free use of all twelve chromatic tones without a central tone or "tonic."

two-part form See *binary form.*

unison Interval between two notes of the same pitch; the simultaneous playing of the same notes.

upbeat Last beat of the measure, a weak beat, that anticipates the downbeat.

verismo Operatic "realism," a style popular in Italy in the 1890s which tried to bring naturalism into the lyric theater.

verse Solo passage from the Gradual which precedes the response (choral answer). In poetry, a group of lines constituting a unit; in liturgical music for the Catholic Church, a phrase from the Scriptures that alternates with the *response.*

verse anthem Anglican devotional work similar to the motet of the Catholic Church, for solo voices with a choral refrain.

vibraphone A percussion instrument with metal bars and electrically-driven rotating propellors under each bar that produces an attractive vibrato sound, much used in jazz.

vibrato Small fluctuation of pitch used as an expressive device to intensify a sound.

vielle Medieval bowed instrument that was primarily cultivated by the privileged classes and was the ancestor of the violin.

viola Bowed string instrument of middle range; the second highest member of the violin family.

viola da gamba Family of Renaissance bowed string instruments that had six or more strings, was fretted like a guitar, and played held between the legs like a modern cello.

violin Soprano or highest-ranged member of the bowed string instrument family.

violoncello Bowed string instrument with a middle-to-low range and dark, rich sonority; lower than a viola. Also *cello.*

virelai Medieval and Renaissance poetic form and chanson type with French courtly texts.

vivace Lively.

vocalise A textless vocal melody, as in an exercise or concert piece.

volume Degree of loudness or softness of a sound. See also *dynamics.*

waltz Ballroom dance type in triple meter; in the Romantic era, a short, stylized piano piece.

whole-tone scale Scale pattern built entirely of whole-tone intervals, common in the music of the French impressionists.

woodwind Instrumental family made of wood or metal whose tone is produced by a column of air vibrating within a pipe that has holes along its length.

word painting Musical pictorialization of words from the text as an expressive device; a prominent feature of the Renaissance madrigal.

xylophone Percussion instrument consisting of blocks of wood suspended on a frame, laid out in the shape of a keyboard and struck with hard mallets.

Appendix III

Attending Concerts

Despite the many ways now available to hear fine quality recorded music, nothing can equal the excitement of a live concert. The crowded hall, the visual as well as aural stimulation of a perfomance, even the element of unpredictability—of what might happen on a particular night—all contribute to the unique, communicative powers of people making music. There are, however, certain traditions surrounding concerts and concert-going—how to chose seats, the way performers dress, the appropriate moment to applaud, are but a few. Understanding these traditions can contribute to your increased enjoyment of the musical event.

Choosing Concerts, Tickets, and Seats

Widely diversified musical events, performed by groups ranging from professional orchestras and college ensembles to church choirs, can be found in most parts of the country. It may take some ingenuity and research to discover the full gamut of concerts available in your area. Both city and college newspapers usually publish a calendar of upcoming events; these are often announced as well on the local radio stations. Bulletin boards on campus and in public buildings and stores are good places to find concert announcements. Often a music or fine arts department of a college will post a printed list of future events featuring both professional and student performers.

Ticket prices will vary considerably, depending on the nature of the event and the geographical location of the theater. Many fine performances can be heard for a small admission price, especially at college and civic auditoriums. For an orchestra concert or an opera in a major metropolitan area, you can expect to pay anywhere from $20 to $75 for a reserved seat. The first rows of the orchestra section, located at stage level, and of the first balcony or loge are usually the most expensive. Although many consider it desirable to sit as close as possible to the performers, these are often not the best seats for acoustical reasons. To hear a proper balance, especially of a large ensemble, you are better off sitting in the middle of the hall. Today, most new concert halls are constructed so that virtually all seats are satisfactory. For the opera, many people bring opera glasses or binoculars if they are sitting some distance from the stage.

Concert tickets may be reserved in advance as well as purchased at the door. Often, reduced prices are available for students and senior citizens. Tickets reserved by telephone, or charged to a credit card, are generally not refundable; they are held at the box office in your name.

Preparing for the Concert

You may want to find out what specific works will be performed at an upcoming concert so that you can read about them and their composers in advance. If this book does not provide enough background, visit the music reference section of your library or ask your instructor for assistance. If you plan to attend an opera, it is especially helpful to read an overview of the plot, since productions are usually sung in the original language of the work. Fortunately, many large opera houses today have monitors that run simultaneous English translations above the stage, a practice that can increase our comprehension and enjoyment enormously.

Suitable attire for a concert depends somewhat on the degree of formality and the location of the event. Although strict traditions of concert dress have long since broken down, you will not feel out of place if you are neatly dressed. If you are attending an opening night of an opera, a musical, or an orchestra season, or if you have seats in a box or founder's circle, you will find most people wearing evening dress. But more usually, dress will be fairly informal.

Arriving at the Concert

Plan to arrive at a concert at least fifteen minutes before it is scheduled to begin. This is particularly important if the seating is open—that is, non-reserved by seat number—so that you can choose your location. The time before a performance is often when people meet with friends, have a beverage at the lobby bar, and are "seen."

Concert programs are generally passed out (and sometimes sold) in the lobby or handed to you by the usher showing you to your seat. The program provides important information about the pieces being performed and about the people performing them. Often you will find English translations of vocal texts as well.

Should you arrive after the performance has begun, you will not be able to enter the hall until the first break in the music. This may occur after the first piece, or following the first movement of a large-scale work. Being late can mean missing as much as twenty minutes or more of a concert. When you finally do enter the hall, it is considerate to take a seat as quickly and quietly as possible.

During the Performance

Certain concert conventions come into play when the performance begins. The house lights will generally go down for the entrance of the performers or the opening of the curtain. Large ensembles, such as an orchestra or chorus, will usually be on stage at this time. The orchestra takes this opportunity to tune their instruments, cued by the *concertmaster* or *concertmistress* (the first chair, first violinist) asking for a pitch from the oboe player. It is customary to applaud the entrance of the conductor or any soloists. There will then be a moment's pause for complete quiet before the concert begins.

Knowing when to applaud during a concert is important. Generally, one applauds after complete works, such as at the close of a symphony, a concerto, a sonata, or a song cycle; it is inappropriate to clap between movements of a multi-movement work. Sometimes, short works are grouped together on the program, suggesting that they are a set. In this case, applause is suitable at the close of the group. If you are unsure, follow the lead of others in the audience. This is also sound advice for performances in a church, where people often feel reluctant to applaud until the close of a performance. One notable exception to the rule of avoiding applause during a work is at the opera, where it is traditional to interrupt the drama with applause after a particularly fine delivery of an aria or an ensemble number.

Most concerts have an intermission, which is indicated on the program. (At the opera, there may be two or more, one after each act.) This is the only time that it is appropriate to leave one's seat or the theater.

The Performers

Newcomers to the concert hall are often surprised at the way the perfomers are dressed. For many years, it has been traditional to wear black—long dresses for the women, tuxedos or tails for the men. While this may seem overly formal, it is still customary, since dark, uniform clothing will minimize visual distraction.

The behavior of the performers on the stage is often as formal as their dress. The entire orchestra generally stands at the entrance of the conductor, who shakes the hand of the first violinist before beginning. A small group, such as a string quartet, will often bow to the audience in unison. The only time a performer will directly address the audience is if, at the close of the program, an additional piece or two is demanded by the extended applause and appreciation. In this case, the *encore* (French for again), or extra work, is generally announced.

It may surprise you to see that some musicians perform from memory. This is particularly common for pianists, singers, and other soloists. To perform without music requires intense concentration and necessitates many arduous hours of study and practice.

This brief explanation is intended to remove some of the mystery surrounding concert going. The best advice that can be given is to take full advantage of the opportunities available—try something completely unfamiliar, perhaps the opera or the symphony, and continue enjoying concerts of whatever music you already like!

Index

Definitions of terms appear on the pages indicated in **bold** type.
Illustrations are indicated by *italic* numbers.